金融学精选教材·双语注释版

国际金融管理
INTERNATIONAL FINANCIAL MANAGEMENT
3E

第 3 版

〔美〕迈克尔·B. 科诺利（Michael B. Connolly） 著

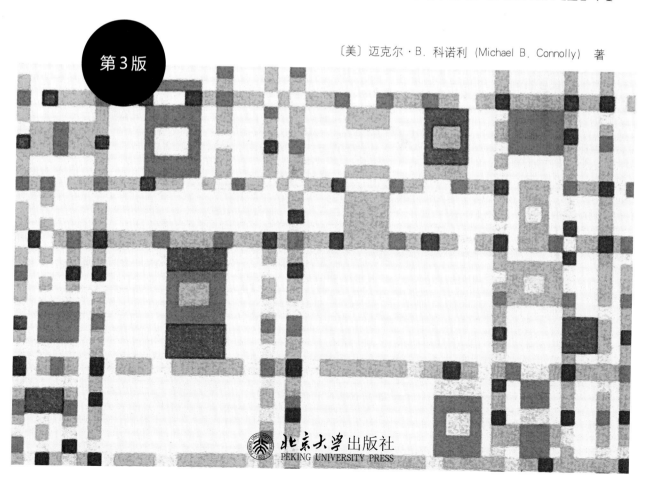

北京大学出版社
PEKING UNIVERSITY PRESS

图书在版编目(CIP)数据

国际金融管理:第3版:英文/(美)迈克尔·B.科诺利(Michael B. Connolly)著. —北京:北京大学出版社,2020.1

金融学精选教材·双语注释版

ISBN 978-7-301-30894-3

Ⅰ.①国… Ⅱ.①迈… Ⅲ.①国际金融管理—高等学校—教材—英文 Ⅳ.①F831.2

中国版本图书馆CIP数据核字(2019)第236764号

书　　名	国际金融管理(第3版) GUOJI JINRONG GUANLI (DI-SAN BAN)
著作责任者	〔美〕迈克尔·B.科诺利(Michael B. Connolly) 著
责任编辑	张　燕
标准书号	ISBN 978-7-301-30894-3
出版发行	北京大学出版社
地　　址	北京市海淀区成府路205号　100871
网　　址	http://www.pup.cn
电子信箱	em@pup.cn　　QQ:552063295
新浪微博	@北京大学出版社　@北京大学出版社经管图书
电　　话	邮购部 010-62752015　发行部 010-62750672 编辑部 010-62752926
印刷者	北京市科星印刷有限责任公司
经销者	新华书店
	787毫米×1092毫米　16开本　23.25印张　484千字 2020年1月第1版　2020年1月第1次印刷
印　　数	0001—3000册
定　　价	58.00元

未经许可,不得以任何方式复制或抄袭本书之部分或全部内容。
版权所有,侵权必究
举报电话:010-62752024　电子信箱:fd@pup.pku.edu.cn
图书如有印装质量问题,请与出版部联系,电话:010-62756370

Preface   前言

This third, bilingual edition of *International Financial Management* with Peking University Press provides a working knowledge of international business finance with applications to real world problems. It is designed not only to introduce modern finance and new financial instruments to Chinese students, but also to provide a solid foundation for the English readers. This edition has case studies, concept boxes, and exercises. The solutions are provided at the back of the book.

Corporate aspects of international finance are analyzed, especially hedging techniques. The book also aims to help readers understand how managers of international corporations do or should behave. It also examine the mechanics of the foreign exchange market, reviewing spots, forwards, futures, and options—the main tools used to hedge exchange rate risk. The book constructs the building blocks of international finance: (1) interest rate parity, (2) purchasing power parity, and (3) the international Fisher equation. It then turns to international management issues and international financial scams, including Ponzi games. We then lay out the optimal portfolio model in an international setting based upon an investor's degree of risk aversion and the reward-risk ratio. It specifically highlights the role of the exchange rate in portfolio decisions.

My students in international finance at Duke University and the University of Miami kindly provided suggestions on the final version of the manuscript. I would specifically like to acknowledge Luyuan Fan, now at McKinsey, Boston and Yiwen Zhu, now at Goldman Sachs, New York for their valuable contributions.

In recent years, I have been teaching international finance at Hunan University, China, as well as doing joint research with colleagues there. It is exciting to witness China's movement toward free markets and the development of new financial markets and instruments. Futures markets in petroleum were only launched in March 2005, and new options markets in the yuan in March 2011 were hampered by prohibitions on investors selling calls and puts, which are more exposed to loss than buying calls or puts. Capital transfers still require approval of SAFE, the State Administered Foreign Exchange System. SAFE approved the withdrawn offer of $18.5 billion by CNOOC Ltd. for UNOCAL. The Chinese government is encouraging direct foreign investment and acquisitions, making available the foreign exchange necessary for this and other investments. These investments are often to secure sure supplies of raw materials for production by state enterprises involving petroleum, copper, or other items. The offshore use of the yuan as a settlement currency is increasing, especially for cross border transactions with China.

I owe thanks to Robert Z. Aliber of the Graduate School of Business, University of Chicago, and to Ed Tower, Duke University, who made significant, detailed suggestions on the content and focus of the volume. Robert Langham, Taylor and Francis Books plc, London, made helpful editorial suggestions in the earlier stages of this project. I owe a debt of gratitude to my thesis advisor at the University of Chicago, Robert A. Mundell, Columbia University, who taught me economics and the fun of learning. Cheng Li, University of Alabama, translated key concepts, explanations, the table of contents and the index into simplified Chinese. Yi Pan, Duke University, proofread and edited the final manuscript for both substance and style. Tie Su, my valued colleague at the Miami Herbert Business School, made significant suggestions improving this third edition.

I am especially indebted to Yan Zhang, Editor of Peking University Press for her steadfast encouragement and professional editing. This third edition could not have been accomplished without her able and constant guidance.

The plan of the book is as follows:

- Chapter 1 introduces the topic of international finance by highlighting its main characteristics, in particular, currency risk and conversion.
- Chapter 2 begins with the history of international finance and monies, stressing the importance of money as a medium of exchange, a store of value, and a unit of account. Bills of exchange are identified as the source of the first financial securities in foreign currency and the origin of the stock exchanges. The concept of seigniorage, i.e. the printing press, to finance fiscal deficits is highlighted as the source of inflation in several countries.
- Chapter 3 deals with the exchange rate. The foreign exchange

market is analyzed, including spot, future, forward, option, and swap markets in foreign exchange. The basic building block for forecasting future exchange rates—interest rate parity—is illustrated as a no-profit arbitrage condition. The bid-ask spread—the difference between the ask and the bid price of foreign exchange dealers—represents the currency dealers' profits, in addition to any commission paid, and a transaction cost in currency conversion for the firm. Unanticipated foreign exchange risk involves the risk that a subsequent spot rate will deviate from its current forward level. Forwards and foreign exchange swaps are analyzed and laid out as a particularly useful way of hedging long-term and operational exposure in foreign exchange.

- Chapter 4 covers the hedging of foreign exchange risk by the firm. To hedge or not is the first issue addressed, then hedging techniques. If a firm or an individual has a "long" position in say euros, foreign exchange risk is said to be hedged or guarded against by acquiring an opposite, offsetting "short" position in euros. A simple hedge of a million euros of accounts receivable in 90 days could involve the sale of one million euros forward for delivery in 90 days. The firm would no longer be subject to foreign exchange risk: neither unanticipated gains if the euro rises relative to the forward price in dollars or pounds, nor unanticipated losses if the euro declines relative to the forward rate. Chapter 4 also covers contractual hedges: futures, forwards, money market hedges, and options, as well as operational, accounting, and transactional hedging by offsetting cash flows, such as foreign exchange swaps, by the international firm.

- Chapter 5 deals with international financial management issues that confront the multinational firms: transfer pricing, working capital management, international taxation, offshore banking, and international mergers and acquisitions. In addition, the currency conversion of free-cash flows in an international business plan is covered in detail.

- Chapter 6 covers financial scams and swindles, including pyramid schemes, insider trading, accounting malfeasance, and other scams that have surged worldwide in recent years. Partly, the problem seems to be old-fashioned greed, but another culprit seems to be the linking of bonus and options compensation with reported earnings, not necessarily actual earnings.

- Chapter 7 reviews the financial crisis of 2007 – 2009, stressing the importance of financial leverage, securitization, and moral hazard in precipitating the rapid near-collapse of the US financial system. The US government played a role in triggering the collapse, through Fannie Mae and Freddie Mac promoting, bundling, and guaranteeing low quality, sub-prime mortgages. The Troubled Asset Relief Program (TARP) rescued the investment banks of Wall Street, but firmly established a moral hazard — "too big to fail."

- Chapter 8 reviews due diligence methodologies in cross border mergers and acquisitions, as well as different structures of ownership and finance. It concludes with a case study of the $43 billion ChemChina acquisition of Syngenta, a high technology Swiss seed and pesticide company, in 2017.

- An appendix on the time value of money follows with several applications.

Problem sets are also provided at the end of every chapter to give the reader confidence in problem-solving with numerical and conceptual analysis.

Solutions to these problems and an index close the book.

I hope you enjoy this volume. My students do and I had fun writing it.

Michael B. Connolly
Department of Economics
Miami Herbert Business School
University of Miami
Florida, USA

Department of Finance
College of Finance and Statistics
Hunan University
Changsha, China

Abbreviations 重要缩写词

ADR	American depositary receipt
ADS	American depositary shares
AMEX	American Stock Exchange
AMR	American Airlines Corp.
APA	advanced pricing agreement
BAC	Bank of America, ticker symbol
BFC	British Finance Centre
BIS	Bank for International Settlements
BOA	Bank of America
BSCH	Banco Santander Central Hispano
CAD	covered arbitrage differential
CAOC	China Aviation Oil Corporation
CAOHC	China Aviation Oil Holding Company
CHIPS	Clearing House Interbank Payments System
CDO	Collateralized debt obligation
CSFB	Crédit Suisse First Boston
DJIA	Dow Jones Industrial Average
EDGAR	Electronic Data Gathering and Retrieval
ETF	exchange traded fund
FASB	Financial Accounting Standards Board
FATF	Financial Action Task Force
FCPA	Foreign Corrupt Practices Act
FED	Federal Reserve System
Footsie	Financial Times Stock Exchange
FOREX	foreign exchange
FSC	foreign sales corporation
GAAP	generally accepted accounting principles
GATT	General Agreement on Tariffs and Trade
GKOs	Gosudarstvennye Kratkosrochnye Obligatsii
HLI	highly leveraged institution
IAS	international accounting standard
IBC	international business corporation

IFOC	international financial offshore center
IMF	International Monetary Fund
IPO	initial public offer
IRR	internal rate of return
IRP	interest rate parity
IRS	Internal Revenue Service
L/C	letter of credit
LSE	London Stock Exchange
LTCM	Long Term Capital Management
MBA	mortgage backed asset
MEI	marginal efficiency of investment
MIGA	Multilateral Investment Guarantee Association
Nasdaq	National Association of Securities Dealers Automated Quotations
NCCTs	Non-Cooperative Countries and Territories
NDF	non-deliverable future
NPV	net present value
NYSE	New York Stock Exchange
OECD	Organization for Economic Cooperation and Development
OFC	offshore financial center
OTC	over-the-counter
PPP	purchasing power parity
RER	real exchange rate index
RIC	Reuters Instrument Code
S&P	Standard & Poor's
SASAC	State Asset Supervision and Administration Commission
SEC	Securities and Exchange Commission
SIMEX	Singapore International Monetary Exchange
SOES	Small Order Execution System
SOX	Sarbanes-Oxley Act
SSE	Shanghai Stock Exchange
SWIFT	Society for Worldwide Interbank Financial Telecommunications
T-bill	Treasury bill
UAL	United Airlines Corporation
UNCAC	UN Convention Against Corruption
USD	US dollars
WACC	weighted average cost of capital
WTO	World Trade Organization

Contents

Chapter 1
Features of International Finance   1
   Currencies   1
   Accounting rules   2
   Stakeholders   3
   Legal framework   3
   Institutional framework   4
   Language   5
   Taxation   6
   Regulatory framework   7
   Political risk   10
   Intellectual property rights   11
   Conclusion   12

Chapter 2
The History of Money and Finance   14
   Prerequisites of good money   15
   Money and exchange rates   16
   History of monies   17
   Foreign exchange history   23
   Banks and banking   25
   The Federal Reserve System   26
   The international monetary institutions   27
   History of the stock exchanges   29
   Conclusion   37

Chapter 3
The Foreign Exchange Market   41
   A floating exchange rate system   42
   A fixed exchange rate system   45
   The euro—"irrevocably fixed" exchange rates   53
   The Chinese yuan   57
   The SWIFT international clearing system   60
   Theories of the long-run movement of exchange rates   60
   Purchasing power parity   61
   The monetary approach to the exchange rate   66
   The IMF's real effective exchange rate   70
   Foreign currency futures versus forward contracts   71
   Forwards and futures in commodities   74
   Arbitrage determination of the spot and future rates   78
   Exchange rate forecasting   87
   Random investing   89
   Conclusion   103

Chapter 4
Hedging Foreign Exchange Risk   113
   Hedging defined   113
   Credit ratings   116
   Default risk premium   120
   Hedging foreign exchange transactions exposure   122
   Related techniques for hedging foreign exchange risk   132
   Hedging operating exposure   134
   Foreign currency swaps   139
   Back-to-back (parallel) loans   140
   Accounting exposure   141
   Financial Accounting Standards Board—FASB 52   141

Hedge accounting 142
Trade finance 143
Hedging interest rate exposure 144
Reference rates 145
Forecasting forward interest rates 146
The yield curve 146
A strip of the yield curve 147
Conclusion 153
Appendix: Risk and Insurance 154

Chapter 5
International Financial Management 166
Capital structure 166
Cross-listing on foreign stock exchanges 169
International liquidity and market integration 170
Transfer pricing 170
International taxation 174
Working capital management 176
Offshore banking 178
An international business plan: the *Azteca Café* 185
Optimal investment analysis 187
Conclusion 200

Chapter 6
International Financial Scams and Swindles 209
Pyramids: an international perspective 209
Corporate governance failures 219
The Sarbanes-Oxley Act of 2002 225
Lessons learned 244
Conclusion 245

Chapter 7
Financial Leverage, Moral Hazard and Counterparty Risk: The Financial Crisis of 2007–2009 249
Financial leverage 250
Securitization 253
Leveraged households 255
The role of the government: Fannie Mae and Freddie Mac 256
Rising and falling home equity 257
Strategic default 262
Counter-party risk 268
Leveraged financial institutions 269
The bankruptcy of Lehman Brothers 271
The macro-economic impact of the financial crisis 276
The Volcker Rule 280
The Dodd-Frank Act of 2010 283
Conclusion 283

Chapter 8
Cross Border Mergers and Acquisitions 287
Motives for M&A activity 287
The ease of doing business abroad 288
M&A structures 290
Due diligence 298
Cash and share consideration 304
The ChemChina acquisition of Syngenta 307
Conclusion 320

Appendix: The Time Value of Money 324

Solutions to Problems 340

Index 355

中文目录

第1章 国际金融的特征 1
 货币 1
 会计准则 2
 利益相关者 3
 法律框架 3
 制度框架 4
 语言 5
 税收 6
 监管体系 7
 政治风险 10
 知识产权 11
 小结 12

第2章 货币和金融历史 14
 良币的必要条件 15
 货币和汇率 16
 货币的历史 17
 外汇交易的历史 23
 银行和银行业 25
 联邦储备体系 26
 国际货币组织 27
 股票交易的历史 29
 小结 37

第3章 外汇交易市场 41
 浮动汇率制度 42
 固定汇率制度 45
 欧元:不可撤销的固定汇率 53
 人民币 57
 SWIFT 国际清算系统 60
 长期汇率变动理论 60
 购买力平价 61
 汇率的货币方法 66

 国际货币基金组织的真实有效汇率 70
 外汇期货与远期合约 71
 商品期货与远期合约 74
 即期汇率与远期汇率的无套利决定
  方法 78
 汇率预测 87
 随机投资 89
 小结 103

第4章 外汇风险的套期保值 113
 套期保值的定义 113
 信用评级 116
 违约风险溢价 120
 外汇交易风险的套期保值 122
 外汇交易风险套期保值的相关
  技术 132
 经营风险的套期保值 134
 外汇互换 139
 背对背(平行)贷款 140
 会计风险 141
 财务会计准则委员会第52号准则 141
 对冲会计法 142
 贸易融资 143
 利率风险的套期保值 144
 相关利率 145
 远期利率的预测 146
 收益率曲线 146
 收益率曲线的剥离 147
 小结 153
 附录:风险与保险 154

第5章 国际金融管理 166
 资本结构 166

在国外证券交易市场交叉上市　169

国际流动性与市场一体化　170

转移定价　170

国际税收　174

营运资本管理　176

离岸银行业　178

国际商务计划：Azteca Café　185

最优投资分析　187

小结　200

第6章　国际金融欺诈与骗局　209

金字塔骗局：一个国际视角　209

公司治理失效　219

2002年《萨班斯-奥克斯利法案》　225

教训　244

小结　245

第7章　金融杠杆、道德风险和对手风险：2007—2009年的金融危机　249

金融杠杆　250

资产证券化　253

杠杆化家庭　255

政府的角色：房利美和房地美　256

房屋所有者权益的上升与下降　257

策略违约　262

交易对手风险　268

杠杆化金融机构　269

雷曼兄弟公司的破产　271

金融危机的宏观经济影响　276

沃克尔法则　280

2010年《多德-弗兰克法案》　283

小结　283

第8章　跨国兼并与收购　287

并购的动机　287

境外经商便利性　288

并购框架　290

尽职调查　298

现金与股份的考量　304

中国化工集团公司收购先正达　307

小结　320

附录：货币的时间价值　324

章后习题答案　340

索引　355

Figures 图形目录

2.1 The birth of coinage: Chinese spade monies of the eastern Zhou Dynasty, 770-256 BC, and Ming knife monies, late 5th century BC   18
2.2 The Lydian Lion Head: 600-575 BC   18
2.3 The world's first banknote—the Jiaozi of the Song Dynasty, 1023 AD   20
2.4 The first European banknote 1661—the riksdalers specie of the Stockholms Banco, Sweden   20
2.5 The first global money—the Spanish peso   21
3.1 A floating exchange rate   42
3.2 Bank profits from the bid-ask spread   44
3.3 The People's Bank of China buys three million dollars at the lower intervention rate   46
3.4 The People's Bank of China sells three million dollars at the upper intervention rate   47
3.5 The PBOC sells USD   48
3.6 The PBOC buys USD   48
3.7 The PBOC sells bonds to neutralize its foreign exchange purchase   50
3.8 The change in domestic credit, ΔDC, and the change in net foreign assets, ΔFX, of the PBOC   51
3.9 The PBOC buys bonds to neutralize its foreign exchange sale   53
3.10 Selected long term interest rates and debt to income ratios in the euro zone   55
3.11 Relative purchasing power parity   66
3.12 Payoff from a short position in gold   75
3.13 A gain from a short position in gold   76
3.14 A loss from a short position in gold   77
3.15 A hedged position in gold   77
3.16 Covered interest rate parity   81
3.17 Covered interest arbitrage with a gain   83
3.18 Uncovered interest rate arbitrage with a loss   84
3.19 Triangular foreign exchange arbitrage   85
3.20 Random investing   90
3.21 The premium on a foreign exchange call option   97
3.22 The premium on a foreign exchange put option   98
3.23 The payoff at maturity from buying a pound call option   99
3.24 The payoff at maturity from selling a pound call option   100
3.25 The payoff at maturity from buying a pound put option   101
3.26 The payoff at maturity from selling a pound put option   101
4.1 Default risk premium   122

4.2 A long position in dollars 123
4.3 A loss on a long position in dollars 124
4.4 A gain on a long position in dollars 124
4.5 A forward hedge of a long position in dollars 125
4.6 A money market hedge of a long position in dollars 126
4.7 A put option hedge of a long position in dollars 127
4.8 An unhedged short loss in dollars 128
4.9 An unhedged short gain in dollars 128
4.10 A forward purchase of dollars to hedge a short position 129
4.11 A money market loan of dollars to hedge a short position 130
4.12 Payoff from buying a call option at the money to hedge a short position 130
4.13 A collar hedge of accounts receivable in dollars 131
4.14 A collar hedge of accounts payable in dollars 132
4.15 An out-of-the-money put option as a partial hedge of a long position 133
4.16 An out-of-the-money call option as a partial hedge of a short position 134
4.17 A re-invoicing center 138
4.18 A natural hedge in dollars 139
4.19 A foreign exchange swap 139
4.20 A back-to-back (parallel) loan 140
4.21 A letter of credit 144
4.22 The US Treasury yield curve: February 4, 2011 146
4.23 An interest rate cap, ignoring the premium paid 149
4.24 An interest rate cap, including the premium paid 150
4.25 An interest rate floor, not including premium paid 151
4.26 An interest rate floor, deducting the premium paid 152
4.27 A collar on an interest rate payment with equal premium 152
4.28 A collar on an interest rate receipt with equal premium 153
4.29 Expected utility with risk aversion 154
5.1 The weighted average cost of capital and financial leverage 167
5.2 Transfer pricing 171
5.3 Abusive transfer pricing 173
5.4 Working cash balances 176
5.5 Offshore banking 178
5.6 Profit maximization by the firm 184
5.7 Portfolio diversification and market risk 188
5.8 The efficient investment frontier 189
5.9 Capital allocation 192
5.10 The optimal complete and market portfolios 194
5.11 A leveraged complete portfolio 195
5.12 The mutual fund theorem 197
7.1 The financial crisis of 2008−2009 250
7.2 The magnification effect of financial leverage on gains and losses 252

7.3	The S&P/Case-Shiller U.S. National Home Price Index (January 2000 = 100)	260
7.4	China: Sales price index of residential and commercial buildings in 70 large and medium size cities	261
7.5	China: Real estate floor space sold	261
7.6	Optimal strategic default with negative equity	263
7.7	A credit default swap with no default	266
7.8	A credit default swap with default	266
7.9	AIG's default swap insurance sold to five major Wall Street Banks	267
7.10	AIG's payments of default swap insurance sold to five major Wall Street Banks (USD billions)	268
7.11	Counterparty risk	269
7.12	Losses to financial institutions in 2007 (USD billions)	272
7.13	Excess reserves held by US depository institutions (USD billions)	274
7.14	Total borrowings from the Federal Reserve System (USD millions)	275
7.15	US GDP growth	276
7.16	The contributions of consumption and investment expenditure to growth in real GDP	277
7.17	Annualized quarterly change in GDP for the euro area	277
7.18	The US economic spending plan of 2009, a consumption smoothing program	284
8.1	The value of Chinese global M&A transactions, 2010 – 2017 (USD billions)	289
8.2	Chinese direct investment in the United States, 2009 – 2017 (USD billions)	289
8.3	A merger—or two firms merge and become one	291
8.4	A stock purchase	292
8.5	An asset purchase—if only specific assets are desired	293
8.6	A spinoff into a subsidiary	294
8.7	An equity carve-out	296
8.8	A joint venture (JV)	297
8.9	A leveraged buyout with cash	298
8.10	Syngenta's weighted average cost of capital	314
A.1	Measuring default risk	336

Tables 表格目录

2.1 The US budget deficit and debt held by the public as a percent of GDP 35
2.2 Negative seigniorage on the US penny 36
3.1 Global daily foreign exchange trading in April 2016 41
3.2 Direct and cross rates in foreign exchange quotations 43
3.3 The balance sheet of the PBOC 48
3.4 *The Economist*'s Big Mac standard 63
3.5 Points and outright forward quotations 73
3.6 European style outright quotations 73
3.7 Basic arbitrage data 82
3.8 A five-year forecast of the future exchange rate 88
3.9 Forecasted free cash flows for a UK acquisition in millions of pounds 89
3.10 Random investment funds 90
3.11 The call and put premium on a stock option 95
3.12 The call and put premium on a foreign exchange option 102
3.13 Foreign exchange option Greeks 103
4.1 Valuation of the firm 115
4.2 S&P's credit ratings 118
4.3 Long term sovereign credit ratings by agency 118
4.4 Treasury spending as a fraction of tax revenues (%) 120
4.5 US deficits and debt as a fraction of Gross Domestic Product (%) 120
4.6 Attitudes toward risk 157
4.7 Fair insurance and risk aversion 158
5.1 Affiliate located in a high-tax jurisdiction 175
5.2 Affiliate located in a comparable tax jurisdiction 175
5.3 Affiliate located in a low-tax jurisdiction 175
5.4 Affiliate located in a tax haven 176
5.5 Decentralized cash management 177
5.6 Centralized cash management 177
5.7 Forecast of the Azteca Café's free cash flow in new Mexican pesos 185
5.8 Discounted free cash flow of the Azteca Café 186
5.9 Discounted free cash flow minus existing liabilities of the Azteca Café 187
5.10 A hypothetical complete portfolio 191
6.1 A hypothetical Ponzi game with rollover at a quarterly rate of return of 50% 210
7.1 Financial leverage of selected US technology and internet firms 255
7.2 Financial leverage of selected Chinese technology and internet firms 255
7.3 Financial leverage of selected US and Chinese electric automobile and computer companies 255

7.4 Rising equity with rising home prices   257
7.5 The boom and the bust in Miami's home prices   258
7.6 Falling equity with falling home prices   258
7.7 China's policies to slow the rise in housing prices   262
7.8 Loan to value and financial leverage   264
7.9 Bank leverage (Levered Bank, Inc.)   270
7.10 Bank leverage and accounting bankruptcy (Levered Bank, Inc.)   270
7.11 Residential investment as a share of GDP in the United States: 1999 – 2009   276
7.12 TARP loans to financial and automobile companies   279
8.1 Ease of doing business index   288
8.2 Standalone values of Firms A and B   305
8.3 An outright cash acquisition of B by A   305
8.4 An acquisition of B by A through an incorrect share offer   306
8.5 An acquisition of B by A through a correct share offer   306
8.6 An acquisition of B by A through a combination of cash and share offer   307
8.7 Calculation of free cash flow   313
8.8 Syngenta valuation assumptions   313
8.9 Calculation of value per Syngenta share   315
8.10 Valuation analysis of Syngenta   316
8.11 Selected Chinese acquisitions terminated in the first half of 2018 due to U.S. regulations   318
8.12 Regulatory guidance on outbound investment issued by Chinese authorities   319
A.1 Accumulated interest after three years depending on the frequency of interest payments per year   326
A.2 The present value of 1,000 dollars paid in year 3 using a discount rate of 5%, depending on the number of conversion periods paying r on P 327
A.3 The effective rate of interest depending on the number of conversion payments   328
A.4 Accumulated values of an initial payment of $1,000 with continuous versus discrete conversion payments of interest r percent per year paid on P 329
A.5 Present values of $1,000 paid in each year   329
A.6 Present values of free cash flow of $1,000 per year every year for 5 years   330
A.7 The internal rate of return   330
A.8 The net present value of free cash flow plus terminal value   332
A.9 The net present value of a semi-annually paid 5% coupon bond with face value of $1,000   333
A.10 The net present value of estimated synergies and integration costs   338
A.11 The internal rate of return on AT&T's offer to Deutsche Telecom   338

CHAPTER 1

Features of International Finance 国际金融的特征

In what sense does international finance differ from finance? In fact, there are many.

Currencies

The key distinction between international finance and finance is the exchange rate issue. Issues of valuation, uncertainty about the future exchange rate, its convertibility and transactions costs lead to market segmentation. Consider the important decision to make a foreign acquisition. To value the foreign firm, it is customary to work up an income statement forecasting free cash flow over the next three to five years and estimate a terminal resale value of the acquisition. This is part of due diligence.

When the forecast is in terms of a foreign currency, say the euro, the forward cash flows must then be converted to the home currency, say the dollar, the pound, or the yuan. This task is easy enough using forward rates for the euro up to two years and interest rate parity to forecast the exchange rate through year five. The corresponding conversion of free cash flows is now in home currency for each year, ready to be discounted by the firm's weighted average cost of capital in home currency. If the net present value is positive and higher than alternative investments, the firm may decide to undertake the acquisition.

In doing so, the firm is faced with foreign exchange risk due to unexpected deviations from forecasted exchange rates. This exchange risk takes different forms: transactions risk associated with a specific transaction in foreign exchange, operational risk associated with ongoing operations in the foreign currency, and translation risk associated with accounting require-

国际金融与金融学的主要差别之一便是不同货币带来的汇率问题。汇率的定价、不确定性、货币的可兑换性问题和外汇的交易成本导致了市场分割。

ments. In addition, reporting requirements are in local currency to the Internal Revenue Service, Inland Revenue, or the Chinese Treasury. In order to hedge exchange risk, there are contractual, operational, and financial hedges, but these add to the costs of risk management of the firm. If done selectively, hedging may lower borrowing costs by reducing the risk of financial distress and bankruptcy.

Accounting rules

影响跨国并购的另一个重要因素是各国会计准则和实务之间的差异。在美国,通用的会计准则是由财务会计准则委员会(FASB)制定实施的美国通用会计准则体系(GAAP),而国际上普遍接受的会计标准是国际会计准则(IAS)。

Another important consideration is the issue of different accounting rules and practices. In the United States, the generally-accepted accounting principles (GAAP) is used and sanctioned by the Federal Accounting Standards Board. FASB 52 governs currency translation and valuation. Overseas, the standard practice is the international accounting standard (IAS) which depends more on concept and principle than on practice.

In general, reporting and disclosure requirements are higher in the U.S., England, and continental Europe than abroad, particularly when compared to emerging markets. In the U.S., Sarbanes-Oxley 2002 (SOX 2002) and Dodd-Frank 2010 regulatory bills have significantly increased compliance costs to US firms. SOX 2002 requires the CEO and CFO of publicly listed firms to sign financial and income statements as to their veracity. In principle, this is to reduce accounting fraud in the United States by increasing the liability of officers.

Regulatory Act: The Sarbanes-Oxley Act of 2002

Corporate responsibility requires that CEOs and CFOs certify in annual or quarterly reports that:

"the signing officer has reviewed the report; based on the officer's knowledge, the report does not contain any untrue statement of a material fact or omit to state a material fact ... the financial statements, and other financial information included in the report, fairly present in all material respects the financial condition and results of operations of the issuer as of, and for, the periods represented in the report;" It also provides for forfeiture of bonuses and profits as a result of mis-reporting, prohibits insider trades during pension fund blackout periods when the firm suspends the right of more than a majority of participants of pension plans from selling their shares in the company, and provides for "disgorgement" or fair funds for investors whose rights are violated.

While these regulations are a response to the Enron and other corporate scandals, they also raise compliance costs to publicly listed firms. Enron employees were locked into pension plans holding Enron shares, unable to liquidate their pension shares before they became worthless. On the other hand, Enron officers, Kenneth Lay and Jeffrey Skilling, sold their shares before the collapse. Europe uses the concept based IAS.

Stakeholders

A related issue is more philosophical; the US firm typically owes its allegiance to its owners, the shareholders. In Europe and elsewhere the firm may have different constituents or stakeholders: the shareholders, management, the government, its unions and its customers. Of course, the government is a majority shareholder in the case of state enterprises. President Dmitry Medvedev of Russia approved a new privatization plan in 2011 reducing the state's participation in 21 enterprises, yet conserving "golden shares" in 6 keeping the government's "right" to veto decisions made by their directors. These six enterprises are the diamond monopoly, Alrosa where the state currently holds 51% of the shares, the largest hydro-electric supplier, Rousguidro, 61% held by the government, Zarouubliejneft foreign drilling and exploration, cereal producer and buyer OZK, and the second largest petroleum company, Rosneft, 75% controlled by the government. Vladimir Putin, previous president, and candidate in 2012 had implemented several re-nationalizations. Medvedev's argument is that innovation and growth will be higher when the companies are privatized, and will also reduce the fiscal deficit, which was 5% of GDP in 2010. The new plan of privatizations was set for 2017, but was changed when Putin was re-elected.

美国企业通常以所有者或股东利益最大化作为经营目标。在欧洲和其他地区,企业可能代表不同委托人的利益,如股东、企业管理人员、政府、工会或顾客。

Legal framework

A number of countries observe Napoleonic rather than Common Law, deriving from the Napoleonic codes which govern business law in France. Spain also implanted the Napoleonic codes in most of Latin America. In Islamic countries, interest is prohibited by the Koran, so financial institutions must arrange for profit-sharing with its depositors-owners. As an amendment to the U.S. Securities Act of 1934, the Foreign Corrupt Practices Act of 1977 (FCPA 1977), prohibits making payments to foreign of-

许多国家遵循拿破仑法律体系,而非英美的普通法体系。

ficials for the purpose of securing contracts or licenses, influencing decisions, evading regulations and law, and obtaining business, retaining business, or directing business to any person. If a director, officer, or shareholder of the firm either knows or should know that a payment is being made as a bribe or kickback to favorably influence a decision, it is illegal and subject to civil penalties up to $100,000 and imprisonment for not more than 5 years, or both. There is an exception for routine governmental action "to expedite or to secure the performance of a routine governmental action by a foreign official." This is known as *grease* money, which is not prohibited unless it is so by the local laws.

If a grease payment is not large and is made to expedite governmental action to grant a license to operate a bank that is granted to everyone qualifying for a bank license, there may be no problem. If the payments are made simply to expedite the request, they are not illegal under FCPA 1977. If the official has some discretion, and few applicants are approved, the payment would be illegal. The Organization for Economic Cooperation and Development (OECD) established in 1997 a Convention Against Bribery of Foreign Public Officials in International Business. The Convention makes it a crime to offer, promise or give a bribe to a foreign public official in order to obtain or retain international business deals. In addition, The UN Convention Against Corruption (UNCAC) is an international treaty that was signed by 113 countries in December 2003.

Institutional framework

There is no question that corruption exists everywhere to some degree. Cleptocracies misappropriate profits and wealth, thereby discouraging enterprise and thrift. Instead, bribery and malfeasance are rewarded. It matters little to have laws against corruption, when it is institutionalized in practice. To combat bribery, on November 21, 1997, OECD Member countries and five non-member countries, Argentina, Brazil, Bulgaria, Chile and the Slovak Republic, adopted a Convention on Combating Bribery of Foreign Public Officials in International Business Transactions. The convention was signed in Paris on December 17, 1997. However, Peter Eigen, Chairman of Transparency International puts it this way (January 20, 2001):

> "The scale of bribe-paying by international corporations in the developing countries of the world is massive. Actions by the majority

of governments of the leading industrial countries to curb international corruption are modest. The results include growing poverty in poor countries, persistent undermining of the institutions of democracy, and mounting distortions in fair international commerce."
Source: www.transparency.org.

Much of the last standby loan to Russia before their sovereign default in 1998 is rumored to have been deposited by Russian officials in an offshore bank in Jersey, which honors banking secrecy and has no income taxes. "The IMF should learn a lesson from the past five years," the former official, Boris Fyodor, said, referring to the International Monetary Fund, "The IMF was pretending that it was seeing a lot of reforms in Russia. Russia was pretending to conduct reforms. The Western taxpayer was paying for it." (*The New York Times*, October 1, 1998) However, "The IMF was surprised by last year's discovery that the central bank was linked to an offshore investment company in the Channel Island of Jersey and that the (Russian Central) bank had misreported its asset levels to the fund. The offshore company, Fimaco, was acquired by a subsidiary of the central bank during Gerashchenko's previous tenure as central bank chief, although the Fimaco operations that have drawn the most attention to date fell during the 1994–1998 period when he did not head the central bank. (Then U. S. Secretary of the Treasury, Larry) Summers continued his public warnings to Russia on Sunday, repeating the line he took at the opening of a congressional inquiry last week into corruption, money-laundering and the still-unsubstantiated charges that IMF funds had been illegally diverted." (*The New York Times*, September 27, 1999)

Language

Language barriers can be an important obstacle or alternatively, an advantage in conducting business abroad. Banco Santander Central Hispano of Madrid is now the largest bank in Latin America. It is closely followed by Bilbao Viscaya of Barcelona in size of assets. No doubt the language, cultural similarities, and the use of Napoleonic Law explain, in part, the comparative advantage of Spanish banks in Latin America. Also, their long banking tradition serves them well in emerging markets in Latin America.

Taxation

International taxation varies from country to country, ranging from zero corporate income taxes and zero personal income tax in some tax havens to a high average of 24% in the OECD countries reported by The Tax Foundation, *Corporate Tax Rates Around the World*. When profits of a US company are repatriated, they are converted into dollars and the U.S. corporate tax rate of up to 21% is applied. If the foreign tax rate is lower, say 20%, the company receives a tax credit of 20% paid to the foreign government, and then pays the remaining 1% to the U.S. Treasury. If it pays over 21% in corporate taxes, the firm will get a full offset up to 21%, its marginal tax rate on U.S. earnings, as well as tax credits, possibly deferred or for other branches, on the additional excess taxes. In some cases, companies are able to transfer profits out of the U.S. to shell corporations in tax havens to escape taxes by transfer pricing. This is not in principle a legal practice if done solely for the purpose of evading taxes.

FYI: OECD Corporate Tax Rates 2019

Country	Percent (%)	Country	Percent (%)
Australia	30	Korea	28
Austria	25	Latvia	20
Belgium	30	Lithuania	15
Canada	27	Luxembourg	25
Chile	25	Mexico	30
Czech Republic	19	Netherlands	25
Denmark	22	New Zealand	28
Estonia	20	Norway	22
Finland	20	Poland	19
France	32	Portugal	32
Germany	30	Slovak Republic	21
Greece	28	Slovenia	19
Hungary	9	Spain	25
Iceland	20	Sweden	21
Ireland	13	Switzerland	21
Israel	23	Turkey	22
Italy	28	United Kingdom	19
Japan	30	United States	26

Note: Combined Federal, State and Local rates.
Source: https://data.oecd.org, July 22, 2019.

Since January 1, 2018, the nominal federal corporate tax rate in the United States of America is 21% due to the Tax Cuts and Jobs Act of 2017.

Corporate tax rates in Asia are generally lower, but not so low as in tax havens at zero percent.

FYI: Asian and Tax Haven Corporate Tax Rates 2019

Asia	Corporate tax rate (%)	Tax havens	Corporate tax rate (%)
Cambodia	20	Anguila	0
China	25	Bahamas	0
India	30	Bahrain	0
Indonesia	25	Belize	0
Japan	30	Bermuda	0
Korea	25	British Virgin Islands	0
Laos	24	Cayman Islands	0
Malaysia	24	Channel Islands	0
Myanmar	25	Cook Islands	0
Pakistan	30	Guernsey	0
Philippines	30		
Singapore	17		
Thailand	20		
Vietnam	20		

Source: KPMG Global, https://home.kpmg.com, July 22, 2019.

Regulatory framework

In the United States, the U.S. Securities and Exchange Commission (SEC) regulates the major exchanges and securities dealers. "The primary mission of the U.S. Securities and Exchange Commission is to protect investors and maintain the integrity of the securities markets. ... The laws and rules that govern the securities industry in the United States derive from a simple and straightforward concept: all investors, whether large institutions or private individuals, should have access to certain basic facts about an investment prior to buying it. To achieve this, the SEC requires public companies to disclose meaningful financial and other information to the public, which provides a common pool of knowledge for all investors to use to judge for themselves if a company's securities are a good invest-

在美国,美国证券交易委员会(SEC)是监管证券市场参与者的主要机构。虽然新兴市场也强调对交易所、公司、证券交易者的监管,但许多国家的监管并没有被严格执行。

ment. The SEC also oversees other key participants in the securities world. ... Typical infractions include insider trading, accounting fraud, and providing false or misleading information about securities and the companies that issue them. ... The SEC offers the public ... the EDGAR database of disclosure documents that public companies are required to file with the Commission." (www.sec.gov, April 30, 2001) While overseas exchanges, firms, and securities dealers are also subject to scrutiny, in emerging markets many of these are recent and the same disclosure and transparency requirements do not apply. Interestingly, the SEC was created during the great depression (1929–1933), precipitated by the October 1929 stock market crash where half of the $50 billion in new securities offered during the 1920s became worthless. Purchases on margin represented over 10% of the market. The main purposes of the security and exchange law of 1933 can be reduced to two common-sense notions:

- Companies publicly offering securities for investment dollars must tell the public the truth about their businesses, the securities they are selling, and the risks involved in investing.

- People who sell and trade securities — brokers, dealers, and exchanges — must treat investors fairly and honestly, putting investors' interests first. (www.sec.gov, April 30, 2001)

U.S. publicly listed companies' income statements and balance sheets can be found on the EDGAR database of corporate filings. Here is a lexicon for some of the common filings by publicly traded companies at www.sec.gov.

登录网址 www.sec.gov, 选择"search for company filings"或者"Quick EDGAR Tutorial"来获取美国上市公司的资产负债表信息。

FYI: The EDGAR Database of Corporate Filings (www.sec.gov)

10K	The official version of a company's annual report, with a comprehensive overview of the business.
10Q	An abridged version of the 10K, filed quarterly for the first three quarters of a company's fiscal year.
8K	If anything significant happens that should be reported before the next 10K or 10Q rolls around, the company files one of these.
12b-25	Request for a deadline extension to file a required report, like a 10K or 10Q. When the late report is ultimately filed, NT is appended to the report's name.

S1	Basic registration form for new securities, most often initial or secondary public offerings. Variants with higher numbers are used for registrations connected with mergers, employee stock plans and real estate investment trusts (REITs).
F6	Foreign companies use similar forms beginning with F; for example, F6 for American Depository Receipts.
Proxy statement	Information and ballot materials for shareholder votes, including election of directors and approval of mergers and acquisitions when required.
Forms 3, 4 and 5	Directors, officers and owners of more than 10 percent of a company's stock report their initial purchases on Form 3 and subsequent purchases or sales on Form 4; they file an annual statement of their holdings on Form 5.

Source: *New York Times*, Sunday June 21, 1998, www.edgar.gov.

The Sarbanes-Oxley Act of 2002 in the United States provided for an independent accounting oversight board, independent auditors, corporate responsibility rules, enhanced financial disclosure, regulations on analyst conflict of interest, and increased criminal and civil penalties for executive and accounting fraud. Many of the enhanced penalties are being served in jail and significant fines and disgorgement penalties have been raised.

This did not, however, solve the problem since the Dodd-Frank Financial Regulation bill (The **Dodd-Frank Wall Street Reform and Consumer Protection Act** was signed into law by President Barack Obama on July 21, 2010), following the 2007–2010 financial collapse and economic recession in the United States. In "A New Foundation Outline", the Administration proposed: The consolidation of regulatory agencies, elimination of the national thrift charter, and a new oversight council to evaluate systemic risk.

Regulatory Act: The Dodd-Frank Act of 2010

1. Comprehensive regulation of financial markets, including increased transparency of derivatives (bringing them onto exchanges);

2. Consumer protection reforms including a new consumer protection agency and uniform standards for "plain vanilla" products as well as strengthened investor protection;

> 3. Tools for financial crises, including a "resolution regime" complementing the existing *Federal Deposit Insurance Corporation* (FDIC) authority to allow for orderly winding down of bankrupt firms, and including a proposal that the Federal Reserve (the "Fed") receive authorization from the Treasury for extensions of credit in "unusual or exigent circumstances";
>
> 4. Various measures aimed at increasing international standards and cooperation, including in this section were proposals related to improved accounting and tightened regulation of credit rating agencies;
>
> 5. The Volcker rule to separate commercial banking and proprietary trading by investment banks was added in January 2010.
>
> Source: *A New Foundation: Rebuilding financial supervision and regulation*, US Congress, Washington, D. C., 2009.

It remains to be seen if the proposed benefits of increased transparency and no more "too big to fail" will outweigh the increased regulatory costs of compliance to the financial industry. There is always the problem of "regulatory capture," where those that are regulated, capture the regulators by more than grease money. In fact, the large banks have become larger since they can afford to comply, and many small banks are too small to survive the increased regulatory cost.

Political risk

政治风险（Political Risk）:因意料之外的政策变化而导致企业的海外分公司遭受经济损失的风险。

Political risk refers to economic exposure to unanticipated changes in governmental policy that affect the earnings and value of your affiliate or subsidiary. Unanticipated nationalization would be an extreme example. The growing global membership in the General Agreement on Tariffs and Trade/World Trade Organization (GATT/WTO) has significantly reduced political risk as a signatory nation must adhere to Article III of the GATT, National Treatment on Internal Taxation and Regulation (see Chapter 5). National Treatment requires that a country adhering to the GATT apply the same internal taxes and regulations to foreign firms as it does to national firms. Consequently, a government cannot levy a 25% corporate income tax on national firms and a 35% tax on foreign firms. Of course, in practice informal taxes may be solicited as "fees" from corrupt officials. Even nationalization is possible when a populist government unexpectedly comes to power. The foreign oil companies in Venezuela faced implicit nationalization by the Hugo Chávez regime through governmental decrees and "purchases" tantamount to nationalization.

The purchases are often done in Venezuelan bolivars at the official rate, thus substantially reducing the compensation for nationalization:

> **In the News: Political Risk in Venezuela**
>
> Hugo Chávez, the president of Venezuela, "has ordered the confiscation of 717,000 acres from a British company amid a disagreement over compensation for earlier seizures of ranchland from the firm. Chávez announced the latest takeover after saying that Venezuela refuses to pay compensation in foreign currency to Agropecuaria Flora, a local subsidiary of Britain's Vestey Group. Chávez said the company had demanded the government pay it in dollars for the previous expropriation of tens of thousands of acres. But the government insists in paying in bolivars, Venezuela's currency. It is difficult for foreign companies operating in Venezuela to repatriate profits and other income in bolivars because of foreign currency controls in the South American country."
>
> Source: "Hugo Chávez orders seizure of British company's land for Venezuelan state," AP Caracas, guardian.co.uk, October 30, 2011.

Chávez also imposed price controls, so that a major CEO, Lorenzo Mendoza, the owner of Empresas Polar SA, Venezuela's largest privately held company, complains that Venezuela is "drowning under regulations." (*Bloomberg*, November 6, 2011)

A subsidiary of the World Bank, the Multilateral Investment Guarantee Agency (MIGA), provides insurance against investment risk in emerging markets.

Intellectual property rights

Software code, Madonna's latest song, Microsoft's latest Windows operating system, Rolex watches, Lacoste shirts are counterfeited worldwide on a regular basis. In some instances, the copying and manufacture of pharmaceuticals is perfectly legal in the home country, but is prohibited by the GATT/WTO articles of agreement. The Software association publishes a blacklist of countries that pirate the most. Acceding to the WTO requires the signatory country to respect international patents, trademarks and brands. In Latin America, Brazil seems to be the greatest culprit. In Asia, China is taking strong steps to enforce intellectual property rights since it acceded to the GATT/WTO in December 2001. In the smart phone industry, Apple and Samsung are pursuing litigation to prevent copying of intellectual property rights. Kodak, short of liquidity, is selling its patents to earn cash flow. Google bought Motorola Mobility in order to acquire patents to avoid patent litigation. International property rights are extremely valuable in encouraging innovation and spreading it worldwide, especially in our global market connected by the internet.

与贸易有关的知识产权协定(TRIPS):该协定规定了知识产权的保护范围,具体来说,它包括版权及相关权、商标、地域标识、工业品外观设计、专利、集成电路布图设计、未公开的信息等七种知识产权。

Trade Related Intellectual Property Rights (TRIPS) were agreed upon in the Final Act of the Uruguay Round of Multilateral Trade Negotiations, April 1994, the WTO. A country which has acceded to the WTO must respect patents, trademarks, copyright, and other intellectual property rights. In addition, industrial designs, software programs, and media and inventions of products or processes are protected for 20 years. That means the owners of protected designs can prevent the manufacture, sale or importation of articles bearing or importing a design that is counterfeit—an unauthorized copy of the protected design.

Conclusion

International finance involves currency conversion and foreign exchange risk issues. In addition, international taxation, the legal framework, and regulation differ across countries. Most countries have acceded to the GATT/WTO, so are required to extend national treatment to foreign banks and financial institutions, including insurance companies. China acceded to the WTO in December 2001, thus celebrating its tenth anniversary of accession in December 2011. Capital market integration equalizes the risk-adjusted rates of return worldwide, thereby increasing global rates of return and economic growth. Corruption remains a crucial issue in global markets: It is a brake on economic growth and foreign direct investment. Business and finance practices vary widely from country to country. The US dollar is still the world's reserve and settlement currency, but the yuan is taking cautious steps, as if in Deng Xiaoping's words "crossing the river by groping for stones," in establishing offshore markets for the yuan for clearance in settlements and holding as a reserve asset.

Questions and problems

1.1 Suppose there were a single world currency, such as gold, that each country could produce and mint. Would there be any need to study international finance?

1.2 What is the purpose of the SEC requiring publicly listed firms to disclose earnings and the financial condition of the firm in its 10Q and 10K forms?

1.3 What is the purpose of the SOX 2002 act requiring the CEO and the CFO to sign the income and balance sheets as to be correct to the best of their knowledge?

1.4 Why is it that hard currencies, such as gold or silver coins, tend to produce less inflation than fiat or paper monies?

1.5 Why would so many US firms incorporate affiliates in Ireland and not repatriate earnings?

References and suggested reading

Bailay, Rasul, "A Ban on Forward Trading Roils Bombay Share Market," *The Wall Street Journal*, May 16, 2001.

"Kim's Fall from Grace: Inside Daewoo's Fraud Scandal," *BusinessWeek*, February 19, 2001.

The International Monetary Fund (2000), *Finance & Development*, Washington, D. C.

Deloitte, "Worldwide Corporate Tax Rates 2011," www. deloitte. com

Fritch, Peter, "Sanborns Official Bought CompUSA Stake Before Buyout," *The Wall Street Journal*, May 18, 2001.

Gordon, Michael R., "I. M. F. Urged by Russian Not to Give More Aid," *The New York Times*, October 1, 1998.

Leggett, Karby, "Lawsuits Flood China's Securities Industry: Shareholders Allege Rife Manipulation," *The Wall Street Journal*, May 30, 2001.

Luo, Yadong (2007), *Guanxi and Business*, World Scientific, 2nd ed.

Sanger, David E., "Russia Hotly Protests Audits Demanded by I. M. F. for Loans," *The New York Times*, September 27, 1999.

CHAPTER 2

The History of Money and Finance

货币和金融历史

价值尺度 (Unit of account):货币的三种重要职能之一,是指货币衡量和表现一切商品价值大小的职能。

交换媒介 (Medium of exchange):货币的三种重要职能之一。货币的产生,使得商品之间的交换由直接的物物交换变成以货币为媒介的交换。

贮藏手段 (Store of value):货币的三种重要职能之一,是指货币退出流通领域作为社会财富的一般代表被保存起来的职能。

Money serves three important roles in an economy. It is a **unit of account**, a **medium of exchange**, and a **store of value**. As a medium of exchange, money avoids barter of one good for another. Barter, where individuals trade goods, requires a double coincidence of wants. You have a bicycle, but want an iPad, and someone you run into in the market has an iPad and wants a bicycle. When you meet by coincidence, you might exchange the goods. This is called barter, countertrade, or bilateral clearing: trade without a medium of exchange.

In the absence of a stable medium of exchange, countertrade flourishes, bringing oranges from Brazil in exchange for cotton from Uzbekistan or wheat from Kazakhstan. Indeed, Minnesota's Cargill in the US is one of the largest firms engaging in countertrade worldwide. In the newly independent states, the ruble was unstable, losing value over 20% a month, so that half of the trades made in the early and mid-1990s involved bilateral clearing and barter. It is still done, but using a medium of exchange—a hard currency—is far more efficient. A double coincidence of wants is not necessary. If you want an iPad, you take cash to the store and buy it. If you want a bicycle, you can pay cash—or nowadays, use a debit card or a revolving credit card, which involves finance.

Money facilitates exchange. It also provides a unit of account—a yardstick by which we measure the value of goods, assets and foreign currencies. When there is high inflation, money loses its effectiveness both as a yardstick of value and as a medium of exchange. The seller is uncertain about the real amount that will be paid upon delivery since high inflation usually means unstable inflation rates. When a contract calls for payment in 30 days, yet there is 20% inflation in the month, the seller receives

20% less in real value. If the rate of inflation unexpectedly accelerates to 40%, the seller receives 40% less, but if it slows to 10%, the receipt is only 10% less. High inflation sometimes moves economies to indexing for inflation. This reduces the resistance to inflation and makes stopping it more difficult. As a store of value, money is replaced by interest-yielding assets, foreign currency, or durables that rise in value along with inflation.

When the peso rapidly falls in value in Latin America, individuals substitute a more stable currency which they hold as a store of value, medium of exchange, and a stable unit of account. Informal **dollarization** takes place in Argentina and Peru. When the home currency becomes worthless as a medium of exchange, countries occasionally abolish it and formally adopt another currency as their own. In 2000, Ecuador formally adopted the dollar, abolishing the sucre.

美元化(Dollarization): 是指作为一种政策, 一国或经济体的政府让美元取代自己的货币并最终自动放弃货币或金融主权的行动。

Prerequisites of good money

A hard currency, such as gold or silver, costs resources to make. The resource cost ensures that too much money will not be produced, thereby checking inflation. If there is inflation, the intrinsic value of the metal in the coin may surpass its face value as money. At that point, the coins are melted down, thus stopping growth in the money supply. The difference between a coin's value as money and the cost to mint it is called **seigniorage** or mint profits. For example, a penny has one cent as its value as money, yet it costs over a penny to produce it. The cost of materials—zinc and copper—is 0.8 cents, while the manufacturing cost is 0.6 cents. The mint costs are thus 1.4 cents. Consequently, seigniorage is negative, −0.4 cents on a penny. However, consider a $100 bill. To make it difficult to counterfeit, its design requires high quality linen with specks, many colored inks and watermarks, yet the marginal cost of an extra $100 banknote is only about 14 cents. However, its value as money is $100. Seigniorage or mint profits are therefore $99.86. It is no wonder that the $100 bill is the banknote that attracts the most counterfeiters. By law, only the realm can strike coinage. That is, a sovereign country enjoys the monopoly issue of the national currency. It consequently also enjoys the seigniorage profits associated with the issue of currency. The US Treasury benefits from the world reserve status of the dollar and its use as a substitute money around the world. It collects seigniorage from the use of the dollar as a store of value and medium of exchange in other countries. Approximately 80% of the printed $100 bills are held abroad. Ecuadori-

铸币税(Seigniorage): 硬币作为货币的价值与铸造它所耗费成本的差额, 也称为铸币利润。

ans, for example, ship coffee and shrimp to the US to earn the $100 bill.

To avoid inflation, the Charter of central banks usually establishes the independence of the Central Bank from the Treasury. That way, the Treasury cannot simply order the Central Bank to purchase its bonds in exchange for the issue of new money, i.e. the printing press, to finance its deficits. However, central bank independence is not always observed.

As a medium of exchange, a good money must be divisible, even down to a penny. This allows a near continuum of prices to be settled upon rather than discrete price increments or the exchange of money plus some candy or gum, as has been the case in Italy in bygone days. It is a "nickels or dimes" problem. A ten-dollar bill is divisible into two fives, a five-dollar bill is divisible into five ones, a one-dollar bill is divisible into twenty nickels, ten dimes, four quarters, or 100 pennies. This divisibility criterion is important to facilitate transactions. Cigarettes have been used in exchange in prisoner of war camps, as well as script that signify money. The UK shilling being worth 12 pence and 20 shillings equal to one pound made for an awkward division and became obsolete with decimalization on February 15, 1971.

不兑现纸币(Fiat money):由政府发行的不能兑换成黄金或白银的纸币。它的目的在于节省采掘金银带来的成本。

Fiat money, paper money not exchangeable for a commodity, such as silver—came about to save on the mint costs of mining gold and silver. It is also easier to change denominations and carry around paper money rather than heavy coin. The first paper money was issued in China during the 11th century, around 1023. Seigniorage is greater with paper money than coin. In some countries, such as Argentina in the early 2001, protestors wore signs in protest of "No mas papel pintado" or "No more painted paper" to voice their opposition to the over-issue of money, the freezing and confiscation of bank accounts, and the ensuing inflation. It is always tempting for government to finance a deficit by fiat money. The broader the currency zone of a money, and the fewer the transactions costs of conversion, the more useful it is. The use of the US dollar in the 50 US states and the euro in 19 European countries makes the liquidity of these currencies greater. Stable monetary policy is the key to having a currency substituted for those that depreciate rapidly in value. Price stability in a currency increases the zones that the particular money is used in. Fiscal convergence within the same monetary zone is also proving to be a necessary condition to avoid financial crises such as those occurring in Europe.

Money and exchange rates

Great central banks, such as the Bank of England and the Banque de

France, had gold windows where they bought and sold gold at a fixed currency price in the 19th century. In doing so, their currency rates were fixed. For example, if the Bank of England sets 10 pounds per ounce of gold as the buy/sell rate and the Banque de France 100 francs, the equilibrium exchange rate is set at 100 francs per 10 pounds or 10 francs a pound.

Arbitrage in gold kept the exchange rates within a narrow band of **gold points**. Let's say the exchange rate falls to 9.5 francs a pound. A gold arbitrageur purchases 10 pounds for 95 francs, presents the 10 pounds to the Bank of England gold window in exchange for an ounce of gold. The arbitrageur then insures and ships the gold to the Banque de France, selling it for 100 francs, pocketing 5 francs less insurance and shipping as profits. This gold arbitrage kept the exchange rates within narrow margins known as gold points, the points at which profitable gold arbitrage took place. Consequently, countries that were on the gold standard had fixed exchange rates between themselves.

黄金输送点（Gold Points）：对于黄金的套利使得汇率在黄金输送点确定的狭窄范围内波动。

Similarly, countries in Asia were on the silver standard so that their currencies were pegged to one another and had corresponding silver points. However, since there was usually no fixed relationship between the price of gold and silver, China, a silver standard country, floated its exchange rate with respect to the gold standard currencies. The silver depreciation kept Chinese exports up during the great depression in the West until 1934, when the US passed the Silver Purchase Act to monetize silver at a significantly higher price. The implicit Chinese revaluation of 25% destroyed their export and import competing industries, sending them into a major recession that caused famine in the countryside (Friedman, 1992).

History of monies

The first money originated in China during the Shang Dynasty from the 13th to the 12th century BC. It was in shell form, cowls connected by string, bone, and copper objects shaped in the form of grain or shells. From 770 to 256 BC, mostly in the later Zhou Dynasty, bronze and copper coins in the shapes of small spades, chisels, hoes and knives were used in place of the articles themselves as hard-bodied money in some of the warring states. Figure 2.1 illustrates the Chinese spade monies of the eastern Zhou Dynasty and Ming knife monies.

历史上第一枚货币出现在公元前13世纪到公元前12世纪的中国商朝。

Figure 2.1 The birth of coinage: Chinese spade monies of the eastern Zhou Dynasty, 770-256 BC, and Ming knife monies, late 5th century BC

It is legitimate to regard Chinese tool coins as the first coinage since they were used as a medium of exchange, unit of account, and store of value. Glyn Davies (1994) believes that Chinese spade, hoe, and knife monies preceded Lydian coinage of 600-575 BC but refers to them as "quasi-coins." Many Zhou period coins have characters indicating denomination in liangs, the Chinese *tael*, but they weigh only about 77% of their official value, indicating a seigniorage system where coins are made to a weight below their circulating value. The seigniorage profits offset the cost of minting, earning a small profit to the minting authority.

最早所知的欧洲硬币出现在大约公元前 600 年到公元前 575 年的利迪亚古国（现在小亚细亚和土耳其的一部分）。它是由琥珀制成的。

The earliest known European coins appeared in Lydia, now Asia Minor, part of Turkey, circa 600-575 BC. These early coins were made of electrum, a precious alloy of gold and silver that: "...consists of about 54 percent gold, 44 percent silver, 2 percent copper, and trace amounts of iron and lead." Figure 2.2 illustrates the Lydian Lion Head, an early electrum coin.

Figure 2.2 The Lydian Lion Head: 600-575 BC

Source: "A Case for the World's First Coin: The Lydian Lion", http://rg.ancients.info/lion

The electrum coins were used to finance transactions between City States based on their weight. Greek coinage followed. The first bronze coins did not appear in Europe until the fifth century BC. Alexander the Great introduced uniform coinage to all the territories he conquered. He confiscated the gold and silver treasuries in these countries and minted coins from them. At this time, the Romans were developing their own metal monies. The Romans reduced the metal content of their coins, making them lighter, but maintaining the same value as money. The government saved precious metals in this way to meet its debts by making greater seigniorage profits: the difference between value as money and mint costs.

The silver penny was first introduced around 760 AD in Britain. Following the Norman invasion in 1066 AD, William the Conqueror continued to mint the Saxon pennies. He introduced the "sterling silver" standard. Silver was the coin of England from the Norman invasion until 1920. The gold sovereign appeared in circa 1500. It was called a sovereign because the coin bore the picture of Henry VII on the royal throne. It was minted until the outbreak of World War I.

Jiaozi, the first uniform paper money in the world, was printed in 1023 AD by the Song Dynasty. Later dynasties issued paper money, but most were over reliant on seigniorage—the printing press—to finance their expenditures. Hyperinflation resulted. Eventually, even the government would not accept paper money in payment of taxes. Round copper and bronze coins replaced paper, but lost their worth due to ease of production and widespread counterfeiting. One ounce silver ingots, called *taels* weighing slightly more than one ounce, supplanted paper and copper money since silver was a better asset not subject to ease of coining. It was also a good international medium of exchange, used in trade payments. Figure 2.3 illustrates the world's first banknote, the Song Dynasty's Jiaozi.

中国的宋朝发明了世界上第一张纸币——"交子"。

In 1661, the first European bank note appeared in Sweden. The Swedish riksdaler banknote is illustrated in Figure 2.4. Before the end of the 17th century, banknotes were being printed and issued in England. London goldsmiths originated the banknote when they began to act as bankers. People deposited gold with them for safe keeping, and the goldsmiths would give them a receipt. The words "or bearer" were added after the name of the depositor in 1670. This meant that the goldsmith would deliver metallic money to the person who presented the note for redemption; thus the notes were used as money.

Figure 2.3 The world's first banknote—the Jiaozi of the Song Dynasty, 1023 AD

Figure 2.4 The first European banknote 1661—the riksdalers specie of the Stockholms Banco, Sweden

Johan Palmstruch, founder and director of the Stockholms Banco obtained a Royal Decree to print banknotes in 1661, agreeing to share the profits of the bank with the Crown. However, overissue of the new banknotes was a problem. When the banknotes were presented in 1664 for redemption in terms of copper coins, redemption was refused by the bank which was insolvent. The bank was then taken over by the government.

The first global money: the Spanish peso 1497 to the 1900s

出现于1497年的西班牙比索是第一种世界货币。

The Spanish peso or silver dollar, contained 0.821791 troy ounce (25.56 grams) of pure silver and was also used as domestic money in China, having been minted in the new world in Mexico, Peru, and Spain, then used in commerce. The so called "pieces of eight," referred to their value of 8 *reales*. The Spanish silver dollars were manufactured in Mexico and Peru, as well as in Sevilla, and transported in bulk back to Spain to pay for wars and commerce. The Manila Galleon shipped Mexican silver to Manila, where it would be exchanged for Chinese goods, since silver was the only foreign commodity money Chinese merchants would accept. Spanish silver dollars were often stamped with Chinese characters known as "chop marks", indicating that the coin had been assayed by a respected merchant and determined to be genuine. Figure 2.5 shows a 1739 Spanish silver dollar.

Figure 2.5 The first global money—the Spanish peso

The use of *taels* reduced significantly the risk of inflation in terms of the silver price of goods because it was widely hoarded as a store of wealth. The weight of a piece of silver determined its value as money, so it had the desired divisibility property. Furthermore, silver was also held in the form of jewelry, thereby reducing its supply as a medium of exchange. Under the silver standard, China experienced 300 years of price stability (Huang, 1974). Paper money was used again from 1875 to 1908 during the Qing Dynasty, the last feudal dynasty in China. It was colorful, ornate and difficult to counterfeit, resembling modern banknotes.

When the first pilgrims arrived in America, they found the Amerindians using strings of shell beads, cowls or "wampum" as money. The colonists traded goods with the Amerindians, but also adopted wampum as money. The Spanish silver dollar coming from Mexico was held as a store of value and used as a medium of exchange for large transactions. The colonists met their everyday needs by paying with sugar and tobacco—commodity monies. Bricks of salt were used elsewhere as commodity money.

The American colonists requested a supply of coins from Britain, but the British Treasury declined. So they set up the first mint in Boston, producing shillings, sixpences, and three-penny pieces in 1652. Private state banks issued their own banknotes until the Civil War of 1861–1865, when both the greenback and the confederate dollar were newly printed to finance the war efforts of the North and the South respectively. At the end of the war, the confederate currency was worthless and the greenback dollar evolved into the modern currency used in the United States. It still has a green back, but is smaller in size than the original issue. The Federal Reserve System was created in 1913, splitting seigniorage profits between the 12 districts.

The latest prominent currency is the euro, created by the Maastricht Treaty whereby Western European countries increased integration of their economies by adopting a common currency. On January 1, 1999, the exchange rates of the existing currencies were irrevocably set and the euro was introduced as a legal currency. Euro area member states began implementing a common monetary policy, but diverged in fiscal policy, debt and borrowing. The eleven existing currencies of the participating member states were converted to euros and withdrawn from circulation January 1, 2002. Greece joined on January 1, 2001, though it required accounting smoke and mirrors. Now 19 member states share the new euro banknotes and coins, but the European sovereign debt crisis of 2011 and 2012 is putting the euro in jeopardy. It is proving difficult to reform spending greater than tax revenues, thus putting no upper bound on debt in countries like Greece. A structured default of Greek sovereigns took place, but even then the fiscal deficit must be eliminated in a sustainable manner.

Foreign exchange history

Foreign trade was initially conducted by barter or with the currency of the importing country acting as the medium of exchange. Foreign merchants accepted payment in local currency and spent the proceeds on the purchase of local goods. Foreign exchange emerged when uniform metallic coins bearing the marks and seal of a banker or merchant came into being. Having gold, silver and copper as the units of account facilitated valuation and conversion.

Bills of exchange made their appearance in Babylonia and Assyria centuries before the invention of marked coinage in China and Lydia. The bill of exchange was used primarily in international trade, and is a written order by one person to pay another a specific sum on a specific date in the future. Since carrying large amounts of coins was risky, bills of exchange were used in order to facilitate currency and trade transactions. The text of some bills of exchange indicates that payment was made in locations other than those of issue. The bill of exchange allowed trade to take place without the use of coinage, a precursor of the modern letter of credit (L/C). Furthermore, the bills were traded as financial instruments in trade fairs. They were discounted and converted into foreign units of account. The trade fairs were the precursors of modern stock and foreign exchanges.

汇票(Bill of exchange): 汇票主要用在国际贸易中,是由一人开出的要求某人在将来某一特定时间支付特定金额给他人的书面命令。它是现代信用证(L/C)的前身。

The first semblance of foreign exchange trading consisted of meeting places in commercial centers. The discrepancies in the relative values of metals were exploited by foreign merchants when choosing their means of payment, a version of Gresham's Law where merchants use the lower valued money in exchange, and hoard the higher valued one. It also confirms the "law of one price" through arbitrage. The role played by money-changers greatly increased in importance during the centuries of Roman debasement of the coinage.

During the Middle Ages and the Renaissance, the bill of exchange could be used to disguise payments of interest in foreign exchange. Since they were discounted, their yield to maturity represented interest payments. These disguised loans were referred to as "fictitious exchange", whereas conventional bill exchanges were referred to as "real exchange". The convention was to quote foreign exchange rates in terms of bills payable at settlement. The pound was quoted in terms of foreign currencies.

Thanks to interest-bearing loans disguised as a foreign exchange transaction, merchants and financiers were able to make loans evading usury laws using a sequence of two bill transactions—a precursor of today's foreign exchange swap.

不可交割的远期外汇市场(Non-deliverable forward market):下注者对将来一个特定时期的外汇汇率作出预测。预期汇率与真实汇率之间的差别决定了在这场预期的博弈中谁是赢家,输家要支付多少给赢家。这种远期外汇交易今天仍然以不可交割远期(NDFs)的形式在新加坡和中国香港市场上存在,并仍以人民币计价。

An important 16th century development was the appearance of a system of "betting" on future exchange rates: a **non-deliverable forward market**. The betters made forecasts on future exchange rates. The difference between the realized rate and the forecasted rate determined who won the bet and how much the loser would pay the winner. This form of forward exchange existed until 2012 in the form of non-deliverable futures (NDFs) in the Chinese yuan, formally the Renminbi, the "People's Currency," in Singapore and Hong Kong SAR of China.

As Rudiger Dornbush noted, Spanish writers of the 16th century discovered the basics of the purchasing power parity theory. They noticed the relationship between the prices of goods exported from Spain to the new World. By the time they reached their destination, the price of these goods was higher, owing to the cost and risk in transport. The purchasing power parities represented the difference between the prices of these goods in Spain and in Mexico and Peru, adjusting for costs of transport. In the 19th century, Paris and London became the leading markets, dealers being in contact throughout business hours. Forward currencies were widely traded. During the U.S. colonial period, no business in dollars was transacted in London, so that trade with Britain was financed exclusively in sterling. Many of the transactions in sterling bills were done in New Orleans where bills earned by cotton traders were sold.

1944年布雷顿森林体系(The 1944 Bretton Woods system):是指第二次世界大战后以美元为中心的国际货币体系。其主要内容包括美元与黄金挂钩,成员国货币和美元挂钩,实行可调整的固定汇率制度。

The 1944 Bretton Woods, New Hampshire system of pegged but adjustable exchange rates triggered automatic foreign exchange intervention in spot markets, but occasional discretionary intervention in forward markets. Forward intervention often inflicts great losses to the Central Banks buying their currency forward "high" when it eventually goes "low". Thailand did this at great loss, initiating the South East Asia crisis of the 1990s. The era of fixed exchange rates came to an end in 1971–1973, in particular when US President Richard Nixon closed the gold window in 1971 and Britain floated the pound in 1973. With the euro's launch in 1999, fixed rates have returned for many countries in the form of a common currency.

The London FOREX market

By the early 1920s, London was considered to be the world's leading foreign exchange center (Atkin, 2005). Floating exchange rates began in the early 1970s, the resulting desire of multinational businesses to hedge their currency exposures caused the rapid growth of foreign exchange trading. London is still by far the largest FOREX market today in terms of daily foreign exchange turnover. Banks located in the United Kingdom accounted for 37% of global foreign exchange market turnover in April 2016, followed by the United States (20%), Singapore (9%), Japan (6%), Switzerland (2%) and Australia (2%). (Bank for International Settlements, 2016)

Banks and banking

In 3000 BC, the temples in Babylon are reported to have accepted deposits of money and made loans. In the Greek states of the 5th and 4th centuries BC, the temples, the city authorities and private individuals engaged in banking (Jones, 1973). In the 12th century banking started again in some Italian cities after the fall of the Roman Empire. Risky lending by banks led to a demand for a bank that would transfer funds for its customers, but not make loans. The first *giro* or transfer banks came into being. These started in the great Italian trading cities: Florence, Siena, and Venice. German cities followed, but Amsterdam and London eventually became the most important financial centers. The first modern bank was the Bank of Amsterdam, founded in 1609. The Amsterdam bank was quickly followed among other major cities. The Bank of Hamburg was formed in 1619 and the Bank of Sweden in 1656. As noted, Sweden issued the first European paper bank notes in 1661.

Until 1640 the Tower of London provided merchants with a reliable deposit service. Other banking services, money transmission and accounting, were provided by scriveners, essentially accountants. The development of "goldsmith bankers" came about when the goldsmiths persuaded the scriveners to deposit money with them in return for a small interest payment. The main purpose was apparently to have an opportunity to pick over the coins (Atkin, 2005).

Charles I seized the assets deposited in the Tower in 1640 when refused a goldsmith loan of 300,000 pounds. The Tower was no longer a safe depository. The goldsmiths become commercial bankers, providing loans of revolving cash balances. The Bank of England was founded in 1694 as a commercial bank by William Paterson with the right to issue notes up to the amount of its capital, initially £1.2 million. It was nationalized by Parliament in 1946. The shareholders received compensation and the Bank of England thereafter ceased its private business, becoming the banker of government and, since 1977, taking responsibility for monetary policy. Prudential oversight of the British commercial banking system was simultaneously transferred to the Securities and Investments Board.

The Federal Reserve System

联邦储备体系(The Federal Reserve System):美国的中央银行体系,它由设在华盛顿特区的联邦储备理事会和位于全国一些主要城市的12个地区联邦储备银行构成。地区银行的行长由每个银行的理事会选择,理事会成员一般来自当地银行和企业界。

The First Bank of the United States was established in 1791, but collapsed in 1811. The Second Bank of the United States was established in 1816 and survived only until 1836. Thereafter, until 1862, only state-chartered banks existed. They issued notes against gold and silver and were regulated by the states in which they were chartered. The National Banking Act of 1863 in the middle of the U.S. Civil War created a system of national banks with higher banking standards than state banks. It also created a national currency, the greenback dollar. National banks were required to accept each others' notes at par. The government imposed a tax on state banks, forcing most to become national banks. Also, the use of checking accounts grew: by the turn of the century, 90% of narrow money, currency outside banks plus demand deposits, was in the form of checking accounts.

In 1907, a banking panic in the U.S. accompanied by runs on deposits bankrupting some banks, led to arguments for the establishment of a U.S. central bank with an elastic currency to provide liquidity to commercial banks in the event of crises. The Federal Reserve Act established the Federal Reserve System (FED) in 1913 with 12 districts. The Federal Reserve Banks provide liquidity, control the money supply, clear transactions and supervise member banks. The FED was established primarily as a reserve institution, a lender of last resort to prevent bank runs and liquidity crises. The FED has developed into a supervisory institution for member banks and savings and loan associations that pay a premium to the Federal Deposit Insurance Corporation, established in 1933, and the Federal Savings and Loan Insurance Corporation, established in 1934. The FSLIC's functions were transferred to the FDIC in 1989.

The FED is also responsible for U.S. monetary policy: open market operations, primarily Federal Funds targets, rediscount rate setting, and reserve requirements of commercial banks. The FED system also serves as a clearinghouse for the transfer of monies by check and draft between banks within the United States and abroad. By law, the FED also has the objective of promoting maximum employment, but cannot achieve this "real" objective with monetary policy, even if it sacrifices its dual goal of price stability.

The international monetary institutions

The International Monetary Fund(IMF) was established in 1944 at the Bretton Woods Conference in New Hampshire. Its purposes were:

- to establish orderly exchange rate arrangements based on a par value system,
- to eliminate exchange controls, especially for current account transactions, and
- to provide temporary short term balance of payments assistance via loans to member countries that are short of foreign exchange reserves.

国际货币基金组织(The International Monetary Fund):国际货币基金组织与世界银行并列为世界两大金融机构之一,其职责是监察货币汇率和各国贸易情况,提供技术和资金协助,确保全球金融制度正常运行;其总部设在美国华盛顿。

The IMF provided for a pegged exchange rate system with central bank intervention required in the foreign exchange market when the rate approached narrow margins around the official, par value. Rather than imposing exchange controls, it was deemed better to make balance of payments adjustment loans that impose macro-economic policy conditions on the sovereign country that agrees to the conditions. If it agrees to the IMF's loan conditions, the finance minister and the governor of the central bank typically sign a memorandum of understanding with the IMF. The loan is disbursed in several "tranches" or slices and satisfaction of the loan conditions is monitored between disbursements. Extended stand-by-loans have a maturity of 36 months and are essentially lines-of-credit that the country can draw from should it wish to or need to do so. There have been several criticisms leveled recently at the role of the IMF in the international financial system. Just before the Russian default, a multi-billion dollar disbursement was made. The IMF country economist called it a FIEF (foreign investor relief facility) since the dollars were sold for 6 rubles shortly before the Russian default and floating of the exchange rate to 18 rubles a dollar. A substantial portion of the IMF loan was also rumored to have been diverted by government officials into their private accounts in the Jersey Islands (Blustein, 2001). The argument is that the IMF creates "moral hazard", encouraging investors to invest in risky, high return jurisdictions knowing that the IMF will bail them out. In a crisis, the IMF often lends foreign reserves to the central bank, which then dumps them in the foreign exchange market at discount prices before the ultimate depreciation takes place. Similarly, in the case of Argentina's currency board crisis of 2001, due to excessive foreign debt, provincial deficits, and spending before a Presidential campaign, the IMF lent to the Argentine government anyway. In response to criticism, the IMF established an "Independent Internal Evaluation" unit. It is now trying to rescue Europe by lending more to insolvent European nations that are not reforming—a harsh example of moral hazard. The Germans are reluctant to finance the deficit of other spendthrift Europeans.

世界银行(The World Bank): 世界银行作为IMF的姊妹机构,创建于1944年的布雷顿森林会议,其最初的使命是帮助在第二次世界大战中被破坏的国家进行重建。今天它的任务是资助国家克服穷困,联合向发展中国家提供低息贷款、无息贷款和赠款。

The World Bank, a sister institution of the IMF, created in 1944 at the Bretton Woods Conference, initially made long term development loans for projects such as dams, airports, rubber and concrete production, water systems, and the like. It got involved in Structural Adjustment Loans (SALs) in the 1990s in tandem with the IMF requiring structural adjustments to economic policy. This could mean privatization of state enterprises, lifting price and exchange controls, and improving monetary and fiscal policies, for instance. Some of its large scale loans for dams in particular were criticized by environmentalists and human rights activists because of damage to the environment by immediate flooding of the dam area, and the wholesale removal of villagers in the way of the projects. In modern times, World Bank lenders are more sensitive to the environment, as is the IMF to corruption, so they go in for micro-lending at the wholesale level. Many economists think IMF and World Bank loans do more harm than good to the residents of the countries that receive them. Ultimately, the loans are the taxpayers' liability. Portfolio investors often count on the multilateral lenders to bail out a country from bankruptcy, a so-called "moral hazard" investor play where the country is guaranteed not to fail by the lenders. The multi-lateral institutions have also not successfully prevented the wholesale theft of loans by officials in corrupt environments: the former Zaire's Mobutu built palaces in the Congo, France, and Switzerland. Of course, maybe the money did not come from IMF and World Bank loans.

The Bank of International Settlements (BIS) is often referred to as the bank of central banks. It was established May 17, 1930 at the Hague convention. As such, it is the oldest international monetary organization. It does not do business with private individuals or corporations; only with central banks and international institutions. The head office is in Basel, Switzerland. In their role of fostering international monetary cooperation, the General Manager of the BIS has seen the need to address issues of the growth of Offshore Financial Centres (OFCs), Highly Leveraged Institutions (HLIs), Large and Complex Financial Institutions (LCFIs), deposit insurance and the spread of money laundering and accounting scandals.

In his statement to the Financial Stability Forum (FSF), Mr. Crockett, then General Manager, specifically mentions Long Term Capital Management (LTCM), a Connecticut hedge fund, as an example of the near-collapse of a highly leveraged institution. He also singles out Enron as an accounting scandal with financial risks. These are the issues that need to be addressed by the international monetary institutions in his view. Additionally, offshore financial centers need to "facilitate efforts to strengthen supervisory, information sharing and cooperation practices in OFCs, which have taken on increased urgency following September 11 attacks and the global efforts to combat terrorism financing." (Crockett, 2001)

国际清算银行(The Bank of International Settlements):于1930年5月17日成立于海牙会议中,因而是最古老的国际货币组织。国际清算银行常被视为中央银行的银行。

History of the stock exchanges

Adam Smith warned in 1776 about mismanagement of companies that issue shares to finance their operations, the primary role of the stock exchanges. He raises the principal-agent problem, where the shareholders are the principals or owners and the managers are the agents:

Applying the Concept: The Principal-Agent Problem

"The directors of such (joint stock) companies, however, being the managers rather of other people's money than of their own, it cannot well be expected that they should watch over it with the same anxious vigilance with which the partners in a private copartnery frequently watch over their own. Like the stewards of a rich man, they are apt to consider attention to small matters as not for their master's honour, and very easily give themselves a dispensation from having it. Negligence and profusion, therefore, must always prevail, more or less, in the management of the affairs of such a com-

> pany. It is upon this account that joint stock companies for foreign trade have seldom been able to maintain the competition against private adventurers. They have, accordingly, very seldom succeeded without an exclusive privilege, and frequently have not succeeded with one. Without an exclusive privilege they have commonly mismanaged the trade. With an exclusive privilege they have both mismanaged and confined it."
>
> Source: Adam Smith, "Of the Expences of the Sovereign or Commonwealth", *An Inquiry into the Wealth of Nations*, Ch. 1, p. 107.

Yet, large corporations with many owners are able to limit the liability of the owners to the value of the shares they hold. The shareholder can enter a venture by buying shares, and exit it by selling them. The manager acts as the shareholders' agent. Under agency law, a corporation is a single entity, a "person" that may sue or be sued without its members being held liable. It is chartered by the state in which it is located. A corporation is a business in which large numbers of people are organized so that their labor and capital are combined in a single venture. Corporations can list and sell their shares on a number of exchanges. This is known as equity finance versus debt finance. Some of these exchanges used the "open-outcry" form of trading where the trader has to continuously shout his or her order until they are out of breath. If a trader stops shouting, the order is assumed no longer in effect. Since many are shouting at the same time, a system of hand signals has come about that effectively convey the order to the pit manager. While some argue that the presence of specialists and market makers on the floor aid in the conveyance of information, others welcome the transparency of the electronic exchanges that took business away from the open-outcry exchanges. Indeed, the NYSE has acquired Archipelago, a state of the art electronic trading system, no longer using open outcry trading.

The main global stock exchanges

The New York Stock Exchange was established on May 17, 1792 on Wall Street. Traders met at the old wooden wall, no longer in existence, but giving its name to the street. The Dow Jones Industrial Average (DJIA) started out with 12 stocks in October 1928. Only General Electric remains of the original twelve. The S&P 500 Index covers the 500 most widely held companies. The exchange is now NYSE-Euronext following its merger on September 22, 2000 with the Amsterdam, Brussels, and Paris exchanges. It has moved to all electronic trading using Archipelago with five trading posts, and various brokers arranged along the side of the exchange. Specialists still monitor trading activity and the brokers send their orders wirelessly.

The **NASDAQ** is an acronym for National Association of Securities Dealers Automated Quotations. An online stock exchange, it began operations in 1971.

纳斯达克证券交易所 (**NASDAQ**)：NASDAQ 是全国证券商协会自动报价系统的缩写。作为在线证券交易所，它于 1971 年开始交易。

The American Stock Exchange (AMEX) is a subsidiary of the National Association of Securities Dealers. The AMEX index is a composite index of the 739 stocks listed.

The London Stock Exchange was established in 1773, formerly Jonathan's Coffee House where trades met. Trading has since moved off the floor with the introduction of the Stock Exchange Automated Quotations (SEAQ) system. The Footsie 100 Index is the Financial Times Stock Exchange Index of the 100 largest companies listed on the London Stock Exchange.

The Tokyo Stock Exchange was established on May 15, 1878. Japan's Nikkei 225 Index is an average of stock market prices similar to the Dow Jones Industrial Average.

The Paris Bourse was established in Paris by the order of the Royal council in 1724. In 1986, the futures exchange—Le MATIF—was established. The CAC 40 Index is the acronym for "Compagnie des Agents de Change 40 Index," 40 French companies listed on the Paris Stock Exchange.

The Shanghai Stock Exchange (SSE) was founded in 1904, mainly dealing in rubber shares. The Japanese occupation brought an end to its operations. The modern Shanghai Stock Exchange was founded in 1990. The Shanghai Composite Index is a composite of foreign currency denominated B shares sold to qualified foreign institutions and yuan-denominated A shares sold to Chinese citizens and institutions. This market segmentation combined with capital controls makes the Shanghai exchange less linked to international exchanges.

The Shenzhen Stock Exchange (SZSE) was founded in 1990. Owned by the Shenzhen Securities Clearing Corporation (SSCC), it is under the regulatory supervision of the China Securities Regulatory Commission. The SZSE has grown significantly to become the second-largest exchange in China after the Shanghai Stock Exchange. It is now owned by the China Securities Depository and Clearing Co., the parent company of the Shanghai Stock Exchange. By May 2008 the SZSE listed 897 securities in 697 companies. In 2009, it agreed with Standard & Poor's to produce benchmark investible indices on the Chinese market. Chinese institutional investors will also be able to invest in a listed fund based on the S&P 500 Index.

点心债券(Dim sum bonds): 在中国香港地区发行的以人民币计价的债券,因其相对于整个人民币债券市场规模很小,所以被称为点心债券。

The Hong Kong Stock Exchange was established in 1891. The Industrial and Commercial Bank of China (ICBC) and the Bank of China (BOC) along with other commercial banks from Chinese mainland were listed on the Hong Kong Security Exchange by issuing H shares denominated in HK dollars. An H share is a share of a company incorporated in the Chinese mainland but listed on the Hong Kong Stock Exchange or another foreign exchange. H-shares are regulated by Chinese law, but when listed on the HKSE are denominated in Hong Kong dollars and traded the same as other equities on the Hong Kong exchange. ICBC was simultaneously listed on both the HKSE and Shanghai Stock Exchange on October 27, 2006. It was the world's largest initial public offer (IPO) at that time, valued at US $21.9 billion. However, in 2010, the Agriculture Bank of China broke its record and became the world's largest IPO by raising US $22.1 billion. ICBC raised at least US $14 billion in H shares and another US $5.1 billion in A shares. The BOC was listed on the HKSE on June 1, 2006, raising US $9.7 billion in H shares. The total value of their IPO was US $11.2 billion.

The great virtue of offering shares on the Hong Kong Exchange in HK $ is the currency board of the Hong Kong Monetary Authority. The HK currency board has a rigidly fixed exchange rate pegged to the USD since 1983 with a parity rate of HK $7.8 per USD, though it may float between HK $7.75 and HK $7.85. Consequently, the shares are effectively USD shares. Under the Special Administrative Law (SAL), Hong Kong retains financial independence for 50 years following its return to Chinese sovereignty in 1997.

Launched on November 17, 2014, the Shanghai and Hong Kong Exchanges *Stock Connect* allows investors to trade securities on each other's markets through the trading and clearing facilities of their home exchange. The *Stock Connect* between Shenzhen and Hong Kong was inaugurated December 5, 2016. The *Stock Connect* now covers over 2,000 listed equities on the exchanges.

Futures exchanges in China

There are four official futures exchanges in China.

The Shanghai Futures Exchange (SFE) trades futures contracts in copper, aluminum, zinc, plumbum, fuel oil and natural rubber. It was established in 1998 in a merger of four previously separate commodity exchanges.

The Dalian Commodity Exchange (DCE), established on February 28, 1993, trades futures contracts in agricultural products such as corn, soybean, egg, palm oil, as well as soybean and corn options. The DCE also trades industrial futures in plastic products such as PVC (Polyvinyl chloride), LLDPE (Linear low-density polyethylene) coke and coke products, iron ore, and ethylene glycol.

The Zhengzhou Commodity Exchange (ZCE) was established in 1990. The ZCE trades futures in agricultural products such as wheat, cotton, cotton yarn, white sugar, rice, rapeseed, rapeseed oil and meal, apple and Chinese jujube. Its non-agricultural futures are in glass, thermal coal, methanol, and ferroalloy, and it also trades options in white sugar and cotton.

The China Financial Futures Exchange, established in Shanghai in 2006, trades in CSI 300 Index Futures.

In the News: Shanghai Yuan Options

In the latest liberalizing step for its foreign-exchange market, China is loosening the rules on yuan options—offering banks and businesses more ways to hedge currency risks, which have grown in recent months with the increasing volatility in the yuan's value. The move could be a shot in the arm for the nascent yuan-options market, virtually dormant since its launch in April. The new risk-reversal option structure, introduced by a State Administration of Foreign Exchange statement dated November 8, 2011 will allow investors to buy and sell options simultaneously, starting December 1, 2011. Under the current rules, investors can buy options only from banks; they can sell options only to exit the position established by their earlier option purchase. To limit risk exposure under the new rules, the cost of the option—called the premium—that the investor sells can't exceed the cost of the option the investor buys. Selling options is riskier than buying them—the buyer's risk is limited to the premium paid. Restricting investors' options sales—or selling a put or a call—is a typical measure adopted in emerging economies, Chinese regulators said.

Source: Esther Fung and Shen Hong, "China Eases Yuan-Option Rules", *Wall Street Journal*, November 11, 2011.

The Frankfurt Stock Exchange dates from the 9th century when trade fairs were authorized. In 1585 it was organized as a bourse to fix exchange rates and by 1894 had become a formal stock exchange. Its main index, the DAX, consists of the 30 largest issues traded on the exchange.

The performances of the international stock markets indices are related. In fact, this is one aspect of the increased globalization of international trade and finance. The major stock indices are positively correlated, suggesting the globalization of the international financial markets. Since we are dealing with the monthly real rates of return adjusted for inflation, the positive and significant correlations suggest that arbitrage is keeping the real rates of return in line. Also, many real shocks are worldwide.

Why is money important?

When the money supply is unstable, prices are unstable. This often happens when the printing press becomes the finance of last resort of the Treasury's deficit. A financing identity illustrates the fact that the printing press can be used for residual finance of the deficit that is not financed by a sale of bonds to the public:

$$H_t - H_{t-1} = [G_t + rB_{t-1} + V_t - T_t] - [B_t - B_{t-1}] \quad (2.1)$$

where $H_t - H_{t-1}$ is new base money issued by the central bank.

$[G_t + rB_{t-1} + V_t - T_t]$ is the total fiscal deficit, including interest on the national debt, rB_{t-1}, V_t is transfer payments (entitlements), G_t is government purchases of goods and services, and T_t is total tax revenues.

$[B_t - B_{t-1}]$ is the amount of the fiscal deficit financed by new borrowing, i.e. the sale of new debt by the Treasury to the public.

The residual of the deficit that is not financed by new bond issue is the printing press, $H_t - H_{t-1}$, the sale of new debt to the FED.

This is a tautology, an identity that must hold, unless the Treasury sells gold of state owned assets. When there are shocks to the deficit or spending greater than tax revenues that cannot be financed by new borrowing, the printing press is engaged and inflation typically follows. As a fraction of GDP, the financing equation can be written as:

$$\frac{H_t - H_{t-1}}{Y_t} = \frac{G_t + r_t B_{t-1} + V_t - T_t}{Y_t} - \frac{[B_t - B_{t-1}]}{Y_t} \quad (2.2)$$

or in terms of small letters:

$$h_t - \frac{h_{t-1}}{(1+\gamma)} = g_t + \frac{r_t}{(1+\gamma)} b_{t-1} + v_t - \tau_t - \left(b_t - \frac{b_{t-1}}{(1+\gamma)}\right) \quad (2.3)$$

where γ is the growth rate in GDP, since $Y_t = (1+\gamma) Y_{t-1}$. If we define the total deficit as a fraction of GDP by d_t as the fiscal deficit as a fraction of GDP, we have:

$$d_t = g_t + \frac{r_t}{(1+\gamma)}b_{t-1} + v_t - \tau_t \qquad (2.4)$$

$$h_t - \frac{h_{t-1}}{(1+\gamma)} = d_t - \left(b_t - \frac{b_{t-1}}{(1+\gamma)}\right) \qquad (2.5)$$

The world reserve and settlement status of the US dollar is put in jeopardy by large deficits financed by the printing of seigniorage, as reported in Table 2.1.

Table 2.1 The US budget deficit and debt held by the public as a percent of GDP

表2.1 给出了2019年美国预算赤字和公众持有的债务占美国GDP的比重。

	Deficit (-) or surplus (%)	Debt held by the public (%)
2007	-1.1	35.2
2008	-3.1	39.4
2009	-9.8	52.3
2010	-8.7	60.8
2011	-8.4	65.8
2012	-6.7	70.3
2013	-4.1	72.2
2014	-2.8	73.7
2015	-2.4	72.5
2016	-3.2	76.4
2017	-3.5	76.1
2018	-3.9	77.8
2019	-4.2	78.2
2020	-4.0	79.5
2021	-4.2	81.0
2022	-4.7	83.0
2023	-4.5	84.8
2024	-4.2	85.9
2025	-4.5	87.2
2026	-4.3	88.5
2027	-4.0	89.4
2028	-4.7	90.8
2029	-4.2	91.8

Note: Estimates from 2019 to 2029.
Source: Congressional Budget Office, May 2019.

Printing money to finance deficits is risky. Hopefully, the US dollar will not suffer the fate of the Zimbabwean dollar!

> **In the News:** **The End of the Zimbabwean Dollar**
>
> Zimbabwe slashed 12 zeros from its currency as hyperinflation continued to erode its value, the country's central bank announced. The move means that 1 trillion in Zimbabwe dollars now will be equivalent to one Zimbabwe dollar. The old notes—with the highest being 100 trillion dollars—not enough to buy a loaf of bread—will remain valid until June 30, 2009 after which they will cease to be legal tender. One US dollar is trading above 300 trillion Zimbabwe dollars. Since many traders no longer accept the ZWD, the acting finance minister authorized payments in foreign currency.
>
> Source: cnn.com/world.

While seigniorage is typically positive, it can indeed be negative, such as on the US penny. In 2018, the unit cost of a penny was US¢ 1.8 and the unit cost of a nickel was US¢ 7!

> **Applying the Concept:** **Negative Seigniorage—US Mint Cost to Produce the Penny and Nickel**
>
> For the past four years, it has cost the **United States Mint** more than face value to produce the penny and the nickel. The cost of the coins was recently 1.62 cents to produce each penny and 5.79 cents to produce each nickel... Seigniorage arises from the difference between the face value and the cost to manufacture and distribute the coins. Amounts earned through seigniorage—are transferred to the United States Treasury General Fund. However, since 2006, it has cost more than face value to produce the cent and nickel due to the increased costs of base metals—the cent is 2.5% copper and 97.5% zinc, and the nickel is 75% copper and 25% nickel.

Table 2.2 calculates the negative seigniorage realized by the US Treasury on the one cent coins since 2017.

Table 2.2 Negative seigniorage on the US penny

Fiscal year	Cost of producing the US penny US mint cost (US cents)	Seigniorage (USD millions)
2018	2.06	−$86
2017	1.82	−$69

Sources: US Mint April 2018, Coin.News.net, May 24, 2019.

While the US Mint loses on the production of the cent and nickel, in 2018, it earned a net $321 million in seigniorage from all coins. Profitable seignorage is earned from the international circulation of banknotes. While the cost of printing a $100 banknote is 14.2 cents in 2018, foreigners must supply goods and services—coffee, shrimp, and tourism, for instance—at the face value of the note. The $100 banknote is held abroad because the entity values it as a *store of value* because of mistrust of the local currency and as *a unit of account* and *medium of exchange* for settling both legal and illegal transactions. The Federal Reserve Board of Governors Flow of Funds reports that at the end of December 2018, $1,340 billion dollars in $100 bills are in circulation, nearly 80% abroad. Foreigners are thus paying a high seigniorage tax to the US Treasury—an accumulated $920 billion.

The negative seigniorage on the penny and the nickel are a wise investment by the US Treasury in maintaining the dollar as a good unit of account and medium of exchange. Rather than exchanging chewing gum to round up or down transactions, the reliable penny is there as the unit of account and means of payment.

Conclusion

Money serves as a medium of exchange, a unit of account, and a store of value. Different monies must be converted into the same unit of account by the exchange rate in order to compare prices and rates of return. This currency conversion gives rise to foreign exchange risk in investing and operating internationally. The foreign exchange markets have arisen to deal with spot and forward transactions in different monies, as well as currency options to either hedge or speculate. The largest FOREX market remains London, accounting for 37% of daily turnover in the foreign exchanges. The exchange costs on the FOREX market are mainly the difference between the *ask* and the *bid* price of foreign currency—*the bid-ask spread*—as well as any commission associated with the conversion. These costs are not insignificant, amounting to approximately a billion USD daily.

The world financial market is becoming increasingly integrated. The adoption of the euro by 12 countries—now 19 countries—as the same currency has removed conversion costs from the financial landscape of Europe, but has not prevented greater credit risk in the PIIGS sovereign bonds—Portugal, Ireland, Italy, Greece, and Spain. Greater openness in trade has brought with it greater openness in finance since current account deficits must be financed, and surpluses provide foreign lending. The decade of the 1990s brought all of Latin American into the GATT/WTO, and in December 2001, China became a signatory as well. Russia acceded in 2012. There have been great foreign direct investment flows that follow trade, as well as portfolio investments. On the other hand, China still has not liberalized the capital account to permit foreign portfolio diversification, though large direct foreign investments and acquisitions have been approved since China's policy of moving toward the socialist market economy and opening the Chinese economy in 1978. There is increasing financial integration in the world financial markets, making for a more efficient distribution of worldwide capital. Shocks to the financial system are now global in nature.

Questions and problems

2.1 The functions of money

a. What are the three main functions of money? (that is, define and explain the different roles of money in an economic system.)

1.

2.

3.

b. How does high inflation damage each of the main roles that money plays?

1.

2.

3.

2.2 Gold arbitrage

Assume country A's central bank has a gold window where it freely sells and/or buys an ounce of gold for 2 dollars of currency, while Country B buys and/or sells an ounce of gold for one pound of currency. There is no bid-ask spread in purchases or sales of gold at the Central Bank.

a. Using the cross rate, what is the par price of the pound in terms of the dollar?

b. If the price of the pound rises to $2.01 on the foreign exchange market, will gold arbitrage take place assuming no costs of arbitrage?

c. If so, explain the steps in a "round trip" beginning and ending in the same currency. That is, explain each transaction in gold arbitrage and indicate your profits:

1. Sell one pound for $2.01 on the foreign exchange market
2.
3.
4.
5.

d. Since gold moves from one country to another, what is the automatic effect on the money supply of the country that receives gold, and on the money supply of the country that loses gold?

e. Could these monetary effects of gold flows be neutralized? How?

References and suggested reading

Aliber, Robert Z. (2002), *The International Money Game*, Chicago: The University of Chicago Press.

Atkin, John (2005), *The Foreign Exchange Market of London: Development Since 1900*, London & New York: Routledge.

Bahng, Seungwook (2003), "The Response of the Indian Stock Market to the Movement of Asia's Emerging Markets: From Isolation Toward Integration," *Global Economic Review*, 32(2): 43–58.

Bank of International Settlements (2011), *Trienniel Central Bank Survey: Foreign Exchange and Derivatives Activity in 2010*, Basel, Table E4:56.

Blustein, Paul (2001), *The Chastening: Inside the Crisis that Rocked the Global Financial System and Humbled the IMF*, New York: Public Affairs.

Chown, John F. (1994), *A History of Money: From AD 800*, London & New York: Routledge.

Damme, Ingrid Van (1998), "The Cradle of the European Banknote Stood in Sweden," Museum of the National Bank of Belgium.

Davies, Glyn (1994), *A History of Money: From Ancient Times to the Present Day*, Cardiff: University of Wales Press.

Donaldson, R. Glen (1993), "Financing Banking Crises: Lessons from the Panic of 1907," *Journal of Monetary Economics*, 31(1): 69–95.

Einzig, Paul (1970), *The History of Foreign Exchange*, New York: Macmillan.

Jones, J. P. (1973), *The Money Story*, New York, Drake Publishers.

Friedman, Milton (1992), "FDR, Silver and China," in *Money Mischief: Episodes in Monetary History*, Orlando, Florida and San Diego, California: Harcourt Brace and Company.

Huang, Ray (1974), *Fiscal Administration During the Ming Dynasty*, London: Cambridge University Press.

Poitras, Geoffrey (2000), *The Early History of Financial Economics, 1478-1776: From Commercial Arithmetic to Life Annuities and Joint Stocks*, Cheltenham & Northhampton: Edward Elgar.

Racine, M. D. and Lucy F. Ackert (2000), "Time Varying Volatility in Canadian and U.S. Stock Index and Index Futures: A Multivariate Analysis," *Journal of Financial Research*, 23(2): 129-143.

Smith, Adam (1776), *An Inquiry into the Wealth of Nations*, London: Methuen and Co., Ltd.

Spahn, Heinz-Peter (2001), *From Gold to Euro: On Monetary Theory and the History of Currency Systems*, Berlin & New York: Springer.

Westermann, Frank (2002), "Stochastic Trends and Cycles in National Stock Market Indices: Evidence from the U.S., U.K. and Switzerland," *Swiss Journal of Economics and Statistics*, 138(3): 317-328.

CHAPTER 3 The Foreign Exchange Market 外汇交易市场

According to the Bank of International Settlements (BIS), average net daily turnover in the over-the-counter (OTC) foreign exchange market in 2016 was over $5 trillion—spot transactions of $1.65 trillion, forwards of $700 billion, foreign exchange and currency swaps of $2.46 trillion, and options of $254 billion. That makes foreign exchange trading one of the largest financial markets in existence. Table 3.1 reports the daily foreign exchange turnover in April 2016.

Table 3.1 Global daily foreign exchange trading in April 2016

Foreign exchange instruments	turnover (USD billions)	Percent (%)
Spot	1,652	33
Outright forwards	700	14
Foreign exchange and currency swaps	2,460	49
Options and other products	254	5
Total	5,066	100

Source: Bank of International Settlements, Triennial Central Bank Survey of Foreign Exchange and Derivatives Market Activity in 2016.

This chapter outlines floating and fixing the exchange rate in the spot market, forward and futures markets, as well as the options market in foreign exchange. As always, it is supply and demand that determines the equilibrium in each market, but arbitrage plays an important role in setting an equilibrium price in both the spot and futures markets. Broadly understood, **arbitrage** is buying low in one market and selling high in another, thereby bringing prices into equilibrium. No further profitable arbitrage is possible.

套利(Arbitrage):在低价市场上买进再到高价市场上卖出,从而调节市场价格达到均衡。在此均衡价格上任何套利行为都将不再赢利。

A floating exchange rate system

浮动汇率制度 (Floating exchange rate system): 央行不进行外汇买卖活动从而不对汇率进行干预的汇率制度。在浮动汇率制度下,外汇市场的供给和需求决定了均衡汇率。

买入价 (The bid): 银行买入一单位外汇的价格。

卖出价 (The ask): 银行卖出一单位外汇的价格。

欧式标价法 (European quotation): 以一单位美元买卖人民币的数量进行标价的方式。

美式标价法 (American quotation): 以一单位人民币买卖美元的数量进行标价的方式。

With a floating exchange rate, supply and demand in the foreign exchange market determine the equilibrium exchange rate. When the central bank neither purchases nor sells foreign exchange, it is said to be a freely floating exchange rate system.

The bid is what a bank pays for a unit of foreign exchange, **the ask** is the price at which it sells the same unit of foreign exchange. Individual firms and persons will pay the ask rate which is slightly higher, and they will receive the slightly lower bid rate. The bank earns the bid-ask spread.

In Figure 3.1, at a spot price of S, the supply and demand for foreign exchange are reconciled, so S is the equilibrium exchange rate in terms of yuan/dollar. This is known as a **European quotation**—foreign currency unit per USD. When a currency is quoted as USD per unit of foreign currency, it is known as an **American quotation**. The equilibrium quantity bought and sold is Q.

Figure 3.1 A floating exchange rate

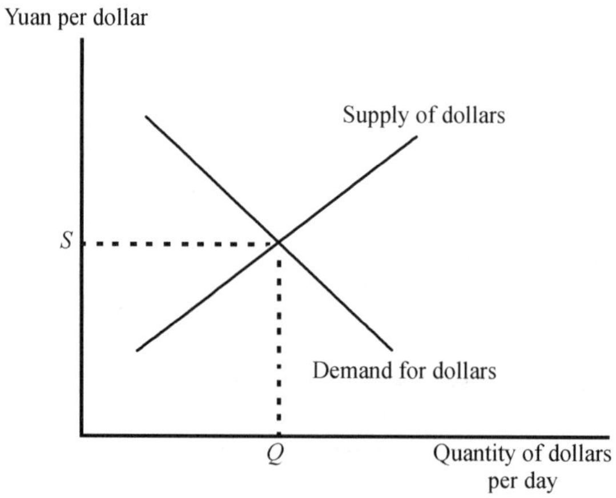

有管理的浮动汇率制度 (Managed float): 中央银行有时会通过增加或减少外汇市场上外汇供给数量的办法来干预外汇市场的浮动汇率制度。

Central banks occasionally intervene in the foreign exchange market by increasing or decreasing the supply of foreign exchange. With intervention, the float is said to be a **managed float**. Foreign exchange dealers quote customers a *bid* and an *ask* (or offer) rate for foreign exchange. A dealer purchases at the bid rate and sells at the offer rate. The *bid-ask spread* (the difference between the ask and the bid rates) represents profits to the foreign exchange dealer.

Day trading in foreign exchange is not likely to be profitable. For one thing, the speculator pays fees per trade and, for another, buys at the ask and sells at the bid when trading. Consider a simultaneous purchase and sale of foreign exchange by a day trader: the trader buys high at the ask and simultaneously sells low at the bid, paying the exchange spread plus any commission on the trade. Table 3.2 indicates the bid and ask rates from a foreign exchange trading platform.

Table 3.2 Direct and cross rates in foreign exchange quotations

	CNY	USD	EUR	JPY
CNY		Bid: 0.15660284 Ask: 0.15699355	Bid: 0.11358405 Ask: 0.11385380	Bid: 12.03100014 Ask: 12.05799961
USD	Bid: 6.36968851 Ask: 6.38558027		Bid: 0.72516000 Ask: 0.72531998	Bid: 76.80491303 Ask: 76.80491303
EUR	Bid: 8.78319424 Ask: 8.80405314	Bid: 1.37870185 Ask: 1.37900601		Bid: 105.91000366 Ask: 105.91999817
JPY	Bid: 0.08293250 Ask: 0.08311861	Bid: 0.01302000 Ask: 0.01302000	Bid: 0.00944000 Ask: 0.00944000	

Source: Xignite Currencies, September 17, 2011.

CNY indicates the yuan or renminbi, while USD, EUR, JPY indicate the United States dollar, the euro, and the Japanese yen respectively. The CNY bid for the USD is 6.36968851, while the ask is 6.38558027, so the bid ask spread is (6.38558027 − 6.36968851) = 0.0158918 or 159 **basis points or** *pips*—measured as the fourth decimal.

The bank is a market maker, ready to either buy or sell dollars. Assume that it trades 1 billion USD per day: That is, it buys 1 billion at 6.36968851 and sells them at 6.3855807, closing out its net position in dollars at the end of the day. Its profits from the spread are thus:

$$1{,}000{,}000{,}000 \times \frac{0.01589176}{} = 15{,}891{,}760$$

Profits in terms of CNY are indicated in Figure 3.2.

基点（Basis points or *pips*）：衡量债券或票据利率变动的最小计量单位。1个基点等于1%的百分之一，即0.01%。

Figure 3.2 Bank profits from the bid-ask spread

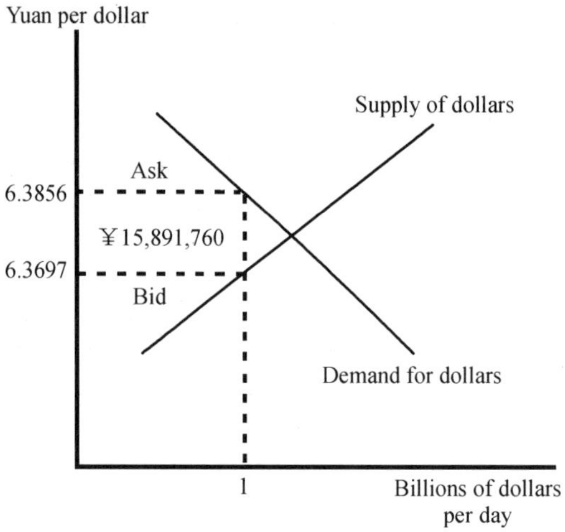

[Figure: Supply and demand diagram with Yuan per dollar on vertical axis, Billions of dollars per day on horizontal axis. Ask = 6.3856, Bid = 6.3697, area labeled ¥15,891,760 at quantity 1.]

American and European quotations

A forex quotation may be in American terms—USD per unit of foreign currency or in European terms—units of foreign currency per dollar. The European quotation of the dollar is:

$$\frac{\text{CNY}}{\text{USD}} \quad \begin{array}{l} \text{Bid: 6.36968851} \\ \text{Ask: 6.38558027} \end{array}$$

while the American quotation of the CNY is:

$$\frac{\text{USD}}{\text{CNY}} \quad \begin{array}{l} \text{Bid: 0.15660284} \\ \text{Ask: 0.15699355} \end{array}$$

美式标价法与欧式标价法之间的转换(Conversion between American and European quotations):一种标价法下的买入价的倒数即为另一种标价法下的卖出价;同样,一种标价法下的卖出价的倒数即为另一种标价法下的买入价。

The **conversion between American and European quotations** is simple since 1/bid in one quotation equals the ask in the other. Similarly, 1/ask equals the bid when changing the style of quotation. To be sure, the ask must always exceed the bid after conversion.

A fixed exchange rate system

A fixed exchange rate system usually has a ceiling and a floor (intervention points). The central bank purchases foreign exchange at the floor and sells it at the ceiling to maintain the exchange rate within a narrow band. When the supply of dollars is greater than the demand for dollars at the floor price, the central bank purchases dollars at the floor price and adds them to its foreign exchange reserves. To facilitate international adjustment, the central bank that purchases dollars with say yuan lets the domestic yuan money supply rise, thus enabling inflation. Occasionally, central banks "sterilize" or "neutralize" the monetary effects of forex purchases by simultaneously selling domestic currency bonds or raising required reserve ratios to take back the increase in the supply of yuan (Hanke, 2002). This neutralizes adjustment and the surplus or deficit continues until policy or a shock changes the circumstances.

固定汇率制度(Fixed exchange rate system): 在该汇率制度下,汇率的变动通常有一个上限和下限,即干预点。央行在汇率变动的下限买入外汇,并在上限卖出外汇,以使汇率稳定在一个狭窄的区间内。

A central bank purchase of dollars

When the supply of dollars is greater than the demand for dollars at the floor price, the central bank purchases dollars at the floor price and adds them to its foreign exchange reserves. For example, in Figure 3.3 the supply of dollars exceeds the demand for dollars at a floor price of 6.3697 yuan per dollar. This triggers central bank intervention (that is, purchases of 3 million dollars by the central bank) at 6.3697 yuan per dollar. The equilibrium exchange rate is thus 6.3697 yuan per dollar, including the central bank's demand for 3 million dollars at the floor rate. Normally, the 3 million dollars are added to central bank reserves in the form of US Treasuries. However, the central bank could sterilize the immediate impact on the domestic money supply by selling 6.3697 × $3,000,000 yuan of domestic bonds on the open market.

央行买进美元(A central bank purchase of dollars): 在下限价格上,美元的供给大于需求,于是央行以下限价格买进美元用以增加外汇储备。

Figure 3.3   The People's Bank of China buys three million dollars at the lower intervention rate

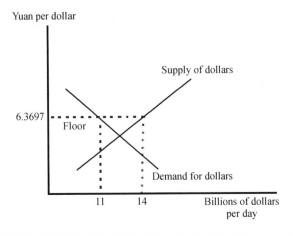

Notice that a central bank's ability to purchase foreign reserves is unlimited since it can always print or supply more domestic money. This is not the case when it comes to selling foreign reserves to support the home currency. It cannot print foreign currency.

A central bank sale of dollars

央行卖出美元(A central bank sale of dollars):在上限价格上,美元的供给小于需求,于是央行动用外汇储备,以上限价格卖出美元。

When the demand for dollars is greater than the supply of dollars at the ceiling price, the central bank draws from its reserves of dollars and sells them at the ceiling price. In Figure 3.4, the demand for dollars exceeds the supply of dollars at a price of 6.3856 yuan per dollar, triggering a sale of dollars by the central bank at the ceiling rate. The sale of reserves just equilibrates supply and demand at a price of 6.3856 yuan per dollar. Neutralization would entail a purchase of domestic bonds equal to 6.3856 × 3,000,000 yuan. With a fixed exchange rate that has a ceiling and a floor the central bank purchases foreign exchange at the floor and sells it at the ceiling to maintain the exchange rate within a narrow band. By appreciating the rates slowly, the central bank can appreciate the currency, yet provide some certainty to exporters.

A central bank's holdings of foreign reserves are limited. Consequently, it may sell reserves until it has sold all its reserves and exhausted its ability to borrow reserves to support its currency, if it chooses to do so. At that point, it must float (or worse yet, impose exchange controls, in which case the parallel market rate floats) its exchange rate.

Figure 3.4 The People's Bank of China sells three million dollars at the upper intervention rate

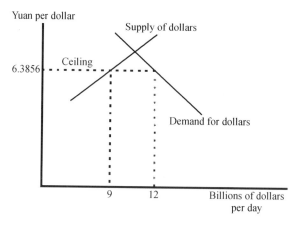

At that point, speculators who had "Bet against the Bank" make their profits. Most empirical studies show that by taking a position opposite to central bank intervention, small systematic profits can be made (Taylor, 1982). The reason for this is that central banks often "lean against the wind", that is, resist changes in the fundamental equilibrium rate. In June 2005, the People's Bank of China (PBOC) held $736 billion in foreign reserves when it abandoned the fixed exchange rate of 8.28 RMB/USD. Afterwards, the PBOC bought reserves steadily, reaching $4 trillion in June 2014 at the peak. The RMB appreciated to 6.06 RMB/USD in January 2014. In 2015, it sold about $1 trillion of reserves, preventing further yuan appreciation. Since 2016, the PBOC has maintained a fairly stable level above $3 trillion in foreign reserves through July 2019, with an exchange rate reaching 6.88 RMB/USD on July 23, 2019 (Source: Federal Reserve Bank of St. Louis). A managed floating exchange rate system allows the exchange rate to float according to the laws of supply and demand, but there are discretionary sales and/or purchases of foreign exchange to maintain the equilibrium exchange rate within small margins as in the PBOC's ±2% around its reference rate.

央行所持有的外汇储备是有限的。因此,它可以选择卖出外汇储备,直至外汇储备全部耗尽而且无法借入外汇储备来支持本币。在这个时候,央行只能允许其汇率浮动。

The effect of a sale in foreign reserves on the domestic money supply

When the demand for money declines, say due to a crisis in confidence in the home currency, the Central Bank must sell foreign exchange reserves, thereby reducing the supply of home currency. **The effect on**

对本国货币供给的影响 (The effect on the domestic money supply): 央行在卖出外汇储备的同时,购进了本国货币。因此,银行体系中的本币减少了,卖出外汇储备便自动减少了本币的供给。当央行购进外汇以增加外汇储备时,同时向银行体系中注入了本币,所以本币供给自动增加。

the domestic money supply is direct: when the Central Bank sells foreign exchange reserves, it simultaneously buys domestic currency. Consequently, domestic currency in the banking system declines. Sales of foreign exchange reserves automatically reduce the domestic money supply as illustrated in Figure 3.5.

Figure 3.5   The PBOC sells USD

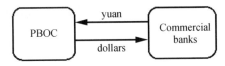

Similarly, when a central bank purchases foreign exchange and adds to reserves, it simultaneously sells domestic currency to the banking system. Consequently, the domestic money supply rises automatically. The effect on the domestic money supply in China can be illustrated in Figure 3.6.

Figure 3.6   The PBOC buys USD

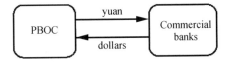

Naturally, the ability of a Central Bank to maintain a fixed exchange rate depends on its holdings of foreign reserves. From the point of view of the balance sheet of the Central Bank in Table 3.3, we have a simplified T-account:

Table 3.3   The balance sheet of the PBOC

Assets (RMB)	Liabilities (RMB)
Foreign reserves	Currency held by the public
Domestic credit	Commercial bank reserves
Base money	Base money

On the asset side, foreign reserves are net foreign assets held by the central bank; domestic credit represents loans made by the Central Bank, usually to the Treasury or the commercial banks. On the liability side, the bank issues domestic currency to the public and it takes in deposits of commercial banks as required reserves. Commercial banks are also allowed to count cash on hand ("vault cash") as part of their reserves.

A decline in the demand for money is reflected by a decline in the demand for base money. By selling its foreign reserves at the spot rate, the Central Bank accommodates the decline in the demand for money by buying the excess domestic supply. Otherwise, the Central Bank could contract domestic credit to reduce base money supply.

Notice that if the demand for money were constant, base money is constant. Any attempt by the Central Bank to expand domestic credit (say to finance a fiscal deficit) under a fixed exchange rate regime would come at the expense of a loss in foreign reserves. The central bank would have to repurchase the excess supply of money on the foreign exchange market. This is the so called "monetary anchor" role of a fixed exchange rate. In principal, a fixed exchange rate prevents the Central Bank from financing the fiscal and quasi-fiscal deficit. An independent expansion of the money supply by the Central Bank triggers excess demand in the foreign exchange market, requiring a sale of foreign exchange reserves to maintain the fixed exchange rate. The Central Bank thus expands credit and hence the money base, but contracts the base by the same amount when it sells foreign exchange reserves. Consequently, a fixed exchange rate serves as a "monetary anchor" on expansionary monetary policy.

Neutralization policy

When the PBOC purchases US dollars to stabilize the exchange rate, it increases the yuan base money supply in the commercial banking system. Normally, this leads to an increase in the yuan money supply and ultimately a higher rate of inflation in China. To offset the effect of the purchase of dollars on the yuan money supply, the PBOC can neutralize by selling Chinese bonds to the commercial banks, or by increasing the domestic required reserve ratio that commercial banks must maintain. Neutralization is thus illustrated in Figure 3.7.

冲销政策(Neutralization policy): 当中国人民银行购入美元来稳定汇率时,商业银行系统中的人民币数量增加。通常,这会导致人民币供给增加和通货膨胀率上升。为了抵消这一效果,中国人民银行可以通过出售中国国债或提高存款准备金率来降低人民币供给数量。

Figure 3.7 The PBOC sells bonds to neutralize its foreign exchange purchase

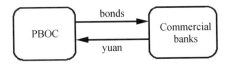

In theory, we know from Mundell (1968) that a central bank can *either* fix the exchange rate and let the money supply float, *or* fix the money supply and let the exchange rate float, but not fix *both*.

From the simplified balance sheet of the PBOC, a change in monetary base, H, the liabilities of the central bank, equals the change in its assets, either caused by a change in net foreign assets, FX, or a change in net domestic assets, DC.

$$\Delta H \equiv \Delta DC + \Delta FX \qquad (3.1)$$

This identity suggests that an increase in foreign assets, due to the PBOC's purchase of foreign exchange, other things constant, tends to increase the monetary base, and hence the overall money supply. However, to limit the impact of an increase of net foreign assets on monetary base, the central bank can neutralize the monetary effects by reducing domestic credit. A direct way to measure the effectiveness of PBOC's neutralization is to test how domestic assets respond to a change in net foreign assets.

Neutralization can be characterized by a sterilization coefficient, θ, representing the fraction of the change in net foreign assets that is neutralized:

$$\Delta DC = -\theta \Delta FX \quad \text{where} \quad 0 \leqslant \theta \leqslant 1 \qquad (3.2)$$

The coefficient of $\theta = 1$ implies full monetary neutralization, or $\Delta DC = -\Delta FX$ so $\Delta H = 0$, while $\theta = 0$ implies no monetary neutralization. Here we define the sterilization coefficient narrowly from the central bank balance sheet perspective. It is the fraction of a change in net foreign assets that is neutralized by a reduction in the PBOC's domestic credit.

We can also test the impact of an increase in net foreign assets on broader monetary supply such as M2. Recall that the money supply M equals monetary base times the money multiplier m:

$$M = mH \qquad (3.3)$$

which implies, for a constant multiplier:

$$\Delta M = m\Delta H = m(\Delta FX + \Delta DC) \qquad (3.4)$$

Substituting equation (3.2) into equation (3.4), we have:

$$\Delta M = m(1-\theta)\Delta FX \qquad (3.5)$$

where ΔM denotes the change in commercial banks' domestic credit due to a change in net foreign assets, ΔFX, and $m(1-\theta)$ is the *effective* money multiplier, which de-multiplies the effect of the purchase of net foreign assets on the money supply. Note that in the case of perfect neutralization $\theta = 1$, so the effective money multiplier for purchase of foreign exchange $m(1-\theta) = 0$. In general, $m(1-\theta) > 0$.

On the complete sample from period, July 1999 to June 2011, OLS regressions yield an estimated sterilization coefficient of 0.66, significant at the 5% level, suggesting that the PBOC only neutralizes 66% of the change in net foreign assets effectively. This is illustrated by the negative slope of the estimated neutralization equation and the regression line in Figure 3.8.

$$\Delta DC = -0.66 \Delta FX + 0.03 \qquad (3.6)$$
$$(0.02) (0.02)$$

Note: Standard errors are reported in parentheses.

Figure 3.8 The change in domestic credit, ΔDC, and the change in net foreign assets, ΔFX, of the PBOC

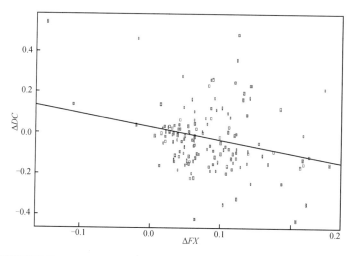

The estimated money multiplier is 4.04. This implies an *effective* money multiplier of 1.4, that is, a one yuan increase in net foreign assets would lead to a 1.4 yuan increase in the money supply due to sterilization. From July 1999 to June 2011, China's foreign reserves rose by 66.9 trillion yuan, at the nominal exchange rate. Given an effective money multiplier of 1.4, this led to an increase of 27.3 trillion yuan increase in the money supply, which is 41% of the total increase of 66.9 trillion yuan during the same period. In other words, 41% of money growth is accounted for by the growth of foreign reserves alone. This high percentage suggests that the PBOC cannot effectively neutralize the change in its net foreign assets, contrary to previous results.

Indeed, if we divide the whole sample into two subsamples using the 2005 currency reform as the break point, the results suggest that the size of the sterilization coefficient decreases considerably in the second period, and the degree of statistical significance is lower, indicating it has become more difficult for the PBOC to pursue a policy of neutralization since August 2005. The estimates are significant at 5% level except for the sterilization coefficient in the second subsample, whose p-value is less than 0.12. Estimated sterilization coefficients for these two subsamples are 0.82 and 0.57 respectively. In the face of rapid growth of foreign reserves, neutralization in China is becoming increasingly difficult, consistent with Mundell's hypothesis.

When a Central Bank has an expansionary monetary policy (say, to finance the fiscal deficit via the printing press), it continuously loses reserves until they are exhausted, usually by a sudden speculative attack or a run against remaining Central Bank reserves. At that point, the exchange rate must float since no further support of the exchange rate is possible—foreign exchange reserves are no longer available. Often, the central bank sees no alternative but to expand domestic credit as the financier of last resort of the Treasury's deficit. Monetary policy becomes dependent on the deficit of the Treasury. Thus foreign exchange reserves are spent until they run out.

Under neutralization or sterilization policy, a central bank sells a million dollars of foreign currency and simultaneously buys with the proceeds a million dollars worth of Treasury debt. In doing so, it neutralizes the natural fall in the money supply triggered by the sale of foreign exchange. Neutralization of the monetary effects of a sale of foreign exchange reserves is illustrated in Figure 3.9.

Figure 3.9 The PBOC buys bonds to neutralize its foreign exchange sale

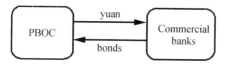

The euro—"irrevocably fixed" exchange rates

Robert A. Mundell, Professor Emeritus at Columbia University and 1999 Nobel Prize Laureate in economics noted in his "A Theory of Optimum Currency Areas" that the "... economists of the nineteenth century were internationalists and generally favored a world currency. Thus John Stuart Mill wrote: 'So much of barbarism, however, still remains in the transactions of most civilized nations, that almost all independent countries choose to assert their nationality by having, to their own inconvenience and that of their neighbors, a peculiar currency of their own.'" John Stuart Mill clearly had in mind transactions costs involved in having separate monies. Not only the bid-ask spread and commissions in foreign exchange, but also problems of exchange controls and currency risk that impede trade, investment, and factor mobility. Rigidly fixed exchange rates under a gold standard provided a nearly universal money for most of the 19th century, although Asia was mainly on a silver standard.

As Mundell put it succinctly: "Money, in its role of medium of exchange is less useful if there are many currencies; although the costs of conversion are always present, they loom exceptionally large under inconvertibility or flexible exchange rates." (AER, 1961) In 1973, he proposed a European currency in "A Plan for a European Currency" and has become known as the "father of the euro." His plan extolled the benefits of a common currency: reserve pooling, less costly more transparent financial intermediation, and policy coordination. The larger the zone of a common currency, the greater are its advantages.

罗伯特·A. 蒙代尔（Robert A. Mundell）：美国哥伦比亚大学教授，1999年诺贝尔经济学奖获得者，因提出"最优货币区理论"和推动欧洲货币一体化而被誉为"欧元之父"。

The launching of the euro

On January 1, 1999, the euro was launched. The 11 member states launching the euro were Belgium, Germany, Spain, France, Ireland, Italy, Luxembourg, the Netherlands, Austria, Portugal and Finland. On January 1, 2000, Greece became the 12th member state to adopt the euro. At inception, the euro was worth $1.18, sank to $0.85, and then rose to a peak of $1.45, before stabilizing somewhat at $1.35. It is now $1.12(July 23, 2019). Costs of conversion are disappearing. The bid-ask spread has gone to zero for banknotes and coins, and wire transfers are less expensive. In addition, exchange rate uncertainty under separate European currencies had led to an active market in London in foreign exchange options, futures, forwards and swaps in cross currency trading in Europe. With the adoption of a single currency, forex risk management is no longer necessary in the euro zone. Exchange rate volatility is zero, so options are worthless. European interest rates initially converged since currency risk in the euro zone was eliminated. However, they diverged significantly in 2011 due to large fiscal deficits in Portugal, Ireland, Greece, and Spain. As a direct consequence of the deficits, sovereign debt in these countries paid a high default risk premium over German sovereigns of the same maturity.

In Figure 3.10, as debt rises to income in Europe, the interest rate on sovereigns rises to reflect the increased risk of default. Greece has the highest interest rates. A joint IMF, EC and ECB plan restructured Greek debt by increasing its maturity to 15 years, and asked banks holding Greek debt to mark it down 52.5%. This represents a sovereign default. In any case, European banks, especially French and Greek ones that hold billions of euros worth of Greek sovereigns have suffered write downs in these assets of 52.5% in 2011. The share price of these banks plummeted.

The interest rate is being targeted at 3.5% for new debt that is bought by the European Financial Stability Facility, and commercial banks in Europe have written down their holdings of Greek debt by 52.5%, representing a default.

Figure 3.10 Selected long term interest rates and debt to income ratios in the euro zone

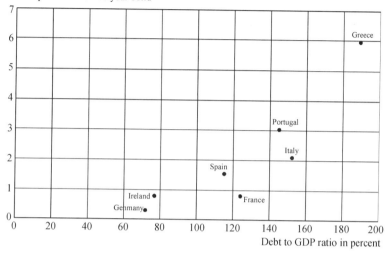

Source: OECD Data, July 2019.

In the News: The euro and the Greek debt crisis

The Greek crisis hasn't proved that the euro was a mistake. But the political reaction to it has placed the experiment in serious danger by abandoning the no-bailout principle and replacing it with a doctrine that sovereign default in a currency zone is unthinkable. This policy makes no more sense than saying that bankruptcy should be impossible, because no one will lend to a company if it might go bust. What's worse is that Europe's leadership has adopted this view for the sake of defending the Greek government from the consequences of its irresponsibility on spending and mendacity about its true level of deficit and debt. The solution is not a return to monetary "sovereignty." Countries don't need unfettered monetary freedom. Only governments do, to bail themselves out of their own bad policies. If the euro should fail, it will be because those governments did too little to hold themselves to the discipline that a hard currency, albeit a paper one, demanded.

Source: *Wall Street Journal*, October 7, 2011.

Benefits of currency unification

Transactions costs should, in theory, disappear in currency conversion and payments transfer within the euro zone. Prior to the Civil War in the Confederated States (1861–1865), state banks issued their own currencies, so each levied seigniorage on its residents. With the outbreak of the Civil War, the North issued the greenback dollar to finance its increased military expenditures, as the South printed the confederate dollar to finance theirs. With the ultimate victory of the North, the confederate dollar became worthless, and the greenback dollar evolved into the US dollar of today. State chartered banks no longer have the right to print seigniorage since there is one central bank, the Federal Reserve Bank of the United States. The 12 Federal Reserve Districts do share in the seigniorage associated with banknote issue, but no State can issue currency. No one would deny the benefits from currency and trade integration of the 50 United States. Capital market integration and liquidity effects have led to a low cost of capital, investment and growth in the United States. The U. S. Constitution prohibits taxes on trade among the states, and a banknote issued in New York is legal tender in California. Similarly, a note issued in San Francisco is accepted in New York.

This is now the case in Europe with the euro. Seigniorage is spread among the member countries by the issue of slightly different banknotes and coins. All are acceptable as the medium of exchange in the member countries. However, the countries within the Euro zone have not met the convergence conditions in terms of budget deficits less than 3% of GDP, and a national debt less than 60% of GDP established by the Maastricht Treaty. National macro-economic policy is supposed to be subjected to the monetary anchor of a common currency. European sovereign debt is denominated in euros, but it is not the common obligation of the European states, but rather the sovereign obligation of each country that issues the debt. There is little chance, however, that an individual country, such as Italy or Greece, would forego the benefits of the common currency zone to be able to run a higher deficit, financed by seigniorage through the printing press. A sovereign country can run a higher deficit, but it then faces default risk since it has difficulty financing its bonds on the open market. When Greece faced a default on its debt obligations in May 2010, the

European's established a European Stabilization Fund hand in hand with the IMF to lend to Greece with conditionality. Since the debt to GDP ratio of Greece cannot go to infinity, further restructuring will be necessary. Technically, Greece could leave the euro zone by re-issuing the drachma, though this is ruled out by three successive bailouts and a policy of austerity in Greece. Furthermore, a new drachma would not be credible. Nevertheless, Greek debt is over 180% of income in 2019.

The Chinese yuan

The following essay makes the case for China maintaining a fixed exchange rate for stability and growth in the Chinese economy, despite much clamor for yuan revaluation of up to 35%. We take the position that a large appreciation would cause a major recession in China, much as the ever-appreciating yen caused recession, a housing and stock market slump, and a liquidity trap as in Japan where interest rates approached zero and became negative.

In the News: China Syndrome

In the 1980s and early 1990s, Japan bashing was the favorite pastime in Washington. Japan's sin: its large "contribution" to a growing U.S. trade deficit. To solve this "problem," the U.S. demanded that Japan either strengthen the yen or face trade sanctions. Japan reluctantly complied. In Tokyo, "voluntary" export quotas and an ever-appreciating yen policy became orders of the day. But that one-two policy punch missed its target. Both the U.S. trade deficit and Japan's surplus continued to grow. The "strong" yen wasn't benign, however. It created a monster of a problem in Japan—a deflationary slump.

Today, the U.S. trade deficit is almost double what it was five years ago. This time around China is the fingered culprit; it accounts for almost 25% of the deficit. To deal with China, Washington has dusted off the same defective game plan used to bash Japan.

Senators Charles Schumer (D., N.Y.) and Lindsey Graham (R., S.C.) have led the mercantilist charge on Capitol Hill. They claim that China manipulates its currency, the yuan. As a result, the yuan is undervalued and Chinese exports are subsidized. To correct for China's alleged unfair trade advantage, Senators Schumer and Graham have sponsored currency revaluation legislation and the Senate has agreed to give it an up or down vote by July. If it becomes law, the Chinese would be given six months to negotiate a yuan revaluation with the U.S. Absent a satisfactory revaluation, all China's exports to the U.S. would be slapped with a 27.5% tariff—a rate equal to the alleged yuan undervaluation.

Not to be outdone, members of the House have also laid the U.S. trade deficit at the yuan's doorstep. Congressmen Duncan Hunter (R., California) and Tim Ryan (D., Ohio) have introduced the China Currency Act. It defines "exchange rate manipulation" as a "prohibited export subsidy" which, if deemed harmful, could—under Article VI of the General Agreement on Tariffs and Trade—trigger an antidumping or countervailing duty to offset the "subsidy." Furthermore, if currency manipulation injured the U.S. defense industry, the importation of Chinese defense products would be prohibited.

The clamor for a yuan revaluation is loud. At one time or another, everyone from President Bush to the G-7 has had a hand in the noisemaking. But the yuan quick fix might just be neat, plausible and wrong. Let's investigate:

- Does China manipulate its currency? It is not possible to give a categorical response to this question because "currency manipulation" is simply not an operational concept that can be used for economic analysis. The U.S. Treasury admitted as much in a March 2005 report that attempted to clarify the statutory meaning of currency manipulation for the Committees on Appropriations.

- Is the yuan undervalued vis-à-vis the dollar? No. The nominal yuan/dollar rate has been set in stone at 8.28 since June 1995. Adjusting for inflation in China and the U.S., the real value of the yuan has depreciated by only 2.4% during the last decade. And today the yuan is in equilibrium in the sense that China's inflation rate has converged to the U.S. rate. Not surprisingly, the IMF's most recent Country Report on China concluded that "it is difficult to find persuasive evidence that the renminbi is substantially undervalued."

- Would a yuan revaluation reduce the U.S. trade deficit? Not much, if at all. After a yuan revaluation, the U.S. demand for foreign goods would simply be shifted from China to other countries.

- Would the House and Senate bills comport with international agreements and U.S. obligations? No. The yuan revaluation required by the Schumer-Graham bill would violate China's rights and sovereignty. Under the IMF Articles of Agreement [Article IV, sec. 2(b)], a member country is free to choose its own currency regime, including a fixed exchange rate. The bill's revaluation mandate would also throw a wrench into what has been an incredibly successful economic performance. Over the last decade, China avoided the great Asian financial maelstrom of 1997–1998 and has realized stable prices and an annual growth rate of over 9%. The yuan's fixed exchange rate against the dollar has provided the linchpin for that outstanding record.

  According to Nobelist Robert Mundell, who is honorary president (along with Xu Jialu, vice chairman of the Standing Committee of the National People's Congress) of Beijing's Mundell International University of Entrepreneurship, a substantial yuan revaluation would cut foreign direct investment, cut China's growth rate, delay convertibility, increase bad loans, increase unemployment, cause deflation distress in rural areas, destabilize Southeast Asia, reward speculators, set in motion more revaluation pressures, weaken the external role of the yuan and undermine China's compliance with World Trade Organization rules. In consequence, a forced revaluation would violate Article IV, sec. 1(i) of the IMF Articles of Agreement, which states that a member shall "endeavor to direct its economic and financial policies toward the objective of fostering orderly economic growth with reasonable price stability."

- If China failed to revalue the yuan, the across the board 27.5% tariff triggered by Schumer-Graham would violate China's Most Favored Nation status under Article I of the GATT. Both the tariff and import prohibition features of the Hunter-Ryan China Currency Act would also violate the MFN treatment of China and would be ruled illegal by the WTO.

- Would it be in China's interest to revalue and get the U.S. politicos off its back? No. The effect of a yuan revaluation—deflation and recession—would even be more damaging to China than trade sanctions. We estimate that a 25% yuan revaluation against the dollar would result in a deflation of at least 15%. China would be forced to relive the terrible economic conditions induced by the 1930s yuan revaluation. In 1934, the U.S. Silver Purchase Act monetized silver. This effectively revalued the yuan by 24% because China was on the silver standard. The price of the yuan against the dollar went from 33 cents at the end of 1933 to 41 cents in 1935. As Milton Friedman concluded in his classic study *Money Mischief*: "Because silver was

> China's money, the rise in the price of silver had produced a major deflation, which in turn had led to severely troubled economic conditions."
>
> It is time for the U. S. to stop rushing to judgment based on false premises. Antagonizing the world's most populous country—and doing so by illegal means to boot—is both irrational and dangerous.
>
> Source: Steve H. Hanke and Michael Connolly, *The Wall Street Journal*, May 9, 2005. (reprinted by permission of the WSJ © 2005.)

The SWIFT international clearing system

SWIFT 清算系统 (SWIFT clearing system): 环球同业银行金融电信协会(SWIFT)开发的清算系统。该系统将各国的银行间清算系统联系起来,并为一千多位成员提供安全的电子汇款和信息传输服务。中国银行(Bank of China)是其成员之一。

In 1977, national inter-bank clearing systems were linked internationally through the **SWIFT clearing system**: an acronym for The Society for Worldwide Interbank Financial Telecommunications. The system has over a thousand members for whom it provides secure electronic transfer of monies and communication of messages internationally. Each member bank has an electronic identification and some handshaking goes on through the international computer centers for identification. When the bank ID is confirmed, transactions and communications can take place swiftly and securely since the computer system is a dedicated one. The CHIPS (Clearing House Interbank Payments System) in the United States handles tens of thousands of transactions and transfers many billions of dollars internationally per day. Member banks make electronic payments in CHIP dollars during the day and at the end of the day the master system nets out the sums to be paid, then transfers only the net amount of real money. This system is connected to the SWIFT system and is run by dedicated computers and member banks having strict code identification. Verification, confirmation, and authentification of transactions is also carried out by the CHIPS.

Theories of the long-run movement of exchange rates

During World War I, a Swedish economist, Gustav Cassel corresponded with John Maynard Keynes, then editor of the *Economic Journal*. Cassel's position was that movements in exchange rates reflected movements in their relative purchasing power. He plotted monthly changes in prices in different countries and compared those to the movements in exchange rates at the same time period. Countries with higher inflation suffered currency depreciations. He dubbed his theory the "Purchasing Power Parity" (PPP) doctrine of the exchange rate in 1918. The PPP theory fit well the wartime facts of high inflation and currency depreciation in the belligerent nations.

Purchasing power parity

If a commodity can be purchased in one place and sold in another without any transport costs, tariffs, nor transactions costs, its price should be the same in both markets. This is the law of one price. It is an arbitrage relationship: arbitrageurs buying low and selling high will equalize commodity prices. That is:

$$P_{us} = SP_j \qquad (3.7)$$

where the price of the product in yen is multiplied by the spot dollar price of the yen to yield the same price in the United States.

购买力平价理论 (Purchasing power parity): 关于汇率决定的一种理论,它要求汇率等于两种货币购买力之比。

Absolute purchasing power parity

By the same token, if all goods are costlessly arbitraged, the spot exchange rate can be deduced from the ratio of any identical commodity price in each currency, or:

$$S = \frac{P_{us}}{P_j} \qquad (3.8)$$

This strong version of PPP is known as absolute PPP, where the prices correspond to consumer price indices of similar commodities in each country.

The spot exchange rate can be inferred from commodity prices in different markets.

This is the reasoning embodied in *The Economist's* Big Mac standard.

绝对购买力平价理论 (Absolute purchasing power parity): 如果所有商品均可以被用于无成本的套利活动,那么根据任何一种同质商品用不同货币所表示出的价格便能够推导出两种货币之间的即期汇率。这个购买力平价理论的一般形式就被称为绝对购买力平价理论。

In the News: The Big Mac Standard

"ITALIANS like their coffee strong and their currencies weak. That, at least, is the conclusion one can draw from their latest round of grumbles about Europe's single currency. But are the Italians right to moan? Is the euro overvalued? Our annual Big Mac index suggests they have a case: the euro is overvalued by 17% against the dollar. How come? The euro is worth about $1.22 on the foreign-exchange markets. A Big Mac costs € 2.92, on average, in the euro zone and $3.06 in the United States. The rate needed to equalize the burger's price in the two regions is just $1.05. To patrons of McDonald's, at least, the single currency is overpriced. The Big Mac index, which we have compiled since 1986, is based on the notion that a currency's price should reflect its purchasing power. According to the late, great economist Rudiger Dornbusch, this idea can be traced back to the Salamanca school in 16th-century Spain. Since then, he wrote, the doctrine of purchasing power parity (PPP) has been variously seen as a "truism, an empirical regularity or a grossly misleading simplification." Economists lost some faith in PPP as a guide to exchange rates in the 1970s, after the world's currencies abandoned their anchors to the dollar. By the end of the decade, exchange rates seemed to be drifting without chart or compass. Later studies showed that a currency's purchasing power does assert itself over the long run. But it might take three to five years for a misaligned exchange rate to move even halfway back into line. Our index shows that burger prices can certainly fall out of line with each other. If he could keep the burgers fresh, an ingenious arbitrageur could buy Big Macs for the equivalent of $1.27 in China, whose yuan is the most undervalued currency in our table, and sell them for $5.05 in Switzerland, whose franc is the most overvalued currency. The impracticality of such a trade highlights some of the flaws in the PPP idea. Trade barriers, transport costs and differences in taxes drive a wedge between prices in different countries. More important, the $5.05 charged for a Swiss Big Mac helps to pay for the retail space in which it is served, and for the labour that serves it. Neither of these two crucial ingredients can be easily traded across borders. David Parsley, of Vanderbilt University, and Shang-Jin Wei, of the International Monetary Fund, estimate that non-traded inputs, such as labour, rent and electricity, account for between 55% and 64% of the price of a Big Mac. The two economists disassemble the Big Mac into its separate ingredients. They find that the parts of the burger that are traded internationally converge towards purchasing-power parity quite quickly. Any disparity in onion prices will be halved in less than nine months, for example. But the non-traded bits converge much more slowly: a wage gap between countries has a "half-life" of almost 29 months. Seen in this light, our index provides little comfort to Italian critics of the single currency. If the euro buys less burger than it should, perhaps inflexible wages, not a strong currency, are to blame."

Source: "Fast food and strong currencies?" *The Economist*, June 11, 2005.

Table 3.4 measures over-valuation and under-valuation of different currencies based on the Big Mac standard. It is a whimsical index, not to be taken seriously.

Table 3.4 *The Economist*'s Big Mac standard

	Big Mac price in dollars*	Implied PPP† of the dollar	Under(−)/ over(+) valuation against the dollar, %		Big Mac price in dollars*	Implied PPP† of the dollar	Under(−)/ over(+) valuation against the dollar, %
United States‡	3.06	—	—	Aruba	2.77	1.62	−10
Argentina	1.64	1.55	−46	Bulgaria	1.88	0.98	−39
Australia	2.50	1.06	−18	Colombia	2.79	2.124	−9
Brazil	2.39	1.93	−22	Costa Rica	2.38	369	−22
Britain	3.44	1.65§	+12	Croatia	2.50	4.87	−18
Canada	2.63	1.07	−14	Dominican Rep	2.12	19.60	−31
Chile	2.53	490	−17	Estonia	2.31	9.64	−24
China mainland	1.27	3.43	−59	Fiji	2.50	1.39	−18
Czech Republic	2.30	18.40	−25	Georgia	2.00	1.19	−34
Denmark	4.58	9.07	+50	Guatemala	2.20	5.47	−28
Egypt	1.55	2.94	−49	Honduras	1.91	11.70	−38
Euro area	3.58**	1.25‡	+17	Iceland	6.67	143	+118
Hong Kong SAR of China	1.54	3.92	−50	Jamaica	2.70	53.90	−12
Hungary	2.60	173	−15	Jordan	3.66	0.85	+19
Indonesia	1.53	4.771	−50	Latvia	1.92	0.36	−37
Japan	2.34	81.70	−23	Lebanon	2.85	1.405	−7
Malaysia	1.38	1.72	−55	Lithuania	2.31	2.12	−24
Mexico	2.58	9.15	−16	Macau SAR	1.40	3.66	−54
New Zealand	3.17	1.45	+4	Macedonia	1.90	31	−38
Peru	2.76	2.94	−10	Moldova	1.84	7.52	−40
Philippines	1.47	26.10	−52	Morocco	2.73	8.02	−11
Poland	1.96	2.12	−36	Nicaragua	2.11	11.30	−31
Russia	1.48	13.70	−52	Norway	6.06	12.70	+98
Singapore	2.17	1.18	−29	Pakistan	2.18	42.50	−29
South Africa	2.10	4.56	−31	Paraguay	1.44	2.941	−53
Korea	2.49	817	−19	Qatar	0.68	0.81	−78
Sweden	4.17	10.10	+36	Saudi Arabia	2.40	2.94	−22
Switzerland	5.05	2.06	+65	Serbia & Montenegro	2.08	45.80	−32
Taiwan, China	2.41	24.5	−21	Slovakia	2.09	21.60	−32

	Big Mac price in dollars*	Implied PPP† of the dollar	Under(−)/ over(+) valuation against the dollar, %		Big Mac price in dollars*	Implied PPP† of the dollar	Under(−)/ over(+) valuation against the dollar, %
Thailand	1.48	19.60	−52	Slovenia	2.56	163	−16
Turkey	2.92	1.31	−5	Sri Lanka	1.75	57.20	−43
Venezuela	2.13	1,830	−30	Ukraine	1.43	2.37	−53
				UAE	2.45	2.94	−20
				Uruguay	1.82	14.40	−40

Source: "Fast food and strong currencies," *The Economist*, London (June 11, 2005).

Notes:

* At current exchange rates. † Purchasing-power parity. ‡ Average of New York, Chicago, San Francisco, and Atlanta. § Dollars per pound. ** Weighted average of member countries. # Dollars per euro.

Arbitraging Big Macs

Let's follow *The Economist's* suggestion and buy Big Macs low in yuan and sell them high in USD! As the article suggests, the costs of arbitrage are high. Firstly, we have to buy yuan to purchase a Big Mac in Shanghai, China. We pay the ask price of the yuan to the bank. Secondly, with our yuan, we buy the Big Mac in Shanghai. Thirdly, we pay insurance and freight charges to ship the Big Mac to New York. Fourthly, we pay any U.S. customs duties on prepared foods. Finally, we sell the Big Mac in Manhattan, paying the sales tax there. Let's write a formula for our arbitrage profits:

$$\pi = P_{us}(1 - t_{us}) - S_{ask}P_c(1 + \tau_{us} + t_{c-us}) \qquad (3.9)$$

When our transactions costs are reckoned in, arbitrage profits are likely to be nil. We incur these additional arbitrage costs:

1. We pay the ask rate, S_{ask}, a premium, for the yuan—these are currency exchange costs.

2. We pay the cost of shipping and insuring the Big Mac, t_{c-us}.

3. We pay US customs rate on the Big Mac, τ_{us}.

4. Finally we pay the NY excise tax, t_{us}.

Net of these costs, we will not make a dime since arbitrage assures that the law of one price holds, assuring that arbitrage profits are zero,

$\pi = 0$, or

$$P_{us}(1 - t_{us}) = S_{ask}P_c(1 + \tau_{us} + t_{c-us}) \quad (3.10)$$

The bid-ask spread is part of the transactions costs that the arbitrageur must cover in order to make the arbitrage profitable. The other transactions costs—import duties and transport costs—are more obvious, but they must also be covered to make arbitrage profitable.

The strict law of one price

For the law of one price to exactly hold, taxes, transports costs, import duties, and the bid-ask spread all must be zero, in which case arbitrage (in either direction) imposes the strict law of one price, or:

$$P_{us} = SP_c \quad (3.11)$$

With non-traded goods (in which no arbitrage takes place due to high transport costs or prohibitive duties), this condition cannot be satisfied. In general, the spot exchange rate, whether bid or ask, will not exactly satisfy the law of one price due to the presence of duties and transport costs on traded goods as well as the prohibitive costs of arbitraging non-traded goods. A weaker form of purchasing power parity-relative PPP—however, may save the day.

严格的一价定律(The strict law of one price): 如果要使一价定律严格成立,那么税收、运输费用、进口关税和外汇的买卖价差都必须为零。在这种情况下,任何方向的套利活动都会使严格的一价定律成立。一般说来,即期汇率可能会因为可贸易商品的关税、运输费用以及不可贸易商品的存在而不严格地满足一价定律。

Relative purchasing power parity

Relative PPP does not require that the level of the exchange rate equal the ratio of purchasing powers, but that the change in the spot rate reflect the inflation rate differential. In other words, there is no change in the real exchange rate. Relative PPP states:

$$E\left(\frac{S_{t+1} - S_t}{S_t}\right) = E\left(\frac{P_{t+1}^{us} - P_t^{us}}{P_t^{us}}\right) - E\left(\frac{P_{t+1}^{j} - P_t^{j}}{P_t^{j}}\right) \quad (3.12)$$

where the left-hand side of equation (3.12) is the expected appreciation of the foreign currency in terms of home currency and the right-hand side is the expected inflation rate differential: That is, the expected rate of inflation at home less the expected rate of inflation abroad. The relative purchasing power parity theory of the exchange rate is depicted in Figure 3.11.

相对购买力平价理论(Relative purchasing power parity): 相对购买力平价理论不要求汇率等于两种货币购买力之比,而是要求即期汇率的变化反映通货膨胀率的差异。

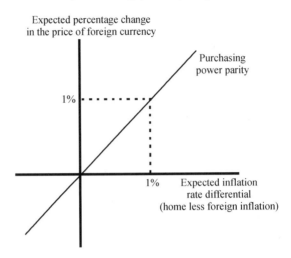

Figure 3.11 Relative purchasing power parity

When inflation at home is expected to be 1% greater than abroad, the expected price of foreign currency rises 1%. In fact, whenever the shocks are mainly monetary in nature, the purchasing power parity theory provides a good forecast of future exchange rates. It is not an arbitrage equation; rather it says that movements in currencies reflect movements in their relative purchasing power.

The monetary approach to the exchange rate

If different movements in price levels cause movements in the exchange rate, it is natural to ask what causes different inflation rates internationally. The old view that "inflation is too much money chasing too few goods" is not far from the truth. When money grows faster than income, prices tend to rise. Consequently, countries that inflate their money supply relative to the supply of goods experience higher inflation and greater depreciation of their currencies. This is known as the monetary approach to the exchange rate.

货币数量理论（The quantity theory of money）:认为货币数量变化与物价变化之间存在因果关系的理论。其核心思想是,当其他因素不变时,货币数量增加会导致物价上升。用公式表示为 $MV = Py$,其中 M 为货币供应量,V 为货币流通速度,P 为价格水平,y 为 GDP 水平。

It follows from **the quantity theory of money**:

$$MV = Py \qquad (3.13)$$

Where M is the money supply (currency plus checking deposits), V is the income velocity of circulation of money, P is the price level, in this case the implicit GDP deflator, and y is real GDP. The price level is thus determined by:

$$P = \frac{MV}{y} \qquad (3.14)$$

An equivalent but insightful way of defining income velocity as the inverse of the demand for money as a fraction of income, that is $k = 1/V$ we may express the price level as the ratio of money supply to money demand:

$$P = \frac{M}{ky} \qquad (3.15)$$

where M is the money supply and ky is the demand for money. The higher the money supply relative to money demand, the higher the price level.

In terms of percentage changes, the rate of inflation is determined by growth in the money supply relative to growth in money demand:

$$\frac{\Delta P}{P} = \frac{\Delta M}{M} - \frac{\Delta y}{y} - \frac{\Delta k}{k} \qquad (3.16)$$

式(3.16)表明,通货膨胀率由货币供给相对于货币需求的增长率所决定。

Inflation is caused by "too much money chasing too few goods", $\frac{\Delta M}{M} - \frac{\Delta y}{y}$, compounded by any percentage fall in the demand for money relative to income, $\frac{\Delta k}{k} < 0$, or, equivalently, an acceleration in the income velocity of money, $\frac{\Delta V}{V} > 0$.

In a sense, money is the root of all inflationary evil. It helps to understand why inflation bursts out here and there periodically. In principle, any third grader as Governor of the Central Bank could follow a simple Friedman rule to maintain a low, constant rate of growth in the money supply to avoid inflation. The problem is that the issue of money, seigniorage, is often the finance of ultimate resort of the fiscal deficit. For example, if the fiscal deficit is 10% of GDP, and 3% can be financed by borrowing at home through the sale of bonds domestically, and 2% can be financed by borrowing abroad by the sale of bonds to foreigners, the residual finance must come from the "printing press" or seigniorage finance, 5%. New money must be issued. That is:

$$H_t - H_{t-1} = [G_t + rB_{t-1} + V_t - T_t] - [B_t - B_{t-1}] \qquad (3.17)$$

除了征税和发行国债,政府还可以通过启动印钞机器来弥补财政赤字。新发行货币的数量如式(3.17)所示。

or new seigniorage, $H_t - H_{t-1}$, must finance the unfinanced residual of the fiscal deficit, $[G_t + rB_{t-1} + V_t - T_t] - [B_t - B_{t-1}]$, where G represents government spending on goods and services, rB represents interest payments on the public debt, V represents transfer payments, and T represents taxes. The change in the debt equals the sale of new bonds: $[B_t - B_{t-1}]$. Another way of expressing inflationary finance is as the inflationary tax, multiplying and dividing the left hand side of equation (3.17) by H_t:

$$H_t \times \left[\frac{H_t - H_{t-1}}{H_t}\right] = [G_t + rB_{t-1} + V_t - T_t] - [B_t - B_{t-1}] \tag{3.18}$$

where $\left[\frac{H_t - H_{t-1}}{H_t}\right]$ is the percentage inflationary tax rate and H_t is the base of the inflationary tax. There is a limit to the amount of inflationary tax since high inflation renders money a poor store of value, so money demand collapses, i.e. velocity accelerates. This exacerbates inflation. Inflationary episodes such as in Peru in the late 1980s were the result of collapsing real GDP, a fiscal deficit residual equal to 20% of GDP, financed almost solely my new money issue, and accelerating velocity. Inflation made the *inti* worthless, so the currency had to be changed. In the context of the exchange rate, countries that rely more heavily on inflationary finance have greater depreciations than those that do not. This suggests that the purchasing power parity relationship has as its foundation the growth of money supply relative to the growth of money demand.

> **Applying the Concept:** Inflation in China in 2005
>
> The percentage increase in China's Consumer Price Index in 2005 was only 1.8%, despite high money growth 17.6%. This is due to some prices being controlled, particularly fuel and gasoline. The implicit price deflator, a broader measure, rose however 3.4% more accurately reflecting inflation in China. A strong factor keeping inflation down, in addition to 9.9% real growth in GDP, is the rise in demand for money relative to income in China, 4.3%, a sign of financial deepening in Ronald McKinnon's terminology. There is greater financial intermediation due to an income elasticity of demand for money equal nearly to 2. Here is the summary for 2005.
>
> - Increase in Implicit GDP Deflator 3.4%, $\frac{\Delta P}{P}$.
> - Increase in Money supply (Money + Quasi - Money) 17.6%, $\frac{\Delta M}{M}$.

> - Increase in Real GDP 9.9%, $\frac{\Delta y}{y}$.
> - Increase in demand for money as a fraction of Nominal GDP 4.3%, $\frac{\Delta k}{k}$.
>
> Had money demand not increased relative to income by 4.3%, the inflation rate would have been 7.7%. In terms of the actual outcome:
>
> $\frac{\Delta P}{P} = \frac{\Delta M}{M} - \frac{\Delta y}{y} - \frac{\Delta k}{k}$ or $3.4 = 17.6 - 9.9 - 4.3$
>
> Source: Author's calculations.

The great advantage of the quantity theory of money is that it provides a basis for estimating the difference in expected inflation rates, thus providing a foundation for the theory of purchasing power parity. The level of the exchange rate in terms of the monetary approach is given by the ratio of internal prices. Consequently:

$$S = \frac{\frac{M}{ky}}{\frac{M^*}{k^* y^*}} \qquad (3.19)$$

That is, the level of the exchange rate is determined by the relative money supplies and money demands.

In general, relative purchasing power parity as a monetary phenomenon can be expressed as:

$$\frac{\Delta S}{S} = \left[\frac{\Delta M}{M} - \frac{\Delta y}{y} - \frac{\Delta k}{k}\right] - \left[\frac{\Delta M^*}{M} - \frac{\Delta y^*}{y} - \frac{\Delta k^*}{k}\right] \qquad (3.20)$$

According to equation (3.20), more rapid monetary growth at home causes the home currency to depreciate, as does slower real economic growth. By the same token, a fall in domestic money demand compared to foreign money demand also depreciates the home currency. This is known as the monetary approach to the exchange rate.

Deviations in exchange rates from purchasing power parity can, however, result from real shocks and changes in the terms of trade. For that reason, it is useful to have a measure of the ***real exchange rate*** (RER) to capture changes in the exchange rate relative to the *PPP* rate. The concept of the real exchange rate is a simple one, measuring the costs of one country's goods in terms of another's. A bilateral real exchange rate is defined as:

实际汇率（Real exchange rate）：将现实汇率经过相对物价指数调整后得到的汇率。

$$\text{RER} = \frac{P}{SP^*} \qquad (3.21)$$

Where P is the price level at home and SP^* is the foreign price level expressed in terms of home currency. When domestic prices rise relative to foreign prices, a real appreciation is said to take place. This means home goods can buy more foreign goods because a positive deviation from purchasing power parity has taken place. A dramatic example of the real depreciation of the dollar in terms of the euro has been the increase in the dollar price of the euro from \$0.90 to \$1.37 from 2005 to 2008, while there has been little difference in the inflation rates. The euro has thus experienced a real appreciation, while the dollar has suffered a real depreciation.

Naturally, there are many currencies, so the best RER measurement is one that takes into account the weight of each currency in terms of trade. The IMF provides such a calculation.

The IMF's real effective exchange rate

国际货币基金组织的真实有效汇率指数（The IMF's real effective exchange rate index）：一个指数加权指数。该指数用外国商品来衡量本国商品的价格。

The International Monetary Fund's (IMF's) real effective exchange rate index, RER (line rec, International Financial Statistics) is an exponentially-weighted index which measures the price of a home country's goods in terms of foreign goods. This type of index has excellent properties and is known as a *harmonic index*, having exponential weights that sum to one:

$$\text{RER} = 100 \prod_{i=1}^{n} \left(\frac{P}{S_i P_i}\right)^{W_i}$$
$$= 100 \left(\frac{P}{S_1 P_1}\right)^{W_1} \left(\frac{P}{S_2 P_2}\right)^{W_2} \left(\frac{P}{S_3 P_3}\right)^{W_3} \cdots \left(\frac{P}{S_n P_n}\right)^{W_n} \qquad (3.22)$$

As the RER rises, the home currency is said to experience a real appreciation while if RER falls, a real depreciation is said to occur. The Π symbol stands for the product of the i terms, in the same way that the Σ stands for the sum of various terms in a summation expression. P indicates the consumer price index of the home country, S_i indicates the home currency price of currency i, and the P_i indicates the consumer price index in country i. The exponential weights for each currency i are the w_i terms and must sum to unity (i.e. the equation is homogeneous of degree one so that a doubling of domestic prices relative to all exchange rate adjusted foreign prices leads to a doubling of the index). The w_i can represent simply trade weights with different countries, or in the case of the IMF's RER, the weights are known as effective trade weights.

Essentially, if the USA trades heavily with China and Mexico, the weights for the yuan and the peso would be relatively high in the US's RER. The International Financial Statistics are published in CD-ROM format monthly by the IMF, but lags in the data are a problem. Bloomberg contains more current financial data on the real exchange rate.

Foreign currency futures versus forward contracts

Futures are standard contracts per currency traded on the floor of an organized exchange. Maturities are usually less than one year and have fixed maturity dates. Until 1992, prices were determined by the Chicago method of "open outcry." In Francesca Taylor's words: "This is very colorful to watch, and conveys 'price transparency' by allowing every trader equal access to the same trade at the same price. Technically the meaning of open outcry is that your bid or your offer is good 'whilst the breath is warm.' What this actually means is that each trader on the exchange will shout out what trade he is trying to execute. He is not able to just shout it once and assume everyone has heard him, he must keep shouting. If he stops shouting, it is assumed that he no longer wishes to execute his trade at that price level. Everyone around him is also shouting, resulting in a lot of noise without too much clarity. The consequence of this is that not only do traders have to shout continuously what trades they are trying to fill, but they must also 'hand-signal' their trades, in case a trader a long way away cannot hear clearly. The hands and the mouth must say the same thing. Traders cannot just trade with hand signals and they must take examinations to comply with the requirements of the respective exchanges." In 1992, the Chicago Mercantile Exchange (CME) developed the Globex automated electronic trading platform, displacing the open pit outcry system of trading in options and futures.

In the futures market, initial margin is required and the position is "marked to market" daily. Delivery rarely takes place—the purchase of an offsetting position unwinds the contract. A single commission is paid for the round trip purchase and sale. There is no counterparty risk as the exchange guarantees the contracts. Trading hours are regular exchange

期货合约(Futures): 在有组织的某种交易所内进行交易的某种标准化合约。合约的期限一般低于一年,并且有固定的到期日。

hours, but electronic trading takes place on a 24-hour basis. While liquid, the futures market is small in size.

远期合约(Forwards):
没有固定的合约规模,合约期限也可以超过一年。

Forwards, on the other hand, are any size desired, with maturities occasionally longer than a year. Trading occurs between firms and banks in the interbank market, with prices determined by bid-ask quotes—the spread providing profits for the banks. Standing bank "relations" are necessary, but not margin collateral. In the forwards market, banks are connected 24 hours a day via the SWIFT system and negotiate forward prices directly. In volume, the forwards market dwarfs the futures markets. As a practical matter, international businesses hedge their risks through the forward market, through money market hedges, and foreign exchange swaps. Forwards give them the flexibility in terms of size of contract, maturity terms, and does not require the firm to tie up working balances in margin deposits. Money market hedges allow for a matching of streams of payments and receipts in a foreign currency, thus reducing exchange rate exposure. Foreign exchange swaps do the same thing, but allow each firm to take advantage of its comparative advantage in borrowing in its local currency, swapping the obligations of the loans through a swap dealer. Both borrowers are able to hedge their ongoing exposure through swaps at a lower cost. Nevertheless, the bid-ask spreads in foreign exchange and interest rates allows the swap dealer to make profits.

In forward markets, money markets, and swap markets, there is counterparty risk, broadly defined as non-fulfillment or downgrading, either partial or complete, of the terms of a financial contract.

Points quotations

A point is the last digit of a quotation. Thus, a point in foreign exchange quotations is typically equal to 0.0001 or 1/10,000 because currencies are usually quoted to four decimal points. A point is sometimes called a *pip* by foreign exchange traders. Consequently, when a forward quotation is given in terms of forward points (also known as swap points), it is necessary to adjust the spot quotation accordingly to obtain an outright forward quotation. For example, consider the following outright spot quotations on the pound sterling and the one-, two-, three-, six-, twelve-month and two-year forward point quotations in Table 3.5, as well as the corresponding outright forward rates.

Table 3.5 Points and outright forward quotations

Spot rate GBP/USD = 1.76048/1.76242.

Forward points			Outright forward quotations(£/$)		
Period	Bid	Ask	Period	Bid	Ask
1 month	−0.00195	−0.00185	1 month	1.75853	1.76057
2 months	−0.00354	−0.00313	2 months	1.75694	1.75929
3 months	−0.00440	−0.00410	3 months	1.75608	1.75832
6 months	−0.00599	−0.00541	6 months	1.75448	1.75702
12 months	−0.00619	−0.00541	12 months	1.75428	1.75702
2 years	−0.00639	−0.00541	2 years	1.75408	1.75702

Source: OzForex Foreign Exchange Services, July 14, 2005.

As a general rule:

- When the bid in points is larger than the offer in points, the reference currency is at a discount, so the points are subtracted from the spot quotations to obtain the outright forward quotation.

- When the bid in points is smaller than the offer in points, the reference currency is at a premium, so the points are added to the spot quotations to obtain the outright forward quotation. Notice again that the reciprocal of the American bid equals the European ask quotation. Likewise, the reciprocal of the American ask equals the European bid. This is obviously the case since when bidding pounds for dollars, a bank or trader is simultaneously offering dollars for pounds. The corresponding European quotation is reported in Table 3.6.

Table 3.6 European style outright quotations

Outright forward quotation(£/$)

Period	Bid	Ask
1 month	0.56800	0.56866
2 months	0.56841	0.56917
3 months	0.56872	0.56945
6 months	0.56915	0.56997
12 months	0.56915	0.57003
2 years	0.56915	0.57010

Source: OzForex Foreign Exchange Services, July 14, 2005.

Forwards and futures in commodities

Like futures, forward contracts are agreements to exchange an underlying asset, such as gold, at an agreed price at some future date. Consequently, futures and forward contracts may be used either to manage risk or for speculative purposes. However, there are important differences between forwards and futures that bear recalling:

1. A forward contract is negotiated directly between counterparties and is therefore tailor-made, whereas futures contracts are standardized agreements that are traded on an exchange.

2. Although forward contracts offer greater flexibility, there is a degree of counterparty risk, whereas futures contracts are guaranteed by the exchange on which they are traded.

3. Because futures contracts can be sold to third parties at any point prior to maturity, they are more liquid than forward contracts.

4. Futures prices are determined by the carrying costs at any time. These costs include the interest cost of borrowing gold plus insurance and storage charges.

5. The cost of a futures contract is also determined by the "initial margin", the cash deposit that is paid to the broker.

Speculative positions in forward contracts

远期合约的投机性头寸（A speculative position in a forward contract）：以今天决定的价格 F 在未来某一特定交割日交割某一特定资产或商品。

A speculative position in a forward contract is the forward purchase or sale of an asset or commodity for delivery at some specified date in the future at a price, F, determined today. If a speculator who sold gold short, purchases gold spot upon the delivery date at a price, S, to cover the short position, the profits/losses per unit of gold are $F - S$. Gold is usually traded forward in large units—metric tons. On the other hand, if the spot price of gold is greater than F the trader loses $S - F$ in covering the forward contract. The payoff for a forward sale of gold at the price F is illustrated in Figure 3.12.

Figure 3.12   Payoff from a short position in gold

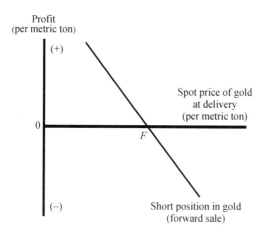

A long position in gold is a purchase of gold for forward delivery. Consequently, if the spot price upon maturity of the forward purchase is higher than the forward price, a speculator gains $S - F$. If the spot price is less than the forward price, the trader loses. A gold mining company that sells its gold forward may not be perfectly hedged. If the spot price of gold rises before maturity, the company may be forced to sell its forward contract at a loss if it needs cash. Similarly, if it has production problems, it may not be able to deliver the gold, so may end up buying and selling spot at the same time.

The cost of carry and the forward arbitrage price

The forward price of an asset may be computed by the cost of carry and a no-profit arbitrage condition. Consider the following steps:

- Borrow S today at interest rate r.
- Purchase today one unit of the security at price S.
- Sell forward today one unit of the security at price F for delivery at time T.
- At maturity T, cash in the dividend, k, on the security, and
- Deliver the security at maturity T at agreed upon price F.
- Pay off loan at T.

资产的远期价格可以通过无套利条件和持仓成本来计算。

The profit from this arbitrage can be computed as the forward sale price, plus the dividend received, less the principal and interest on the borrowed funds. That is:

$$\pi = F + [(1+k)^T - 1]S - (1+r)^T S \qquad (3.23)$$

Zero arbitrage profits imply: $F = [(1+r)^T - (1+k)^T + 1]S$

Or, subtracting S from both sides of the equation yields *the cost of carry*:

$$F - S = [(1+r)^T - (1+k)^T]S \qquad (3.24)$$

When $T = 1$, the cost of carry is simply:

$$F - S = [r - k]S \qquad (3.25)$$

持仓交易 (Carry trade): 要求当借款利率高于红利率, 也即 $r > k$ 时, 远期价格出现溢价。

The **carry trade** requires that the forward price be at a premium when the borrowing rate is greater than the dividend rate or $r > k$. When the security has zero coupon $k = 0$, or is a commodity with storage costs, $k < 0$, arbitrage pricing requires a premium over spot on the forward sale.

Let's take a few examples. First, suppose you sell 500 ounces of gold short for delivery in the futures market at $1,680 in three months. In a short sale, an investor borrows shares or gold from a brokerage firm and sells them, hoping to profit by buying them back at lower prices. If they rise, the investor faces a loss. Uncovered short sales are those shares or gold that have been borrowed and sold, but not yet covered by repurchase. If the spot price falls to $1,660, three months later when you cover your short position, gaining $20 per ounce or $10,000, as illustrated in Figure 3.13.

Figure 3.13 A gain from a short position in gold

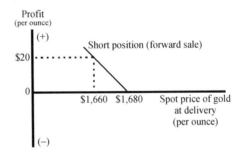

However, if the price of gold rises in the spot market to $1,700, you will lose $20 per ounce, or $10,000, as shown in Figure 3.14.

Figure 3.14 A loss from a short position in gold

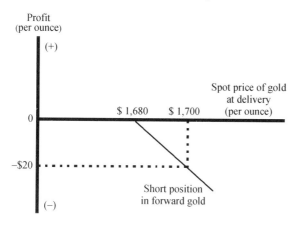

Since the forward rate is centered at the expected future value of gold, it is as likely you will gain at least $11,000 as you will lose at least $11,000. A **hedged position** combines a short with a long position, guaranteeing neither gains nor losses. However, you will pay the ask for the long forward and receive the bid for the short forward—that is, you will pay the spread. In addition, there is a commission. Since the hedged position is the combination of a long and a short position for the same amount and maturity of a security or asset, what is gained on the long position is lost on the short position, and vice versa. Graphically, the hedged position, ignoring transactions costs, is the sum of the long and short positions, yielding the horizontal axis in Figure 3.15—a zero payoff.

对冲头寸(Hedged position)将一个多头头寸与一个空头头寸结合起来,从而保证既无收益也无损失。

Figure 3.15 A hedged position in gold

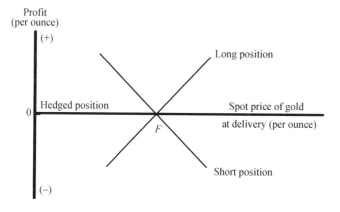

By the same token, a long position—i. e. a forward purchase, gains when the spot price rises and loses upon covering when the spot price falls.

Gold is a hedge against inflation, as evidenced by these observations: "Crude's coming back up, and gold is getting more buying," said Frank McGhee, head trader at brokerage Alliance Financial LLC in Chicago. 'Oil's stability is allowing gold to regain some of the price that it shed,' he said. Gold futures for August delivery rose 50 cents to $420.70 an ounce at noon on the Comex division of the New York Mercantile Exchange." (*Bloomberg*, July 15, 2005) Of course, this writer was right, gold is currently in December 2019 $1,465 a troy ounce.

Arbitrage determination of the spot and future rates

Arbitrage—buying low, selling high and profiting from differences in price when the same security, currency, or commodity is traded on two or more markets. An arbitrageur simultaneously buys one contract of say gold in New York and sells one contract of gold in Chicago, locking in a small profit because at that moment the price on the two markets is different. Arbitrageurs perform the economic function of making markets trade more efficiently by eliminating different prices for the same item. **Covered interest arbitrage** hedges the foreign currency risk, thus covering the arbitrage from exchange rate losses in the future spot market. The hedge takes the form of a forward sale for foreign currency today at an agreed upon rate for delivery in the future, thus locking in the exchange rate conversion to home currency.

抛补套利 (Covered interest arbitrage) 能够对冲外汇风险,通过这种办法可以抵补在未来即期外汇市场上的潜在汇率损失。

非抛补套利 (Uncovered interest arbitrage) 不对冲外汇风险。

Uncovered interest arbitrage does not hedge foreign currency risk. The arbitrageur purchases foreign Treasuries on the expectation that when they mature, the foreign exchange proceeds—interest plus principal in pounds, for example—will be sold on the spot market in say 30 days for more dollars than would otherwise be earned by holding US 30-day Treasuries. The uncovered arbitrageur may expect to sell at the forward rate in effect today, but the spot rate for the pound may be higher or lower than the forward rate today. If it is higher, the arbitrageur-speculator gains by selling pounds at the higher rate, but if it is lower, there are unanticipated losses on the exchange conversion. Since the arbitrager does not cover foreign exchange exposure by selling pounds in the forward market, this type of interest arbitrage is called uncovered.

Covered interest arbitrage

Let's jot down some preliminary notation. To focus on strict interest rate parity, we will initially ignore the foreign exchange and Treasury bid-ask spreads. As we shall later see, these spreads are not insignificant and add substantially to the cost of arbitraging for an individual investor. Banks and financial intermediaries trading on their own accounts are spared the spreads and can arbitrage large amounts to take advantage of small deviations from interest rate parity.

Spot rate for the pound: $S = (\$/\pounds)$ spot = number of dollars paid today for one British pound sterling today. Forward rate for the pound: $F = (\$/\pounds)$ forward = number of dollars received in three months for the sale of one pound sterling. This rate is agreed upon today.

The US Treasury bill (T-bill) interest rate: r_{us} = the interest rate on the three-month US T-bill (the quarterly rate). US T-bills are issued with maturities of three months in denominations beginning at $1,000. T-bills do not bear interest nor pay coupons. Instead, investors purchase bills at a discounted price from their face value. At maturity, the Treasury redeems the bills at full face or par value. The difference between the discounted price paid and the face value of the bill is paid when redeemed. T-bills are also quoted by price. An investor pays the ask when buying T-bills and receives the bid when selling them. For the moment, we set the bid-ask spread at zero. The UK T-bill interest rate: r_{uk} = interest rate on a three-month UK T-bill. To simplify the notation, this is the three-month interest rate, i.e. the quarterly rate, not the interest rate per annum. To convert the annual interest rate to a 90-day interest rate, the convention is to multiply the annual rate by 90/360 or 1/4 to convert to a quarterly rate: that is, just divide it by four.

To take advantage of small profit opportunities by arbitraging short term liquid capital, take the following two steps:
- **Step I. Compare dollars to dollars**

1. Route one: With one million dollars, buy 90-day US T-bills. At maturity, they will yield principal plus interest of $(1 + r_{us})$ million dollars. Each dollar invested yields $1 + r_{us}$ dollars in 90 days.

2. Route two:

a. Buy $[1/(S)]$ million pounds sterling in the spot market at S.

b. Invest $[1/(S)]$ pounds sterling in 90-day UK T-bills, yielding $[(1/S)(1+r_{uk})]$ million pounds in three months.

c. Sell $[(1/S)(1+r_{uk})]$ pounds sterling in the forward market at F, yielding $F[(1/S)(1+r_{uk})]$ million or $\left(\dfrac{F}{S}\right)(1+r_{uk})$ dollars at settlement in three months.

- **Step II. Select the higher dollar return**

If $(1+r_{us}) > \left(\dfrac{F}{S}\right)(1+r_{uk})$, place short term capital in US T-bills due to the higher yield. That is, sell UK T-bills from your portfolio, buy dollars spot, buy 90-day US T-bills, sell the proceeds 90 days forward. You have completed a round trip in pounds and gained the covered arbitrage differential.

If $(1+r_{us}) < \left(\dfrac{F}{S}\right)(1+r_{uk})$, place short term capital in UK T-bills due to the higher yield. That is, sell 90-day US T-bills from your portfolio, buy pounds spot, buy 90-day UK T-bills, sell the pound proceeds forward for delivery in 90 days. You have completed a round trip and gained the covered arbitrage differential.

However, if

$$(1+r_{us}) = \left(\dfrac{F}{S}\right)(1+r_{uk}) \tag{3.26}$$

covered interest rate parity holds: there are no unexploited arbitrage profit opportunities, so do nothing!

Covered interest parity can be expressed in terms of the percentage interest rate differential versus the percentage premium or discount on the forward pound. Subtract $(1+r_{uk})$ from both sides of the interest rate parity equation and simplify:

$$(r_{us} - r_{uk}) = \left(\dfrac{F-S}{S}\right)(1+r_{uk}) \tag{3.27}$$

which says that the interest rate differential in favor of US T-bills is just (approximately) offset by the premium on the pound sterling. If interest rates on US T-bills are two percent higher than on UK T-bills, the forward pound will be at a 2% premium. Covered interest rate parity can be illustrated in Figure 3.16.

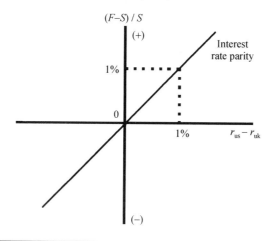

Figure 3.16 Covered interest rate parity

Along the interest rate parity line, it does not matter whether you invest your short term funds in U.S. Treasuries or UK T-bills. To the right of the interest parity line, the covered arbitrage differential is in favor of US Treasuries. To the left, the covered arbitrage differential is in favor of UK T-bills.

The covered arbitrage differential

The **covered arbitrage differential** (CAD) in favor of 90-day US T-bills is measured by:

$$CAD = (1 + r_{us}) - \left(\frac{F}{S}\right)(1 + r_{uk}) \qquad (3.28)$$

which may be positive or negative. If positive, sell UK T-bills, buy dollars spot with the pound proceeds, buy US T-bills, sell the dollars forward (buy pounds forward), thus gaining the CAD in the round trip arbitrage. If negative, sell US T-bills, buy pounds spot, buy UK T-bills and sell pounds forward (buy dollars forward), to gain the CAD in favor of UK T-bills.

Transaction costs

Of course, there are transactions costs since the investor must pay the ask when buying and receives the bid when selling, effectively paying the bid-ask spreads on forex to the financial institution. Similarly, when buying US or UK T-bills, the investor pays the ask price, while when selling, the investor receives the bid. For this reason, slight deviations from interest rate parity do not trigger covered arbitrage movements, except possibly by financial institutions. Ignoring transactions costs, capital will arbitrage until interest rate parity holds since the assets are risk-free. The CAD, including transactions costs, equals zero, yielding covered interest parity. Otherwise, unexploited risk less profits from arbitrage would exist.

套利成本(Arbitrage costs):进行无风险套利时所支付的交易费用,例如,买入和卖出的价差、交易佣金以及其他任何交易费用。

Just what are these **arbitrage costs**? We can identify three spreads and commissions in the forex and treasuries markets:

1. The forex spread.
2. The US T-bill spread, and
3. The UK T-bill spread.
4. Commissions on foreign exchange and Treasuries.

Taking into account the rates at which an individual transacts, the interest rate parity condition is a bit more complex. It should be borne in mind that when you purchase pounds, you pay the ask, when you buy UK T-bills you again pay the ask, but when you sell pounds forward you receive the bid. That is, there are transactions costs in short term money arbitrage.

An example of covered interest arbitrage

When the interest differential does not exactly offset the forward discount, it is possible to make small gains by arbitraging money. Consider an example of either investing $10,000 in three-month US T-bills, or converting into euros, purchasing euro T-bills, and selling the euro proceeds in the three month futures market. The basic data are given in Table 3.7.

Table 3.7 Basic arbitrage data

US T-bill rate(3 months)(%)	0.9625
Euro T-bill rate(3 months)(%)	0.9000
Sport price of the euro($/€)	1.2500
Forward price of the euro(3 months)($/€)	1.2700

In this case, the interest rate differential against euro T-bills is less than the percentage future premium on the euro. Consequently, small gains ($33.41) can be made by arbitraging toward euro T-bills, and selling the euro proceeds three months forward. Once again, we are covered in the futures market. Thus this riskless arbitrage (buying low, selling high) will eliminate arbitrage gains. The steps in covered interest arbitrage are illustrated in Figure 3.17.

Figure 3.17 Covered interest arbitrage with a gain

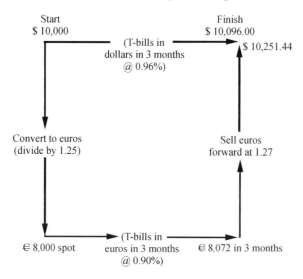

For arbitrage activity to be truly profitable to the investor, the correct rate quotation must be used for each transaction. When US T-bills are sold, the bid rate is received, when pounds are bought spot, the dollar bid—pound ask rate is used, the ask rate for UK T-bills is paid and the forward bid price of the pound is received (or equivalently, the forward ask price of the dollar is paid). Every transaction has a transactions cost. The round-trip must cover all the transactions costs to be worthwhile.

It is also possible to buy and hold euro T-bills for three months, then at maturity sell the euro proceeds in the spot exchange market. This type of arbitrage is called uncovered interest arbitrage because it is subject to unexpected gains or losses.

Uncovered interest arbitrage equilibrium occurs when the expected returns are equal. When there are riskless assets, it is generally true that $E(S_{90}) = F_{90}$. Consequently, when covered interest arbitrage equilibrium holds, the uncovered interest arbitrage equilibrium condition does too. Figure 3.18 illustrates an example of realized uncovered interest arbitrage where the euro proceeds are multiplied by the actual spot exchange rate realized after three months.

If the realized spot rate of the euro is higher than the expected rate in one year, there are unanticipated gains, while if it is less, there are unanticipated losses. Hence, the term uncovered interest arbitrage. In Figure 3.18, the spot price of the euro has unexpectedly fallen to $1.20, so the arbitrage return is only \$9,686.40. A loss of \$409.85 is realized relative to the investment is US T-bills.

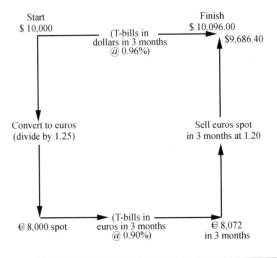

Figure 3.18 Uncovered interest rate arbitrage with a loss

Of course, the arbitrageur could liquidate the position at any time before maturity, thereby locking in any gains or losses. In general, we may define the unanticipated gain (+)/loss (−) by the difference between the spot price of the euro in 90 days (the bid) S_{90} and the future bid price of today. The unanticipated gain, if positive, or loss, if negative, in uncovered interested arbitrage activity is measured as $S_{90} - F_{90}$ per unit of foreign exchange. We must still bear in mind that the rates refer to the dollar bid price of the euro in the spot and futures markets respectively, i.e. American quotation, and that the bid-ask spread is also paid on Treasuries.

Cross rates and triangular arbitrage

三角套利 (Triangular arbitrage) 能够消除两种货币之间直接汇率与交叉汇率的不一致,从而确保一价定律的成立。它能够使即期与远期外汇市场上的汇率保持一致。

Another type of arbitrage that is done by multinational financial institutions is known as **triangular arbitrage**. Triangular arbitrage eliminates inconsistencies between direct and cross rates between two currencies, thereby enforcing the law of one price. It can take place in the spot or the futures markets to keep rates consistent.

• The direct rate for the purchase of pounds by dollars is simply the American style quotation \$/£. For an investor, this is the ask in dollars for one pound.

The cross rate, American quotation, between dollars and pounds via the yen is indicated by ($/¥)(¥/£) since this is the number of pounds obtained by buying yen for dollars, then buying pounds with the yen.

Naturally, an investor pays the ask rate in dollars for yen, then the ask price in yen for pounds.

Triangular arbitrage equilibrium

There are no profit opportunities via triangular arbitrage when ($/¥)(¥/£) = ($/£).

Whenever this condition is not satisfied, profit opportunities exist. Consider the following inconsistent quotations:

Direct rate:

Dollars per pound sterling ($/£)   1.7669

Cross rate:

Dollars per Japanese Yen ($/¥)   0.009434

Japanese yen per pound sterling (¥/£)   186.3543

Therefore, the cross rate is (0.009434)(186.3543) = 1.7581

An arbitrage opportunity exists! Buy yen with dollars, then pounds with yen. This will cost you $1.7581 per pound. Sell the pounds at $1.7669, earning one half of a US penny per pound. If you trade $1,000, your net profits are $5.02.

In Figure 3.19, start with $1,000 in the upper right hand starting position. Buy yen with dollars, then pounds with yen. At the end of the triangular arbitrage, you will have made about one cent per pound.

Figure 3.19   Triangular foreign exchange arbitrage

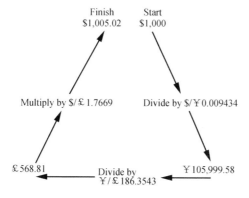

Profitable arbitrage will eliminate this price inconsistency, establishing the law of one price. Arbitrageurs take advantage of these opportunities until profit disappears and arbitrage equilibrium is satisfied, increasing the dollar price of the yen and the yen price of the pound, until no further arbitrage profits exist.

Consider another arbitrage example: You have two prices for a pound:

$$(\$/¥)(¥/£) = \$1.7669$$
$$(\$/£) = \$1.7642$$

In this case, buy a pound directly with dollars, and then sell it indirectly through yen for dollars, earning profits of ($1.7669 - $1.7642) = $0.0027 per pound. Recall that you will pay the forex spread three times in converting currency in this example.

The law of one price

一价定律(The law of one price): 当同种商品在不同的市场有不同的价格时,就存在套利机会。低价买进而高价卖出的套利活动使得商品价格在不同的市场上趋于一致。这就是一价定律。

Interest rate arbitrage is another way of looking at the law of one price. A dollar is a dollar. You should only pay one dollar for it! In general, the same item must have the same price, adjusting for transactions and shipping costs. An ounce of gold is worth the London fixing price all over the world. Even gold panners in Brazil know the day's market price of gold.

When prices for the same item are out of line, that is, are different in two markets, an arbitrage opportunity exists. Buy low in the low market and sell high in the high market, making sure your transactions and/or transportation costs are covered in doing so. Buying in the low market makes the price rise there and selling in the high market makes the price fall there. The equilibrium requires the law of one price, accounting for transactions costs, to hold for the same item. Arbitrage makes markets more efficient, moving goods and assets from markets with lower returns to markets with higher returns. In the process, wealth and income are increased.

This is particularly true for riskless financial arbitrage where the transactions costs are low and the commodity is currency. While the individual investor loses the spreads by paying the ask price when buying and receiving the bid when selling, multinational financial institutions trading on their own account have minute transactions costs and will therefore push the equilibrium back towards the interest rate parity line whenever there are slight deviations. This keeps markets efficient, moving capital from low return environments to high return environments. Bear in mind, naturally, that we are speaking of riskless assets that are otherwise identical.

When riskless assets do not exist, the interest differential is no longer a good predictor of the percentage rate of depreciation because a risk premium is imbedded into the risky asset. Yet the interest rate is the best predictor available.

Exchange rate forecasting

If a forward rate, F, exists, it is centered at the expected exchange rate. Consequently, just buy the *Wall Street Journal* or the *Financial Times* and look up the forward rate. In the euro and the pound, there are futures up to two years. Consequently, today's forward quotations provide every bit of known information about the future, so they are unbiased predictors of the future spot exchange rate.

汇率预期（Exchange rate forecasting）：我们可以利用利率平价公式来预测远期汇率,即能够使套利利润为零的远期汇率。

However, forward and futures markets do not always exist for future delivery of foreign currency and their maturity is only up to two years. A forward bid and ask quotation could be gotten from a foreign exchange dealer, but the spread would be greater, the further the quote is in the future. The foreign exchange dealer limits risk by widening the spread.

Forecasting the future exchange rate is conveniently done by the interest rate parity equation. First, let's create a hypothetical one-year Treasury Bill that is composed of a six month bill rolled over for an additional six months. That is: $(1 + r_{us_{180}})(1 + r_{us_{180}}) = (1 + r_{us_{360}})$ yields an estimate of the comparable risk free one year rate, r_{us}. Alternatively, we could strip the interest rate futures to predict the 180 to 360 day 6-month T-bill forward rate, or we could use the rate on a 2-year T-bill with one year to maturity remaining. The main point of the exercise is to construct a one-year riskless Treasury rate, r_{us}.

According to interest rate parity one year forward:

$$\left(\frac{F}{S}\right) = \frac{(1 + r_{us})}{(1 + r_{uk})} \qquad (3.29)$$

Or equivalently

$$F = S \frac{(1 + r_{us})}{(1 + r_{uk})} \qquad (3.30)$$

We can therefore use the interest rate parity equation to forecast the forward spot rate in one year—it is a no profit arbitrage condition that must hold. Similarly, by rolling over the Treasury asset an additional year or in general, n years, we can forecast the future spot rate in n years by repeated application of interest rate parity.

式(3.31)给出了预测 n 年后即期汇率的公式。

$$F = S \left[\frac{(1+r_{us})}{(1+r_{uk})} \right]^n \quad (3.31)$$

All information needed to make a five year forecast of the future spot rate of the pound is available today: the spot rate, a one year riskless interest rates in the U.S. and the U.K.

For example, if one year risk less rate were 3.5% in the United States and 4% in the U.K., interest rate parity implies that the dollar would be expected to appreciate approximately one half of a percent in a year relative to the pound. By rolling over the riskless pound investment each year, the successive dollar pound future spot rates can be predicted using interest parity. That is, given the spot bid of $1.7609 per pound, we may predict the future spot bid rates by applying the n period forward interest parity formula, yielding a five-year forward forecast of the price of the pound in Table 3.8.

Table 3.8 A five-year forecast of the future exchange rate

$$F_1 = 1.75243$$
$$F_2 = 1.74401$$
$$F_3 = 1.73562$$
$$F_4 = 1.72728$$
$$F_5 = 1.71898$$

The use of interest rate parity conditions—that is, the no expected profit arbitrage condition—as a forecasting tool is powerful and based in the best available finance theory. Despite the absence of a futures market five years ahead, a market based forecast is still possible. It can be used to convert expected future cash flows in foreign currency, for instance.

An application to international capital budgeting

自由现金流(Free cash flow):税后收入加上折旧(非现金费用)再加上净营运资本的变化。

Free cash flow is defined as earnings after tax, plus depreciation, a non-cash expense, minus changes in net working capital, minus capital expenditures. Table 3.9 indicates the forecasted free cash flows for a possible expansion in the United Kingdom by a US firm in millions of pounds.

Table 3.9 Forecasted free cash flows for a UK acquisition in millions of pounds

	Year						Terminal value
	0	1	2	3	4	5	
Earnings before financing charges and taxes	—	10.0	12.5	15.0	16.5	18.0	
Taxes*	—	—	3.5	4.4	5.3	5.8	
Earnings before financing charges, after taxes	—	10.0	9.0	10.6	11.2	12.2	
Depreciation expense†	—	5.0	5.0	5.0	5.0	5.0	
Capital expenditures	(50.0)	(4.0)	(4.4)	(5.0)	(5.3)	(5.7)	
Investment in net working capital	(6.0)	(0.6)	(0.7)	(0.9)	(1.0)	(1.1)	
Total free cash flow	(56.0)	10.4	8.9	9.7	9.9	10.4	78.0‡

  * Taxes are incurred locally at the full marginal corporate tax rate of 35 percent, and paid 9 months following the end of the tax year. US Inc. receives a tax credit on income remitted from UK plc up to the full marginal U.S. corporate tax rate of 35 percent.

  † Initial capital expenditures of £50 million are depreciated on a straight-line basis over 10 years, beginning in the first year.

  ‡ Estimated as a level, no-growth perpetuity of £11.7 million that begins in the sixth year of the project.

  Source: W. Kester & T. Luehrman (1993), "Note on Cross Border Valuation," *Case Problems in International Finance*, McGraw-Hill.

Their approach is to estimate foreign-currency cash flows, then discount to the present at the weighted average cost of capital in pounds, assumed to be 15%. Table 3.9 estimates the cost of acquisition of a subsidiary in the U.K. at 50 million pounds. In the first year of operations, it will generate a free cash flow of £10.4 million, then to £10.4 in its fifth year of operations. During its fifth year, the firm is sold. Its terminal value is estimated to be £78.0 (a £11.7 million perpetuity discounted at 15%, the pound discount rate). Alternatively, the terminal value could be the scrap value of the operation. Then discount at the firm's cost of borrowing in pounds, given as 15%. This yields a positive net present value of £15.76 million, representing a 20% internal rate of return (the rate of discount of free cash flows in pounds that sets the net present value of the investment equal to zero). Clearly, this expansion is worthwhile.

Random investing

Are darts better than financial advisors? Consider the following three tosses of a true (fair) coin that has a fifty percent (0.5) probability of landing heads and a fifty percent probability of landing tails. There are 8 possible outcomes after three tosses as illustrated by the binomial tree illustrated in Figure 3.20.

Figure 3.20 Random investing

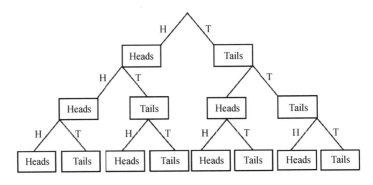

There are eight investment funds associated with each branch of the binomial tree in Table 3.10. *Ex ante*, before the coin tosses, each has a 12.5% chance of winning the forecast, assuming three tosses of a fair coin. *Ex post*, after the coin tosses, there will only be one winner.

Table 3.10 Random investment funds

	Branches	Probability	Investment Fund
1.	HHH	12.5%	Fudelity
2.	HHT	12.5%	Local
3.	HTH	12.5%	Simpleton
4.	HTT	12.5%	Dubious
5.	THH	12.5%	Ponce de Leon
6.	THT	12.5%	GuarVan
7.	TTH	12.5%	T. Rut Price
8.	TTT	12.5%	Christopher Columbus

Only one of the investment funds will be the successful investor, the others will be wrong. Nevertheless, the outcome was randomly determined. This random-walk view of investment suggests that indexed funds managed passively with low fees will do better on the average than actively managed funds with high fees (Reinker and Tower, 2004). This is the efficient market hypothesis. For instance, if the winner gets $100, a fair investment would be $12.50. Notice that this example is a "fair" investment—neither bid-ask spread, nor fees associated with it—each investor pays the expected value of investing. However, the house usually charges an entry fee and an ask price, so the investment is biased against the investor. This is especially true when a portfolio is actively managed and charges management fees. Yes, darts are better than financial advisors, unless the advisor uses expert witnesses to trade on inside information.

Stock options

A call option contract carries the right, but not the obligation, to buy a specified amount of shares of stock at an agreed upon price at settlement on or before a specified future date. **A put option** contract carries the right, but not the obligation, to sell a specified amount of shares of stock at a settlement price on or before a set future date.

The specified price is called the option's exercise or strike price. The specified future date is called the option's expiration date or maturity. Options are therefore derivatives whose value derives from the value of an underlying asset.

An ***American* style option** can be exercised anytime between the moment the option is purchased and its expiration. A ***European* style option** can be exercised only on its expiration date. The terms *American* and *European* refer to the existence of the early exercise feature or not of the options, not to where they are traded.

The cost of an option is known as the **premium**, which has both an intrinsic value and a time value. The **intrinsic value** is the profit from an immediate exercise of an option if it is in the money, i.e. profitable if exercised. Otherwise, the intrinsic value of the option is zero. Mathematically, intrinsic values can be easily summarized by the follow expressions:

$$\text{Intrinsic value of a call} = \max(S - X, 0)$$
$$\text{Intrinsic value of a put} = \max(X - S, 0)$$

where S is the stock price and X is the exercise price of the option.

The time value of an option is also called the speculative value of an option. It is the difference between the option premium and the option's intrinsic value. Because the option holder does not have to exercise the option immediately, the time value reflects the holder's right to exercise the option on a later date when the stock price moves higher.

An option is **in the money** if its intrinsic value is positive. An option is at the money when the underlying stock price is equal to the option's exercise price and an option is **out of the money** when it is not profitable to exercise.

The buyer of an option pays a premium to purchase the option, but does not risk any further monies. If the option finishes at the money or out of the money, the buyer loses 100% of the initial investment. The maximum payoff of a put option is the option's exercise price when the underlying stock becomes worthless. The maximum payoff of a call option is unlimited because the underlying stock price can, in principle, be infinite.

The seller of an option receives a premium for selling, or writing the option. In exchange for the option premium, the seller agrees to stand ready to satisfy an option exercise if the buyer chooses to do so. As the option moves further into the money, the seller's liability increases. As the option moves further out of the money, his liability remains zero. If the option finishes in the money, the buyer will exercise and the seller must fulfill the exercise and lose the intrinsic value of the option.

The maximum loss to a put option seller, or writer, is the exercise price should the underlying stock becomes worthless. The seller of a call option faces potentially unlimited losses as the price of the asset could conceivably rise towards infinity.

Options are risky investments for two reasons. First, option positions are highly leveraged and consequently, small changes in the underlying stock may cause large percentage changes in the option price. Second, since the life of the option is usually no longer than nine months, option traders are forced to close out their positions at expiration. They don't have the ability to continue to hold their positions until the market "recovers or comes back."

投资者可以在**交易所**(**Exchange**)购买期权,交易所内进行的期权交易是标准化的,且不存在违约风险,因为清算所保证了这种交易的顺利进行。

If an investor buys an option on an **exchange**, the buyer does not run counterparty risk since a clearinghouse for the exchange guarantees the option. Options cannot be bought on margin since there is no supporting stock. Instead, the full premium must be paid. The seller (writer) of the option has to post a margin account, which is marked-to-market by the clearinghouse on a daily basis. Stock options are traded on a number of U.S. exchanges, including the Chicago Board Options Exchange (www.cboe.com), the Pacific Exchange (www.pacificex.com) in San Francisco, the Philadelphia Stock Exchange (www.phlx.com), and the American Stock Exchange (www.amex.com). Exchange-traded options are standardized options in terms of underlying asset, contract size, expiration dates, exercise prices, delivery, and exercise settlement, among others. The cost of an option is always known as the premium. The contract size is a pre-specified amount of the underlying asset. The quoted exercise price is per unit of the underlying asset, for example per share. Standardization of options dramatically increases the liquidity of options. Because the Options Clearing Corporation (OCC) (www.optionsclearing.com) guarantees the performance of every option, exchange-traded options essentially do not carry any counterparty default risk.

Over-the-counter (OTC) options are sold by financial institutions to institutional buyers and are tailored to their needs in terms of amount (notional principal), delivery conditions, and expiration date. These are mainly hedging transactions between enterprises and banks. There is counterparty risk of non-performance if an option is purchased over-the-counter from a dealer, broker, or bank, since these can go bankrupt or default.

场外交易期权 (Over-the-counter options): 由金融机构向机构投资者销售,它根据投资者的需要来确定金额和到期日。场外期权交易存在交易对手风险。

The Black-Scholes formula for a call option premium, C, is given by:

$$C = SN(d_1) - Xe^{-rT}N(d_2) \quad (3.32)$$

where $\quad d_1 = \dfrac{\ln(S/X) + (r + \sigma^2/2)T}{\sigma\sqrt{T}}, \quad d_2 = d_1 - \sigma\sqrt{T}$

This result is derived from the basic relationship that the value of the option today is the discounted value of the expected payoff at expiration:

$$C = e^{-rT}E[\max(0, S_T - X)] \quad (3.33)$$

The Black-Scholes formula for a put option premium, P, is given by:

$$P = Xe^{-rT}N(-d_2) - SN(-d_1) \quad (3.34)$$

This is similarly derived from the discounted value of the expected payoff of the put at expiration:

$$P = e^{-rT}E[\max(0, X - S_T)] \quad (3.35)$$

The notation for the call and put options on a share is:

C = the value of the European call option

P = the value of the European put option

T = the time to maturity (when the option matures, in years)

e = exponent, base of the natural logarithm (the number 2.718281828 where $\dfrac{de^x}{dx} = e^x$)

S = the spot market price of the underlying asset

X = the exercise or strike price of the option

r = the continuously compounded risk-free interest rate

σ = volatility (the standard deviation of the returns on the underlying asset)

$N(d)$ = the cumulative standard normal distribution function (see Equation (3.36) below)

ln = the natural logarithm ($\ln e^x = x$)

For any number z, where z can be negative, $N(z)$ is indicated by the area under the standard normal distribution to the left of the value z. Due to the symmetry of the normal distribution, the following relation holds for the cumulative normal distribution function: $N(z) = 1 - N(-z)$.

That is:

$$p(z < d) = N(d) = \frac{1}{\sqrt{2\pi}} \int_{-\infty}^{d} e^{\frac{-z^2}{2}} dz \qquad (3.36)$$

which is indicated by the mass of the area under the normal distribution to the left of the value d.

The probability of a critical value less than d can be looked up in the cumulative normal distribution tables, or consulted in Microsoft Excel under the function wizard, f_x, as NORMSDIST(d), where you are prompted to enter the d value. Simply enter the d value you are seeking to input into the Black-Scholes formula. For example, if you input the value -1 into the NORMSDIST function, your result is 15.8655%. That is:

= NORMSDIST(-1) in Excel displays 0.15865526

meaning that the probability of an observation being below one standard deviation from the mean is about 16%. NORMSDIST(1) yields 0.84134474, so that $1 - N(1) = 1 - 0.84134474 = 0.15865526 = N(-1)$. Similarly, $N(-2) = 0.022750062$, so that the probability of an observation falling outside two standard deviations is about 2.3%, or nearly 5% for a two-tailed test.

The more general NORMDIST(x, mean, standard deviation, cumulative) in Excel gives the probability of a value being less than x, given the mean and standard deviation specified and whether it is cumulative (true) or not (false). This is essentially the JPMorgan's Riskmetrics approach. That is, indicate "T" when prompted for cumulative or "F" if it is the probability density distribution, rather than the cumulative distribution. For example:

= NORMDIST(80,100,10,TRUE) = 0.022750062

indicates that if the mean or expected value is 100 and the standard deviation (volatility) is 10, there is a probability of a value of less than 80 of 2.3%. The logical statement "TRUE" is to indicate that we are dealing with the cumulative normal distribution.

If "FALSE" were indicated, it would be the standard normal distribution and would indicate the height of the probability density at 80. With "FALSE", the probability density of 80 equals 0.005399097 or approximately 0.54%.

Table 3.11 provides a numerical example of options pricing of a stock.

Table 3.11 The call and put premium on a stock option

Equity options		
Strike price($)	X	100
Time to expiry	T	0.25
Spot price($)	S	100
Interest rate	r	0.05
Volatility	σ	0.3
	d_1	0.1583
	d_2	0.0083
Call($)	C	6.5831
Put($)	P	5.3409

Options on this non-dividend paying stock with 90 days to maturity and a strike price of $100 yield a call option premium of $6.5831 and a put option premium of $5.3409.

Foreign currency options

A foreign currency call option is the right, but not the obligation, to buy a specified amount of foreign currency, known as the contract size, at an exercise price on or before the expiration date. A forex put option is the right to sell a specific quantity of foreign currency at a strike price on or before maturity. Therefore, foreign currency options are derivatives whose value derives from the value of the underlying foreign currency. Like options on stocks, a European style option cannot be exercised before the expiration date, while an American style option can be exercised anytime between the moment it is written and its expiration.

- A call is an option to buy a foreign currency
- A put is an option to sell a foreign currency

The buyer of a foreign currency option pays a premium to purchase the option, but does not risk any further monies beyond the premium paid. Holding option positions can be risky and expensive. If the option expires "out-of-the-money," not profitable if exercised, the buyer loses all of the investment in the option premium. If the option expires "in-the-money," profitable if exercised, the buyer realizes a positive profit if the payoff of the option exceeds its cost, the premium.

The seller or writer of a foreign exchange option must honor the option

外汇期权(Foreign currency options): 在合约到期日或者之前, 按照一定的执行价格, 购买(或卖出)一定数量的外汇的权利。

contract if it is presented for exercise. Consequently, the seller of a put option risks the amount equal to the exercise price times the option contract size, should the currency become worthless. The seller of a call option faces potentially unlimited losses as the spot price of the underlying foreign currency could conceivably rise to infinity.

Exchange options in foreign currency are traded on the Philadelphia Stock Exchange (www.phlx.com), and the International Money Market of the Chicago Mercantile Exchange (www.cme.com). Exchange-traded options are standardized. The price of the option on an exchange is known as the premium. The contract is for a specified amount and the quoted exercise price is per unit of the underlying foreign currency, for example per pound sterling. Exchange-traded foreign exchange options do not carry default risk as the clearing house guarantees their performance.

Over-the-counter (OTC) options are sold by financial institutions to institutional buyers and are tailored to their needs in terms of amount (notional principal) and expiration date. These are mainly hedging transactions between multinational enterprises and banks. Once again, with over-the-counter options, there is counterparty risk—the risk of deterioration in the terms of repayment, including default.

The valuation of European style foreign exchange options

An option is worth its expected present value. The Fischer Black and Myron Scholes formula is used for the valuation of a European style option, and there are binomial tree pricing models for the valuation of American style options.

If the foreign interest rate is indicated by φ and the domestic interest rate by r, interest rate parity is expressed:

$$F = Se^{(r-\varphi)T} \qquad (3.37)$$

The Black-Scholes formula can then be written as:

$$C = Se^{-\varphi T}N(d_1) - Xe^{-rT}N(d_2) \qquad (3.38)$$

where $d_1 = \dfrac{\ln(S/X) + (r - \varphi + \sigma^2/2)T}{\sigma\sqrt{T}}$, $d_2 = d_1 - \sigma\sqrt{T}$

C = the value of the European style foreign exchange call option
T = the time to option's maturity, in years
S = the spot price of the underlying foreign currency
X = the option's exercise price
r = the continuously compounded US risk-free interest rate
φ = the continuously compounded foreign risk-free interest rate

σ = volatility (the standard deviation of the returns on the exchange rate)

Graphically, the premium on a foreign exchange call option is illustrated in Figure 3.21.

Figure 3.21 The premium on a foreign exchange call option

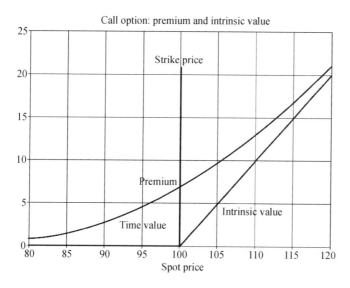

In general, the expected value of the underlying asset is given by its forward price. Its volatility or standard deviation indicates how likely it is that the subsequent spot rate deviates from its expected value. The greater the volatility of the underlying asset, the greater is the likelihood of large movements in its value. With large movements, options are likely to be more "in the money." Therefore, they are worth more, the greater the volatility of the underlying asset.

Options further away from expiration are worth more. Indeed, at the time of expiration, the option is worth only its intrinsic value—the value if immediately exercised. The time value of the option is extinguished at expiration.

The value of an option equals the sum of its intrinsic value and its time value. The intrinsic value is its value if exercised immediately. It is zero if the option is out of the money, then rises cent for cent as the option moves into the money. The time value is the difference between the premium and the intrinsic value. It reflects the possibility that the option could move into the money or even further into the money.

A put option on foreign exchange

The put option formula also uses continuous interest rate parity in the Black-Scholes equation:

$$P = Xe^{-rT}N(-d_2) - Se^{-\varphi T}N(-d_1) \qquad (3.39)$$

where $d_1 = \dfrac{\ln(S/X) + (r - \varphi + \sigma^2/2)T}{\sigma\sqrt{T}}$, $d_2 = d_1 - \sigma\sqrt{T}$

P = the value of the European style foreign exchange put option
T = the time to option's maturity, in years
S = the spot price of the underlying foreign currency
X = the option's exercise price
r = the continuously compounded US risk-free interest rate
φ = the continuously compounded foreign risk-free interest rate
σ = volatility (the standard deviation of the returns on the exchange rate)

Graphically, the premium on a foreign exchange put option is illustrated in Figure 3.22.

Figure 3.22 The premium on a foreign exchange put option

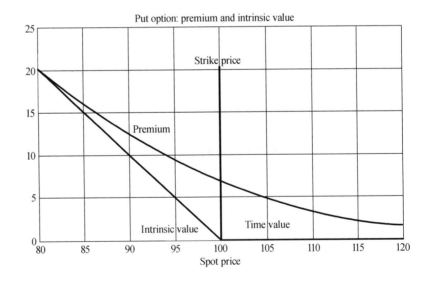

We use a call option on pounds sterling to demonstrate the terminal profit to a long (buy) and a short (sell) call option position. Suppose that the call option premium is ¢1 per pound when the option positions were established. The exercise price of the call option is $1.77 per pound. Figure 3.23 demonstrates the profit/loss to an investor who bought the call option and held it to the option's expiration date. As we can see, the payoff is a negative ¢1 per pound when the option expires at $1.77 per pound or lower. The more the call option is in the money, the higher is its payoff. The breakeven point is at $1.78 per pound, which is the sum of the exercise price and call option premium. The payoff is potentially unlimited because the exchange rate could go to infinity.

Figure 3.23 The payoff at maturity from buying a pound call option

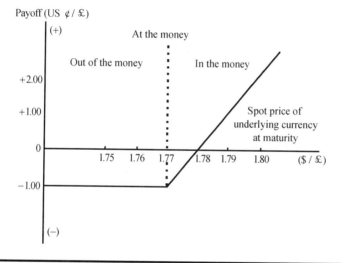

At expiration at a spot price of $1.79 per pound, the call holder exercises the call option, buying pounds at $1.77 and selling them spot at $1.79, making ¢2 per pound. Net profits are one cent since the holder paid a premium of ¢1 per pound. The break-even point is $1.78 per pound. At a spot price of $1.75 per pound, the option would finish out of the money. The call expires unexercised, leaving the holder with a net cost of ¢1 per pound of notional value. Because options are zero-sum games to their buyers and sellers, the seller of the call option has a profit diagram mirroring that of the buyer, but opposite in value, as in Figure 3.24.

Figure 3.24 The payoff at maturity from selling a pound call option

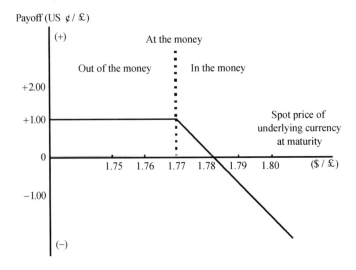

The seller earns the premium of ¢1 per pound if the terminal spot exchange rate is no higher than $1.77 per pound. Beyond the exercise price of $1.77 per pound, the seller pays the difference between the spot price and the exercise price, keeping the option premium paid earlier. At $1.78 the seller pays out the premium collected, so $1.78 per pound represents the seller's break-even point also. At a price of $179, the seller of the call loses ¢2 per pound on the exercise, but keeps the ¢1 premium per pound. Since the price of the pound can in theory rise to infinity, the seller's potential losses are unlimited.

Profits from a foreign exchange put option

We use a put option on pounds sterling to demonstrate the terminal profit to a long and a short put option position. Suppose that the put premium was ¢1 per pound when the put option position was bought. The exercise price of the put option is $1.77 per pound. The put holder paid ¢1 per pound for the put. On expiration, the holder benefits if the spot exchange rate drops below $1.76 per pound, the breakeven point. The lower the terminal spot rate, the higher are profits. The maximum profit is $1.77 per pound when the pound exchange rate drops to zero. The holder's maximum loss is the put option premium, ¢1 per pound if the put expires out of the money—above $1.77 spot at maturity, as shown in Figure 3.25.

Figure 3.25 The payoff at maturity from buying a pound put option

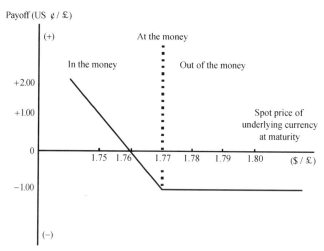

The put seller collected ¢1 per pound of premium, which is the maximum profit the seller can expect to realize. If the put option finishes out of the money (when the spot exchange rate is more than $1.77 per pound), the seller keeps the premium without any further obligation. However, as the spot exchange rate decreases, so does the seller's liability up to $1.77 per pound. Because of the symmetry in payoffs, the seller's profit break-even point is also $1.76 per pound. Figure 3.26 illustrates the payoff for the seller of a put option.

Figure 3.26 The payoff at maturity from selling a pound put option

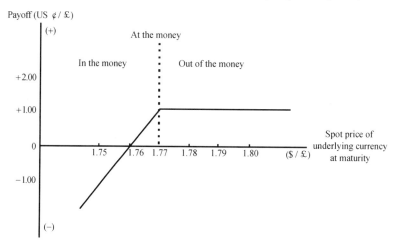

The seller earns the premium of ¢1 per pound if the terminal spot exchange rate is no lower than $1.77 per pound. Below the exercise price of $1.77 per pound, the seller pays the difference between the spot price and the exercise price. At $1.76 the seller pays out the premium collected, so $1.76 per pound represents the seller's break-even point also. The seller of the put has a maximum liability of the exercise price of the currency, should its spot value fall to zero.

Table 3.12 illustrates the premium of a 180 day European style call option with a strike price of $100, an annual volatility of 25%, and domestic and foreign interest rates at 6% per annum. If the current spot price is at-the-money, or $100, the premium of an at-the-money call is $6.835 according to the Black-Scholes formula. Figures 3.22 and 3.23 illustrate the premium for the buyer of a put and a call with these characteristics.

Table 3.12 The call and put premium on a foreign exchange option

Foreign exchange option		
Strike price($)	X	100
Time to expiry	T	0.5
Spot price($)	S	100
Domestic interest rate	r	0.06
Foreign interest rate	φ	0.06
Volatility	σ	0.25
	d_1	0.0884
	d_2	-0.0884
Call($)	C	6.835
Put($)	P	6.835

The at-the-money put option with the same maturity has the exact same value $6.835 since the expected forward value is $100 with the same standard deviation.

As the spot price rises to $105, for example, the intrinsic value of the call option is $5 if exercised immediately. It would be held, however, since its time value is $4.696, for a total premium value of $9.696. The put option is out-of-the-money at a spot price of $105, and thus has an intrinsic value of zero. It could still move back into the money, so its time value (and premium) would now be $4.84.

Foreign exchange option Greeks

In general, the value of a call option is summarized in Greek terms. Option Greeks measure the sensitivity of option price changes with respect to small changes in underlying parameters. For example, by raising the spot price of the foreign currency a very small amount, the call option premium rises. The rate at which the call option premium rises with respect to small increases in the underlying spot price of the currency is known as the option's delta. Table 3.13 summarizes the effect of changes in various parameters and the change in an option premium.

Table 3.13 Foreign exchange option Greeks

Greeks	Meaning	Interpretation
Delta	The change in the option premium due to a small change in the spot rate	The higher the delta the more (less) likely a call (put) option will move into the money
Theta	The change in the option premium due to a small change in the time to expiry	Premia deteriorate in value as the time to expiration approaches
Vega	The change in the option premium due to a small change in volatility of the asset	An increase in volatility increases the value of call and put premia
Rho	The change in the option premium due to a small change in the domestic interest rate	An increase in the domestic interest rate causes rising call and falling put premia
Phi	The change in the option premium due to a small change in the foreign interest rate	An increase in the foreign interest rate causes falling call and rising put premia

Note: Vega is not a Greek language term, but is used for convenience.

Options may be used to hedge foreign exchange exposure, as we will see in Chapter 4 on hedging techniques.

Conclusion

The foreign exchange market is huge: average net daily turnover in the over-the-counter foreign exchange market in 2016 was nearly 5 trillion US dollars. These transactions facilitate trade and finance, and allow hedging of both transactional and operational exposure. We have tried to emphasize the idea that there is a bid-ask rate for nearly every forex transaction, as well as a commission. Unanticipated changes in exchange rates can cause large financial losses to unhedged international businesses. Yet hedges are not free. It is too costly to hedge all risk, but prudent risk management is in order when the firm has substantial foreign exchange revenues from transactions and operations. Often natural or matching hedges will do the trick, at less cost.

The Bank for International Settlements, the central bank's bank, has called for global currencies as we had under the silver and gold standards. So has Nobel Laureate Robert Mundell of Columbia University. This would remove exchange rate risk and reduce transactions costs considerably. However, nations would have to forego seigniorage, an important source of tax revenue for many. Their monetary and fiscal policies would also have to converge, a seemingly Sisyphean task in Europe, thus giving up discretionary economic policy. In the meantime, as an asset, good monies will drive out bad monies and various currency unions are to be expected.

Questions and problems

3.1 The time value of money

Consider the following cash flows from today (year 0) to year 3 in pounds sterling.

Cash flow in pounds sterling	Year
−100	0
50	1
50	2
50	3

Your interest rate (or discount rate) in pounds is 10%.

a. Compute the net present value (NPV) at a 10% discount rate and the internal rate of return of this investment in pounds.

b. If you were to sell this investment today (its NPV in pounds), how much would it be worth in USD at 1.76 dollars per pound?

3.2 The equilibrium exchange rate

Consider the following quantity of dollars demanded and supplied in millions as a function of the dollar's peso price, S.

Quantity demanded $Q_D = 90 - 2S$

Quantity supplied $Q_S = -10 + 3S$

a. Solve for the equilibrium exchange rate under a freely floating exchange rate regime, S (pesos per dollar). What is the quantity sold at the equilibrium price?

b. If the Central Bank maintained a fixed exchange rate of 15 pesos per dollar, how many millions of dollars of foreign reserves would it have to sell to maintain the fixed exchange rate regime? (Hint: Solve for $Q_D - Q_S$ at $S = 15$ pesos per dollar.)

c. If the Central Bank only had $15 million left in foreign reserves, what would its policy alternatives be?

d. If it instead wished to add $10 million to its holdings of foreign reserves, to what exchange rate would the Central Bank have to devalue the peso?

3.3 Intervention in the foreign exchange market

Argentina pegged its currency, the peso, to the US dollar at a rate of 1 to 1 from April 1991 to November 2001. Under the rules of the currency board, the central bank must intervene to buy and sell dollars at this rate. For this reason, the Banco de la Republica Argentina backed its domestic currency issue with foreign exchange by the *Convertibility Law*, principally dollars. The supply and demand for dollars is indicated below. Answer the following questions.

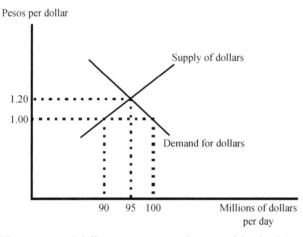

a. What amount of dollar reserves must the central bank of Argentina sell to the foreign exchange market daily in order to maintain its rigidly fixed exchange rate to the US dollar?

b. What is the impact of the sale of dollars on the Argentine money supply? Does this cause any adjustment process?

c. When the Argentine government abandons the currency board, what is the equilibrium exchange rate and the volume of dollars traded daily?

3.4 The bid-ask spread

In the table below, consider the following bid and ask spot quotations in dollars per pound ($/£), i.e. in American terms.

	European terms(£/$)		American terms($/£)	
	Bid	Ask	Bid	Ask
Spot			1.7669	1.7675
Spread				
Mid-point				

a. Compute the bid and quotations in European terms, i.e. in pounds per dollar (£/$).

b. Compute the bid-ask spread in terms of £ and $.

c. Compute the mid-point quotations in both European and American terms (Hint: mid-point = (bid + ask)/2).

d. Compute the bid-ask spread as a percent of the mid-point quotation.

3.5 The bid-ask spread

Consider the following spot quotations in pounds per dollar (£/$) and dollars per pound ($/£) in the table below.

	European terms(£/$)		American terms($/£)	
	Bid	Ask	Bid	Ask
Spot		0.5660		1.7675
Spread				
Mid-point				
Spread/Mid-point(%)				

a. Compute the bid quotations in American and European terms.

b. Compute the bid-ask spread in terms of £ and $.

c. Compute the mid-point quotations in both European and American terms.

d. Compute the bid-ask spread as a percent of the mid-point quotation.

3.6 Point quotations

Consider the following spot quotations in dollars per pound ($/£) and the forward quotations in basis points (1/10,000).

	American terms ($/£)	
	Bid	Ask
Spot	1.7669	1.7675
Points	Bid	Ask
1 month	214	220
2 months	283	298
3 months	388	416

On the basis of the points quotations above, derive the outright quotations.

3.7 Interest rate parity

Consider the figure below indicating (approximately) the difference between interest rates in the United States (U.S.) and the United Kingdom (U.K.), $r_{us} - r_{uk}$, on a one-year Treasury Bill (i.e. a two-year Bill with one year left to maturity) on the horizontal axis, and the forward premium on the pound for delivery in one year, $(F-S)/S$ on the vertical axis. If you wish, assume you already hold a portfolio of both Treasuries. Note:

F is the US dollar price of the British pound for delivery in 1 year (the bid);

S is the US dollar price of the British pound for spot delivery (the ask);

r_{us} is the interest rate on a hypothetical US one year Treasury Note (the ask);

r_{uk} is the interest rate on a hypothetical UK one year Treasury Note (the bid).

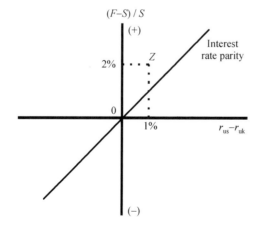

a. At point Z, in what direction will short term arbitrage capital flow and what will be the arbitrage profits?

b. What steps will arbitrageurs take from point Z in order to make their profits and what will be the consequences on the forward discount on the pound and the interest rate differential?

3.8 Purchasing power parity

You are given the following data on prices in local currency in the United States, Mexico, and England:

	Shoes	Hats	Haircuts
U.S.	$20	$10	$5
England	£10	£10	£3
Mexico	N$200	N$100	N$20

Suppose that a representative consumer bundle of these goods is:

Shoes	Hats	Haircuts
2	1	2

a. What are the rates of currency exchange suggested by the absolute version of the purchasing power parity doctrine?

b. Would you be surprised to learn that the equilibrium exchange rates were 0.566 pounds per dollar and 11 pesos per dollar?

c. Why might the PPP prediction for the peso be further off than for the pound?

d. Now suppose that all prices doubled in the U.S. and tripled in England and Mexico in the next 10 years. What would you predict to be the equilibrium exchange rates in 10 years?

e. How might real shocks to say the world price of wheat or oil modify your answer?

References and suggested reading

Abuaf, Niso and Philippe Jorion (1990), "Purchasing Power Parity in the Long Run," *Journal of Finance*, 45(1): 157–174.

Ahtiala, Pekka and Yair E. Orgler (1995), "The Optimal Pricing of Exports Invoiced in Different Currencies," *Journal of Banking and Finance*, 19(1): 61–77.

Aliber, Robert Z. (1973), "The Interest Rate Parity Theory: A Reinterpretation," *Journal of Political Economy*, 81(6): 1451–1459.

Antl, Boris ed. (1983), *Swap Financing Techniques*, London: Euromoney Publications.

Beidelman, Carl R. (1991), *Cross-Currency Swaps*, Homewood, IL: Irwin.

Bilson, John F. O. (1983), "The Evaluation and Use of Foreign Exchange Rate Forecasting Services," in *Management of Foreign Exchange Risk*, R. J. Herring, ed. Cambridge, UK: Cambridge University Press.

Black, Fisher and Myron Scholes (1973), "The Pricing of Options and Corporate Liabilities," *Journal of Political Economy*, 45(1): 637–659.

Cassell Gustav (1918), "Abnormal Deviations in International Exchanges," *Economic Journal*, 81(3): 413–415.

Cincibuch, Martin (2004), "Distributions Implied by American Currency Futures Options: A Ghost's Smile," *Journal of Futures Markets*, 24(2): 147–178.

Connolly, Michael, Alvaro Rodriguez and William Tyler (1994), "The Use of the Exchange Rate for Stabilization: A Real Interest Arbitrage Model Applied to Argentina", *Journal of International Money and Finance*, 13(2): 223–231.

Connolly, Michael and Dean Taylor (1984), "The Exact Timing of the Collapse of an Exchange Rate System," *Journal of Money, Credit and Banking*, 16(2): 194–207.

Connolly, Michael (1983), "Optimum Currency Pegs for Latin America," *Journal of Money, Credit and Banking*, 15(1): 56–72.

Connolly, Michael (1982), "The Choice of An Optimum Currency Peg for a Small, Open Country," *Journal of International Money and Finance*, 1(2): 153–164.

Cox, J. C., Stephen A. Ross, and M. Rubinstein (1979), "Option Pricing: A Simplified Approach," *Journal of Financial Economics*, 7(3): 229–263.

DeRosa, David F. (1992), *Options on Foreign Exchange*, Chicago: Probus Publishing.

Giddy, Ian H. and Guner Dufey (1995), "Uses and Abuses of Currency Options," *Journal of Applied Corporate Finance*, 8(3): 49–57.

Fama, Eugene F. (1976), "Forward Rates as Predictors of Future Spot Rates," *Journal of Financial Economics*, 3(4): 361–377.

Fernald, Julia D. (1993–1994), "The Pricing and Hedging of Index Amortizing Rate Swaps," *Quarterly Review of the New York Federal Reserve Bank*, 18(4):71–74.

Frenkel, Jacob A., and Richard M. Levich (1975), "Covered Interest Arbitrage: Unexploited Profits?" *Journal of Political Economy*, 83(2): 325–338.

Friedman, Milton and Anna J. Schwartz (1993), *Monetary History of the United States: 1867–1960*, Princeton: Princeton University Press.

Geman, Helyette (2005), *Commodities and Commodity Derivatives*, John Wiley & Sons.

Giddy, Ian H. (1979), "Measuring the World Foreign Exchange Market," *Columbia Journal of World Business*, 14(4): 36–48.

Globecom Group, LTD. (1995), *Derivatives Engineering: A Guide to Structuring, Pricing and Marketing Derivatives*, Homewood, IL: Irwin.

Goodhart, Charles A., and Thomas Hesse (1993), "Central Bank Forex Intervention Assessed in Continuous Time," *Journal of International Money and Finance*, 12(4): 368–389.

Hanke, Steve H. (2002), "On Dollarization and Currency Boards: Error and Deception," *Journal of Policy Reform*, 5(4): 203–222.

Hull, John C. (1997), *Options, Futures, and Other Derivatives*, 3rd ed., Upper Saddle River, N. J.: Prentice Hall.

W. Carl Kester and Julia Morley (1993), "Note on Cross Border Valuation," in W. Carl Kester, Timothy A. Luehrman (eds.), *Case Problems in International Finance*, New York: McGraw-Hill.

Lessard, Donald R. (1979), "Evaluating Foreign Projects: An Adjusted Present Value Approach," in D. R. Lessard, ed. *International Financial Management*, Boston: Warren, Gorham & Lamont.

Levich, Richard M. (1998), "Interest Rate Parity and the Fisher Parities," *International Financial Markets: Prices and Policies*, Boston: Irwin-McGraw-Hill.

Mahlotra, Davinder K., Rand Martin and Vivek Bhargava (2004), "An Empirical Analysis of Yen-dollar Currency Swap Market Efficiency," *International Journal of Business*, 9(2): 143–158.

Marshall, John F., and Kenneth R. Kapner (1993), *The Swaps Market*, Miami, FL: Kolb Publishing.

Melvin, Michael (2004), *International Money and Finance*, Addison-Wesley.

Melvin, Michael, and David Bernstein (1984), "Trade Concentration, Openness, and Deviations from Purchasing Power Parity," *Journal of International Money and Finance*, 3(3): 369–376.

Mill, John S. (1848), *Principles of Political Economy*, London: John W. Parker, West Strand, Book III, Chapter XX: 10.

Mundell, Robert A. (1961), "A Theory of Optimum Currency Areas," *American Economic Review*, 51(4): 657–665.

Mundell, Robert. A. (1968), "Barter Theory and the Monetary Mechanism of Adjustment," *International Economics*, New York: Macmillan.

Mundell, Robert A. (1973), "Plan for a European Currency" in Harry G. Johnson and Alexander K. Swoboda (eds.), *The Economics of Common Currencies*, Cambridge, Massachussets: Harvard University Press.

Officer, Lawrence H. (March 1976), "The Purchasing Power Parity Theory of Exchange Rates: A Review Article," *IMF Staff Papers*, 23(1): 1–60.

Ong, Li Lian (2003), *The Big Mac Index: Applications of Purchasing Power Parity*, Palgrave MacMillan.

Pan, Ming-Shiun, Angela Y. Liu, and Hamid Bastin (1996), "An Examination of the Short-Term and Long-Term Behavior of Foreign Exchange Rates," *Financial Review*, 31(3): 603–622.

Popper, Helen (1993), "Long-Term Covered Interest Parity: Evidence from Currency Swaps," *Journal of International Money and Finance*, 12(4): 439–448.

Reinker, Kenneth and Edward Tower (2004), "Index Fundamentalism Revisited," *The Journal of Portfolio Management*, 30(4): 37–50.

Riehl, Heinz and Rita Rodriguez (1989), *Foreign Exchange and Money Markets*, Englewood Cliffs, N. J.: Prentice Hall.

Rolnick, Arthur J., Bruce D. Smith, and Warren E. Weber (2001), "Establishing a Monetary Union in the United States," Federal Reserve Bank of Minneapolis.

Rosenberg, Michael (2003), *Exchange Rate Determination: Models and Strategies for Exchange Rate Forecasting*, McGraw-Hill.

Sercu, Piet, Raman Uppal, and Cynthia Van Hulle (1995), "The Exchange Rate in the Presence of Transaction Costs: Implications for Tests of Purchasing Power Parity," *Journal of Finance*, 50(4): 1309–1319.

Shapiro, Alan C. (1978), "Capital Budgeting for the Multinational Corporation," *Financial Management*, 7(1): 7–16.

Solnik, Bruno (1990), "Swap Pricing and Default Risk: A Note," *Journal of International Financial Management and Accounting*, 2(1): 79–91.

Stapleton, Richard C., and Marti Subrahmanyam (1997), "Market Imperfections, Capital Asset Equilibrium, and Corporation Finance," *Journal of Finance*, 32(2): 307–319.

Sweeney, Richard J., and Edward J. Q. Lee (1990), "Trading Strategies in Forward Exchange Markets," *Advances in Financial Planning and Forecasting*, 4: 55–80.

Tan, Zhuo and Shenggang Yang (2012), "Neutralization in China: Evidence from the Balance Sheet of the People's Bank of China," *Journal of Economic Policy Reform*, 15(1): 25–31.

Taylor, Dean (1982), "Official Intervention in the Foreign Exchange Market, or Bet Against the Bank," *Journal of Political Economy*, 90(2): 356–368.

Taylor, Francesca (1996), *Mastering Derivatives Markets*, London: Financial Times-Pitman Publishing.

Wong, Kit (2003), "Currency Hedging with Options and Futures," *European Economic Review*, 47(5): 833–839.

CHAPTER 4 Hedging Foreign Exchange Risk 外汇风险的套期保值

Hedging defined

A firm or an individual hedges by taking a position, such as acquiring a cash flow, an asset, or a contract, including a forward one, that will rise (or fall) in value to offset a drop (or rise) in value of an existing position. A **perfect hedge** is one eliminating the possibility of future gain or loss due to unexpected changes in the value of the existing position.

Why hedge? Shareholders can, in principle, perform any foreign exchange hedging that the corporation can. Consequently, the corporation need not devote resources to the elimination of diversifiable or hedgeable risk. Indeed, hedging might be counterproductive by harming the interests of shareholders. Similarly, a firm which takes over other firms in different industries might displease shareholders who can diversify their portfolio directly by purchasing shares themselves in those industries.

When there are neither transactions costs, nor bankruptcy costs, shareholders with perfect information on the firm's foreign exchange exposure can undertake any hedging they feel necessary. In short, a cogent argument can be made that the firm should not hedge foreign exchange risk—that is, exposure to unexpected changes in the exchange rate.

However, the majority of international firms hedge foreign exchange risk selectively, if not completely. Furthermore, shareholders do not have the same information that the firm has regarding its foreign exchange risk. Or it would involve considerable search costs to ascertain the foreign exchange risk exposure of the firm. This is a question of asymmetric informa-

套期保值(Hedging):公司或个人建立一个新的头寸,并通过其价值的上升(或下跌)来抵消一个现有头寸价值的下跌(或上升)。

完全的套期保值(Perfect hedge):能够完全消除因现有头寸价值的意外变动而在将来获利或受损的可能性的套期保值。

tion. It is unlikely that pension fund managers, for example, have any idea about the currency flows involved in global operations of firms such as IBM, General Motors or Ford.

A counterargument in favor of foreign exchange hedging is made by Ian Giddy:

> Exchange-rate volatility may make earnings volatile and thus increase the probability of financial distress. If hedging reduces the nominal volatility of the firm's earnings, it will in turn reduce the expected value of the costs of financial distress (including bankruptcy)... Some of these costs are borne by creditors, in which case a reduction in expected distress costs will reduce lenders' required rate of return. In addition, for a given level of debt, lower earnings volatility will entail a lower probability of bankruptcy.
>
> (Source: Ian H. Giddy, *Global Financial Markets*, © DC Heath and Company 1994: 481.)

In bankruptcy, there is a discrete drop in the return to creditors. Their return declines more as the value of its assets is further downgraded. For instance, under Chapter 7 or liquidation proceedings, the return on the dollar to creditors deteriorates as the value of remaining assets to be liquidated by the court decreases.

Increased volatility in earnings and the risk of financial distress, in general, lead creditors to charge a higher risk premium on loans to the firm. Greater leverage becomes more expensive and thus there are lower gains from tax shields. As Giddy argues:

> The double taxation of corporate income and the worldwide practice of tax deductibility of interest payments provide an incentive for debt finance. This incentive is weakened, however, by the direct and indirect costs of financial distress and bankruptcy; the greater the volatility of earnings, the greater the costs. More leverage means more volatile earnings, so the tax shield gains from leverage are, at some point, offset by the deadweight costs of financial distress. The greater the probability of distress, the lower the leverage level that is optimal for the firm and the lower the tax shield. Because **currency matching** reduces the probability of financial distress, it allows the firm to have greater leverage and therefore a greater tax shield and lower borrowing costs. Thus, the greater the degree of bankruptcy-cost-hedging, the greater the value of the firm and the lower the cost

货币配对（Currency matching）降低了企业出现财务困境的可能性,因为它允许公司使用更高的财务杠杆进而获得更多的税盾收益和更低的借款成本。

of capital.

(Source: Giddy, *op. cit.* : 482)

In this simple framework, the value of the firm to shareholders can be divided into the parts in Table 4.1.

Table 4.1 Valuation of the firm

	The value of a firm to shareholders
equals	the value of existing assets
less	the value of existing debt and obligations
less	the present value of the expected costs of financial distress
less	the present value of the cost of hedging
plus	the present value of tax shields
plus	the present value of lowered borrowing costs
plus	the present value of growth and operating options

Consequently, in comparison to the unhedged firm, Giddy argues that a firm which hedges selectively may increase its net worth rather than reducing it. This would be the case when the reduced costs of financial distress and the lowered borrowing costs offset the costs of the hedges. Indeed, if this were true, the net cost of hedging would be negative, Giddy argues. While possible, this is unlikely since managing risk usually entails a cost.

Another way of putting the argument is that foreign exchange hedging reduces the β, or market risk, of a company by reducing the volatility of its earnings, thus reducing the risk premium at which expected earnings are discounted. With hedges, a company's β is lower so its risk premium is lower.

To summarize the arguments: On one hand, expected earnings are discounted at a lower interest rate; On the other hand, earnings may also be lower due to the costs of the hedges. The firm's net worth could therefore conceivably be higher or lower. The theory of comparative advantage should shed some light on this unsettled issue. A firm that does not hedge its foreign exchange exposure is not only producing goods and services, but is also a currency speculator by taking unhedged positions in foreign currencies. It may have a comparative advantage in producing its goods, but surely does not as a currency speculator. To focus on its core business, production, it should selectively hedge through foreign exchange forwards, swaps, and offsetting currency flows that do not leave it exposed to large unexpected losses in foreign exchange that could put it in financial distress.

Consider now a specific example of long exposure to dollars by a Chinese battery firm, Corum batteries. Corum has an ongoing automobile battery contract for delivery of one thousand units each month in exchange for monthly payment of one million dollars upon delivery. Corum's reporting and functional currency is the Chinese yuan, so it is exposed to the risk that the dollar might continuously depreciate, Corum may not want to run the risk of large losses, and consequently could hedge by a number of means, such as a sequence of forward sales of the one million dollars on the forward over-the-counter market with a bank. However, a better way to hedge ongoing flow of receipts in dollars is by a foreign exchange swap of yuan for dollars, thus giving it a debt obligation to service in terms of dollars, In other words, an offsetting currency flow. Each million dollars of accounts receivable monthly could be used to pay one million dollars of interest and principal on the dollar denominated loan. Any losses on dollar depreciation from accounts receivable would be recouped by gains on the loan payments in dollars.

Credit ratings

信用评级 (Credit rating):对公司债务(股份权益或公司债券)、机构债券或政府(包括中央、省级或地方政府)债务信誉的评估。

In addition to foreign exchange risk, there is also credit or default risk. Credit ratings are an assessment of the creditworthiness of a corporation's debt, whether equities or corporate bonds, agency debt or that of sovereign, state and local governments. The definitions of creditworthiness are based on how likely the firm, agency, or government is to default and the protection that creditors receive in the event of a default. Creditworthiness is rated by Standard & Poor's, Fitch, and Moody's.

The highest rating a firm or government can have is AAA or Aaa, and such debt is judged to be the best quality and to have the lowest degree of risk. This rating is not awarded very often; AA or Aa ratings indicate very good quality debt and are much more common. Low quality, speculative and "junk" (below BBB -) bonds have higher probabilities of default than investment grade (BBB - or above) bonds. S&P reduced General Motors two notches to BB and Ford to BB + , both junk bond statuses. The downgrading in light of their low earnings, high pension liabilities and outstanding debts, caused their bonds to plunge in value. (*New York Times*, May 6, 2005)

> **Applying the Concept**: The Bankruptcy of General Motors
>
> On June 1, 2009, General Motors (GM) filed for Chapter 11 Bankruptcy. The filing reported US $82.29 billion in assets and US $172.81 billion in debt, with US $2 billion cash in hand. The company received debtor-in-possession financing of US $15 billion from the US Treasury to complete the bankruptcy. The "new GM" is mostly owned by the United States Government, whose further Treasury loans of $50 billion gave the government a 60.8% stake. The Canadian Government owns 11.7% and the United Auto Workers, a further 17.5% through its health-care trust. The remaining 10% is held by unsecured creditors. Under the reorganization process, a *363 sale* (for Section 363, Title 11, Chapter 3, United States Bankruptcy Code), the purchaser of the assets of a company in bankruptcy proceedings is able to obtain approval for the purchase from the court prior to the submission of a reorganization plan, free of liens and other claims. On November 17, 2010, the new GM realized the biggest initial public offering in U.S. history, raising $20.1 billion. The new GM sold 478 million common shares at $33 each, raising $15.77 billion, as well as $4.35 billion in preferred shares. On December 28, 2011, its common shares were worth $20.07 on the NYSE, nearly 40% below the IPO price.
>
> Source: *Reuters*, November 17, 2010; *Yahoo Finance*, December 28, 2011.

In the 1980s, a growing part of corporate borrowing has taken the form of low-grade, or "junk" bonds. The lowest corporate rating is D for debt that is in default. For sovereign debt that is in default, the rating is SD. Both Moody's and Standard & Poor's (S&P) use adjustments to these ratings. S&P uses plus and minus signs: an A + is higher than an A rating and an A − is lower. Moody's uses a 1, 2, or 3 designation, with 1 being the highest. A favorable creditworthiness rating reduces the interest that a borrower has to pay for new loans because the risk premium is lower, while an unfavorable rating increases the interest that investors require. Table 4.2 illustrates the twenty-one notches of the S&P's ratings.

Table 4.2 S&P's credit ratings

	S&P	S&P's Credit Rating Notches
Upper Investment Grade	AAA	Capacity to pay interest and principal is extremely strong.
	AA +	Very strong capacity to pay interest and repay principal.
	AA	
	AA –	
	A +	Strong capacity to pay, but susceptible to adverse economic conditions.
	A	
	A –	
Lower Investment Grade	BBB +	Adequate capacity to pay, but likely to have weakened ability to pay.
	BBB	
	BBB –	
Non Investment Grade	BB +	Speculative or "junk" with respect to payment.
	BB	
	BB –	
Lower Non-investment Grade	B +	Large uncertainties regarding ability to pay. Some issues in default.
	B	
	CCC +	
	CCC	
	CCC –	Income bonds on which no interest is being paid.
	CC	
	C	
Default	D	Default, payment of interest and or principal is in arrears.

Source: S&P.

Table 4.3 shows several long term sovereign bond ratings by agency in July 2019.

如表 4.3 所示,标准普尔在近期下调了美国国债评级,将其从 AAA 级降至 AA + 级。

Table 4.3 Long term sovereign credit ratings by agency

	Moody's	S&P	Fitch	Dagong
China	A1	A +	A +	AA +
United States	Aaa	AA +	AAA	A –
Canada	Aaa	AAA	AAA	AA +
Russia	Baa3	BBB –	BB –	A
United Kingdom	Aa2	AA	AA	A +
France	Aa2	AA	AA	A
Japan	A1	A +	A	A –
Italy	Baa3	BBB	BBB	BB +
Spain	Baa1	A –	A –	BBB +
Greece	B1	B +	BB –	CCC
Portugal	Baa3	BBB	BBB	BB +

Source: Countryeconomy.com, Sovereign Ratings List, July 2019; Dagong Global Credit Rating Co. LTD, Sovereign Ratings, dagongcredit.com, August 2019.

Independent sources expect growth in US spending surpassing growth in revenues. Both Moody's and S&P had a negative outlook, however, on the AAA rating of U.S. Treasuries. In the event, S&P reduced the credit rating of US Treasuries by one notch to AA +, while maintaining the negative outlook, suggesting that further downgrades are likely. The S&P forecast of future deficits was immediately challenged by the US Treasury, but the Chinese agency, Xinhua News Agency, pointed out that when a state "issues new debt to finance repayment of old debt" ... it is taxing Peter to pay Paul. In their words, Xinhua said in a commentary that Mr. Biden—who visited China—had repeatedly told Chinese leaders and students that its U.S. dollars assets were safe.

"Yet that is far from enough to soothe the concerns of China and the world as concrete actions are badly needed from the United States to honor its promises," the commentary said. It urged Washington to "end its excessive reliance on overseas borrowing, make substantial reforms and cuts to its bloated entitlement programs, reduce budget deficits and restructure its economy." (*Wall Street Journal*, August 22, 2011) The Chinese government, whose People's Bank of China holds over a trillion dollars worth of US Treasuries, wants "concrete measures."

Applying the Concept: A US Treasury Ponzi Game

The largest Ponzi game in world history, far surpassing that of Bernie Madoff, is being run by the US Treasury. Worse yet, the People's Bank of China may be left holding the bag. When cash flow from operations is not sufficient to cover interest and redemptions, and old debt is being repaid by funds from new borrowing, we have "Ponzi finance" as defined by MIT's Charles Kindleberger. In terms of sovereign debt, Ponzi finance is the issue of new debt to finance government spending plus net interest on existing debt. Failure to make an interest payment would represent a sovereign Treasury default.

The "non-partisan" U.S. Congressional Budget Office (CBO) suggests that the U.S. Treasury is currently running a pyramid scheme. Treasury debt held by the public (52% US residents, 48% foreign residents) is projected to nearly double in the next 10 years as a percent of U.S. GDP, rising from 78% in 2019 to 92% in 2028.

A CBO forecast is shown in Table 4.4.

庞氏骗局 (Ponzi Game) 实质上是将后一轮投资者的投资作为投资收益支付给前一轮的投资者，以此类推，使卷入的人和资金越来越多。当投资者和资金难以为继时，资金链便会骤然断裂。

Table 4.4 Treasury spending as a fraction of tax revenues (%)

	2019	2020	2021	2022	2023
Spending/Revenues	126	124	125	126	127

Note: As a percentage of total tax revenues.
Source: Congressional Budget Office projections, May 2019.

Table 4.5 US deficits and debt as a fraction of Gross Domestic Product (%)

	2019	2020	2021	2022	2023
Deficit (−) or Surplus	−4.2	−4	−4.2	−4.7	−4.5
Debt Held by the Public	78	80	81	83	85

Note: As a percentage of Gross Domestic Product.
Source: Congressional Budget Office projections, May 2019.

The likely consequence of this Ponzi Game is US Treasury default, either explicitly by failing to make a payment when due or implicitly by unexpected inflation. When U.S. bondholders, domestic and foreign, reach a maximum US debt they are willing to hold, new borrowing by the Treasury must be financed by the "lender of last resort," the Federal Reserve Bank, by printing of new seignorage. Printing press finance of the Treasury deficit will catch bondholders by surprise, erasing the real value of their bonds by the percentage that realized inflation exceeds expected inflation. This is the warning of Sargent and Wallace (1982).

Source: Written by Michael Connolly, Finance, Hunan University and Wei Lai, Economics, Shenzhen Polytechnic.

Default risk premium

违约风险溢价(Default risk premium): 为了吸引投资者，债券的收益率通常会高于同期的市场无风险利率，两者之差即为该债券的违约风险溢价。

Consider a corporate coupon bond with a face value of $100 and a coupon of $5 payable at maturity in one year. The risk free rate is 5% for T-bills with one year before expiration. If there is no default risk, its present value is $100:

$$PV = \$100 = \frac{\$105}{1.05} \qquad (4.1)$$

Now consider the same coupon bond, but having a probability of complete default of p, in which case nothing is paid, and a probability of $(1 - p)$ of no default in which case $105 is paid at maturity. The expected payment is a weighted average of zero with weight p and $105 with weight

$(1-p)$. That is:
$$E(V) = [p \times (0)] + [(1-p) \times 105] = (1-p) \times 105 \tag{4.2}$$

For instance, suppose that the probability of default is 0.3 or 30%. Then the expected value of the payment at maturity is given by:
$$E(V) = 0.7 \times (105) = \$73.5 \tag{4.3}$$

Therefore the present value of the expected payment at maturity is:
$$PV = \frac{\$73.5}{1.05} = \$70 \tag{4.4}$$

This should equal the market value of the bond, given that there is a 30% chance of full default. Accordingly, the yield to maturity, r, is given by the internal rate of return which sets the present value of face plus coupon equal to the market price of the bond, or:
$$\$70 = \frac{\$105}{1+r} \quad \text{or} \quad r = \frac{105}{70} - 1 = 0.5 = 50\% \tag{4.5}$$

Therefore the default risk premium, ρ, for this bond is approximately 45% since $(50\% - 5\%)$ approximately yields the risk premium. The exact risk premium, found by solving $(1+R)(1+\rho) = (1+r)$, is 42.9%, very close to the approximate value, 45%, given by the rule of thumb.

An equivalent technique for measuring the default risk premium on a corporate bond is to simply use the market price discount of the bond to compute the risk premium. That is:

(1) compute the present value of the riskless bond and compare it to the market price of the risky bond.

(2) Compute the risk premium, ρ, from the ratio of the market price of the asset to its present value discounted at the risk free rate, and subtract one.

Default risk graphically

Default risk is measured by the percentage discount of the market value of an asset relative to the present value of its payments at a risk-free interest rate (say U.S. Treasury rate). In Figure 4.1, the present value of the bond is indicated along the horizontal axis, discounted by the risk-free rate. If there is no default risk, the market value of the bonds plotted on the vertical axis would be the same, as plotted along the 45 degree line from the origin. When there is default risk, the market value falls below the risk free value indicated along the 45 degree line.

违约风险（Default risk）：违约风险可由一种资产的市场价值除以它的报酬以无风险利率（例如美国国库券利率）贴现获得的现值所得到的折扣百分比来度量。

Figure 4.1 Default risk premium

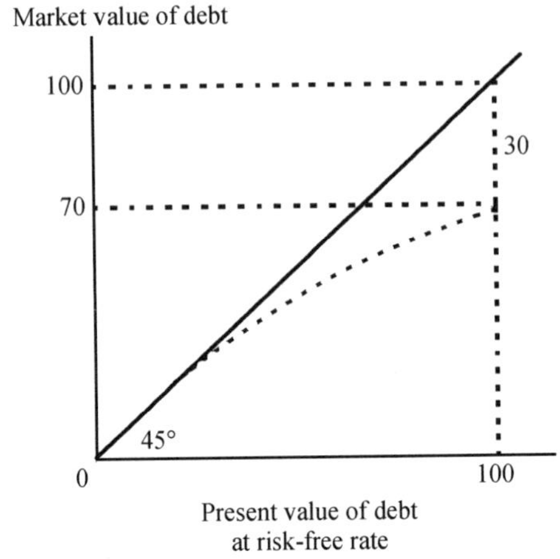

Market value of debt

100 ┈┈┈┈┈┈┈┈┈
                                  30
70 ┈┈┈┈┈┈┈

45°
0   100
Present value of debt
at risk-free rate

As indebtedness increases, holding other things such as income constant, it becomes more difficult to service the debt, so a discount emerges. It is entirely conceivable that additional debt might reduce the expected present value of repayment—more debt would have in fact less market value. In that case, the market value curve slopes downward. In the previous example of a risky coupon bond with a present value of $100 at the risk free rate, the present value of expected repayment is only $70 in one year since there is a 30% chance of full default.

In general, bonds that are rated poorly have a high yield to maturity, incorporating a risk premium.

Hedging foreign exchange transactions exposure

A firm may have foreign currency exposure, either long or short, due to a future receipt or payment of a specified amount in a foreign currency. For example, when a Chinese firm has accounts receivable in dollars at some point in the future, say 90 days, it is exposed to transactions exposure—losses or gains due to unexpected changes in the exchange rate—in the yuan price of the dollar. The Chinese firm is said to be long dollars. If the firm has accounts receivable in dollars, it will have to sell them for yuan—renminbi (CNY)—at the bid rate for the dollar in yuan. Let's indicate the expected exchange rate (yuan price of the dollar) in 90 days by

F_{90}, the futures or forward bid rate. If a forward rate does not exist, just forecast the rate using interest rate parity. In 90 days, there will be a realized spot rate, S_{90}, the bid spot rate for the dollar.

Consequently, the unanticipated change in the exchange rate or forecast error is indicated by $(F_{90} - S_{90})$. This represents the gain or the loss per dollar in which the firm has foreign exchange exposure. If the firm is long 1,000,000 dollars, accounts receivable, for example, it will gain if the spot price of the dollar is above the forward price upon receipt and sale of the dollars. If the spot price is less than the forward, the firm will lose $(F_{90} - S_{90})1,000,000$ in terms of yuan. If unhedged, the long position in dollars due to accounts receivable has the following payoff diagram in Figure 4.2.

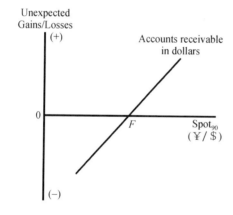

Figure 4.2 A long position in dollars

For example, let's say the 90 day yuan bid price of the dollar is 6.380. This would be the expected rate of settlement of the $1,000,000 accounts receivable. If the firm goes unhedged, it risks possible losses or gains from unanticipated changes in the exchange rate. For instance, the dollar may fall in the spot market to 6.300 so we would lose ¥0.08 per dollar, or 8 fen, when we sell in the spot market. On $1,000,000, this amounts to ¥ −80,000. This is illustrated in Figure 4.3.

图 4.3 显示了美元多头的损失,如果公司不进行套期保值,90 天后即期市场中的美元汇率跌至 6.30,则公司将在每美元上损失 0.08 元人民币。

Figure 4.3 A loss on a long position in dollars

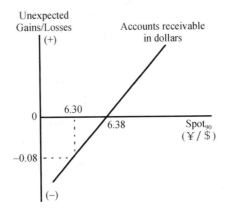

On the other hand, by going unhedged, the firm also may gain from a rise in the spot price of the dollar, to say 6.46 CNY per USD. In this case, the firm would gain ￥80,000 from the sale of our dollar receipts, eight fen per dollar. This is illustrated in Figure 4.4.

图 4.4 显示了美元多头的获利,如果公司不进行套期保值,90 天后即期市场中的美元汇率升至 6.46,则公司将在每美元上获利 0.08 元人民币。

Figure 4.4 A gain on a long position in dollars

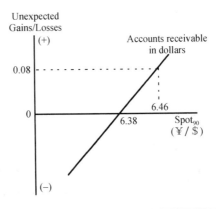

持有 90 天期的 100 万美元应收账款,对于一次性交易,可以选择如下的合约套期保值策略:在远期市场上出售 100 万美元;采取货币市场套期保值,借入 100 万美元的现值;为 100 万美元购买一份看跌期权。

With $1,000,000 accounts receivable in 90 days, a one-time transaction, the hedging choices would be to acquire one of the following contractual hedges:

- A forward market sale of $1,000,000;
- a money market hedge by borrowing the present value equivalent of $1,000,000;
- purchase a put option to sell $1,000,000.

These three contracts would be short positions offsetting the initial long position in USD.

A forward market sale

To hedge the long position in dollars using a forward market hedge, sell $1,000,000 in the forward market for delivery in 90 days. The forward sale is a short position in dollars that exactly offsets the existing long position from accounts receivable. What is gained on the short position is lost on the long position. Or what is gained on the long position is lost on the short position. The combined position is perfectly hedged—no chance of either gain or loss from unanticipated movements in the dollar. The forward market sale is illustrated in Figure 4.5.

远期市场出售（A forward market sale）：利用远期市场对美元多头进行套期保值，在远期市场上出售 90 天后交割的 100 万美元。远期卖出形成一个美元多头，正好抵消应收账款产生的已存在的美元多头。

Figure 4.5 A forward hedge of a long position in dollars

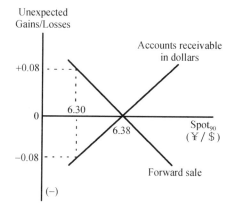

What is lost on the long position—accounts receivable—is just offset by gains on the short position—the forward sale—if the spot price of the dollar falls to 6.30 CNY in 90 days, for example. The horizontal axis is the hedged position, the sum of the long and the short positions, showing neither gains nor losses, independent of the subsequent spot rate in 90 days.

A money market hedge

To hedge the long position in dollars using a money market hedge, borrow dollars today for 90 days, and then sell them immediately in the spot market. In 90 days, repay your loan with the $1,000,000 accounts receivable. How many dollars would you need to borrow today? That would depend on the cost of borrowing. Say you can borrow dollars for 90 days at 2% quarterly interest. Borrow exactly $1,000,000/1.02 = 980,392.16$ dollars today, repay the loan with $1,000,000 in 90 days. This is a per-

可以利用货币市场对美元多头进行套期保值。例如，今天借入 90 天期美元，并在即期市场马上出售；90 天后用 100 万美元应收账款归还贷款。

fect hedge using the money market. Be sure to sell the dollars you borrow in the spot market—otherwise you acquire another long position in dollars. Your intent is to acquire a short position, the payment of the dollar loan, to offset your existing long position, accounts receivable in dollars in 90 days.

The money market hedge is depicted graphically in Figure 4.6, exactly as the forward sale is illustrated, assuming the firm can borrow or lend at the risk free rate.

Figure 4.6 A money market hedge of a long position in dollars

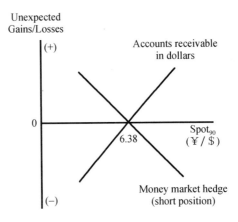

Buying a put option

买入一个执行价格为 6.38 元人民币/美元的看跌期权(put option), 这是一个针对意外损失的套期保值,但仍然保留了意外获利的可能性。

Buying a put option at a strike price of 6.38 CNY per USD would be a hedge against unforeseen losses, while retaining the possibility of unexpected gains. The cost of the hedge is the option premium. Figure 4.7 illustrates a put option hedge of a long position in dollars.

When the positive put option and the losing position below 0.638 per dollar are added, and a hypothetical cost per dollar of 1 jiao or 10 fen of the hedge is subtracted, the net position of the put option hedge is illustrated in Figure 4.7. The breakeven point is at a spot price of the dollar of 6.48, the 10 fen gain in the long position in accounts receivable just offsetting the cost of the option.

An existing short position in dollars

如果你的公司90天后有100万美元的应付账款, 你可以选择不进行套期保值,或者你可以选择下列合约套期保值中的一种:购买90天后交割的远期美元,这是远期市场保值;购买3个月美元国库券,这是货币市场套期保值;为100万美元购买一份看涨期权。

Consider now a short position in dollars. If your firm has a $1,000,000 accounts payable in 90 days, the choices are as follows:
- Do nothing, remaining unhedged.

or acquire one of the following contractual hedges:

- buy dollars for delivery in 90 days, a forward market hedge,
- buy 3 month US Treasuries, a money market hedge, or
- purchase call options for $1,000,000.

Figure 4.7 A put option hedge of a long position in dollars

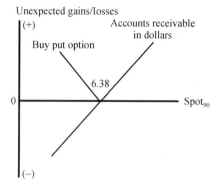

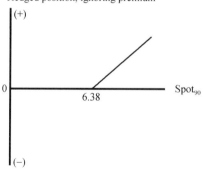

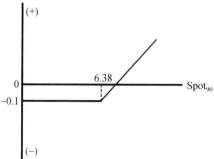

Remain unhedged

The payoff diagram if unhedged is a straightforward short position in dollars, as illustrated in Figure 4.8. The expected spot rate in 90 days is the forward ask rate for the dollar in terms of yuan, which, for simplicity, we assume is 6.39 yuan per dollar. This is because we are short dollars and will have to pay the ask price in yuan when we purchase dollars spot in three months. The difference between the bid and the ask rates is typically around less, but this facilitates the analysis. As drawn in Figure 4.8, we lose 0.08 yuan per dollar when we cover our short position in dollars at a spot price of 6.47, once again amounting to a loss of 80,000 yuan.

如图4.8所示,如果公司不进行套期保值,90天后即期市场上的美元汇率为6.47元人民币/美元,公司将在每美元上损失0.08元人民币。

Figure 4.8　An unhedged short loss in dollars

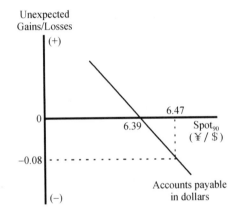

On the other hand, if we do not hedge, we may cover our short position at a lower spot price, say 6.31 yuan per dollar, should the dollar fall by 0.08 yuan on the spot market as illustrated in Figure 4.9.

如图4.9所示,如果公司不进行套期保值,90天后即期市场上的美元汇率为6.31元人民币/美元,公司将在每美元上获利0.08元人民币。

Figure 4.9　An unhedged short gain in dollars

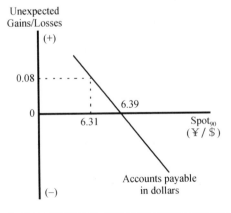

In this case, we gain 80,000 yuan by not hedging our short position.

A forward hedge

We can simply cover our short position by a forward purchase of $1,000,000 at 6.39 yuan per dollar. That is, by acquiring an offsetting long position in dollars, we have a perfect hedge. Any loss made in one position is recovered in the other position, as illustrated in Figure 4.10.

远期套期保值(Forward hedge):一个现货市场和远期(期货)市场的资产组合。它包含一个现货市场的多头和一个远期市场的空头,或者一个现货市场的空头和一个远期市场的多头。

Figure 4.10   A forward purchase of dollars to hedge a short position

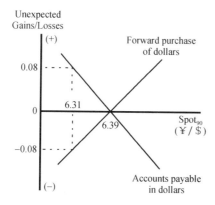

As illustrated in Figure 4.10, the gains from the short position—accounts payable in dollars—are just offset by the forward purchase of dollars, the long position.

A money market hedge

The short position in dollars could be covered by a money market loan made by the firm. It would simply lend enough principal in dollars so that principal plus interest repaid in 90 days would represent $1,000,000. If the rate of return were 1% quarterly, the firm would have to lend $1,000,000/1.01 or $990,099.01.

公司可以通过发放一笔货币市场贷款来弥补美元空头。

The money market hedge is illustrated in Figure 4.11.

Figure 4.11 A money market loan of dollars to hedge a short position

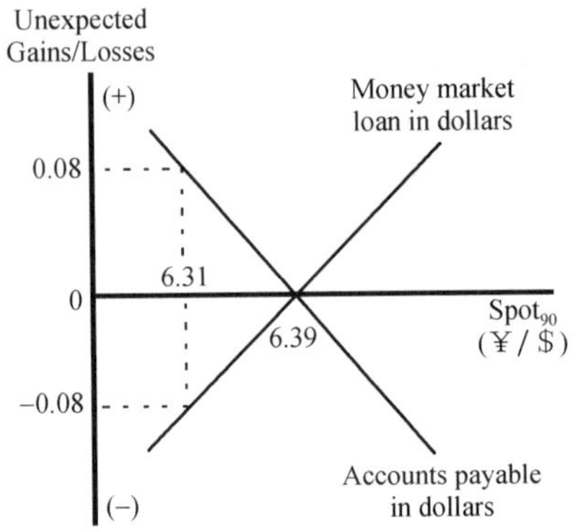

The payoff from the money market hedge exactly cancels any gains or losses from the short position in accounts payable.

Buying a call option

买入一个执行价格为 6.39 元人民币/美元、期权费为 10 分人民币/美元的**看涨期权**（**call option**）。这是一个针对意外损失的套期保值，但是仍然保留了意外获利的可能性。

Finally, we sketch the purchase of a call option with a strike price of 6.39 costing 10 fen per dollar. To simplify, we only sketch the net position in Figure 4.12 with a breakeven point of 6.29 yuan per dollar.

Figure 4.12 Payoff from buying a call option at the money to hedge a short position

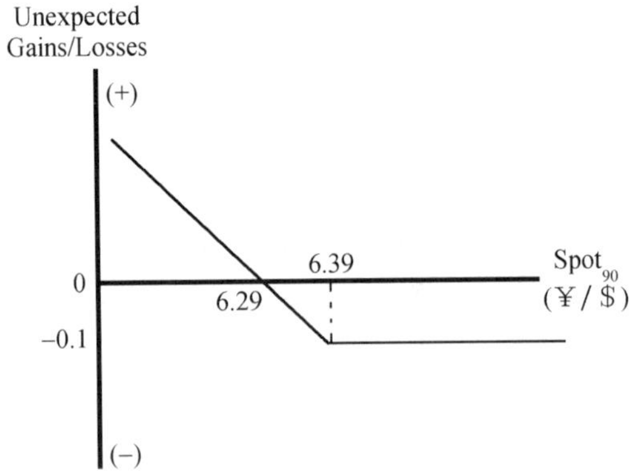

领子期权（**Collar**）：一种期权套期保值，它在放弃一个方向上的获利的同时，限制另一个方向上的损失。

零期权费领子期权（**Zero premium collar**）：一种套期保值，它出售一个期权所获的期权费，正好用于支付购买一个相反期权所需的期权费。

Collars as hedges

A **collar** is an options hedge that simultaneously limits a loss in one direction by giving up a gain in the other direction. A **zero premium**

collar is a hedge in which the premium received from selling one option exactly offsets the premium paid for purchasing an opposing option. For example, consider again 1 million dollars accounts receivable in 90 days. This transaction represents long exposure in the dollar. The firm could simultaneously buy an at-the-money put and sell an at-the-money call for 1 million dollars expiring in 90 days. The premium paid for the put would just equal the premium received for the call—i. e. the hedge is known as a zero premium collar. In Figure 4.13, the payoff from the put eliminates losses and the payoff from the call offsets the gains. Since both are at-the-money, the premium received for selling the call equals the premium paid for the put.

Figure 4.13 A collar hedge of accounts receivable in dollars

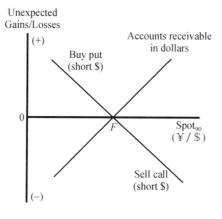

To summarize the steps in financing a hedge by a collar: The initial position is long dollars—accounts receivable of $1,000,000 in 90 days. Buy an at-the-money put to sell $1,000,000 in 90 days at-the-money rate. Simultaneously sell an at-the-money call for $1,000,000 in 90 days. The collar is equivalent to a sale of dollars at the forward price, with the exception that the sale of the call finances the purchase of the put. IBM uses this financing strategy for its hedges.

Hedging a short position in dollars by using a collar

A collar can be used to hedge a short position in foreign exchange. Consider one-million dollars accounts payable in 90 days, a short dollar position. To hedge short foreign exchange exposure, the firm simultaneously sells a put and buys a call, both with 90 days maturity. If the sale

领子期权可以被用来对外汇空头进行套期保值。考虑一个美元空头,例如90天后的应收账款100万美元。为了一个外汇空头风险进行套期保值,公司同时出售一个看跌期权、购入一个看涨期权,期限都为90天。如果售出的看跌期权和购入的看涨期权都是平值的,那么期权费相同。因此,出售看跌期权为购买看涨期权提供了资金,这是一种零期权费领子期权。

of the put and the purchase of the call are both at-the-money, the premium is the same. Thus, the sale of the put finances the purchase of the call—another zero premium collar. This collar is illustrated in Figure 4.14.

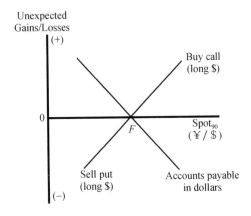

Figure 4.14 A collar hedge of accounts payable in dollars

Related techniques for hedging foreign exchange risk

Risk-shifting by currency invoicing

By invoicing in pounds, a British firm can shift the foreign currency exposure to the European importer. The pound may be specified as the currency of payment in the letter of credit. However, In the process of the shifting of the foreign exchange exposure to the European importer, the British exporter may risk the loss of the contract since it raises the cost to the European firm. The latter may shift its source of supply to another European firm.

Risk-sharing by currency contingency clauses

In the terms and conditions of the letter of credit, a risk-sharing currency clause may pass part of the currency risk onto the European firm. For instance, if the euro declines by more than 10% between today and settlement, the European firm may agree in advance to pay 5% more euros at settlement. Thus, at settlement, the European firm pays 5% more in euros and the European firms receives 5% less in pounds if the euro declines more than 10%.

A single large transaction involving foreign currency can be best and efficiently hedged by a contractual hedge. However, when the accounts receivable or payable are on an ongoing, operational basis, a natural, matching flow of offsetting amounts of the foreign currency is more appropriate.

Out-of-the-money options hedges

If your firm is willing to take some limited losses, an out-of-the-money options hedge is less expensive in terms of the premium paid. For instance, consider a long position in euros in 90 days. Rather than purchasing an at-the-money put option, an out-of-the-money option to sell the euros at an exercise price of X would be less expensive. This would limit losses to the amount of $F - X$ per unit of foreign exchange. The idea is to pay a smaller premium for the purchase of the put. The hedged position is indicated by the dashed line in Figure 4.15.

Figure 4.15   An out-of-the-money put option as a partial hedge of a long position

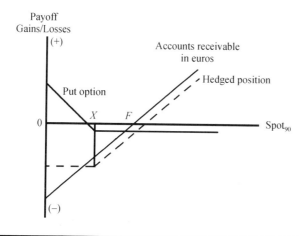

Similarly, if you had a short position in euros, say accounts payable in 90 days, you could purchase an out-of-the-money call at a strike price of X, thus saving on the premium paid to buy the call, and limiting potential losses to $X - F$. The hedged position is indicated by the dashed line in Figure 4.16.

Figure 4.16 An out-of-the-money call option as a partial hedge of a short position

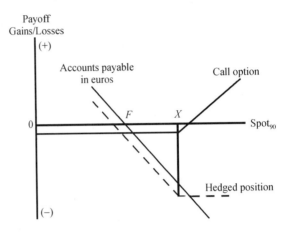

Hedging operating exposure

经营风险(Operating exposure)度量汇率意外变动导致的公司净现值的变动。

Operating exposure measures the changes in the net present value of a firm due to unexpected changes in exchange rates. It is a forward looking concept which re-estimates the discounted cash flow in home currency from overseas operations in a local currency following an unexpected change in the exchange rate. Nissan Motor experienced unexpected losses from its overseas automobile sales in US dollars:

> **In the News**: The Dollar Eats into Nissan's Profits
>
> Nissan Motor Co.'s chief operating officer said Tuesday that the auto maker is working "with a sense of crisis" to lessen the impact of the strong yen on its business, as the currency's surge threatens to eat into profits in one of Japan's key export industries. "We can't adequately express our concern about the sharp yen rise on our earnings by simply saying ... We are worried about it. The company is now working with a sense of crisis," Toshiyuki Shiga said at a news conference for the hybrid version of Nissan's Fuga luxury sedan. The comments are the latest in a series of warnings from Japanese companies ahead of the country's fiscal second-fiscal-quarter earnings season, which starts this week. The dollar fell to 80.41 yen Monday, its lowest since April 1995 and near its record low of 79.75 yen, before rebounding Tuesday. Each one-yen fall in the dollar slashes Nissan's operating profit

> by 15 billion yen, the company has said. Mr. Shiga declined to comment on whether the company would change its assumption for the dollar for this fiscal year from the current 90 yen, saying only that Nissan will explain further when it reports its July-September earnings on Thursday next week.
>
> Nissan said in July that it earned nearly half its expected operating profit for the full fiscal year in the first quarter, but it didn't lift its full-year forecast at the time partly because of the difficult outlook for the yen. The auto maker is reducing exports from Japan while increasing imports as a short-term measure to cope with the strong yen, Mr. Shiga said. The company needs to speed up shifting production overseas in the long term, he added. The car maker plans to produce 1.1 million vehicles in Japan during the current fiscal year through March.
>
> Source: Yoshio Takahashi, "Nissan Tries to Blunt Yen 'Crisis'," *Wall Street Journal*, October 27, 2010.

Nissan motor's problem is that it is long dollars in its operational exposure. Its profits in dollars have been reduced in yen by the yen appreciation (dollar depreciation) relative to expectations. In its fiscal year business plan, Nissan used 90 yen to the dollar but has unexpectedly received 80 yen per dollar, suffering an unexpected 11% loss from its U.S earnings. While much of Nissan's earnings are in dollars, the lion's share of its costs are in yen since it produces automobiles in Yokohama. This operational exposure to the US dollar can be dealt with in several ways, including economical, financial and operational hedges.

日产汽车的美元多头头寸给其带来了经营风险。具体表现为当日元相对美元升值时,日产汽车以日元计价的利润减少。

Economic hedges

Nissan can make economic decisions in its operations to offset the effect of the change in the exchange rate on its earnings when translated into dollars. Firstly, Nissan can raise the dollar price of its automobiles sold in the US market. If it were able to raise the price 11%, yet sell the same volume, it would recoup its foreign exchange losses. This would be more feasible if other auto prices were rising in dollars in the United States.

Alternatively, Nissan could hold the line on prices, yet sell 11% more automobiles in the US. If its costs in yen remain the same, it could recoup its exchange rate losses this way. However, it may require Nissan acquiring a larger share of the US market. Thirdly, it could pursue a strategy of both raising dollar prices somewhat and increasing sales.

The change in Nissan's business plan can involve:

日产汽车可以进行以下商业计划的调整:通过提高价格,提高以美元计价的利润率;通过增加产量,提高美元收入;提高价格与增加产量相结合。

- A rise in the profit margin in dollars by raising prices
- A rise in revenues in dollars by expanding the volume of output
- A combination of higher prices and increased output

Free cash flow in dollars could conceivably increase to offset the unanticipated dollar depreciation.

Each of the three cases is plausible since the devaluation of the dollar will be inflationary, so prices of all goods and services will rise. However, other operational hedges are available.

Diversifying operations

生产、原料供应与销售的国际化分散(**International diversification of production, sourcing and sales**):以日产汽车为例,日产汽车可以从国外进口更多部件,减少汽车出口,还可以加速海外建厂与生产的步伐。

The firm can diversify its production, sourcing and sales internationally. As suggested in Mr. Shiga's remarks, Nissan can import more parts from abroad, export fewer automobiles from Japan, and speed up its plans to locate and produce abroad, as other Japanese automobile companies, notably Honda and Toyota have done. Nissan could shift the production and assembly of its automobiles to the United States, purchasing parts, renting plants, and hiring labor there. Nissan could then use the dollars from its sales to pay for parts, assembly, distribution and after-sales service on a matching basis. This is a natural operational hedge. Nissan's net income would be less adversely affected by the yen appreciation relative to the dollar. The decline in yen revenue due to dollar devaluation is offset in large part by the decline in costs when reckoned in yen. Net income, however, is still adversely affected, particularly since the Japanese auto makers have difficulty increasing their price due to competition from US auto makers.

Another example of operational hedging is the low cost US carrier, Southwest Airlines. In the first quarter of 2005, "Southwest said it saved $155 by capping 86% of its fuel expenses at the equivalent of just $26 a barrel of crude oil, close to half the actual cost of oil during the quarter." (*Wall Street Journal*, April 15, 2005, p. A2) Its fuel hedges run through 2009, but cover a smaller portion of its fuel needs. In 2006, an estimated 60% of fuel use is capped at the equivalent of $30 a barrel, falling to 20% at $35 in 2009. In hindsight, these hedges have led to Southwest being one of the few profitable airlines in 2004 and 2005.

通过选择计价货币转移风险(**Risk-shifting by currency invoicing**):例如,通过以日元作为计价货币,日产汽车原则上可以将外汇风险转嫁给美国分公司的批发采购商。

Risk-shifting by currency invoicing

By invoicing in yen, Nissan could in principle shift the foreign currency exposure to the wholesale purchasers and distributors in the United

States. The yen would be specified as the currency of payment. However, the shifting of foreign exchange exposure to the wholesale purchasers imposes currency risk on the importer, requiring the importer to take hedging actions and costs.

Risk-sharing by currency contingency clauses

In the terms and conditions of a letter of credit, a risk-sharing currency clause may pass part of the currency risk onto the foreign importer. For instance, if the dollar declines by more than 10% between today and settlement for exports of the automobile, the importer may agree to pay 5% more dollars for the automobiles at settlement. Thus, at settlement, the importer pays 5% more in dollars and Nissan receives 5% less in yen if the dollar declines more than 10%.

Leads and lags in currency payments

A firm can pay its "hard" foreign currency commitments early with "soft" currency before the latter's anticipated devaluation. The idea is to spend the "soft" currency before it loses value.

提前或延期支付(Leads and lags in currency payments):在"软币"的预期贬值发生之前,一个公司可以用"软币"提前偿还其以"硬币"计算的外币债务。

Similarly, it can delay paying its "soft" currency liabilities by lagging the payment so as to purchase the soft currency after it loses value. That is, it delays its payment, waiting to purchase the currency at a lower rate. Leading and lagging payments on liabilities benefits the firm actively managing the timing of the transfer of funds, but worsens the position of the corresponding firm. If the latter is a subsidiary that is affected, the profits are transferred from the subsidiary to headquarters. If it is between the firm and a totally separate firm, the latter could easily be bankrupted from currency losses and delays in payments. This procedure may also be used to transfer profits to a subsidiary for example. Early repatriation of profits by Nissan could save the company some unanticipated exchange rate losses.

Re-invoicing centers

A re-invoicing center is a corporate subsidiary that has no inventory but centralizes invoices and manages operating exposure in one center. Manufacturing affiliates ship goods directly to distribution affiliates, but invoice the re-invoicing center that then receives title to the goods and invoices the distribution affiliate in a separate currency.

再开票中心(Re-invoicing centers):是公司的分支机构,它并没有存货,而只是负责开具发票和集中管理经营风险。

Transactions exposure thus resides in the re-invoicing center. Naturally, some of its accounts receivable and accounts payable will be in the same currency, providing a natural hedge. The invoicing center thus centralizes the net exposure to each currency.

A re-invoicing center could also transfer profits from a high tax affiliate to a low tax affiliate, i.e. practice aggressive transfer pricing. This is not the purpose of the re-invoicing center and it violates "arm's length" pricing rules established by the US Internal Revenue Service. A re-invoicing center's purpose is to centralize and manage foreign exchange risk in one place. Diagrammatically, Figure 4.17 depicts the flow of invoices and payments.

Figure 4.17   A re-invoicing center

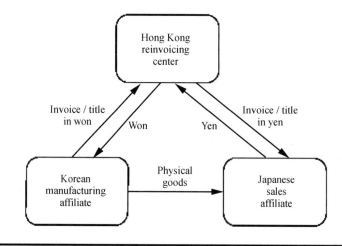

Diversifying financing

Natural hedges

自然套期保值(Natural hedge):如果一家公司有一笔提供持续外币收入的应收账款,那么它可以借入该种外币,产生一个相匹配的应付账款,从而形成一个自然套期保值。

A firm that has an ongoing inflow of foreign currency as accounts receivable, can borrow the same currency so as to have a matching accounts payable as a natural hedge. This is illustrated in Figure 4.18, where a Chinese firm sells goods for dollars in the U.S., but offsets its operating exposure by obtaining a loan in US dollars. This would be a natural hedge of its earnings in dollars—the cash inflow from its sales in dollars would be a cash outflow of offsetting payment of interest and principal in dollars. The loan, when disbursed in dollars, should be immediately sold for yuan to avoid a long cash position in USD.

Figure 4.18 A natural hedge in dollars

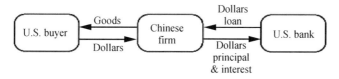

Foreign currency swaps

A foreign currency swap is an agreement between two parties to exchange a given amount of one currency for another and to repay these currencies with interest in the future. One counterparty borrows under specific terms and conditions in one currency while the other counterparty borrows under different terms and conditions in a second currency. The two counterparties then exchange the net receipts from their respective issues and agree to service each other's debt. Diagrammatically, the currency flows of a foreign exchange swap are illustrated in Figure 4.19.

外汇互换(Foreign currency swaps): 一种协议,协议的双方互换数额一定的两种货币的本金,并且约定在将来相互偿还两种货币的本息和。

Figure 4.19 A foreign exchange swap

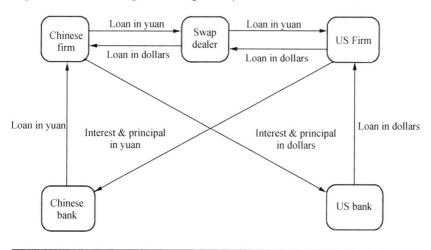

In Figure 4.19, an American firm borrows dollars, a Chinese firm borrows yuan. The two firms exchange the debt obligations through the swap dealer, agreeing to service each other's debt. This swap arrangement benefits each due to their comparative advantage in borrowing in their respective national markets. The swap enables both firms to have lower borrowing costs in foreign currency. The Chinese firm may have dollar receipts from its exports and the American firm may have yuan receipts from its exports, so the swap dealer arranges for matching payments in foreign currency at a lower interest rate. Thus, a currency swap is a way of managing foreign exchange risk. The swap dealer captures some of the lowered borrowing costs by earning the bid-ask spread on foreign currency, the interest rate spread, and other fees from serving as an intermediary. Alternatively, the two firms could have done the swap directly with each other, had they known of each other's matching needs and maturities, but then would have counterparty risk. A swap dealer can provide insurance against non-performance of the counterparty as well as general intermediation.

Back-to-back (parallel) loans

背对背（平行）贷款
[Back-to-back (parallel) loans]：比如，我们可以通过中国企业向美国企业的中国分公司提供人民币贷款，同时美国企业向中国企业的美国分公司提供美元贷款的形式，在两家企业之间开展间接融资。背对背（平行）贷款又被称为信用互换贷款，因为公司彼此借入对方的货币，在一定期限内使用。

Indirect financing can be done by a Chinese firm lending yuan to the US affiliate in China and simultaneously a US firm lends dollars to the Chinese affiliate in the United States. At an agreed upon time, each return the other's currency. A parallel loan is also known as a credit swap loan since the firms are borrowing each other's currency for a specified period of time. It is illustrated in Figure 4.20.

Figure 4.20 A back-to-back (parallel) loan

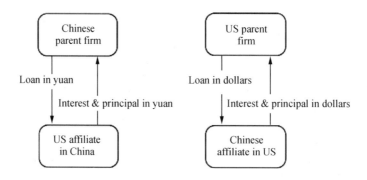

The firms do not go through the foreign exchange market, so do not pay the foreign exchange spread, nor fees. Neither firms wish to hold the cash in foreign currency disbursed by the loan, they are mainly interested in acquiring the interest and principal as an offsetting liability. Consequently, they sell the proceeds from the loan on the spot market.

The firms also benefit from lowered interest rates. In short, they save intermediation costs and benefit from comparative advantage in lending. At the same time, they may use a parallel loan to hedge their foreign exchange risk. Naturally, there is counterparty risk, but the right of offset—to revert to paying your original loan—exists. A swap dealer is better able to match the size, timing, and condition of foreign exchange swaps by avoiding the "double coincidence of wants" implicitly involved in direct counterparty swaps.

Accounting exposure

Accounting exposure arises from changes in the parent's net worth due to changes in exchange rates. Accounting exposure is also known as translation exposure since it is associated with the translation of foreign currency assets and liabilities. Foreign currency financial statements must be translated into the parent company's reporting currency to consolidate worldwide financial and income statements. If exchange rates have changed since the previous reporting period, the restatement of financial and income statements that are denominated in foreign currencies will result in foreign exchange gains or losses. Re-measurement of different line items using different exchange rates results in changes in current income or equity reserves.

会计风险（Accounting exposure）：汇率变动导致母公司净值发生变化而产生的风险。会计风险又称为转换风险，因为它与外币资产和负债的转换相联系。

A firm is long in a currency if its net exposed assets in the currency are positive (i.e. its exposed assets in a currency are greater than its exposed liabilities in that currency). It is short if its exposed liabilities exceed exposed assets in the currency.

Financial Accounting Standards Board—FASB 52

The rules that govern translation in the United States are devised by the Financial Accounting Standards Board. FASB 52—*Foreign Currency Translation* established US translation standards, requiring a functional currency and a reporting currency. A functional currency must be selected for each subsidiary. That is the currency of its primary working environment. Any foreign currency income is translated into the functional currency at current exchange rates if measured at current cost and at historical rates if measured at historical cost. Then, all amounts are translated at the current exchange rate from the functional currency into the reporting currency. The reporting currency is the currency in which the parent firm prepares its own financial statements: that is, US dollars for a US firm. In the case of a hyperinflationary country—defined as one that has cumulative inflation of approximately 100% or more over a three-year period—the functional currency of a US affiliate must be the dollar. Translation gains and losses bypass the income statement and are accumulated in a separate equity account on the parent's balance sheet called a *cumulative translation adjustment*.

Translation methods vary from country to country, but most use a cumulative translation adjustment equity line to account for translation gains or losses.

A simple technique is to multiply the difference between exposed assets and exposed liabilities by the change in the exchange rate in each currency. The resulting number is the gain/loss due to translation exposure in that currency. That is

$$(A_i - L_i)(S_i^2 - S_i^1) \qquad (4.6)$$

Where $(A_i - L_i)$ represents the net position in currency i. If $A_i > L_i$, the firm is long in currency i, if $A_i < L_i$, the firm is short in currency i, while if $A_i = L_i$, the firm is hedged in currency i from an accounting point of view. $(S_i^2 - S_i^1)$ represents the change in the spot price of currency i terms of USD or the home currency between re-measurement periods.

The total gain or loss between reporting periods due to translation at new exchange rates is the sum of the gains or losses in each individual currency, or

$$\sum_{i=1}^{n}(A_i - L_i)(S_i^2 - S_i^1) \qquad (4.7)$$

This amount is added to or subtracted from the cumulative translation adjustment item.

Hedge accounting

对冲会计法(Hedge accounting): 在记录由资产价值变化导致的损益的同时,包含由套期保值金融工具产生的损益。

Hedge accounting refers to the inclusion of gains and losses in earnings from financial hedge instruments at the same time losses and gains from changes in the value of the asset are recorded. FASB 52, paragraph 21 indicates that the financial hedge must be designated as and be effective as a hedge of a firm, foreign currency commitment. That is, the value of the hedge must move opposite to the value of a definite foreign currency commitment.

Trade finance

Trade finance can play a useful role in hedging. A letter of credit specifies, for example, the currency of payment as well as the conditions of payment. When it is confirmed, the bank substitutes its credit for that of the importer should the importer default on payment. Naturally, there are fees associate with a letter of credit, but it assures the payment for international trade, a very important role in the world trade and financial system.

In general, trade can be financed by:

- **cash-in-advance**: the seller receives cash from buyer prior to shipment.

This shifts the credit risk to the buyer.

- **an open account**: goods are shipped to the buyer then payment made to account. This shifts the credit risk to the seller.

- **collections**: goods are shipped to the buyer, the seller's draft and documents covering the shipment are presented through his/her bank to the buyer's bank for payment. In this case, both share in the credit risk.

- **a letter of credit**: After the seller receives a L/C with acceptable terms, the seller ships the goods. The bank which issued the L/C assures the seller of payment when the terms of the L/C are met by confirming the letter of credit. A confirmed letter of credit is a negotiable instrument.

Steps in obtaining a letter of credit

1. The importer obtains a letter of credit promising to pay on the importer's behalf.

2. The bank promises the exporter to pay on behalf of the importer by advising and/or confirming the letter of credit.

3. The exporter "ships to the bank" trusting the bank's promise.

4. The bank pays the exporter.

5. The bank "turns over" the merchandise to the importer.

Diagrammatically, a letter of finance can be depicted in Figure 4.21.

预付现金(**Cash-in-advance**):发货前卖方从买方那里收取现金。这将信用风险转移给了买方。

赊销(**Open account**):货物先被发送给买方,然后再付款。这将信用风险转移给了卖方。

托收(**Collections**):货物发送给买方,卖方的汇票以及运输单据则由其银行递交给买方的付款行索偿货款。在这种情况下,信用风险由双方共同承担。

信用证(**Letter of credit**):卖方收到信用证并接受其所列条款后,将发送货物给买方。在确认信用证的条款得到满足后,信用证开证行通过对信用证进行保兑向卖方提供付款保证。经过保兑的信用证是可以转让的。

Figure 4.21 A letter of credit

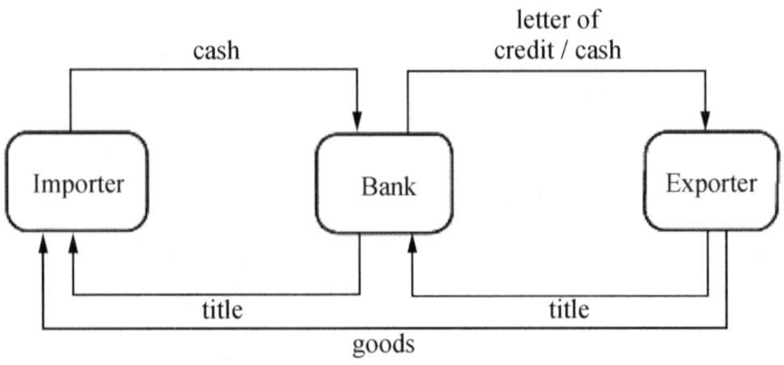

Documents in trade finance

• Letters of credit are documentary or standby, irrevocable or revocable, confirmed or unconfirmed, and revolving or non-revolving. A letter of credit may be transferable to a second party, i.e. discounted on a secondary market. It is typically irrevocable and confirmed to be marketable on the secondary market.

• The exporter ships the merchandise to the importer's country. Title to the merchandise is given to the bank on an order bill of lading.

• The exporter asks the bank to pay for the goods and the bank (or its correspondent or affiliate) does so. The document to request payment is a sight draft (also known as a bill of exchange). The bank passes title to the importer. At that time, or later, depending upon the terms of the agreement, the importer reimburses the bank.

• Both sight drafts and time drafts are negotiable instruments, if properly drawn. When a time draft is drawn upon and accepted by a bank, it becomes a banker's acceptance. When a time draft is drawn on and accepted by a business firm, it becomes a trade acceptance.

• Countertrade takes place when "... the sale of goods and services by a producer is linked to an import purchase of other goods and services." Countertrade is thus a form of barter or bilateral clearing resulting from shortages of hard currency, central planning, political risk, and barriers to international trade and investment. It is also a vehicle for avoiding taxation.

Hedging interest rate exposure

Foreign and interest rate risk management focuses upon hedging existing or anticipated cash flow exposures of the firm. Treasurers have the job of managing interest rate expenses and exposures.

Interest rate risk is of two types:

• **Basis risk** is the mismatching of interest rate reference rates on assets and liabilities. A firm's asset may be indexed to LIBOR, but its corresponding liability is indexed to US PRIME. An unanticipated movement in interest rates will affect the spread on the net interest income—the difference between interest receipts on assets and interest payments on liabilities.

基本风险（Basis risk）：利率风险的一种，是指由资产和负债的利率基准不匹配而引起的风险。

• **Gap risk** arises from the mismatched timing of the re-pricing of interest rate referenced liabilities and assets. A bank may possess long-term interest sensitive assets but be funded by a large amount of short-term interest sensitive debt. Thus, the bank has financial exposure to an unanticipated rise in short-term interest rates when it has to frequently rollover or re-set its short-term debt. For example, the Fed's "operation twist" of the U.S. yield curve involves a purchase of long-term debt and a corresponding sale of short-term Treasury debt. The purpose of the operation is to lower long-term rates. The banks, however, suffer when short-term rates rise and long-term rates fall due to gap risk.

缺口风险（Gap risk）：一个公司的负债与资产不匹配而产生的利率风险。如果一家银行的贷款期限长于存款期限，即借短贷长，那么该银行市场价值的变动方向将与市场利率的变动方向相反。如果该银行的贷款期限短于存款期限，即借长贷短，那么该银行市场价值的变动方向将与市场利率的变动方向一致。

Interest rate practices

Interest rate practices vary but the *international practice* (and US practice) is to use the exact number of days for the day count and 360 days in a year. Consequently, 180 days represents half a year.

On the other hand, the United Kingdom, while using the exact number of days for the day count, has 365 days in a year. The Swiss have 30 days in a month and 360 days in a year.

Reference rates

Reference rates such as US dollar LIBOR are used in quotations and loan agreements. **LIBOR** is the London Interbank Offered Rate determined by the British Banker's Association as the mean of 16 multinational banks' interbank offered rate at approximately 11:00 am London time.

伦敦同业拆借利率（LIBOR）：伦敦的一流银行之间短期资金借贷的利率，是国际金融市场中大多数浮动利率的基础利率。

Yen LIBOR is calculated at the same time in London using an average of interbank yen and DM offer rates. Other financial centers have interbank offer reference rates, such as PIBOR (Paris Interbank Offer Rate), MIBOR (Madrid Interbank Offer Rate), and FIBOR (Frankfurt Interbank

Offer Rate), which refer to reference rates on domestic currency agreements in those countries.

Forecasting forward interest rates

The first step in managing interest rate risk is to formulate a forecast of forward interest rates. For this, a strip of the yield curve is the standard technique. Second, a firm's net cash flow exposure to unanticipated changes in the interest rate is measured, then hedged.

The yield curve

收益率曲线(The yield to maturity curve):收益率曲线表现了利率的期限结构。它刻画了同种类型但有不同到期期限的债券的收益率。

The yield to maturity curve depicts the term structure of interest rates. It plots the yields of bonds of the same class (corporates, treasuries, etc.) with maturities that range from the shortest to the longest term. The curve indicates whether short-term interest rates are higher or lower than long-term interest rates.

In general, the yield curve has a positive slope because investors usually receive a higher yield for the extra risk of tying up their money long term. Figure 4.22 depicts the current yield curve for US Treasuries. In the year 2011, the yield curve exhibits a positive slope with higher long term interest rates on the *long bond* (30-year Treasury) than on the 10-year Treasury.

Figure 4.22 The US Treasury yield curve: February 4, 2011

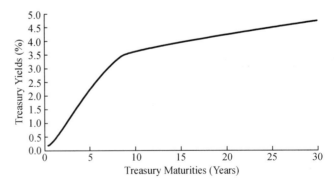

Source: Bloomberg, November 25, 2011.

A strip of the yield curve

Consider a 5.125% per annum yield on a 6-month US Treasury bill versus a 4.850% p.a. yield on a 3-month US Treasury bill. It would be possible to hold the 3-month T-bill, then roll it over for a second three months. Ignoring transactions costs, arbitrage pricing should yield the same rate of return. That is:

$$\left[1 + r_{90}\left(\frac{90}{360}\right)\right]\left[1 + r_{90,180}\left(\frac{90}{360}\right)\right] = \left[1 + r_{180}\left(\frac{180}{360}\right)\right] \quad (4.8)$$

or

$$r_{90,180}\left(\frac{90}{360}\right) = \frac{\left[1 + r_{180}\left(\frac{180}{360}\right)\right]}{\left[1 + r_{90}\left(\frac{90}{360}\right)\right]} - 1$$

$$= \frac{1.025625}{1.012125} - 1 = 0.013338 \quad (4.9)$$

or 1.3338 percent.

Multiplying by 4, we have

$$r_{90,180} = 5.333531\% \text{ p.a.}$$

In continuous time, the answer differs slightly.

$$(1 + r_{90})^{1/4}(1 + r_{90,180})^{1/4} = (1 + r_{180})^{1/2} \quad (4.10)$$

yielding

$$r_{90,180} = 5.401\% \text{ p.a.}$$

Thus, the implicit forecast of the future short term interest rate is a "strip" of the implied forward rates from any yield curve. The interest rate forecast from 3 to 6 months forward is therefore 5.3%. This rate is called the ***forward interest rate*** or the *forward spot rate*. These rates are useful in obtaining contractual or hedge commitments for interest rate obligations of the firms that begin at future dates.

远期利率(Forward interest rate):隐含在给定的即期利率之中,从未来的某一时点到另一时点的利率。

The forward yield curve

The forward interest rate curve derived point by point from the traditional yield curve is used to price many interest rate derivative instruments. The forward yield curve shows the implied forward interest rate for each period covered by the yield curve.

Outright techniques

- Mismatched maturities—a firm interested in locking in a future rate on investments that are more attractive than current rates can borrow short and lend long. With a positive sloping yield curve, a firm could reduce its borrowing costs by borrowing short and lending long, rolling over its short term debt continually. A firm wishing to borrow at a fixed rate from 6 to 12 months in the future can borrow now for one year, then lend for 6 months, thereby locking in the future interest rate.

- **Forward rate agreement (FRA)**—a contract settled in cash to buy or sell interest rate payments on a notional principal. The buyer of an FRA locks in an interest rate for a desired term that begins at a future specified date. The seller of the FRA pays the buyer the increased interest cost on a nominal amount of money if the interest rate rises above a specified rate, but the buyer pays the seller the interest differential if the interest rate falls below the agreed rate. The contract is priced on the basis of the strip rates of the yield curve.

- **A foreign currency swap**—Two offsetting forwards with different maturities can lock in a future interest rate in a foreign currency. Consider two simultaneous forward contracts:
  - Buy 100 euros 180 days forward at $1.15 per euro.
  - Sell 100 euros 360 days forward at $1.17 per euro.

The firm receives 100 euros in 180 days then returns them in 360 days, effectively borrowing the euros forward for 6 months (and lending dollars forward for 6 months). Because the exchange rate is specified on both ends of the contract, the cost of the forward euro funds has been locked in. The actual net cost of the euro funds to the firm is calculated by the internal interest rate that equates the dollar amount put up at the beginning of the 6-month period with the funds returned at the end of the 12-month period. The net interest rate for this foreign currency swap is thus (the difference between the US interest rate and the euro interest rate, from interest rate parity) illustrated in equation (4.11). It is also known as the "cost of carry."

$$\frac{1.17}{1.15} - 1 = 0.171913 \approx 3.49\%$$

or

$$\frac{F_{360} - F_{180}}{F_{180}} = r^{USD}_{180,360} - r^{Euro}_{180,360} \quad (4.11)$$

Interest rate uncertainty is thus removed by the foreign currency swap.

- **Interest rate swaps**—A **swap** is a contract to exchange debt service obligations. An **interest rate swap** is an agreement to exchange fixed for floating interest rate payments in the same currency. A **currency swap** is an agreement to swap interest obligations in different currencies. In both types of swaps, each borrower obtains a payment structure that is preferred, while still retaining the obligation for the principal payment.

货币互换（Currency swap）：不同货币债务间的调换。

Options based interest rate hedging techniques

• Caps, floors and collars are traded over the counter and on the exchanges. Interest rate options have a specified maturity, in practice up to 10 years for the over-the-counter market and from 1 to 5 years in the options market, and *reset dates* or *fixings*, for instance every 3 months during the lifetime of the interest rate option.

An **interest rate cap** is an option to fix a ceiling or maximum on a short-term interest rate payment. The buyer pays a premium to the seller of the cap. If the market interest rate rises above the strike rate, the buyer receives a cash payment equal to the difference between the actual market interest rate and the cap strike rate on the notional principal. If the market rate falls below the strike rate, the option expires out of the money and is not exercised. A cap on an interest rate payment is depicted in Figure 4.23.

利率上限（Interest rate cap）：通过购买利率上限,购买者可以锁定短期利息支付的最大值。

Figure 4.23 An interest rate cap, ignoring the premium paid

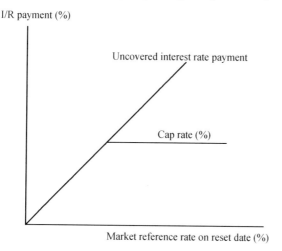

Ignoring the premium paid at the initial purchase of a cap option, the effect of the cap is to reset the interest payment at the fixing when the market rate of interest is above the strike rate. The interest rate payment is thus capped at the strike rate. The borrower pays the market interest rate but receives from the seller of the cap a payment equal to the difference between the market rate and the strike rate. Effectively, therefore, the interest rate payment is capped.

When the market rate of interest is below the strike rate, the borrower pays the market rate of interest since the cap is out-of-the-money. There are thus no compensating interest payments from the seller of the cap to the buyer. The buyer thus loses the premium paid for the purchase of the cap. Figure 4.24 illustrates the effect on interest payments at a fixing date of an interest rate cap.

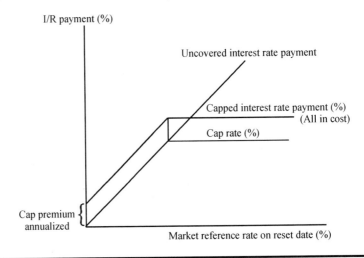

Figure 4.24 An interest rate cap, including the premium paid

An interest rate guarantee (IRG) is similar to a cap but differs in that it provides interest rate protection for a single period. There is thus at most one interest rate resetting. An interest rate cap provides for multiple reset dates. The premium is paid in full upon the purchase of the interest rate cap, but may be annualized to arrive at an all-in-cost (all included) interest rate payment. The standard amortization formula is used to derive a quarterly or annual amortized premium equivalent.

$$\text{Period payment} = \frac{\text{premium}}{\left[\frac{1}{r} - \frac{1}{r(1+r)^t}\right]} \qquad (4.12)$$

which is the amortized loan payment formula for a fixed interest rate r where the premium is the equivalent of the current loan amount, and t is the number of periods or resets. The amortization allows the calculation of the premium on a quarterly or annual basis, for instance, to measure an all-in-cost—the resulting amortized payment that services both principal and interest in a single cash payment per period. Figure 4.24 depicts the all-in-interest payments with the interest rate cap.

The value of an interest rate cap is determined by three factors: (1) the uncovered interest payment, (2) the amount of the cap payment if the reference rate rises above the cap rate, and (3) the annualized cost of the cap.

An **interest rate floor** is an option to fix a floor or minimum on a short-term interest rate receipt. The buyer pays a premium to the seller of the floor. If the market interest rate falls below the strike rate, the buyer receives a cash payment equal to the difference between the strike rate on the notional principal and the market interest rate. If the market rate rises below the strike rate, the option expires out of the money and is not exercised. Figure 4.25 illustrates a floor on interest rate earnings, ignoring the premium paid.

利率下限(Interest rate floor):通过购买利率下限,购买者可以锁定短期利息收入的最小值。

Figure 4.25 An interest rate floor, not including premium paid

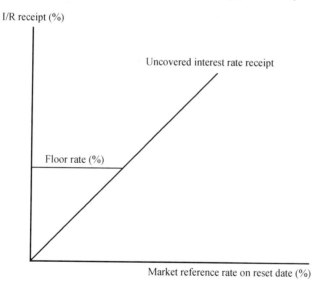

In Figure 4.26, we deduct the interest paid for the premium for a floor on an interest rate receipt.

When an interest rate collar is constructed by the purchase of a cap to protect interest payments and the simultaneous sale of a floor with an equal premium, the combined position is depicted in Figure 4.27.

Figure 4.26 An interest rate floor, deducting the premium paid

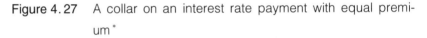

Figure 4.27 A collar on an interest rate payment with equal premium*

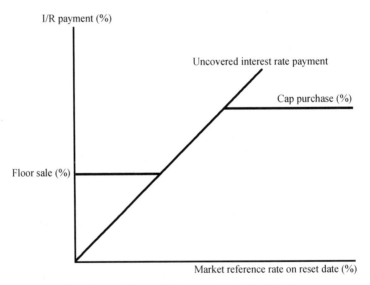

* including offsetting premium paid for cap and received for floor.

An interest rate collar is the simultaneous purchase of a call option and sale of a put option, or the purchase of a put option and the sale of a call option. A zero-cost interest rate collar would have equal premiums so there is zero initial payment. Figure 4.28 outlines a zero-cost collar.

Figure 4.28 A collar on an interest rate receipt with equal premium*

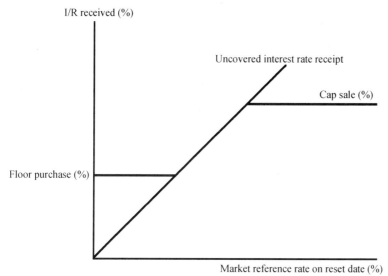

* including offsetting premium received for cap and premium paid for floor.

- Swap options. A swap option gives the firm the right to enter into a swap on a predetermined notional principal at some defined future date at a specified strike rate. A firm might purchase a *payer's* swap option giving it the right to enter into a swap in which it pays the fixed rate and receives the floating rate (Eitemann *et al.*, 2000). A firm might sell a *swapoption*, a *receiver's swap option*, giving the purchasing bank or swap dealer the right to receive the fixed rate from the firm. When the swap is exercised for cash, it is said to be *swap settled*. Cash settlement for the intrinsic value of the swap eliminates ongoing counterparty risk. The firm purchasing a swap option can lose at most its initial premium, ignoring counterparty risk.
- Options on interest rate futures are essentially *caps*, *collars and floors* but traded via an exchange using futures.

Conclusion

A firm's free cash flow from overseas operations is subject to exchange rate risk. By changing economic variables or seeking offsetting matching currency flows, the firm can hedge against exchange rate losses. To hedge, there are contractual hedges, operational hedges, and trade documents that cover against unexpected changes in exchange rates. The contractual hedges are mainly useful for one-time large future receipts or expenses in foreign exchange, while operational hedges provided matching natural offsetting flows in foreign currency on an ongoing basis. Accounting hedges insulate the balance sheet and income statement from translation losses, and trade finance can set up risk sharing contingency clauses or invoicing in the reporting currency of the exporter. While the case for hedging may be debated, large multinational businesses hedge their foreign exchange exposure on a routine basis. Their core business and comparative advantage is in the production of goods and services, not in speculating on movements in the exchange rate by implicitly taking long or short positions in different currencies.

Appendix: Risk and Insurance

Consider a risky investment project that has a good return indicated by $(1 + r_a)$ and a bad return indicated by $(1 + r_b)$. The good outcome has probability p while the bad outcome has probability $(1 - p)$. The expected return from the project is thus indicated by

$$E(W) = p(1 + r_a) + (1 - p)(1 + r_b) \qquad (4.13)$$

Figure 4.29 indicates the levels of utility associated with the two returns, d and h, as well as the utility associated with the expected return, $E(W)$.

Figure 4.29 Expected utility with risk aversion

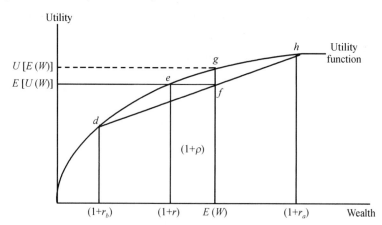

Risk aversion

Risk aversion refers to the assumption that, given the same return and different risk alternatives, a risk averse investor will seek the security offering the least risk—or, put another way, the higher the degree of risk, the greater the return that a rational investor will demand.

When there is diminishing marginal utility of wealth, $U''(W) < 0$, the individual, a proprietor of a firm, for example, is risk averse. This is the case depicted in Figure 4.29 where the utility curve is concave downward. The expected utility is indicated by point f, while the utility of the expected outcome is indicated by the point g. Risk aversion is seen graphically since the utility of the expected outcome is greater than the expected utility, or $U[E(W)] > E[U(W)]$. That is:

$$U[p(1+r_a) + (1-p)(1+r_b)] > pU(1+r_a) + (1-p)U(1+r_b) \quad (4.14)$$

The coefficient of relative risk aversion, Θ, is indicated by

$$\Theta = -\frac{U''(W)}{U'(W)}W \quad (4.15)$$

where $U'(W)$ is the first derivative of the utility function, which is always positive, while $U''(W)$ is the second derivative, which is negative with risk aversion. Consequently, the coefficient of risk aversion is positive when the individual is risk averse.

Attitudes towards risk

When the second derivative of the utility function is zero, the individual is said to be **risk neutral**. The utility function is a straight line, linear in wealth. When there is rising marginal utility of wealth, $U''(W) > 0$, and $\Theta < 0$, the individual is said to be a **risk lover**. When the second derivative is negative, $\Theta > 0$, the utility function displays diminishing marginal utility of wealth. In this case, the individual is said to be risk averse. Naturally, the individual could have an S-shaped utility function, being a risk lover over some range of wealth and being a risk hater over another.

The certainty equivalent ratio

The certainty equivalent level of wealth is indicated by $(1 + r)$ where r is the risk-free rate of return. The certainty equivalent approach yields a certain dollar equivalent ratio between zero and one that is equal to

$$\alpha = \frac{(1+r)}{E(W)} \qquad (4.16)$$

or

$$\alpha = \frac{(1+r)}{p(1+r_a) + (1-p)(1+r_b)} \qquad (4.17)$$

The profits, Π, from a risky project may be multiplied by α, then discounted by the risk-free rate, that is, divided by $(1+r)$:

$$\text{NPV} = \sum_{i=1}^{n} \frac{\alpha \Pi_i}{(1+r)^i} \qquad (4.18)$$

The higher the risk of the project, the lower the certainty equivalent, α. This can be seen by increasing the variance of the project, so that the good outcome involves higher wealth, while the bad outcome involves lower wealth, yet preserving the expected wealth level—the mean. As a result of the risk-increasing spreading of outcomes, the certainty equivalent level of income falls, therefore α declines.

A risk adjusted interest rate

A risk-adjusted interest rate can be used instead by adding a risk premium, ρ, to the risk-free rate of interest, and then discounting by the risk-adjusted interest rate. That is, let

$$\alpha = \frac{1}{1+\rho}$$

where ρ is the risk premium. Multiplying by Π yields:

$$\alpha \Pi = \frac{\Pi}{1+\rho}$$

Consequently, a stream of uncertain receipts may be equivalently discounted at the rate $(1+r)(1+\rho)$ to calculate the net present value of the risky project using

$$\text{NPV} = \sum_{i=1}^{n} \frac{\Pi_i}{[(1+r)(1+\rho)]^i} \qquad (4.19)$$

Once again, profits from projects with higher risk—greater standard deviations—are discounted at a higher risk premium.

高风险的项目(也即收益具有更高标准差的项目)需要用更高的风险溢价率来折现。

Now consider the square-root utility function:

$$U = \sqrt{\Pi} = \Pi^{1/2}$$

The coefficient of relative risk aversion can be computed to be $1/2$ from equation (4.14).

Constant risk aversion

In general, if the utility function has the following form:

$$U = \Pi^\theta \quad \text{where} \quad \theta > 0$$

The coefficient of relative risk aversion is indicated by

$$\Theta = 1 - \theta$$

which yields the constant coefficients of relative risk aversion given by table 4.6.

Table 4.6 Attitudes toward risk

θ	Θ	Attitude toward risk
1/2	1/2	risk averse
3/4	1/4	risk averse
1	0	risk neutral
3/2	−1/2	risk lover
2	−1	risk lover

Risk aversion and fair insurance

An individual or firm owns an asset, say a house or an office building, that is worth $100 thousand, but, if uninsured, risks a fire with a 10% probability of reducing the building's value to $9 thousand (i.e. a loss of $91 thousand). Consequently the expected loss is 0.1 × $91 = $9.1 thousand. The expected value of the asset is $100 − 9.1 = $90.9 if uninsured. This is a single proprietorship with a square root utility function:

$$U = \sqrt{\Pi} = \Pi^{1/2}$$

That is, utility rises as the square root of the value of the building. Consequently, if uninsured the entrepreneur in the good state (no fire) enjoys utility of $\sqrt{100} = 10$ and in the bad state (fire) enjoys $\sqrt{9} = 3$ utils. Expected utility is therefore $(0.9 \times 10) + (0.1 \times 3) = 9.3$ utils.

This entrepreneur displays risk aversion due to the diminishing marginal utility of his/her utility function, and would therefore seek insurance against fire to protect against the low state of utility (3 utils). An insurance company might offers a premium rate per dollar of losses equal to γ, so that full insurance against the loss would cost $\gamma 91$ thousand dollars. Consider the expected profit, Π_c, of the insurance company. It is equal to the premium less the expected payout, $p91$, if a fire occurs.

$$\Pi_c = \gamma 91 - p91$$

Fair insurance

公平保险(Fair insurance):如果保险公司设定的保险费率能够保证其期望利润为零,则称这种费率为公平保险费率,这种保险就是公平保险。

A "fair" insurance policy would imply zero profits for the insurance company and thus the premium per dollar of insurance would be 10% in a competitive insurance industry. That is, $\gamma = p = 0.10$ or 10%. To insure the building against fire, the entrepreneur would therefore pay a premium of \$9.1 to enjoy a certain value of the home of \$90.9, after payment of the premium. Instead of an expected value of utility of 9.3 utils, he/she now enjoys a certain utility level of 9.53, which is preferred.

It is optimal for the risk averse manager/entrepreneur to fully insure when insurance rates are "fair". However, this entrepreneur would be willing to pay up to \$13.51 or a rate of 13.51% per dollar of insurance since this would yield a certainty-equivalent after-premium value of the building equal to \$86.49. This would be the value that corresponds to an expected value of \$90.9.

To summarize the states of nature and the choices of this risk averse manager (Mr./Ms. Square Root), Table 4.7 summarizes expected wealth and utility outcomes when the entrepreneur is uninsured, and then computes the outcomes with fair insurance.

Table 4.7 Fair insurance and risk aversion

State of nature	Probability	Wealth (no insurance)	Utility
Good(No fire)	90%	100	10
Bad(Fire)	10%	9	3
		90.9	**9.3**
		Expected wealth uninsured	Expected utility uninsured
State of nature	Probability	Wealth (fair insurance)	Utility
Good(No fire)	90%	90.9	9.53
Bad(Fire)	10%	90.9	9.53
		90.9	**9.53**
		Expected wealth fair insurance	Expected utility fair insurance

逆向选择(Adverse selection):投保者的投保意愿与其面临的风险正相关,通常低风险承担者不愿意投保,而高风险承担者愿意投保,保险公司难以甄别每类人群所面临的风险。

With fair insurance, the manager fully insures.

Key concepts in insurance

- **Adverse selection** occurs when higher risks seek insurance claiming to be low risks. Low risks may not see the need to insure. Often, insurance companies deny insurance to those they identify as high risks (an example is the denial of new homeowner insurance and the huge increase in homeowner's premium after Hurricane Andrew in 1992 in South Florida).

• **Moral hazard** occurs when the owner of the building does not install fire detectors, hoses, etc. since he/she has insured against fire. An extreme case of moral hazard would be the owner of the building burning it down for its insurance value when its market value falls from $100 thousand to below $91 thousand.

道德风险(Moral hazard):当某人获得保险后,其行为方式可能发生改变。例如,房屋拥有者可能不安装烟雾探测器,因为他已经购买了火灾险。此时,道德风险就发生了。

• Risk diversification can be accomplished by purchasing assets or pursuing projects that tend to vary oppositely in value. Let $Z = X + Y$ be the sum of two random variables, stock Y and stock X for example. The variance of Z is indicated by

$$V(Z) = V(X) + V(Y) + 2\text{Cov}(X,Y) \quad (4.20)$$

Consequently, reducing US portfolio holdings from 100% to 80% by acquiring 20% foreign assets that vary negatively with US assets, the expected rate of return can be increased at the same time the overall portfolio volatility (the square root of the variance) reduced.

In general, a simplifying formula for the variance of a random variable, Z, is given by

$$V(Z) = E(Z^2) - [E(Z)]^2 \quad (4.21)$$

• Risk-spreading or pooling in the example above, individuals faced with a risk of fire could self-insure in a cooperative insurance arrangement. If say 1,000 individuals faced the same risks as above, they could all agree in advance to pay $91 thousand to any of its members that suffer from a fire. Similarly, a stock market allows owners to spread the risk of the firm among many shareholders.

Other decision making rules under uncertainty

• The maximin criterion has the manager determine the worst possible outcome under each strategy, then choose the strategy that provides the best of the worst possible outcomes. This is a very conservative, pessimistic decision rule.

• The minimax regret criterion postulates that the decision maker should select the strategy that minimizes the maximum regret or opportunity cost of the wrong decision, whatever the state of nature that actually occurs. Regret is measured as the difference between the payoff between a given strategy and the best strategy under the same state of nature. This is a more optimistic decision rule than the maximin criterion.

Questions and problems

4.1 Hedging

There are several schools of thought regarding hedging and its impact on the value of the firm. One school argues that if the owners of the firm wish to hedge, they can do so in their own portfolios. If the firm hedges, the costs outweigh any benefits. Another school argues that the comparative advantage of the firm is production of goods and services, and that if it does not hedge, it is essentially speculating. However, not all risk can be hedged by contracts and the cost of reducing some risks is prohibitively expensive. Write two short essays defending the following opposing positions:

a. "I never hedge, since it reduces my bottom line!"

b. "I always hedge, since I cannot take the risk of exchange rate losses bankrupting my firm."

4.2 Default risk

Consider the following basic data on a one-year Ecuadorian Brady Bond (dollar denominated sovereign obligation). It has a face value of USD 100 payable at maturity, but no coupon. Today it is trading at $80. Your risk free rate is 5%. Answer the following questions:

a. What is the Brady Bond's "yield to maturity" (that is, its internal rate of return)?

b. What is its "risk premium"?

4.3 Stock options as executive compensation

You were hired by Sparkle.com, a telecommunications company, last year (exactly one year ago). The company agreed to pay you £12,000 annual salary plus an option to buy in one year (i.e. today) 1,000 shares in Sparkle.com at £80. Today's share price on the market is £50. Answer the following questions:

a. What was your total annual compensation?

b. What percent of your compensation was in the form of stock options? Now answer questions a. and b. above on the assumption that today's share price is £100 instead.

4.4 Foreign exchange options

a. Claudia Speculator, IB Investments LTD bought a €100 call options at $0.01 per option (i.e. one cent per option) with a strike price of

$1.25. She exercised them and sold the proceeds at a spot price of $1.27. How much profit did Claudia make?

b. Thomas Banker, NPI Bankers, sold €100 put options with a strike price of $1.25, receiving a premium of $.005 (i.e. one-half of one cent per option). The put expired when the spot price was $1.20. Answer the following questions:

1. Was the put in or out of the money from the point of view of the buyer?

2. How much money did Tomas make or lose as the seller (what is his P/L on the put he sold)?

3. Did he have to honor the put?

4.5 Hedging

Martha Exporter, *Miami Baking*, LTD. exports her delicious Martha's Brownies to the United Kingdom and has accounts receivables in pounds sterling of £100 thousand in 90 days. What are the various contractual hedges that Martha might purchase to hedge her pound exchange exposure?

You are given the following basic data:
- U.S. interest rate at which Martha can borrow dollars 10% p.a.
- U.K. interest rate at which Martha can borrow pounds 8% p.a.
- Spot price of pound $1.7603, bid
- Spot price of pound $1.769, ask
- Forward bid price of pound $1.78 for 90 day delivery
- Premium on pound put option at $1.78 (at-the-money) strike price $0.0028 per pound

Now suppose that Martha decides to invoice British Baking Imports in US dollars to shift the exchange rate exposure to the importer. She thus invoices $178 thousand dollars deliverable in 90 days. British Baking is assumed to face the same market conditions as Martha's Brownies, namely:

- U.S. interest rate at which British Baking can lend dollars 10% p.a.
- U.K. interest rate at which BB can borrow pounds 8% p.a.
- The spot ask price of the dollar is £0.56527 per dollar
- The forward ask price of the dollar is £0.5618 per dollar for 90 day delivery
- A £0.5618 at-the-money call option to buy dollars costs £0.0028 per dollar

What are the various contractual hedges that British Baking might purchase to hedge their dollar exchange exposure?

4.6 Balance sheet hedging

Gateaux Antoinette, Société Anonyme, a subsidiary of Antoinette Cakes,

Inc., New York, had cash of 100,000 euros and accounts receivable of 100,000 euros each on its books (or 200,000 euros in total) when the euro suddenly appreciated from $1 per euro to $1.20 per euro.

a. Indicate what effect of the revaluation would have on the translation of these assets into US dollars on the consolidated balance sheet of the US parent firm.

b. How could Antoinette Cakes have acquired a "balance sheet" hedge for its cash and accounts receivable in euros prior to the revaluation (even though it benefited from the exposure in this instance)?

4.7 **Operating exposure**

You are a French company exporting widgets to the U.S. from your plant in France where the widgets are produced. You sell them for dollars in the United States. Last year you sold 100,000 widgets in the US for 10 dollars a widget, converting your dollar revenues to euros at 0.90 euro per US dollar. Next year you expect the dollar to be worth less, 0.8 euros but to export 110,000 widgets to the U.S. You are considering selling them at $10 a widget, but may reconsider the U.S. price.

a. Are you subject to operating exposure in dollars for the next year? If so, by how much?

b. What are some techniques you can use to hedge against this operating exposure in the United States?

4.8 **Operating exposure**

Tiny Tots Toys of Miami, Florida projects second quarter 2006 sales in Argentina to be 10,000 pesos, and expects the exchange rate to be $0.5 per peso (dollar earnings are therefore expected to be $5,000).

a. If the exchange rate unexpectedly changes to $0.25 per peso and Tiny Tots has not hedged, what are losses due to "operating exposure"?

b. How could Tiny Tots eliminate its operating exposure?

c. Suppose that Tiny Tots relocates production to Argentina and expects second quarter costs of production and distribution to be 5,000 pesos, leaving a net profit of 5,000 pesos if sales remain constant. Would you recommend that Tiny Tots hedge the entire 10,000 pesos?

d. In either event, what will Tiny Tots hedging activity do to the expected profitability in US dollars and in Argentine pesos of Tiny Tots? Explain.

4.9 **Accounting exposure**

Your European subsidiary has cash and accounts receivable of 100 and 300 euros respectively, and accounts payable and short term debt of 100 and 200 euros respectively. U.S. headquarters re-measures these line items in dollars on November 1, when the dollar price of the euro rose from $1.20 per euro to $1.30 per euro.

a. Did headquarters experience translation losses or gains in terms of US dollars?
b. How are any such translation gains or losses entered into the balance sheet?
c. How could the European subsidiary have acquired balance sheet hedge against losses or gains from translation exposure?

References and suggested reading

Akemann, Michael and Fabio Kanczuk (2005), "Sovereign Default and the Sustainability Risk Premium Effect," *Journal of Development Economics*, 76(1): 53–69.

Aliber, Robert Z. and C. P. Stickney (1975), "Accounting Measures of Foreign Exchange Exposure: The Long and Short of It," *Accounting Review*, 50(1): 44–57.

Ball, Ray (1995), "Making Accounting International: Why, How, and How Far Will it Go?" *Journal of Applied Corporate Finance*, 8(3): 19–29.

Banks, Gary (1983), "The Economics and Politics of Countertrade," *World Economy*, 6(2): 159–182.

Bilson, John F. O. (1994), "Managing Economic Exposure to Foreign Exchange Risk: A Case Study of American Airlines", in *Exchange Rates and Corporate Performance*, Y. Amihud and R. Levich, eds., Burr Ridge, IL: Irwin Publishing.

Bishop, Paul, and Don Dixon (1996), *Foreign Exchange Handbook: Managing Risk and Opportunity in Global Currency Markets*, New York: John Wiley & Sons, Inc.

Clark, Ephriam (2004), *Arbitrage, Hedging, and Speculation: The Foreign Exchange Market*, New York: Praeger.

Donnenfeld, Shabtai and Alfred Haug (2003), "Currency Invoicing in International Trade: An Empirical Investigation," *Review of International Economic*, 11(2): 332–345.

Eiteman, David K., Arthur I. Stonehill, and Michael H. Moffett (2000), "Translation Exposure," in *Multinational Business Finance*, 10th edition, Massachusetts: Addison-Wesley Publishing Company.

Knight, Martin, James Ball, and Andrew Inglis-Taylor, eds. (1998), *The Guide to Export Finance*, London: Euromoney Publications.

Financial Accounting Standards Board (1981), *Foreign Currency Trans-*

lation, *Statement of Financial Standards No. 52*, Stamford, Connecticut.

Francis, Dick (1987), *The Countertrade Handbook*, Westport, Conn: Quorum Books.

Friedman, Milton, and Leonard Savage (1948), "The Utility Analysis of Choices Involving Risk," *Journal of Political Economy*, 56(4):279-304.

Giddy, Ian H. (1994), *Global Financial Markets*, Illinois: Houghton Mifflin.

Schwartz, Robert, and Clifford W. Smith (1990), *Handbook of Currency and Interest Rate Risk Management*, New York: New York Institute of Finance.

Heckerman, Donald (1972), "The Exchange Rate Risks of Foreign Operations," *Journal of Business*, 45(1): 42-48.

Henderson, Callum (2002), *Currency Strategy: The Practitioner's Guide to Currency Investing, Hedging, and Forecasting*, New York: John Wiley & Sons.

Jesswein, Kurt R., Chuck C. Y. Kwok, and William R. Folks, Jr. (1995), "Corporate Use of Innovative Foreign Exchange Risk Management Products," *Columbia Journal of World Business*, 30(3): 70-82.

Jokung, Octave (2004), "Risky Assets and Hedging in Emerging Markets," *Economic and Financial Modeling*, 11(2): 66-98.

Kerkvliet, Joe and Michael H. Moffet (1991), "The Hedging of an Uncertain Future Foreign Currency Cash Flow," *Journal of Financial and Quantitative Analysis*, 26(4): 565-578.

Lecraw, Donald J. (1989), "The Management of Countertrade: Factors Influencing Success," *Journal of International Business Studies*, 20(1): 41-59.

Lintner, John (1965), "The Valuation of Risk Assets and the Selection of Risky Investments in Stock Portfolios and Capital Budgets," *Review of Economics and Statistics*, 47(1): 13-37.

Pilbeam, Keith (2004), "The Stabilization Properties of Fixed and Floating Exchange Rate Regimes," *International Journal of Finance and Economics*, 9(2): 113-123.

Ross, Stephen A., Randolph W. Westerfield, and Bradford D. Jordan (2003), *Corporate Finance*, 5th ed., New York: McGraw-Hill Irwin.

Sharpe, William. F. (1964), "Capital Asset Prices: A Theory of Market Equilibrium Under Risk," *Journal of Finance*, 19(3): 425-442.

Smith, Clifford W., Jr., and Rene M. Stulz (1995), "The Determinants of Firms' Hedging Policies," *Journal of Financial and Quantitative Analysis*, 20(4): 391-405.

Soenen, Luc A. (1991), "When Foreign Exchange Hedging Doesn't Help," *Journal of Cash Management*, 11(6): 58-62.

Solnick, Bruno (1990), "Swap Pricing and Default Risk: A Note," *Journal of International Financial Management and Accounting*, 2(1): 79-91.

Stultz, Rene M. (1984), "Optimal Hedging Policies," *Journal of Financial and Quantitative Analysis*, 19(2): 127-140.

Stultz, Rene M. (1996), "Rethinking Risk Management," *Journal of Applied Corporate Finance*, 9(3): 8-24.

CHAPTER 5 International Financial Management

国际金融管理

International financial management deals with valuation of cross border acquisitions, cash pooling, offshore accounts, transfer pricing, international taxation, and other matters that impact the global firm's balance sheet, income statement, and its business plan. Special tax regimes are considered, as well as the issue of repatriation of profits earned abroad. A concluding section extends the Markowitz (1952) optimal investment portfolio analysis to international portfolio investments taking into account foreign currency risk.

Capital structure

Apart from internal savings, there are two ways to finance your firm: by contracting debt (business loans) or issuing equity (shares). Creditors have senior debt that must be paid in full, except in the case of bankruptcy. They only share in bankruptcy risk. Shareholders participate in ownership of the firm, so they share in both business risk and risk of bankruptcy, in which case they usually get nothing. Due to the greater risk, shareholders typically require a higher rate of return to their equity. Interest payments to creditors are treated as an expense, so they are a "**tax shield**" for the firm. **The cost of capital** is thus a weighted average of the after-tax cost of borrowing (D) and the cost of issuing equity (E):

$$\text{WACC} = r_D(1 - t_C)\left(\frac{D}{D+E}\right) + r_E\left(\frac{E}{D+E}\right) \qquad (5.1)$$

- where WACC indicates the weighted average cost of capital, r_D is the cost of debt, r_E is the cost of equity, t_C is the marginal corporate tax rate, $D/(D+E)$ is **the degree of financial leverage**, the ratio of debt to

税盾(Tax shield):支付给债权人的利息在财务上是按照费用来处理的,所以它们是公司的税盾。

资本成本(The cost of capital):税后举债成本(D)以及发行股票成本(E)的加权平均。

金融杠杆度(The degree of financial leverage):负债与资产的比率,即$D/(D+E)$,是三种金融杠杆度之一。

the value of the firm, and E is the value of equity shares in the firm. For example, assume your corporation has 30% debt and 70% equity. It can borrow at 10% by selling its corporate bonds. Its shareholders require a return on investment based on the market risk premium. The cost of equity can be estimated using the Capital Asset Pricing Model (CAPM):

$$r_E = r_f + \beta(r_M - r_f) \qquad (5.2)$$

Where r_f is the risk-free rate, β is the covariance between the equity return, r_E, and the market rate of return, r_M, divided by the variance of the market rate of return r_M, and $(r_M - r_f)$ is the market risk premium. The equity's β or *beta* is thus a measure of the degree of market risk of the equity. It is measured as $\text{Cov}(r_E, r_M)/\text{Var}(r_M)$. With a 5% risk-free rate, an equity *beta* equal to one, and a market risk premium of 10%, yielding an r_E equal to 14%, the weighted average cost of capital is:

$$11.75\% = 10\%(1 - 0.35)(0.3) + 14\%(0.7)$$

Due to the tax shield of borrowing and to the low degree of risk to the initial loans, the WACC initially declines with greater financial leverage, $[D/(D+E)]$. With a high degree of financial leverage, $[D/(D+E)]$ approaching one, the risk of financial distress and bankruptcy increase. This causes both the borrowing rate and the equity rate to rise sharply. Consequently, there is an **optimum capital structure** which minimizes the weighted average cost of capital, indicated in Figure 5.1.

最优资本结构(Optimal capital structure): 能够最小化资本加权成本的资本结构。

Figure 5.1 The weighted average cost of capital and financial leverage

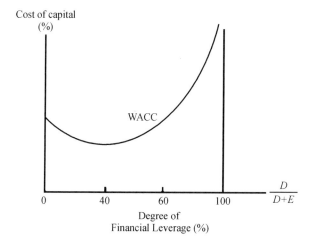

The optimal degree of leverage appears to be around 40% in Figure 5.1. The degree of curvature is exaggerated for illustration purposes. In practice, the WACC is likely to have fairly flat ranges. Start-ups are often too leveraged and fail to reach their break-even point due to fixed interest and principal payments on debt. Equity-based finance is less risky to the firm because shareholders participate in operational and economic risk. Dividends need not be paid out should profits be small or negative. However, venture capitalists often seek management fees and some management control, in addition to an ownership control. Marketing is often the greatest challenge to the start-up firm. The four Ps of marketing: product design, pricing, promotion and placement (distribution), are critical in generating positive cash flow as soon as possible.

Tight financial controls are indispensable. A monthly, if not weekly, profit/loss statement (P/L) should be accurately done, including the opportunity cost of the owners, if they are involved in the management. Positive cash flow is the aim of the firm and its owners. Records must be kept and discussed at regular meetings of the board of directors and managers.

代理人(Agent)受委托人委托,必须忠于后者,采取措施增加企业价值。

This is what gives value to the firm and ultimately dividends to its owners. The managers can enjoy their jobs, but as **agents**, they must be loyal to the principals, taking decisions that increase the value of the firm. Revenue growth is good, but costs should grow at a lower rate. The tax shield advantage of additional debt must be weighed against the rising cost of financial distress. Theoretically, a firm has an optimal level of debt which balances increased value of the tax shield against the increased cost of borrowing with greater leverage.

International capital structure

Some basic rules apply to the optimal capital structure from an international point of view. First, the basic rule for conversion of the WACC in dollars to say pounds for purposes of discounting pound cash flows is the interest rate parity rule:

在这里,我们遵循利率平价原则,将以美元计价的资本的加权平均成本转化成以英镑计价。

$$\left(\frac{1 + \text{WACC}_£}{1 + \text{WACC}_\$}\right) = \left(\frac{1 + r_{uk}}{1 + r_{us}}\right) \quad (5.3)$$

or equivalently:

$$\text{WACC}_£ = (1 + \text{WACC}_\$)\left(\frac{1 + r_{uk}}{1 + r_{us}}\right) - 1 \quad (5.4)$$

If your weighted average cost of capital is 10.7% in USD, r_{us} = 4.5% in USD, and r_{uk} = 3%, the WACC in GBP is 9.11%, reflecting the lower expected inflation in the UK. That is:

$$9.11\% = (1.107)\left(\frac{1.03}{1.045}\right) - 1$$

The key idea is to seek the appropriate WACC for discounting cash flows. It is important to use the interest rate on risk-free Treasury Bills for conversion purposes. Even though U.S. Treasuries are rated by S&P's at AA +, they are still default risk free. Their real value may be depreciated by inflation, but the Treasury will not miss a payment. The FED will purchase excess debt that cannot be sold to the public, so there is a risk of implicit default by seignorage, leading to high unexpected inflation. That allows the costs of capital to be adjusted for different inflationary expectations, as in the Fisher equation. It is appropriate to consolidate all debt and equity at current exchange rates in order to correctly measure the debt-to-equity ratio for global operations.

Cross-listing on foreign stock exchanges

By cross-listing its shares on foreign stock exchanges—despite additional disclosure, listing and reporting costs—a firm can improve the liquidity of its existing shares by making it easier for foreign shareholders to acquire shares at home in their own currencies. Cross-listing may also increase the share price by overcoming mispricing in a segmented, illiquid, home capital market.

在国外证券交易所交叉上市(Cross-listing on foreign stock exchanges):指既在境外证券市场上市,又在境内证券市场上市。

There are other advantages to cross-listing: (1) It may also provide a liquid secondary market to support a new equity issue in the foreign market and, (2) establish a secondary market for shares used to acquire local firms or to compensate local management and employees in foreign affiliates.

American Depositary Receipts (ADRs)

Cross listing is often accomplished by depositary receipts. In the United States, many foreign shares are traded through American Depositary Receipts, or ADRs. These are negotiable certificates issued by a U.S. bank in the United States to represent the underlying shares of stock in the overseas firms which are held in trust. "Sponsored" ADRs are created at the request of a foreign firm wanting access to equity finance in the United States. The firm applies to the Securities and Exchange Commission and a U.S. bank for regis-

美国存托凭证(American Depositary Receipts, ADRs):美国本土银行所发行的代表基础股份的可转让凭证,以信托的形式由托管银行保存。

tration and issuance. The firm bears the costs of creating sponsored ADRs.

International liquidity and market integration

By seeking access to international capital markets, a firm can benefit from two distinct, important effects: first, increased liquidity of its own securities, and second, overcoming market segmentation. Both effects tend to lower the cost of capital to the firm compared to borrowing from solely domestic sources. The firm has a list of investment projects ranked according to the marginal rate of return on investment, sometimes called the marginal efficiency of investment (MEI). High return projects are taken on before low return projects. As the firm spends more of its capital budget, the marginal efficiency of investment declines. Its level of capital expenditure, therefore, is constrained by the marginal cost of borrowing. Increased liquidity increases the supply of capital at existing interest rates, so that an increase in borrowing causes a smaller rise in the cost of borrowing. In addition, market integration overcomes market segmentation, thus additionally lowering the cost of borrowing.

Transfer pricing

转移定价(Transfer pricing):对于国内外相关公司间转移商品、劳务和技术进行定价,它同时存在于国内和国外的交易中。

Transfer pricing refers to pricing of the transfer of goods, services, and technology between related units of the firm. Transfer pricing takes place both domestically and internationally. In the case of the international firm, several considerations come into play. In principle, there is an optimal transfer price to provide the right incentives to the affiliate to supply the appropriate quantity of the intermediate input.

Optimal transfer prices

Assume there are a marketing division and a production division. Each unit of output requires one unit of marketing production, that is, marketing and production are joint products. The marketing division purchases the intermediate input from the production division, then markets the final product. The intermediate input is neither sold to other firms, nor bought from other firms, by assumption. In Figure 5.2, the marginal cost of the marketing and the production divisions are summed vertically to yield the marginal cost of the final product. Setting marginal cost of the final product equal to its marginal product yields the profit-maximizing level of production, 100, and a market price of $8 for the final good.

Figure 5.2 Transfer pricing

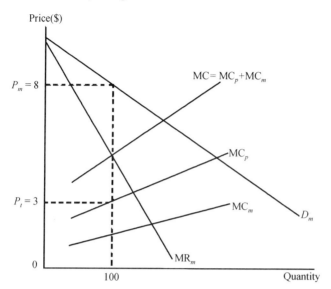

在图5.2中,最优转移价格所对应的产出水平是使利润最大化的产量。

To provide the correct incentives to the production division, a transfer price of $3 is optimal. In its production decisions, the production division sets marginal cost equal to $3 to maximize profits. It produces exactly the required amount of intermediate inputs and sells them to the marketing division. Any other transfer price would distort the incentives of the overseas affiliate.

Transfer pricing with external sales or purchases

When there is a possibility to buy or sell the intermediate input externally to other firms at a fixed price, the firm should regard this price as the opportunity cost of the intermediate input. In this case, the marketing department will maximize profits by having a transfer price equal to the market price of the intermediate input. Any excess supply of the intermediate input at the market price would be sold externally, while any excess demand for the intermediate input would be outsourced; that is, purchased externally.

Imperfectly competitive market for the intermediate good

When the market for the intermediate good is not competitive, the marketing division should set a higher transfer price to its internal division, and restrict its purchases slightly from the external market. Indeed, profit-maximization requires:

$$\frac{P_t}{P_x} = 1 + \frac{1}{\varepsilon} \tag{5.5}$$

where P_t represents the transfer price, P_x represents the price at which the firm purchases the input on the external market, and ε the elasticity of supply of the intermediate input to the marketing division. Equation (5.5) reflects the fact that by curtailing purchases on the external market somewhat, the marketing division pays a lower price for outsourced intermediate goods. For example, if $\varepsilon = 2$, the transfer price would be 50% higher than the external price. If the external market were perfectly competitive, ε approaches infinity, and the optimal transfer price equals the market price of the intermediate good.

If the production division produces more of the intermediate input than sold to the marketing division and has monopoly power in the market for the intermediate input, its optimal transfer price is below the price at which it sells the intermediate input to the external market.

$$\frac{P_t}{P_x} = 1 - \frac{1}{\eta} \tag{5.6}$$

where η is the absolute value of the elasticity of market demand for the intermediate good. For example, if $\eta = 2$, the optimum transfer price is 50% below the price at which the intermediate input is sold on the external market. Again, if the external market were perfectly competitive, η approaches infinity, and the optimal transfer price would equal the market price of the intermediate good.

Transfer pricing may be also a technique by which funds may be relocated. A lowering of transfer prices may finance the foreign affiliate. On the other hand, a parent firm wishing to transfer funds out of a particular country can charge higher prices on goods sold to its affiliate there, thus evading exchange controls. By setting transfer prices to shift taxable income from a country with a high income tax rate to a jurisdiction with a low income tax rate, the firm may also lower its taxable income. It may do so legally since profits earned in the lower tax jurisdiction may not be taxed until repatriated under some circumstances. However, according to the IRS guidelines, the "correct transfer price" is one that reflects an arm's-length price for a sale of the same goods or service to an unrelated customer. An advanced pricing agreement (APA) may be negotiated with the tax authorities of both home country and host country. An APA may save trouble and litigation resulting from an IRS challenge to transfer prices. The incidence of import duties may also offset the favorable income taxes in transfer pricing, an additional consideration.

The aggressive use of transfer pricing can transfer profits from high tax jurisdictions to **tax havens**, thereby reducing global tax liabilities. Profits can be accumulated in an offshore tax haven, no income taxes being paid in the home country of headquarters. Say you are a hardware equipment manufacturer, XYZ Hardware Corp., USA where you are not only subject to federal taxes, but also state and local taxes. You export hardware equipment to Europe through a Foreign Sales Corporation(FSC) in Nassau, the Bahamas. Take a hammer, for example, that costs a constant $2.00 per unit to produce. XYZ Hardware sells it to the FSC in Nassau for $1.00, thereby incurring losses of $1.00 per hammer exported. Thus far, headquarters has saved $0.21 in corporate income taxes. Next, the FSC sells it in euros to its affiliate in Europe for $5.00 which in turn distributes it for $3.75, or €3.38, losing $1.25 per hammer.

Consequently, the affiliate's taxes are down approximately $0.37. The FSC bought the hammer at $1.00 and sold it to the affiliate at $5.00, making $4.00 in profits on each hammer. These profits are deposited in an offshore bank and are deemed repatriated taxes are down $0.58 ($0.21 + $0.37), and the affiliate accumulates $4.00 of profits in Nassau taxed at $0.155 \times \$4.00 = \$0.62$ if cash and $0.08 \times \$4.00 = \$0.32$ if securities. Clearly, this would be an example of abuse of the national and international laws of taxation. Yet, it takes place. Figure 5.3 depicts this example of abusive transfer pricing.

避税天堂(Tax haven): 税率很低,甚至是免征税款的国家和地区。

Figure 5.3 Abusive transfer pricing

XYZ Hardware, Inc. could be fined.

* Tax Cut and Jobs Act, December 22, 2017. Deemed repatriated taxes may be paid over eight years.

转移定价的滥用(Abusive transfer pricing)将使企业把利润由高税率国家转移到那些避税天堂,从而在全球范围内减轻税负。

International taxation

关贸总协定(The General Agreement on Tariffs and Trade, GATT)规定了国外分支机构和子公司应享受的税收待遇。

The General Agreement on Tariffs and Trade (GATT) of the World Trade Organization (WTO) governs the tax treatment of branches and subsidiaries located abroad. If a branch or subsidiary is located in a signatory country, it is entitled to "national treatment": that is, tax and regulatory treatment no less favorable than that accorded to national enterprises. Article III *National Treatment on Internal Taxation and Regulation* explicitly forbids discrimination against foreign subsidiaries. Consequently, a firm with a foreign subsidiary may appeal any discriminatory treatment to the GATT/WTO in Geneva, Switzerland. Its corporate income tax cannot be higher than that of local companies, it cannot be charged higher duties to import intermediate goods, nor be required to purchase inputs locally to protect domestic production.

U.S. taxation of foreign income

Income derived from a minority-controlled foreign affiliate was taxed when remitted to the U.S. parent until 2018. This treatment sometimes led to tax avoidance by the creation of tax-shelter affiliates such as Foreign Sales Corporations (FSCs) and International Financial Offshore Centers (IFOCs) located in offshore banking havens. In 2017, The Tax Cut and Jobs Act was passed, deeming profits abroad repatriated at 15.5% if cash or 8% if securities.

Examples of taxation of international operations

A foreign majority-controlled branch is treated as part of the parent firm and thus must repatriate profits and pay home taxes contemporaneously. A subsidiary incorporated locally need not repatriate profits, nor paid home country taxes unless it remits the profits until 2017. Foreign income tax credits apply in both cases. The value-added tax and sales taxes are deducted from income, and thus treated as expenses. The following examples attempt to capture these various aspects of international taxation. Country A, where the affiliate is located is a high-tax country, so that the home country, assumed to be the US, issues an excess tax credit to the parent firm in Table 5.1.

Table 5.1 Affiliate located in a high-tax jurisdiction

	Country A (credit)*
Foreign income	$100
Foreign taxes paid	$40
Home taxes paid	$0
Net income	$60

*Excess tax credit of 19.

Country B in Table 5.2 is a comparable tax country.

Table 5.2 Affiliate located in a comparable tax jurisdiction

	Country B (credit)
Foreign income	$100
Foreign taxes paid	$21
Home taxes paid	$0
Net income	$79

No U.S. taxes would be paid, the firm receiving a full tax credit for the 21% corporate income tax. The tax burden would thus be the same as in the U.S.

Table 5.3 depicts a low tax country.

Table 5.3 Affiliate located in a low-tax jurisdiction

	Country C (credit)
Foreign income	$100
Foreign taxes paid	$15
Home taxes paid	$6
Net income	$79

A U.S. subsidiary that re-invested dividends in the host country would be exempt from U.S. taxes; a branch would receive a tax credit of 15, and pay an additional 20 to the US Treasury on its repatriated profits. The tax treatment of affiliates located in tax havens is shown in Table 5.4.

Table 5.4 Affiliate located in a tax haven

	Country D (tax haven, repatriation of profits)	Country D (tax haven, profits deemed repatriated)
Foreign income	100	100.0
Foreign taxes paid	0	0.0
Home taxes paid	21	8/15.5*
Net income	79	92/84.5

* Low rate/high rate

The value-added tax (VAT) is treated as an expense, so that the firm cannot receive a full deduction for value added taxes paid. The VAT is imposed on the value of the final product less the cost of the intermediate inputs; that is, on the value that is added by the firm. Suppose a firm adds 10 euros of value to a product, and pays a VAT of 20%, or 2 euros. If it is in the 21% marginal corporate tax bracket, it would receive a tax reduction of $0.21 \times 2 = 0.42$ euros, about \$0.51 at current exchange rates.

Working capital management

营运资本净额(Net working capital)包括现金、应收账款、存货减去应付账款以及流动负债。

Net working capital consists of cash, accounts receivables plus inventories less accounts payable and other current liabilities. A firm must have operating balances to manage its receivables, inventories and payables. Its net working capital finances the cash conversion cycle from raw inputs to final product and sale. As indicated in Figure 5.4, short term borrowing and repayment plays an important role in the cash management process.

Figure 5.4 Working cash balances

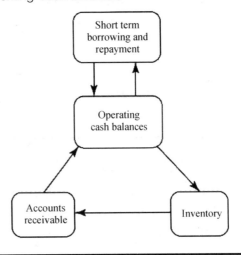

In addition, the international firm may hold cash reserves for its anticipated cash needs (*transactions motive*) and its unanticipated cash needs (*speculative motive*). A multinational firm with many affiliates may, for example, reduce its cash reserves by pooling them in a centralized facility (Eitemann et al., 2000).

Cash pooling maintains the same level of protection, while reducing the amount of cash necessary to hold. Take the example in Table 5.5 of three subsidiaries whose operations have different expected cash requirements.

Table 5.5 Decentralized cash management

	Expected cash requirement	Three standard deviations	Cash management pool
Subsidiary A	$100	$12	$112
Subsidiary B	$50	$6	$56
Subsidiary C	$200	$18	$218
		Total	$386

When the three subsidiaries hold one common cash pool, they are able to hold $13.56 less while maintaining the same level of protection, as illustrated in Table 5.6.

Table 5.6 Centralized cash management

	Expected cash requirement	Three standard deviations	Cash management pool
Subsidiary A	$100	$12	
Subsidiary B	$50	$6	
Subsidiary C	$200	$18	
		Total	$372.45

集中的现金管理(Centralized cash management)减少了所需的现金持有额,同时保证了相同的安全等级。

The analysis assumes that the cash requirements of each subsidiary are independent, normal distributions so that the standard deviation of the sum of the expected cash requirement, σ, equals:

$$\sigma = \sqrt{4^2 + 2^2 + 6^2} = \$7.48 \quad (5.7)$$

Consequently, a centralized cash reserve facility need only hold the sum of the expected cash needs, plus three standard deviations of the sum, or:

$$\$350 + 3(\$7.48) = \$372.45$$

While the cash requirements may be positively correlated, provided they are not perfectly so, gains to pooling can be realized.

Cash netting

现金净额交易(Cash netting)可以减少现金交易的次数,从而降低拥有多个分支机构的跨国公司的结算成本。

Cash netting may also reduce the settlement costs of a multinational firm with several affiliates having separate foreign exchange transactions between themselves and the parent firm. For instance, if subsidiary A must pay 150 euros to subsidiary C for widgets, and C must pay 100 euros to subsidiary A for intermediate inputs for assembling widgets, rather than having two separate transactions, subsidiary A (or a centralized facility) can simply pay subsidiary C 50 euros. The single transaction netting the payment saves the multinational firm transactions and spread fees in its cash operations. In short, the cash management process attempts to not tie up cash unnecessarily, without risking liquidity crises. A centralized invoice center can facilitate cash netting considerably.

Offshore banking

离岸银行业务(Offshore banking):存款人和借款人在本国之外进行的存储业务。

Offshore banking refers to deposits and loans that are made in a country other than the depositor's or borrower's country of origin. The Eurodollar market was one of the earliest examples of an offshore banking market.

Diagrammatically, an offshore deposit or loan is simply characterized in Figure 5.5.

Figure 5.5 Offshore banking

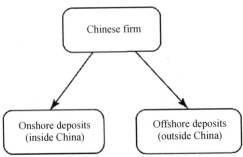

The key differences between offshore banking and domestic banking are the currency of denomination, the tax jurisdiction and the regulatory framework. For accounts payable and hedging purposes, it is often convenient to hold cash balances in a foreign currency. In some cases, however, offshore banking is used for money-laundering. A recent example is a shell Argentine bank in the Cayman Islands which had no personnel in the Cayman Islands, but was used to launder money. It was ordered closed recently by the Cayman banking regulators. The Bank of New York has experienced regulatory trouble resulting from the alleged laundering of Russian monies, as have some Swiss Banks.

In the United States, an **Edge Act Bank** is a branch of a foreign bank that is allowed to take in offshore deposits, but not domestic deposits. Edge banks are subject to the regulation and the supervision of the US monetary authorities (the Federal Reserve Bank and the Comptroller of the Currency), who are keen to discover money laundering and close the offending banks.

埃奇法案银行(Edge Act Bank): 外国银行的分支机构,该银行可以吸收离岸存款,但是不能吸收国内存款。

An Edge bank may make US and foreign loans and investments for its offshore clients. Examples are Banco Santander Central Hispano which has Edge Act facilities for private banking in New York and Miami. Its depositors are mainly from Europe, primarily Spain, and Latin America. It complies with international and U.S. banking regulation and best banking practices which it has observed since the 15th century. Today, Banco Santander Central Hispano has the greatest volume of assets of any bank in Latin America. Its policy is to acquire 100% of existing or new banks, and to install BSCH management to avoid taking the risk of a partner doing illegal or irresponsible banking. Additionally, they take no deposits from politicians nor former-politicians from Latin America.

International Financial Offshore Centers

The primary purpose of an International Financial Offshore Center (IFOC) is to centralize, net, and track international cash flow and defer taxes on profits before repatriation or investment. It may also serve as an invoicing center. The Internal Revenue Act of 1962 and the Tax Reform Act of 1984, which created Foreign Sales Corporations (FSCs), permit this in an attempt to reduce the tax burden on exports from the United States.

离岸国际金融中心(International financial offshore center)的主要目的是集中、结算并追踪国际现金流以及延迟汇回或投资前利润的税收。

However, by the use of aggressive transfer pricing, shell banks and corporations, IFOCs have been vehicles for tax avoidance rather than deferment, and, even worse, money laundering. The Edge Act for the US created IFOCs inside the US for the rest of the world, so this is not a statement only about a few small Caribbean islands. The larger jurisdictions, the United States and Europe, are pressuring smaller offshore banking centers to remove coveted banking secrecy laws that have shielded money laundering. However, it is clear that a great deal of money is laundered through New York and Miami, despite mandatory notification to the Treasury of deposits over $10,000, an amount so small that it triggers too many notifications.

Other special regimes

A US Possessions Corporation is not subject to US income tax on income received in the US possession, provided it is not received in the United States. This is an incentive for US firms to set up separate corporations in the US possessions. These special incentives are being phased out gradually.

Blacklisted countries (Non-Cooperative Countries and Territories)

金融特别行动组 (The Financial Action Task Force):由七国集团成立的一个旨在反洗钱及反恐怖主义融资的国际组织。

The Financial Action Task Force (FATF) to combat money laundering and terrorist financing, an international body created by the G-7 to deter money laundering—the movement of profits from illicit activities through the banking system or legitimate businesses—has established a blacklist of countries that do not take enough action to curb money-laundering. It also requires greater identification of customers involved in wire-transfers to combat terrorism. The currently blacklisted countries are few. Iran and Democratic People's Republic of Korea are listed as not taking enough measures against money laundering and the transfer of terrorist monies. While the FATF cites considerable progress in this respect, there is no hard evidence that money laundering or terrorist finance has abated.

An international business plan

独资企业 (Sole proprietorship):业主根据自身利益而独立经营的企业。

The principal ways of organizing a business are:
- a **sole proprietorship** involves an individual acting on his or her

own behalf in a business context. It is the least specially regulated and least complex form of business, but has greatest asset exposure.

- a **partnership** is formed by the independent action of the partners whose rights and duties are spelled out in business charters.

- a **limited partnership** involves one or more investing partners and at least one operating partner. There are restrictions on the formation of limited partnerships that are designed to ensure that creditors are aware that an investing partner will be liable only to the extent of that partner's investment.

- a **corporation** is a single entity, a "person" that may sue or be sued without its members being held liable. It is chartered by the jurisdiction in which it is located. A corporation is a business in which large numbers of people are organized so that their labor and capital are combined in a single venture. They may enter or withdraw from the venture at any time, by buying or selling shares, leaving it to others to carry on.

The principal-agent problem

The legal cornerstone of business transactions is agency law.

An **agent** is a person empowered to act so as to legally bind another, the principal. An agent must be loyal to the principal, act with reasonable care, follow reasonable instructions, and make an appropriate accounting. So long as the agent acts with authority, the principal is bound to perform the obligations to third parties. The third parties are similarly liable to the principal. There are several possible solutions to the principal-agent problem: Each tries to align the interests of the agent with those of the owners.

- Ownership—sell part of the firm to the agent, or have the agent buy shares in the corporation, or grant the agent shares or options to buy shares.

- Incentive pay—include incentives in the agent's compensation package that reflect the principal's interest. However, there are several problems with stock options as solutions to the principal-agent problem. First, the holdings of current shareholders are diluted since the firm issues more shares to fulfill a stock option plan. The existing shares will decline in value relative to what they would otherwise be. Second, when the market turns downward, many of the manager's call options are under the water—that is, way out-of-the-money and are practically worthless. Thus, their incentive effect is nearly nil. Under some conditions, the exercise price may be reset so as to restore managerial incentives, but this seems unfair to shareholders that have purchased their stock on the open market. At times, the shares have also been backdated to a lower exercise price to build in intrinsic profits. Third, when a manager has inside information, he/she may exercise early or book earnings for goods not delivered so as to cash in the options before the bad news hits the market. Fourth, managers have an incentive to book earnings early, to exaggerate them, or remove negative items from income statements in order to cash in their bonus or stock options. In short, stock options may distort incentives.

• Monitoring—but who will "monitor" the monitor? Many international accounting firms have been fined for signing off on obviously fraudulent earnings and income statements. Partly this is due to conflicts of interest when the auditing firm also seeks investments from the firm.

Financial distress and bankruptcy

Financial distress can be defined in several ways:

• Business failure (a business has terminated with a loss to creditors).

• Legal bankruptcy (Firms or creditors bring petitions to a court for bankruptcy).

• In Chapter 7, or liquidation, the debtor's property is sold off by a trustee to pay the debts owed to creditors. An individual debtor can keep a modest amount of household property or realty under federal or state exemptions. The states of Texas and Florida are famous for its bankrupt managers and owners with multi-million dollar homes sheltered from the bankruptcy court due to "Homestead Laws."

• In Chapter 11, or business reorganization, the business is continued by its management or a trustee while creditors' claims are frozen pending approval of a plan. With court approval, the plan can modify or forgive debts, recapitalize a corporation, provide for mergers or takeovers, or dispose of assets.

• In Chapter 13, or adjustment proceedings, individuals with a regular income who cannot pay their debts may elect adjustment proceedings instead of liquidation. In these cases, claims of creditors are frozen until the individual presents a plan to pay off the creditors from income that is approved by a trustee. With court and creditor approval, debts may be stretched out or compromised while the debtor still retains all property.

• Technical insolvency occurs when a firm defaults on a legal obligation, for example, by not paying a bill. **Solvency** means the ability of the firm to pay its liabilities on time. The short-term solvency of a firm is measured two ways: the current solvency ratio (the ratio of its current assets to its current liabilities), and the quick solvency ratio (the ratio of its liquid assets to its current liabilities). Rules of thumb suggest a minimum current ratio of 2 to 1, and a minimum quick ratio of 1 to 1.

偿债能力(Solvency):公司按时偿还债务的能力。

• Accounting insolvency occurs when the total book value of liabilities exceed the book value of total assets. Owner's equity, the difference between assets and liabilities, is negative.

The break-even point and the profit-maximizing point

In principle, the valuation of a firm requires only three things: a forecast of its profits or free cash flow, an estimate of its terminal value when sold in say 5 years, and a weighted average cost of capital of the firm with which to discount free cash flows and the terminal value. This exercise is part art, part science. When these three variables are estimated, the net present value of the firm is given by substitution into the standard NPV formula:

$$\text{NPV} = \pi_0 + \frac{\pi_1}{(1+i)} + \frac{\pi_2}{(1+i)^2} + \frac{\pi_3}{(1+i)^3} + \frac{\pi_4}{(1+i)^4} + \frac{\pi_5}{(1+i)^5} + \frac{T_5}{(1+i)^5} \quad (5.8)$$

where π represents profits (or rather free cash flow) in each year, T_5 represents the terminal value when the firm is sold in the fifth year, and i represents the weighted-average cost of capital. In the start-up year, costs typically exceed revenues, or $\pi_0 < 0$. For the NPV to be positive there must be positive cash flow in at least one of the future years. In each period, it is assumed that production is at the profit-maximizing level requiring that marginal revenue equal marginal costs. (The slope of the revenue curve equals the slope of the cost curve, as depicted in Figure 5.6.)

Figure 5.6 Profit maximization by the firm

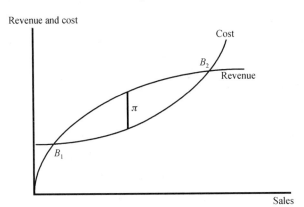

Note that a second-order condition requires that costs be rising faster than revenues, otherwise the marginal cost equals marginal revenue would imply a profit minimum. This can easily occur with economies of scale where average cost is declining.

Financial and operating leverage

A start-up business faces two serious questions—how much financial leverage and how much operating leverage it should take on? Higher financial leverage, as measured by the debt to debt plus equity ratio, benefits the owners greatly when the firm does well. Earnings per share are more responsive to a rise in earnings before interest, because the debt obligations—interest and principal payments to bondholders—are fixed. Shareholder dividends thus rise elastically with respect to earnings before interest. That is the positive side of financial leverage.

However, if the firm does poorly after getting started, the creditors are nevertheless legally entitled to interest and principal payments, but the shareholders can only hope for dividends. Earnings per share can easily be negative while the firm is making losses and yet paying creditors as its business is growing. However, it may be forced into bankruptcy after only a few months if it does not reach a break-even point quickly. New restaurants often do not stay in business for over a year, partly due to financial leverage, as was the case of the Azteca Café, whose start-up was 100% debt financed.

The degree of operating leverage at start up is another critical decision that may jeopardize a firm's survival. Operating leverage is the extent to which a company's costs of operating are fixed—rent, insurance, and salaries—as opposed to variable—materials and direct labor—costs that vary with output, such as wages, and the costs of material inputs. Operating leverage is measured by the ratio of fixed to fixed plus variable costs. In a company whose costs are virtually all fixed, every dollar of increase in sales is a dollar of increase in operating income once the breakeven point has been reached. In contrast, a company whose costs are largely variable would show relatively little increase in operating income when production and sales increased because costs and production rise together. Operating leverage comes into play because a small change in sales has a magnified effect on operating income. The degree of operating leverage—the ratio of the percentage change in operating income to the percentage change in sales—measures the sensitivity of a firm's profits to changes in sales volume. A firm with a high degree of operating leverage has a break-even point at a relatively high sales level.

An international business plan: the Azteca Café

This is all very well and good, but how is it put into practice, particularly abroad? Let's take the example of the Azteca Café whose revenues and costs are in Mexican pesos, its functional currency. As a start-up in 2001, its initial investment costs were N$500,000 for the oven and hood with fire extinguisher, grease trap, tables, chairs and dinnerware, plus renovation of the existing facility. The owner/manager, Juan Olive elected straight line depreciation of his investment over five years. His forecast of free cash flow in pesos in indicated in Table 5.7.

Table 5.7 Forecast of the Azteca Café's free cash flow in new Mexican pesos

	2001	2002	2003	2004	2005
Free cash flow	N$(332,683)	N$(108,046)	N$60,553	N$123,615	N$82,554

He had borrowed from a local bank the entire amount at 22% in pesos, which gives us the weighted average cost of capital (no equity was brought to the project). The Azteca Café's forecasted revenue and costs yielded a free cash flow projection for five years. In addition, a terminal value was predicted as a no-growth perpetuity of its fifth year's free cash flow. Unfortunately, the business plan was done at the end of the Azteca Café's first year of operations. Had it been done earlier, the project would not have taken place.

In the first year, Juan accumulated arrears in his rent, his loan and in payment of the 15% value-added tax in Mexico. His cash flow was negative so he sought finance by running arrears. The business plan was prepared in May 2001 to value the restaurant in pesos. Naturally, the value of debt arrears had to be subtracted from the net present value of forecasted free cash flow.

The business plan summary is presented in Table 5.8.

Table 5.8 Discounted free cash flow of the Azteca Café

Valuation of the Azteca café	2001	2002	2003	2004	2005	Terminal value 2005
Free cash flow in Mexican pesos	N$(332,683)	N$(108,046)	N$60,553	N$123,615	N$82,554	N$375,247
Present value in Mexican pesos	N$(272,691)	N$(72,592)	N$(33,347)	N$(55,799)	N$(30,545)	N$(138,841)
PV of free cash flow in Mexican pesos	N$(86,750)	22.0% WACC in N$				
Spot exchange rate (USD per peso)	$0.1098					
PV of free cash flow in US dollars	$(9,525)					

In addition, the landlord could padlock the restaurant door at any moment with a court order, and the lender could seize the oven and equipment on which he held the lien. The state was about to file criminal charges for tax evasion. The Azteca Café was clearly in serious financial distress. Could it be sold? The net present value of free cash flow was negative, but the restaurant was even worth less. Let's deduct debts from the net present of free cash flow in Table 5.9.

Table 5.9 Discounted free cash flow minus existing liabilities of the Azteca Café

Present value of free cash flow	N$(86,750)
Rent arrears	N$(225,000)
Loan arrears	N$(50,000)
Value-added tax arrears	N$(60,000)
Estimated NPV of the Azteca Café(in N$)	N$(421,750)
Spot exchange rate(USD per peso)	$0.1098
Estimated NPV of the Azteca café(in USD)	$(46,308)

New equity financing was sought to recapitalize the restaurant and repay the loan and rent arrears. Meetings of potential investors took place, but the decision was taken that any more money put into the venture would be lost. In any case, ignoring the arrears, the net present value of cash flow was negative. The potential investors informed the restaurant's lawyer that they would not invest in the Azteca Café. The owner declared a liquidation bankruptcy in June 2001, turning in his keys to the landlord. The bank took the equipment and sold it in auction. It also required the owner, Juan, to sell his home and took its equity. Finally, it rescheduled the remaining balance of his loan, with penalties. Moral of the story: look before you leap! That is, do a reasoned business plan.

International financial management covers the international cost of capital, working capital balance management, offshore banking, international tax management, transfer pricing, mergers and acquisitions and currency forecasting and conversion. There are perfectly legal and reasoned ways of reducing tax liabilities, yet there may be the temptation to abuse some of these tools. Chapter 6 deals with some of the more abusive international financial deals that cross the line in terms of accounting, legal, and ethical standards.

Optimal investment analysis

Market risk, also known as systematic risk, represents risk factors that are common to the whole economy. **Firm specific risk**, also known as diversifiable risk, represents risk factors that can be eliminated by diversification. The variance of security i, σ_i^2, can be written as the sum of the market risk and the firm specific risk, ε_i^2:

$$\sigma_i^2 = \beta_i^2 \sigma_M^2 + \varepsilon_i^2 \qquad (5.9)$$

市场风险（Market risk）：也称为系统风险，表示与整体经济状况相关的风险因素。

公司特定风险（Firm specific risk）：也称为可分散风险，表示可以通过分散投资消除的风险因素。

where

$$\beta_i^2 = \frac{\sigma_{iM}}{\sigma_M^2}$$

and σ_{iM} is the covariance between security i's return and the market return, and σ_M^2 is the variance of the market return. The *beta* (β) of an individual security i measures the security's sensitivity to market movements and therefore is known as its market risk. For example, the *beta* of the S&P 500 index share should be about one since it reflects a broad selection of market stocks. A riskier security would have a *beta* greater than one, and a less risky security would have a *beta* less than one.

Portfolio diversification

The level of market risk is dealt with by choosing the *betas* in the portfolio since the systematic risk is a weighted average of the individual security *betas*. Systematic variance equals $\beta_P^2 \sigma_M^2$, where β_P is the average of the individual security *betas*. By choosing β_P^2, we decide the systematic variance of the portfolio. A choice of domestic and international *betas* can reduce systematic risk relative to a choice of only domestic *betas*. In short, systematic risk is manipulated by choosing the average *beta* of the securities, but the number of securities does not matter.

Non-systematic risk is diversifiable by increasing the number of securities. By sufficiently diversifying, the investor can virtually eliminate firm-specific risk. By holding both domestic and international securities, portfolio diversification is more efficient since the universe of assets is the choice set. Figure 5.7 illustrates the reduction of portfolio risk as the number of securities in the portfolio increases.

Figure 5.7 Portfolio diversification and market risk

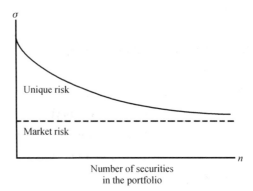

Asset allocation with one domestic and one foreign asset

Here we consider the allocation of the investment budget between two risky funds, a domestic fund and a foreign fund. If the proportion invested in the domestic fund is w_d, then the remainder is invested in the international (g for global) fund, $w_g = 1 - w_d$.

Some basic relationships hold:

$$r_P = w_d r_d + w_g r_g \quad (5.10)$$
$$E(r_P) = w_d E(r_d) + w_g E(r_g) \quad (5.11)$$
$$\sigma_P^2 = (w_d \sigma_d)^2 + (w_g \sigma_g)^2 + 2(w_d \sigma_d)(w_g \sigma_g)\rho_{dg} \quad (5.12)$$

That is:

- The rate of return on the portfolio is a weighted average of the rates of return on the domestic and global funds.
- The expected rate of return on the portfolio is a weighted average of the expected rates of return on the domestic and global funds.
- The variance of the portfolio is the sum of the square of weighted volatilities plus a term involving the correlation coefficient, ρ_{dg}, between the domestic and the global funds. In general, the efficient investment portfolio has the shape depicted in Figure 5.8.

Figure 5.8 The efficient investment frontier

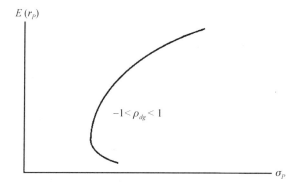

The **correlation coefficient** is the term that permits efficient diversification. Only in the case of a perfectly positive correlation, $\rho_{dg} = 1$ are there no gains to be had from diversification. Initially, by diversification, a higher rate of expected return can be obtained at a lower volatility.

相关系数 (Correlation coefficient) 决定了风险分散的有效性。当完全正相关时,分散化并不会带来收益;只有当完全负相关时,分散化的潜在收益才达到最大。

The minimum risk portfolio

The minimum risk portfolio is found by differentiating equation

(5.12) with respect to the portfolio weights, setting the result equal to zero, and solving. The weight of global shares in the minimum variance portfolio is given by:

$$w_g^* = \frac{\sigma_d^2 - \sigma_g \sigma_d \rho_{dg}}{\sigma_d^2 + \sigma_g^2 - 2\sigma_g \sigma_d \rho_{dg}} \quad (5.13)$$

The minimum risk portfolio, while a point on the efficient investment frontier, will not be chosen because higher expected reward can be achieved by a small increase in risk.

The efficient investment frontier

有效投资前沿(The efficient investment frontier):在给定风险水平下最大化预期回报,或者在给定证券组合预期回报下最小化风险得到的投资组合。

The efficient investment frontier is derived by maximizing the expected return, subject to a given risk. Alternatively, it can be derived by minimizing the risk for a given expected rate of return on the portfolio. For a given level of risk, $\overline{\sigma}_P^2$, the efficient weight of the global asset is given by:

$$w_g = \frac{E(r_g)\sigma_d^2 - E(r_d)\sigma_g \sigma_d \rho_{dg}}{E(r_g)(\sigma_d^2 - \sigma_g \sigma_d \rho_{dg}) + E(r_d)(\sigma_g^2 - \sigma_g \sigma_d \rho_{dg})} \quad (5.14)$$

Note that this is the share of the global asset necessary to be on the efficient investment frontier, a purely technical condition. This share maximizes expected portfolio return for each level of risk. Our next step in the optimal efficient portfolio analysis is to maximize the Sharpe "reward to risk" ratio.

The asset allocation decision

Investors may be risk averse, demanding a higher rate of return—a risk premium—for holding risky assets. Risk may be reduced either by converting risky assets into safe assets such as money market assets or by constructing a risky portfolio efficiently, diversifying away unsystematic risk. Consider an investor holding a risky portfolio, P, along with a risk-free asset, T, such as US T-bills. The risky portfolio consists of some domestic and some foreign assets.

For example, a hypothetical portfolio might be as illustrated in Table 5.10.

Table 5.10 A hypothetical complete portfolio

Company	Assets (US $)	Complete portfolio weights	Risky portfolio weights
General Motors, US	50	0.5	0.625
Tiger International	30	0.3	0.375
Portfolios (Portfolio P)	80	0.8	1.0
US T-bills (Portfolio T)	20	0.2	
Complete portfolio (Portfolio C)	100	1.0	

This investor is holding 62.5% of her risky portfolio in General Motors, U.S. and 37.5% of P in Tiger International. Let w represent the holdings in US securities and w^* indicate the holdings of international securities in the risky portfolio, so that $w + w^* = 1$. Thus, $w = 0.625$ and $w^* = 0.375$. The weight of the risky portfolio, P, in the complete portfolio, C, including risk-free investments is denoted by z. Thus the weight of the risk-free asset in the complete portfolio is $1 - z$. T-bills represent 20% of the complete portfolio, or $1 - z = 0.2$, and risky assets 80% of C, or $z = 0.8$. General Motors, US represents 50% of the complete portfolio and Tiger International 30%.

The investor is thus holding a risk-free asset and a bundle of risky assets which can be thought of as one risky asset. In this way, the investor can keep the relative shares of the two risky assets constant in the risky portfolio P, and at the same time reduce risk by selling them off proportionately to acquire more of the risk-free asset, Treasuries.

By changing the distribution of the risky asset relative to the risk-free asset, yet maintaining the mix of assets in the risky portfolio, the investor can reduce the risk of the complete portfolio yet remain on the efficient investment frontier. That is, z can be reduced in C while maintaining w and w^* fixed in P.

Portfolio expected return and risk

Notation:

r_P—Rate of return on the risky portfolio

r_f—Rate of return on the **risk-free asset**

$E(r_P)$—Expected rate of return on the risky portfolio

σ_P—The standard deviation (*volatility*) of the risky portfolio

无风险资产(Risk-free asset): 通常是指短期政府债券。

$E(r_f) = r_f$ —Expected rate of return on the risk-free asset

$E(r_C)$ —Expected rate of return on the complete portfolio

Consequently, with a fraction z of risky assets in the portfolio and $1 - z$ of risk-free assets, the rate of return on the complete portfolio is:

$$r_C = zr_P + (1 - z)r_f \qquad (5.15)$$

Consequently, the expected rate of return on the complete portfolio is:

$$E(r_C) = zE(r_P) + (1 - z)r_f \qquad (5.16)$$

or equivalently,

$$E(r_C) = r_f + z[E(r_P) - r_f] \qquad (5.17)$$

Which has a perfectly natural interpretation: The complete portfolio has a base return equal the risk-free rate, r_f, plus an expected market risk premium, $[E(r_P) - r_f]$ on its exposure to risky assets, z. Risk-averse investors demand a positive market risk premium. The standard deviation of the complete portfolio is indicated by

$$\sigma_C = z\sigma_P \qquad (5.18)$$

since the volatility of the risk free asset is zero. Substituting $z = \dfrac{\sigma_C}{\sigma_P}$ into (5.18), we have:

$$E(r_C) = r_f + \left[\frac{E(r_P) - r_f}{\sigma_P}\right]\sigma_C \qquad (5.19)$$

资本配置线(Capital allocation line) 反映了相对于风险资产的标准差, 预期组合收益的上升。

which is the **capital allocation line (CAL)**. Figure 5.9 plots the capital allocation line depicting the rise in expected portfolio return against the standard deviation of the risky asset. It is the investment opportunity set resulting from different values of z.

Figure 5.9 Capital allocation

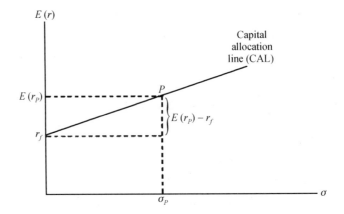

When $z=0$, the CAL begins at r_f and $\sigma_C=0$. When $z=1$, the portfolio has only the risky asset and its standard deviation is σ_P and its expected rate of return $E(r_P)$.

The slope of the investment opportunity schedule is **the Sharpe "reward to risk" ratio**:

$$\frac{E(r_P) - r_f}{\sigma_P} \quad (5.20)$$

夏普回报-风险比率 (The Sharpe "reward to risk" ratio): 又称为回报-波动比率，它是市场风险溢价对风险证券组合标准差的比率。

The slope is also called the reward-to-volatility ratio since it is the ratio of the market risk premium to the standard deviation of the risky portfolio.

Financial leverage (purchases "on margin")

By borrowing, an investor can invest on the CAL line to the right of point P, thereby levering her investment in the risky asset. Our investor has an investment budget of \$100 and borrows, for example, on margin an additional \$50 at the risk free rate, thereby investing \$150 in the risky asset. In this case, $z=1.5$, reflecting a levered position in the risky asset, and $(1-z)=-0.5$ reflecting a short or borrowed position in the risk-free asset.

保证金 (Margin): 在证券市场融资购买证券时，投资者所需缴纳的自备款。

Borrowing to invest in the risky asset requires a margin account with a broker. Purchases "on margin" may not exceed 50% of the purchase value. If the net worth of the margin account is \$100, the investor can borrow up to \$100, for a total investment of \$200. In this case, $z=2$, assets in the account would equal \$200 and liabilities \$100. In practice, an investor can borrow from his or her credit card, deposit this with a broker, and lever the borrowed sum. In most instances, the leveraged borrower cannot borrow at the risk free rate, so therefore faces a lowered CAL line beyond P because she pays a higher interest rate to borrow. That is, there is a kink at the point P.

Risk aversion and asset allocation

Consider the following utility (happiness or choice) function:

$$U = E(r_C) - \frac{A\sigma_C^2}{2} \quad (5.21)$$

This investor enjoys higher expected return, $E(r_C)$, but dislikes higher risk, σ_C. The level of risk aversion is A, a positive number. The higher A, the more risk averse the investor.

Utility maximization: mathematically

The investor's objective is to maximize utility (utils!) by selecting the fraction, z, of the investment budget to be invested in the risky portfolio, P. The expected return and variance of the complete portfolio are $E(r_C) = r_f + z[E(r_P) - r_f]$ and $\sigma_C^2 = z^2 \sigma_P^2$ respectively. To choose the best allocation to the risky asset, we maximize utility, equation (5.21) with respect to z. That is, maximize the quadratic utility function by differentiating with respect to z and setting the result equal to zero:

$$U(z) = E(r_C) - \frac{A\sigma_C^2}{2} = r_f + z[E(r_P) - r_f] - \frac{Az^2\sigma_P^2}{2} \quad (5.22)$$

which yields z^* the optimal share of the risky portfolio in the complete portfolio:

$$z^* = \frac{E(r_P) - r_f}{A\sigma_P^2} \quad (5.23)$$

最优的风险资产持有份额(The optimal share of the risky asset)具有以下特点:随着市场风险溢价的上升而上升;随着风险厌恶程度的上升而下降;随着市场波动率的上升而下降。

The optimal share of the risky asset:
- Rises with increases in the market risk premium, $E(r_P) - r_f$.
- Falls with increases in the degree of risk aversion, A.
- Falls with increases in market volatility, σ_P^2.

Notice that risk aversion, a negative sign attached to the variance of the portfolio, guarantees a maximum rather than a minimum utility.

Utility maximization: graphically

Figure 5.10 illustrates the optimal allocation of assets for a risk averse investor who chooses to hold approximately half the portfolio in the risky asset and half in the safe asset. This optimal allocation yields the highest level of utility (at point C, the tangency of the capital allocation line and the highest indifference curve).

Figure 5.10 The optimal complete and market portfolios

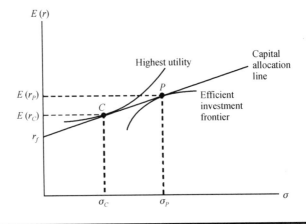

Figure 5.11 illustrates a levered portfolio where the investor has borrowed on margin of approximately 50%. In our example, if the net worth in the account is $100, margin purchases may be up to 50% of the purchase, so the investor can buy "on margin" an additional $100 of the risky asset. The investor would then have $200 on the asset side of the account and $100 on the liability side, yielding $z = 2$.

Figure 5.11 A leveraged complete portfolio

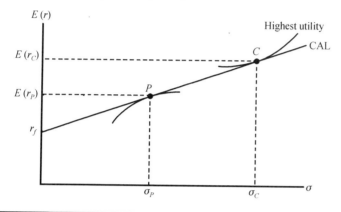

Naturally, a levered portfolio has a greater expected rate of return and a higher risk than an unlevered one.

The tangency of the capital asset line to the investment opportunity frontier at point P yields the highest expected reward-risk ratio. It is therefore the optimal risky portfolio. The optimal risky portfolio is found by the CAL with the steepest slope tangent to the efficient investment frontier at P. The optimal complete portfolio is found by allocating z percent of the portfolio to the risky asset composed of domestic and international assets. The remainder of the optimal complete portfolio, $(1-z)$, is composed of US Treasury bills.

Let's consider an application of the theory of the optimal complete portfolio. The risk-averse investor has the following utility function:

$$U = E(r_C) - 0.5A\sigma_C^2 = E(r_C) - \sigma_C^2 \quad (5.24)$$

Once again, $E(r_C) = r_f + z[E(r_P) - r_f]$. This investor has a degree of risk aversion, $A = 2$, since $0.5A = 1$. We are also given the following data: $E(r_P) = 0.15$, $r_f = 0.05$, $\sigma_P^2 = 0.10$. Consequently, the market risk premium is 10%, as is the variance of the market portfolio. We may directly substitute the data into the optimal share of the risky portfolio of the investor:

$$z^* = \frac{E(r_P) - r_f}{A\sigma_P^2} = \frac{0.15 - 0.05}{2 \times 0.10} = \frac{0.10}{0.20} = \frac{1}{2} \quad (5.25)$$

The optimal solution for this investor is to hold half her portfolio in the optimal risky asset and half in the risk-free asset. The expected return on the complete portfolio is $0.05 + \frac{0.10}{2} = 0.10$ or ten percent. The variance of the complete portfolio is $\left(\frac{1}{2}\right)^2 (0.10) = 0.025$. Its volatility is the square root of 0.025, or 0.158. Finally, the utility of the investor is $0.100 - 0.025 = 0.075$.

The separation property

证券组合选择决策可以分离为两个独立的部分：第一，在 **P** 点选择最优风险组合；第二，个人选择风险组合与无风险资产的最优组合 **C**。这种性质称为**分离性质**(The separation property)。

Portfolio choice is separated into two separate parts: first, selection of the optimum risky portfolio at (P) which is a purely technical consideration and second, the personal investor choice of the best mix of the risky portfolio and the risk-free asset (C). Risk aversion plays no role in the first part; it enters into play in the second part of the portfolio choice. The optimum risky portfolio is the same for all investors, independent of their degree of risk aversion. It is point of tangency of the highest CAL line to the efficient investment portfolio. The second part, construction of the complete portfolio composed of US Treasury bills and the risky portfolio, depends on personal preference, that is, risk tolerance. This separation theorem is due to James Tobin (1958), the 1983 Nobel Laureate in Economics. Since the optimal investment portfolio comprised of domestic and global securities is the same for all investors, a passive index fund of domestic and global securities will usually yield better results than an actively managed fund since the latter have higher management and trading fees.

Determination of the market risk premium

市场风险溢价 (Market risk premium)：市场平均收益与无风险资产收益之差。

共同基金定理 (Mutual fund theorem)：由市场上全部证券所构成的证券组合，其中每一种证券的权重都是依据其市场价值在股票市场总价值中所占的比例确定的。这个证券组合代表了一个市场风险回报有效的基金。

The market portfolio of all assets in the universe, each held in proportion to its market value, represents an efficient fund of risky assets. This is known as the **mutual fund theorem**. A passive index fund holding both domestic and international assets may therefore be viewed by the rational investor as a close approximation to the optimal risky portfolio. In addition, a passive index fund saves management and transaction fees.

Net aggregate lending (borrowing) is zero, viewing Treasuries as the liabilities of the citizens who both issue and hold Treasuries. Some investors are net lenders $z_i < 1$ while others are net borrowers $z_j > 1$, but on aggregate, the average z must equal 1. Therefore, for the average global investor $z = 1$. Since the optimal portfolio of the individual investor with average risk aversion, A^*, is:

$$z^* = \frac{E(r_P) - r_f}{A^* \sigma_P^2} \qquad (5.26)$$

and the average investor has $z = 1$, the risk premium on the market portfolio is proportional to its risk and average risk aversion.

$$E(r_P) - r_f = A^* \sigma_P^2 \qquad (5.27)$$

which states that the market risk premium depends on the average degree of risk aversion times the riskiness of the market portfolio, as measured by its volatility. The average investor's portfolio is thus the market portfolio having expected value $E(r_P)$ and volatility σ_P as illustrated in Figure 5.12.

Figure 5.12   The mutual fund theorem

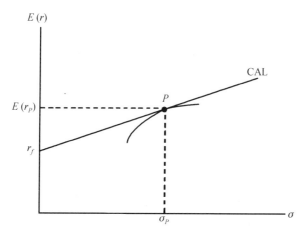

The CAPM (Capital asset pricing model)

The individual contribution of an individual security to the standard deviation of the market portfolio is $\beta_i \sigma_P$. Furthermore, by definition, $\beta_P = 1$ for the market portfolio. The investor's trade-off between risk and return should be the same for the market portfolio and an individual security's per unit contribution to the market portfolio's risk:

$$\frac{E(r_P) - r_f}{\beta_P \sigma_P} = \frac{E(r_i) - r_f}{\beta_i \sigma_P} \qquad (5.28)$$

Noting that $\beta_P = 1$ and re-arranging (5.28), yields the *CAPM's expected return to beta* relationship:

资本资产定价模型 (Capital asset pricing model, CAPM):由美国学者威廉·夏普(William Sharpe)等人在现代投资组合理论的基础上发展起来的一个模型。它是现代金融市场价格理论的支柱,被广泛应用于投资决策和公司理财领域。

$$E(r_i) = r_f + \beta_i[E(r_P) - r_f] \quad (5.29)$$

Which states that the expected return on asset i equals the risk free rate plus the market risk premium times the market risk coefficient, β_i, of the individual security.

Exchange rate volatility in the reward to risk model

The rate of return on the global portfolio is the sum of the rate of appreciation of foreign currency, s, and the rate of return in foreign currency on the foreign asset, r_{g*}, or

$$r_g = s + r_{g*} \quad (5.30)$$

ignoring cross product terms, sr_{g*}, as small.

Consequently, the expected rate of return on the foreign asset in terms of home currency is the expected sum of the percentage appreciation of foreign currency and the rate of return in foreign currency on the foreign asset:

$$E(r_g) = E(s) + E(r_{g*}) \quad (5.31)$$

Thus, the expected rate of return of the risky portfolio may be written:

$$E(r_p) = w_d E(r_d) + w_g[E(s) + E(r_{g*})] \quad (5.32)$$

and the variance of the risky portfolio is

$$\sigma_p^2 = w_d^2 \sigma_d^2 + w_g^2[\sigma_s^2 + \sigma_{r_{g*}}^2 + 2\mathrm{Cov}(s, r_{g*})] + 2w_d w_g \mathrm{Cov}(r_d, s + r_{g*}) \quad (5.33)$$

Where

$$\mathrm{Cov}(r_d, s + r_g) = E[(r_d - E(r_d))((s + r_{g*}) - E(s + r_{g*}))]$$

That is, the expected return on the risky portfolio includes a foreign exchange term as well as the returns in the different currencies. Due to interest rate parity, the expectation is that:

$$\mathrm{Cov}(r_d, s + r_{g*}) > 0$$

while

$$\mathrm{Cov}(s, r_{g*}) < 0$$

also due to IRP.

Our basic result in an international setting is therefore that the optimal share of domestic assets and foreign assets in the risky portfolio is given by

$$z^* = \frac{E(r_p) - r_f}{A\sigma_p^2}$$

$$= \frac{w_d E(r_d) + w_g[E(s) + E(r_{g*})] - r_f}{A\{w_d^2 \sigma_d^2 + w_g^2[\sigma_s^2 + \sigma_{r_{g*}}^2 + 2\mathrm{Cov}(s, r_{g*})] + 2w_d w_g \mathrm{Cov}(r_d, s + r_{g*})\}} \quad (5.34)$$

Changes in the exchange rate play a central role in optimum portfolio allocation. However, according to interest rate parity, the expected change in the exchange rate reflects interest rate differentials, or expected inflation rate differentials. That is:

$$E(s) = E(r_g) - E(r_{g^*})$$

Nevertheless, deviations in exchange rate movements from interest rate differentials or, equivalently, deviations in movements in the exchange rate relative to expected inflation rates raise the issue of currency risk. In reality, the real exchange rate frequently differs from relative purchasing power parity, so that returns on foreign assets converted into home currency can deviate significantly from returns expected from IRP.

Home bias

本国偏好(Home bias): 即使有相对较佳的海外投资机会,人们仍倾向于投资于本国。

Residents seem empirically to have a strong preference for home assets over foreign assets. For instance, an optimal risky portfolio for US residents might have 30% foreign assets, but US residents hold only 12.5%. This puzzle cannot be fully explained by the various reasons offered:

● Asymmetric information and search costs regarding the expected return and volatility of foreign assets.

● Conversion costs due to the bid-ask spread on foreign currencies.

● Hedging against risk from deviations in exchange rates from purchasing power and interest rate parity. Investors may be "short" home goods in their planned consumption baskets, so therefore hold domestic assets primarily as a hedge against unanticipated exchange rate depreciations of their foreign assets.

In the case of China, home bias is absolute since capital controls still exist on individual holdings of assets abroad. The SAFE (State Administered Foreign Exchange) system does not yet permit purchases of foreign exchange for individual investments in securities abroad. As capital controls are liberated, the Chinese investor will diversify some of her holdings of assets toward foreign securities so as to maximize its expected rate of return for a given level of risk, or, equivalently, to minimize its variance for a given expected rate of return. By the same token, world investors will beat a path to the Shanghai and Shenzhen exchanges to diversify their portfolios and take advantage of the high expected return in China. It is hard to predict if inflows will exceed outflows, but that is likely with high returns in China and low returns in Europe and America.

Conclusion

The Markowitz-Sharpe model of risk aversion is a powerful tool for application to the analysis of the optimal portfolio of a client, based upon her degree of risk aversion. It rests solidly on the idea of portfolio diversification, showing that portfolios offer higher returns for given risk than do individual securities, thereby revolutionizing the theory of investment finance. In 1990, Merton Miller, William Sharpe, and Harry Markowitz were jointly awarded the Nobel Prize in Economics for their contributions.

Questions and problems

5.1 The international weighted average cost of capital

Consider the data in of a European IBM subsidiary (in euros). The borrowing rates represent those of the subsidiary in terms of Euros. The parent firm has its headquarters in New York.

Cost of debt	10
Cost of equity	15
Capital structure:	
Debt	30
Equity	70
Corporate tax rate:	
United States	35
Europe	45
Expected inflation:	
United States	3
Europe	2

a. Calculate the weighted average cost of capital (WACC) to IBM in euros.

b. Convert the WACC to US dollars.

5.2 Transfer pricing

Consider the Figure below indicating the marginal costs of production of an intermediate good as well as the marginal cost of marketing the final good. The intermediate good and the marketing are bundled as a joint product, one-to-one. The demand (average revenue) and the marginal revenue curves are drawn as well.

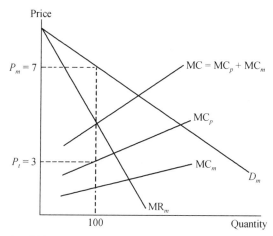

Answer the following:

a. What is the profit maximizing level of sales (units of production)?

b. What will your firm charge the final customer?

c. What is the optimal transfer price that the marketing division will pay for intermediate goods supplied to the marketing division?

5.3 Foreign currency conversion of free cash flows

Consider the data on the U.S. and the U.K. Assume the required real rates of return are the same.

U.S. and U.K. data (percent per annum)	
U.S. inflation rate	3%
U.K. inflation rate	2%
U.S. Treasury	5%
U.K. Treasury	4%
WACC$_£$	15%
WACC$_\$$	

a. If the WACC in US dollars is 15%, what is the WACC in pounds sterling, given the above data? Recall that the conversion rule for the WACC is:

$$\left(\frac{1 + \text{WACC}_£}{1 + \text{WACC}_\$}\right) = \left(\frac{1 + r_{uk}}{1 + r_{us}}\right)$$

and the interest rate parity rule for forecasting the exchange rate is:

$$F = S\left[\frac{(1 + r_{us})}{(1 + r_{uk})}\right]^n$$

Now consider the estimated free cash flows in British pounds of a two-year project by a UK subsidiary.

Method A

- Discount foreign currency flows to the present at the foreign currency discount rate, then convert the NPV in FOREX to home currency at the spot rate.

Year	0	1	2
Free-cash flows (£)	-100	60	70
Present value of cash flow (£)	-100		
NPV (£)			
Spot exchange rate ($/£)	1.77		
NPV ($)			

Method B
- Convert foreign currency cash flows to home currency, and discount to the present at the home currency discount rate.

Year	0	1	2
Free-cash flows (£)	-100	60	70
Exchange rate forecast	1.77		
Free-cash flows ($)	-177		
Present value of cash flow ($)			
NPV ($)			

b. On the basis of the inflation rate, interest rate and weighted average costs of capital ($WACC_\$$), should the US parent firm undertake this project? (i.e. compute the net present value (NPV) in dollars using the two methods.)

5.4 Trade finance

You intend to export 100 computers worth $2,000 each from Miami, FL to Cochabamba, Bolivia. This is the first shipment to a new client, and naturally, you hope to be paid in USD for the computers. Essentially, your options are cash-in-advance, an open account, or a letter of credit. List below the advantages and disadvantages of each, spelling out who bears the counterparty risk in each case.

a. Cash-in-advance

b. An open account

c. A letter of credit

5.5 Trade finance

You have received a confirmed standby letter of credit indicating that Citibank, Nassau will pay you $1,000,000 (one million dollars) every 30 days for one year beginning in 30 days.

a. If you need Bahamian dollars now for payments today, what can you do with the letter of credit immediately?

b. What proceeds in Bahamian dollars would you expect (the Bahamian dollar has since inception been rigidly pegged to the US dollar at one-to-one)?

5.6 Offshore banking

You are the head of new accounts in Citybank, New York, when one fine afternoon Raúl, appears in your office with you bank's external relations officer in México. Raúl happens to have a big suitcase full of money, $100 million, and wishes to deposit the money in Citybank, NY, an Edge Act Bank.

a. How much would Citybank stand to make annually on Raúl $100 million dollars transfer?

b. Would you have to report the deposit? If so, to whom?

c. Apart from reporting requirements, is it worth it to Citybank to take the deposit?

d. Answer the above on the assumption that Raúl instead just wants to transfer the money to his account in Switzerland through Citybank, N.Y.

5.7 Optimal portfolio analysis

Consider the following utility function of an investor:

$$U = E(r_C) - \frac{A\sigma_C^2}{2} = E(r_C) - 2\sigma_C^2$$

Where $E(r_C)$ is the expected rate of return on her complete portfolio (composed of a risky asset and a risk-free asset), σ_C^2 is the variance (the squared standard deviation (volatility) of the complete portfolio), and A is the coefficient of risk aversion. Answer the following:

a. What is the coefficient of risk aversion, A, of this particular investor?

The expected return on the complete portfolio is given by:

$$E(r_C) = r_f + z[E(r_P) - r_f]$$
$$= 0.05 + z(0.15 - 0.05) = 0.05 + 0.1z$$

where z is the proportion of the complete portfolio held in the risky asset, which has an expected rate of return, $E(r_P)$, of 15%, while $(1 - z)$ is the percent held in the risk-free asset, US Treasuries. Treasuries bear a risk-free rate, r_f, of 5%. Furthermore, the variance of the risky asset is given by $\sigma_P^2 = 0.1$ or 10%.

b. Find the optimal proportion of assets held in the risky asset and the proportion held in the risk-free asset.

c. Compute the expected rate of return on the complete portfolio.

d. Compute the variance of the complete portfolio.

e. Compute the level of utility (happiness) of this investor.

5.8 Optimal investment analysis

Consider the following data on a complete portfolio composed of 50% (that is $z = 0.5$) risky assets with $\sigma_p^2 = 0.4$ and $E(r_p) = 0.20$, The complete portfolio thus also has 50% risk-free assets with certain return 5%, that is 0.05. Answer the following:

a. What is the expected rate of return on the complete portfolio?
b. What is the variance of the complete portfolio?
c. What is the standard deviation of the complete portfolio (its volatility)?

5.9 Double marginalization

A firm monopolizing a market would set marginal cost equal to marginal revenue to maximize its profits, as shown below.

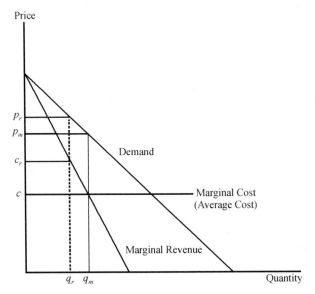

Demonstrate the following proposition:

"If the firm sold instead to a downstream retailer at a transfer price above c, the retailer would charge a higher price, p_r, and sell a lower quantity, q_r, thereby reducing total profits."

This phenomenon is known as "double marginalization", providing an incentive for the upstream producer to acquire the downstream retailer, thereby maximizing profits. Coca-cola and Pepsi are both attempting to acquire their downstream bottlers.

References and suggested reading

Abdallah, Wagdy (2004), *Critical Concerns in Transfer Pricing and*

Practice, Westport, CN, Praeger.

Al-Eryani, Mohammed F., Pervaiz Alam, and Syed H. Akhter (1990), "Transfer Pricing Determinants of U. S. Multinationals," *Journal of International Business Studies*, 21(3): 409–425.

Adler, Michael (1974), "The Cost of Capital and Valuation of a Two-Country Firm," *Journal of Finance*, 29(1): 119–132.

Aliber, Robert Z. (1980), "The Integration of the Offshore and the Domestic Banking System," *Journal of Monetary Economics*, 6(4): 509–526.

Anderson, Ronald (2002), "Capital Structure, Firm Liquidity, and Growth," in *Firms' Investment and Finance Decision: Theory and Empirical Methodology*, Cheltenham, UK; Northhampton, MA: Edward Elgar.

Azzara, Thomas (2003), *Tax Havens of The World*, New Providence Press.

Bangs, David H. Jr. (1998), *The Business Plan*, Chicago: Upstart Publishing, Inc.

Barrett, Edgar M. (1977), "The Case of the Tangled Transfer Price," *Harvard Business Review*, 55(3): 20–36.

Bradshaw, Mark, Brian Bushee, and Gregory Miller (2004), "Accounting Choice, Home Bias, and U.S. Investment in Non-U.S. Firms," *Journal of Accounting Research*, 42(5): 795–841.

Cumming, Douglas (2005), "Capital Structure in Venture Finance," *Journal of Corporate Finance*, 11(3): 550–585.

Dixit, Avinash, Susan Skeath and David H. Reiley, Jr. (2009), *Games of Strategy*, 3rd edition, New York and London: W. W. Norton and Co.

Dye, Ronald and Sri Sridhar (2005), "Moral Hazard Severity and Contract Design," *RAND Journal of Economics*, 36(1): 78–92.

Eckbo, Espen B. (1983), "Horizontal Mergers, Collusion and Stockholder Wealth," *Journal of Financial Economics*, 11(2): 241–276.

Eiteman, David K., Arthur I. Stonehill, and Michael H. Moffett (2000), "Principles of Multinational Taxation," in *Multinational Business Finance*, 10th ed., Reading MA: Addison-Wesley Publishing Company.

Emery, Douglas, R., John D. Finnerty, and John D. Stove (1998), *Principles of Financial Management*, Upper Saddle River NJ: Prentice Hall.

Ganguin, Blaise (2005), *Fundamentals of Corporate Credit Analysis*, New York: McGraw-Hill.

Ghauri, Pervez and Peter Buckley (2003), "International Mergers and Acquisitions: Past, Present, and Future," in *Advances in Mergers and Acquisitions*, Volume 2, Amsterdam: Boston and Oxford Elsevier Science.

Grauer, Robert R., and Nils Hakansson (1987), "Gains from International Diversification: 1968–1985 Returns on Portfolios of Stocks and Bonds," *Journal of Finance*, 42(3): 721–739.

Gup, Benton (2004), *Too Big to Fail: Policies and Practices in Government Bailouts*, Westport, CT: Praeger.

Harris, Milton and Artur Raviv (1991), "The Theory of Capital Structure," *Journal of Finance*, 46 (1): 297–355.

Harvey, Campbell R. (1991), "The World Price of Covariance Risk," *Journal of Finance*, 66(1): 111–158.

Haugen, Robert A., and Lemma W. Senbet (1988), "Bankruptcy and Agency Costs: Their Significance to the Theory of Optimal Capital Structure," *Journal of Financial and Quantitative Analysis*, 2(3): 73–86.

Ioannou, Lori (1995), "Taxing Issues," *International Business*, 8(3): 44–45.

Isenbergh, Joseph (2002), *International Taxation: U. S. Taxation of Foreign Persons and Foreign Income*, New York: Aspen Publishers.

Jensen, Michael C. (1986), "Agency Costs of Free Cash Flow, Corporate Finance, and Takeovers," *American Economic Review*, 76(2):323–330.

Kane, Edward (1987), "Competitive Financial Re-regulations: An International Perspective," in *Threats to International Financial Stability*, R. Portes and A. Swoboda, eds., London: Cambridge University Press.

Keen, Michael (2004), "Pareto-efficient International Taxation." *American Economic Review*, 94(1): 259–275.

Levich, Richard M. (1990), "The Euromarkets After 1992," in *European Banking in the 1990s*, J. Dermine, ed., Oxford: Basil Blackwell.

Lowengrub, Paul and Michael Melvin (2002), "Before and After International Cross-listing: An Intraday Examination of Volume and Volatility," *Journal of International Financial Markets, Institutions, and Money*, 12(2): 139–155.

Marino, Anthony and John Matsusaka, (2005), "Decision Processes, Agency Problems, and Information: An Economic Analysis of Capital Budgeting Procedures," *Review of Financial Studies*, 18(1): 301–325.

Markowitz, Harry (1952), "Portfolio Selection," *Journal of Finance*, 7 (1): 77–91.

Maroney, Neal, Naka Atsuyuki and Theresia Wansi (2004), "Changing Risk, Return, and Leverage: The 1997 Asian Financial Crisis," *Journal of Financial and Quantitative Analysis*, 39(1): 143–166.

Masson, Dubos, J. (1990), "Planning and Forecasting of Cash Flows for the Multinational Firm: International Cash Management," *Advances in Financial Planning and Forecasting*, 4(2): 195–222.

Meyers, Stewart C. (1976), "A Framework for Evaluating Mergers," in Stewart C. Meyers, ed., *Modern Developments in Financial Management*, New York: Praeger.

Miller, Merton (1977), "Debt and Taxes," *Journal of Finance*, 32(2): 261-275.

Modigliani, Franco, and Merton H. Miller (1958), "The Cost of Capital, Corporation Finance, and the Theory of Investment," *American Economic Review*, 48(3): 261-298.

Modigliani, Franco, and Merton H. Miller (1963), "Corporate Income Taxes and the Cost of Capital: A Correction," *American Economic Review*, 53(3): 433-443.

Moffett, Michael H., and Arthur Stonehill (1989), "International Banking Facilities Revisited," *Journal of International Financial Management and Accounting*, 1(1): 88-103.

Mork, Randall, Andrei Schleifer, and Robert W. Vishney (1990), "Do Managerial Objectives Drive Bad Acquisitions," *Journal of Finance*, 45(1): 31-48.

OECD (2005), *E-commerce: Transfer Pricing and Business Profits Taxation*, Paris: Organization for Economic Cooperation & Development.

Ostro-Landau, Nilly (1995), "Avoiding the Global Tax Web," *International Business*, 8(9): 12.

Plasschaert, S. R. F. (1985), "Transfer Pricing Problems in Developing Countries," in *Multinationals and Transfer Pricing*, A. M. Rugman and L. Eden, eds., New York: St. Martins Press, 247-266.

Ross, Stephen A., Randolph W. Westerfield, and Jeffrey F. Jaffe (2005), *Corporate Finance*, 3rd ed. Irwin IL: McGraw-Hill, Chapters 15-16, 415-492.

Roll, Richard, and Stephen A. Ross (1984), "The Arbitrage Pricing Theory Approach to Strategic Portfolio Planning," *Financial Analysts Journal*, 40(3): 14-26.

Ross, Stephen A. (1974), "Return, Risk and Arbitrage," in Friend and Bicksler, eds., *Risk and Return in Finance*, New York: Heath Lexington.

Solnick Bruno, and B. Noetzlin (1982), "Optimal International Asset Allocation," *Journal of Portfolio Management*, 9(1):11-21.

Salvatore, Dominick (1996), *Managerial Economics in a Global Economy*, 3rd edition, New York: McGraw-Hill, Inc.

Sharpe, William F. (1964), "Capital Asset Prices: A Theory of Market Equilibrium Under Risk," *Journal of Finance*, 19(3): 425-442.

Shirreff, David (2004), *Dealing with Financial Risk*, New York:

Bloomberg Press.

Soenen, L. A., and Raj Aggarwal (1987), "Corporate Foreign Exchange and Cash Management Practice," *Journal of Cash Management*, 7(2): 62-64.

Srinivsan, VenKat, and Yong H. Kim (1986), "Payments Netting in International Cash Management: A Network Optimization Approach," *Journal of International Business Studies*, 17(2): 1-20.

Stillman, R. (1983), "Examining Antitrust Policy toward Horizontal Mergers," *Journal of Financial Economics*, 11(2): 225-240.

Stultz, Rene M. (1995), "Globalization of Capital Markets and the Cost of Capital: The Case of Nestlé," *Journal of Applied Corporate Finance*, 8(3): 30-38.

Tobin, James (1958), "Liquidity Preference as Behavior Towards Risk," *Review of Economic Studies*, 26(1): 65-86.

Yunker, Penelope J. (1983), "A Survey of Subsidiary Autonomy, Performance Evaluation and Transfer Pricing in Multinational Corporations," *Columbia Journal of World Business*, 18(3): 51-64.

Yunker, Penelope J. (1982), *Transfer Pricing and Performance Evaluation in Multinational Corporations: A Survey Study*, New York: Praeger.

CHAPTER 6 International Financial Scams and Swindles 国际金融欺诈与骗局

Pyramids: an international perspective

Financial history is full of **Ponzi schemes**, where pyramids of investors invest in notes with no or scant underlying assets. The scheme Carlo Ponzi devised in 1919 is today called a "Ponzi Pyramid." In December, Mr. Ponzi initiated an investment scheme in Boston, establishing his business as The Security Exchange Company promising 50% interest in ninety days on his notes. The Ponzi note declared:

> **FYI: The Ponzi Note**
>
> The Securities Exchange Company, for and in consideration of the sum of exactly $1,000 of which receipt is hereby acknowledged, agrees to pay to the order of _____, upon presentation of this voucher at ninety days from date, the sum of exactly $1,500 at the company's office, 27 School Street, room 227, or at any bank. The Securities Exchange Company, Per Charles Ponzi.
>
> Source: Mark C. Knutson(1996).

Hundreds of initial investors purchased the Ponzi notes. At first, many were redeemed at maturity, some even before after 45 days, and many were rolled over. The word got out. New investors beat a path to his door, their cash permitting redemption of his first issues. He had a gimmick that attracted gullible investors, arguing that he could buy international postal reply coupons in Italy and then sell them to the US post office for five times what he paid. According to Ponzi, the arbitrage opportunity was due to misalignment of postal exchange rates. He claimed to cash in the stamps, thus profiting up to 400%. After fees, he could "plausibly" pay 50% quarterly yet keep about 200% in profits, so he said.

Indeed, he kept a few postal coupons on hand in his office to show to investors. With the money he collected from old and new investors, he repaid those that redeemed their principal plus the promised 50% return, a classic pyramid scheme with no underlying assets. Naturally, the initial investors promoted the scheme by word of mouth. It rapidly mushroomed.

There is always one problem with Ponzi schemes: The last investors who are brought into the scheme ultimately find that there are not enough new investors since the flow of new investment must increase exponentially. The cash flow stops—leaving them holding worthless Ponzi notes. A run to redeem the notes takes place, forcing insolvency bankruptcy. Let's take a simple example of an initial investment in a 3 month Ponzi note of $1,000, which we will rollover in each period. The quarterly interest rate is 50%, equivalent to an annual rate of 406%. For the sake of argument, suppose we rollover the Ponzi note for two years, assuming the scheme has not collapsed by then. Table 6.1 illustrates the growth in the liabilities of the Ponzi scheme were the initial $1,000 rolled over every three months into new Ponzi notes.

Table 6.1 A hypothetical Ponzi game with rollover at a quarterly rate of return of 50%

	Initial Investment $1,000	Principal	Interest
3 months	$1,500	$1,000	$500
6 months	$2,250	$1,500	$750
9 months	$3,375	$2,250	$1,125
12 months	$5,063	$3,375	$1,688
15 months	$7,594	$5,063	$2,531
18 months	$11,391	$7,594	$3,797
21 months	$17,086	$11,391	$5,695
24 months	$25,629	$17,086	$8,543

Within two years, Ponzi would be liable for $25,639 to repay both principal and interest on the initial $1,000 investment. Since there is no underlying asset yielding a positive return, the rate of growth of new deposits would have to be over 400% a year, that is $[(1.5)^4 - 1]$, for Ponzi to be able to redeem his notes. New investments would have to more than quintuple yearly. For this reason, Ponzi schemes usually collapse within a year.

Bernie Madoff's Ponzi game lasted much longer—over 40 years—in part, because the promised rate of return was between 1 and 2 percent per month, between 12.7% and 26.8% per annum respectively. If the Madoff fund could grow at 25% per year, it could sustain such promised rates of return. His reputation grew over the years and he served as Chairman of the Board of the NASDAQ.

In the case of Carlo Ponzi, the cash flow was stopped after nine months by an investigation by the District Attorney of Boston, even though Ponzi had not defaulted on a single note. The scheme broke down in July 1920 when he was ordered not to take any new deposits, pending the results of the investigation. Consider a $1,000 Ponzi note investment bearing 50% in three months. If no more Ponzi investments were made, at the end of three months, Ponzi would pay $500 dollars in interest. At the end of six months, he would pay the remaining $500, thus being insolvent since he has no underlying investments. He would have to default on the initial note. Clearly, new investors are required at an increasing rate to pay interest and redemptions by previous investors.

In general, assuming a constant interest rate, r, **the no Ponzi game (NPG) condition** requires that debt not grow faster than the rate of interest on the debt, or:

$$\lim_{t \to \infty} D(t) e^{-rt} = 0 \qquad (6.1)$$

无庞氏骗局条件 [No Ponzi game (NPG) condition]:负债的增长率低于负债的利率。

If debt is growing at a faster rate than the interest rate, interest is being paid by the new debt and the debt is not sustainable. If $D(t) = D_0 e^{gt}$, $\lim_{t \to \infty} D_0 e^{(g-r)t} = 0$ when $g < r$.

Why would so many people invest in a scheme that ultimately had to collapse? The reason seems to be that the early investors did see great returns on their money. Those in early on a speculative bubble gain by cashing out early. It was, however, the age-old pyramid scheme. Since investors had their notes redeemed until the investigation, not a single complaint had been filed.

On July 26, 1920, Ponzi's house of cards collapsed, The Boston District Attorney ordered Ponzi to suspend taking in new investments until an auditor examined his books. This was the death knoll to the Ponzi game since there were no underlying investments. The public continued to support Ponzi until August 10, 1920, since he attempted to pay off an investor run from his cash deposits in banks. On August 10, the auditors, banks, and newspapers declared that Ponzi was bankrupt. A final audit of his books concluded that he had taken in enough funds to buy approximately 180,000,000 postal coupons, of which they could only confirm the purchase of two. On the witness stand in his trial, Ponzi discussed locations of various safety deposit boxes in the U.S., deposits overseas, and responded evasively to questions about his solvency. Miss Lucy Mell, his 18 year old assistant office manager, testified that she only had knowledge of transactions within the office, not of Ponzi's outside dealings. When asked if there were any postal reply coupons in the office, she replied "Yes, one or two for samples." (www.mark-knutson.com) Ponzi's family reported that his attorneys were preparing a defense of "financial dementia." At the trial, Charles Rittenhouse, an accountant employed by the receivers of Ponzi's estate, testified that $9,582,591 was invested in Ponzi's scheme reflecting notes with a face value of $14,374,755. When the business shut down, $4,263,652 of investments were outstanding, with a face value of $6,396,353.

Imposing a maximum five year sentence for a mail fraud count, Judge Hale added these words: "The defendant conceived a scheme which on his counsel's admission did defraud men and women. It will not do to have the public, the world, understand that such a scheme as his through the United States' instrumentality could be carried out without substantial punishment." The same issue of "substantial punishment" arises in the cases of Enron, Parmalat, Vivendi, BCCI, Barings, WorldCom, and Tyco, to name some of more recent financial abuses. After three and a half years in prison, Ponzi was sentenced to an additional seven to nine years by Massachusetts's authorities. He was released on $14,000 bond pending an appeal. He turned up in Jacksonville, Florida under the assumed name of Charles Borelli and immediately launched a pyramid land scheme. He purchased land at $16 an acre, subdividing it into twenty-three lots, and sold each lot at $10 apiece. Ponzi promised investors that their initial $10 investment would translate into millions of dollars in just two years. Much of the land was underwater and worthless marsh or swamp land. The land boom in Florida was petering out, too late to rescue Ponzi. In February 1926 the Duval County Grand Jury returned a four count indictment against Ponzi and his *Charpon, Florida Land Syndicate*. He was charged with violating Florida regulations for conducting business as a trust, offering securities for sale without filing a declaration of trust, selling units of indebtedness without a permit from the State Controller, and doing real-estate business without paying a $150 license fee. Once again, he jumped bail on June 3, 1926 and ran to Texas. He was captured on June 28th in the port of New Orleans while fleeing to Italy and sent back to Boston to complete his jail term. After seven years, Ponzi was released on good behavior and deported to Italy on October 7, 1934. Back in Rome, Benito Mussolini offered him a position with Italy's new national airline. He served as the Rio de Janeiro branch manager from 1939 to 1942. The airline failed during WWII and Ponzi was unemployed. He passed away January 15, 1949 in a Rio de Janeiro charity ward at the age of 67. (www. mark-knutson. com)

Parmalat(a multi-national Italian dairy and food corporation)

Parmalat, though having underlying assets and operations, ultimately sought Ponzi finance. As Gianfranco Tabasso of the EACT Payment Commission poignantly remarks: "In situations like Parmalat, it is evident how critically important they (treasurers and CFOs) are in detecting and perpetrating frauds. A serious corporate fraud cannot be carried out without the connivance of the treasurer and the CFO. Put another way, the treasurer and the CFO are more important than internal audit and accounting, in the detection of possible frauds, even when perpetrators are CEOs, board members, or other top brass." (*op. cit.*, 25)

What really defines a Ponzi scheme? Gianfranco Tabasso of the EACT Payment Commission notes: "This is the second time in a hundred years that a Parmesan has cheated American investors. In the early 1920s, Carlo Ponzi did it in Boston with the 'postal coupon scheme' and became so famous that Ponzi Games and Ponzi Finance are in all university textbooks and Ponzi has his own dedicated website www. mark-knutson. com. Carlo Ponzi's was a pure high-risk financial scheme with no underlying assets. Parmalat is a dairy and food company, with real assets, which produces and sells real goods, in a sector traditionally considered low risk. Carlo Ponzi operated his scheme alone from a central office of two rooms attended by twelve clerks. Parmalat is a multibillion dollar multinational listed on the Milan Stock Exchange which has over 250 companies around the world; its boss, Calisto Tanzi had lots of interested helpers, bankers, auditors, family, managers, tax and legal professionals, and consultants.

Carlo Ponzi's swindle lasted nine months before it was discovered; Parmalat's went on for more than ten years, an unbelievable length of time in a world where listed companies are subject to corporate governance, reporting, anti-money laundering regulations, market abuse legislation, auditing, external regulations and rating companies. Banks place bonds on the market and earn commission, corporations collect the money and don't have to find new shareholders and answer embarrassing questions. Only investors, who lay out capital but remain far away from the game, are at risk." (*op. cit.*, pp. 21–22) But serious problems started right after the Parmalat stock listing, so Tonna (Parmalat's CFO who ran Parmalat Finanziaria, the holding company) created a network of financial companies, all based in fiscal paradises—tax havens. They would be used to issue bonds, channel funds back and forth, create firewalls and, last but not least, concoct fake balance sheets to shore up the consolidated balance sheet and sell nearly EUR 8 billion of new Parmalat bonds.

Parmalat started in 1962 when Calisto Tanzi inherited a small ham factory from his father near Parma. At 22, he opened a pasteurization plant selling milk for the first time in Tetrapack triangular cartons. The milk cartons were a success: sales grew rapidly from EUR 100,000 in 1962 to 50 million in 1970. It was declared insolvent in December 2003, with Enrico Bondi replacing Calisto Tanzi and later becoming official liquidator. There were: "Public attorneys pursuing various kinds of crimes and misdemeanors, from money laundering to collusion in fraud, false communication to markets, insider trading, market abuse, obstruction of justice etc. It appears almost all the money went to cover operating losses, particularly in South America, but ... some of it was diverted to the family's private businesses and to the personal accounts of family members, top managers and various professionals who were privy to and participated in the Parmalat fraud." (*op. cit.*, p. 23)

庞氏融资(Ponzi finance):在一个经营单位的利息支付超过其营业所得的现金流时,采用发行新债的办法来偿还旧债的一种金融活动。

"**Ponzi finance**" is defined by Charles Kindleberger (1989) "as a type of financial activity engaged in when interest charges of a business unit exceeds cash flows from operations ... with the repayment of debt with the issuance of new debt."

Clearly, an unintentionally unsuccessful operation could have negative cash flow and thus not be able to pay interest charges. To constitute the payment of old debt from the issue of new debt must be present. This was an aspect common to both the Ponzi game and the Parmalat fraud, though the latter had real operations. WorldCom executives were also involved in borrowing to repurchase stock, but were subject to margin calls they ultimately could not meet. Stocks in WorldCom were collateral for the debt, but triggered the margin calls when they lost value.

Lest we think that Ponzi schemes are a thing of the past, "Investors ... had allocated at least $115 million to Mr. Wright's hedge-fund firm, International Management Associates LLC. Over the prior seven years, which included the worst bear market since the Great Depression, Mr. Wright had reported average annual returns of more than 27% ... The Securities and Exchange Commission and International Management investors filed separate lawsuits against Mr. Wright, accusing him of fraud. The SEC estimates that Mr. Wright, who handled International Management's investments, managed somewhere between $115 million and $185 million of client money. After more than two weeks of searching, the hedge fund's court-appointed receiver and the SEC have found only about $150,000 of it ... in two Ameritrade accounts." Kirk S. Wright, an African American, "... may have taken advantage of the city's black professionals," including "... successful black professionals from Atlanta, and former football players" from the Denver Broncos and the Tennessee Titans American football teams (*The Wall Street Journal*, March 9, 2006: A1, A12). Two Atlanta anesthesiologists turned hedge-fund partners claim they were also duped out of $1.5 million by Wright. They and others were recruited for the aggressive marketing of the hedge fund, which seems not to have had any underlying investments. "In 2004, it hired Thomas H. Birk, a Los Angeles-based salesman who had previously raised money for several major brokerage firms. Mr. Birk, who is white, would troll Western golf courses talking up Mr. Wright's investment record. ... Mr. Birk eventually raised more than $10 million." (*op. cit.*, A12) "Mr. Wright is missing," although his lawyer says that "he speaks to him regularly on the phone ... Regulators believe that virtually all the assets of the funds have been dissipated. Mr. Wright's older brother ... has urged his brother to turn himself in." (*op. cit.*, A12) Carlo Ponzi must be smiling from his grave in Brazil.

The Bernie Madoff Ponzi Game

The Madoff Ponzi game is remarkable both in terms of its longevity and its shrewdness. The scheme began as *Bernard L. Madoff Investment Securities LLC*, founded in 1960, and came to a dramatic end during the 2008 financial crisis. Bernie Madoff reportedly told his sons on December

10, 2008 that he was struggling to meet $7 billion in redemption requests and that his hedge fund was "One big lie, a giant Ponzi game." Mark and Andrew turned their father in on December 11, 2008, when Bernie was arrested by the FBI. He is now serving a federal prison sentence of 150 years in North Carolina. Trustee Irving Picard, the lawyer in charge of recovering assets for Madoff's investors, is aggressively trying to "claw back" monies from those who exited early with profits or who served as "feeder" funds to the Madoff scheme. One of his sons, Mark, committed suicide in December 2010. Bernie Madoff's lavish lifestyle has come to a humbling end, leaving his family and reputation in tatters.

The U.S. Securities and Exchange Commission (SEC) is, in principle, charged with uncovering securities fraud to protect investors. In 1999, Harry Markopolos, a financial analyst, was asked by a managing partner at *Rampart*, Dave Fraley, to design a financial product that would, like Madoff's, consistently deliver net returns of 1–2 percent a month. Markopolos later said that he knew within five minutes that Madoff's numbers didn't add up—always rising in a volatile market. It took him another four hours to prove that the reported returns could have only been obtained through fraud, in particular, a Ponzi game. In 1999, Harry Markopolos informed the SEC that he believed it was legally and mathematically impossible to achieve the gains that Madoff claimed. He also filed a formal complaint with the Boston office of the SEC in the spring of 2000. Markopolos then sent a more detailed submission to the SEC a year later. Finally, Markopolos sent a 21-page memo in November 2005 to SEC regulators, entitled "The World's Largest Hedge Fund is a Fraud." It outlined 30 red flags that alleged Madoff's returns could not possibly be legitimate. Markopolos reported to the branch chief of the SEC's New York office, to whom he gave his 21-page report, claiming that Madoff was paying off old investors with money from new investors. However, the SEC's New York chief approved an internal memo in November, 2007 to close an SEC investigation of Madoff without bringing any claim. The SEC did nothing until Madoff turned himself in to the FBI, despite ten years of warnings by Markopolos. George Stigler, Nobel Laureate in 1982, was right: the regulators are "captured" by those they regulate!

Two back officers in Madoff's operation created false trading reports to support the returns claimed to each customer, including an initial false trade and the fictitious closing trade to fit the client's statement. Trades were backdated and account statements manipulated.

In his March 2009 guilty plea, Madoff admitted that his scheme was to deposit client money into a Chase account, rather than invest it. When clients wanted to redeem their money, "I used the money in the Chase Manhattan bank account ... to pay the requested funds." In the meantime, he purchased many homes, a boat, a watch collection and nice cars.

Size of loss to investors

About $36 billion was invested into the Madoff scam, returning $18 billion to investors, with $18 billion missing. Half of Madoff's investors earned more than their investment. The withdrawal amounts in the final six years were subject to "clawback" or return of money lawsuits filed by trustee Irving Picard. Of the total amount, Picard said that the total amounts owed to customers were $57 billion, of which $17.3 billion was actually invested by the customers, $7.6 billion has been recovered, but pending lawsuits, only $2.6 billion would be available to repay victims. If all the recovered funds are returned to those who lost, their net loss would be just under $10 billion. The US Internal Revenue Service ruled that investors' capital loss in this and other fraudulent investment schemes can be treated as a business loss for tax purposes. This will allow the victims to claim them as net operating losses, to reduce their tax liability if they have income tax liabilities otherwise.

Affinity fraud

同族诈骗 (Affinity fraud) 往往针对具有相同种族、相同宗教信仰或其他相同背景的人。

Madoff was a prominent philanthropist, who served on boards of non-profit institutions—many of which entrusted his firm with their endowments. The collapse and freeze of his personal and business assets, and those of his firm pushed charitable foundations into bankuptcy, such as the *Chais Family Foundation*, the *Robert I. Lappin Charitable Foundation*, the *Picower Foundation*, and the *JEHT Foundation*. Sheryl Weinstein, former chief financial officer of *Hadassah*, called Madoff a "beast" at his sentencing hearing.

According to the *New York Post*, Madoff "worked the so-called 'Jewish circuit' of well-heeled Jews he met at country clubs on Long Island and in Palm Beach." In this type of affinity fraud—taking advantage of your own ethnic, religious, or related group members—he also defrauded institutions such as *Yeshiva University*, *Kehilath Jeshurun Synagogue*, the

Maimonides School, *Ramaz* and the *SAR Academy*.

Ponzi games are like mushrooms after the heavy rains, they just pop up miraculously. While the SEC has now begun to scrutinize them more vigorously, Ponzi games are part of the fabric of humankind, offering quick riches to aspiring "Madoffs" that prey upon gullible investors.

In his testimony to the U.S. congress, Markopoulus said: "My experiences with other SEC officials proved to be a systemic disappointment and led me to conclude that the SEC securities' lawyers, if only through their investigative ineptitude and financial illiteracy, colluded to maintain large frauds such as the one to which Madoff later confessed." Furthermore, "Government has coddled, accepted, and ignored White-collar crime for too long," he testified to congress, "It is time the nation woke up and realized that it's not the armed robbers or drug dealers who cause the most economic harm, it's the white collar criminals living in the most expensive homes who have the most impressive resumes who harm us the most. They steal our pensions, bankrupt our companies, and destroy thousands of jobs, ruining countless lives."

Madoff's scheme stands out in its longevity. At its inception, Madoff may have developed a trading platform that was developed further by the NASDAQ. Surely, by not promising exorbitant returns, the rate at which he needed to recruit new money was not nearly so high as in Carlo Ponzi's case. A 1% monthly rate of return would yield 12.8% per annum, 1.5% produces an annual yield of 19.6%, while a 2% monthly rate yields 26.8% per annum. By keeping returns below 2% and increasing new investor's monies by 25% per year, Madoff could satisfy redemptions without any underlying investment. During the 2008 financial crisis, redemption requests rose significantly at all hedge funds, revealing Madoff's scheme and putting him into bankruptcy and jail.

Other affinity Ponzi games

Affinity frauds can target any group of people who take pride in their shared characteristics, whether they are religious, ethnic, or professional.

The "gimmick": Ponzi games typically have a gimmick that tricks gullible investors who are unable or unwilling to do due diligence. Here are some stories they tell potential investors:

Ponzi supposedly arbitraged Italian international reply postage coupons, realizing over 400% profits since the exchange rate was misaligned.

Scott Rothstein, a Fort Lauderdale lawyer, sold fictitious structured legal settlements that promised the holder a stream of cash flow from the structured settlement. He is currently serving a 50-year prison sentence.

Neil Shapiro, Miami, fraudulently claimed to arbitrage food and commodities in bulk, buying low and selling high in different regions of the United States. He is currently serving a 20-year sentence.

The MMM corporation of Russia promised high returns on their investments, much like Ponzi, only to go bankrupt, leaving thousands of investors holding worthless notes.

Consolidated General, Inc. sent you beads to braid into jewelry which they would buy back if you didn't sell them at a good price.

A nationwide scheme primarily targeted African-American churches and raised at least $3 million from over 1,000 churches, believing they would receive large sums of money from the investments—between 7% and 30% annually, from building projects in the US.

Corporate governance failures

Adam Smith made an interesting observation concerning **the principal-agent problem**:

委托–代理问题 (Principal-agent problem)：因为委托人和代理人的目标不一致和信息不对称而导致的委托人利益受损的情况。

> **Applying the Concept**: Adam Smith on the Principal-Agent Problem
>
> The directors of such (joint stock) companies, however, being the managers rather of other people's money than of their own, it cannot well be expected that they should watch over it with the same anxious vigilance with which the partners in a private copartnery frequently watch over their own. Like the stewards of a rich man, they are apt to consider attention to small matters as not for their master's honour, and very easily give themselves a dispensation from having it. Negligence and profusion, therefore, must always prevail, more or less, in the management of the affairs of such a company.
>
> Source: Adam Smith (1776), *An Inquiry into the Nature and Causes of the Wealth of Nations*, London: W. Strahan and T. Cadell. Ch.1, "Of the Expences of the Sovereign or Commonwealth".

It is appropriate to begin discussion of corporate governance failures with Smith's perceptive observation.

United Airlines

Unsecured creditors and executives at the United Airlines Corporation agreed to a deal in which 400 executives will be awarded 10 million shares, 8% of the number to be issued in total upon emergence from bankruptcy. UAL stakeholders, including employees have on the other hand been asked to make great sacrifices, for example to their pension plan. Elizabeth Warren, Professor at Harvard Law School said on January 12, 2005: "Chapter 11 was traditionally about sharing the pain, but now it is more a game of feast and famine—starving the shareholders and creditors while the management team grows fat on big salaries." Annual salaries for the top eight UAL executives will total $3.5 million when UAL exits bankruptcy, rounded up by target bonuses equal from 55 to 100 percent of salary, depending on the executive. There are also $1.39 million in retention bonuses earmarked for seven top executives. Ms. Warren continues: "The lawyers and management team are running the show. Shareholders are out of the picture and creditors are often unsure about the overall financial stability of the company. That is a perfect set of circumstances for the management to extract much higher compensation than they would get if other people were competing for those management jobs." As Ms. Morgenstern, the *New York Times* journalist put it: "Got your airsickness bag handy?" (*The New York Times*, January 15, 2006) Let's now look back on corporate scandals. Keep your airsickness bag handy.

Enron

安然公司（Enron）于2001年12月2日正式破产,这是美国当时最大的一宗商业破产案。

Enron filed for bankruptcy on December 2, 2001. Its accountant, Arthur Andersen, LLP, went bankrupt. Enron is a story of one of the largest business failures of its time in the United States. To call it a failure of governance would be an understatement. The story has many facets:

1. Fraudulent accounting which escaped taxes, booked loans as profits and estimates of future profits as current income from deals, and moved losses off the books, recording them as operational profits.

2. The creation of the Raptors, four private investment partners, was managed by Andrew Fastow, the CFO of Enron, a clear conflict of interest. These partnerships drained profits from Enron and moved losses off the Enron books. The partnerships were an accounting trick to appear to book profits as a hedge. However, they were funded by Enron shares, so did not provide the insurance of a hedge.

3. The large scale shredding and forging of documents, and deletion of e-mails that might compromise Enron in a SEC investigation.

4. Insider trading with the early selling of shares for "estate planning" by CEO Jeffrey K. Skilling, who was indeed found guilty of insider trading.

5. The misleading of employees and investors as to the true financial condition of Enron.

6. The "locking in" or freezing of the employees' right to sell Enron shares from their pensions in an effort to keep its price from falling further.

7. The payments of large bonuses to executives based on improper accounting reports of earnings.

Accounting and legal firms knowingly approved illegal accounting and business practices, including conflict of interest partnerships, the Raptors in particular. David D. Duncan, head of the Andersen audit team went along with the deals provided that Enron's board of directors approve them. (*The Washington Post*, July 30, 2002)

In 2000, Enron was burning cash at a rate of $700 million a year. It is difficult to sustain negative cash flow at this rate. It declared bankruptcy in December 2001. When the Raptor's losses and accounting errors (for example a $1.2 billion equity loss) came to light, Enron's shares sank. In a Hyatt ballroom filled with several thousand Enron employees, Kenneth Lay is quoted: "Let me say right up front, I am absolutely heartbroken about what's happened. Many of you were a lot wealthier six to nine months ago, are now concerned about the college education for your kids, maybe the mortgage on your house, maybe your retirement, and for that I am incredibly sorry. But we are going to get it back." (*The Washington Post*, July 31, 2002) The same day, Lay is reported to have taken a $4 million cash advance from the company. Over the next three days, he withdrew an additional $19 million. He immediately repaid $6 million of the amount by transferring his Enron stock to the company. That allowed him to sell stock but avoid an immediate reporting requirement. (*The Washington Post*, op. cit.)

In a last ditch effort to save Enron, Lay attempted to sell the company to Dynergy, Inc., a smaller Houston based company. Enron misled Dynegy before their proposed merger, saying that its European trading operations had a $53 million operating profit in the previous quarter. In its disclosure, Enron reported that its European operations had actually incurred a $21 million loss. Chuck Watson, the founder and CEO of Dynergy was surprised by the debt disclosure, which he called a " $690 million bullet in the head," killing the merger deal.

Ex-Enron Chairman and CEO Kenneth Lay surrendered to FBI authorities July 8, 2004 after being indicted in the government's crackdown on corporate scandals. On May 25, 2006, a federal jury found Lay and Skilling guilty of conspiracy, wire and securities fraud, and Skilling one count of insider trading in connection with Enron's 2001 collapse. (*The Washington Post*, May 25, 2006) Lay has since passed away, not serving any time in jail. Skilling was released from custody in February 2019.

Enron's Chapter 11 business re-organization plan received court approval in 2004. The July 15, 2004 Enron press release stated: "At the conclusion of the claims reconciliation process, the allowable claims against the company are expected to be approximately $63 billion, Cooper (Stephen F. Cooper, Enron's acting CEO and chief restructuring officer) said. The cash and equity assets available for ultimate distribution are expected to be around $12 billion, he added, not including recoveries from litigation." (www.enron.com) In May 2006, Kenneth Lay, Enron Chairman, was found guilty of one count of conspiracy, two counts of wire fraud, and three counts of securities fraud. CEO Jeffrey Skilling was found guilty of one count of conspiracy, twelve counts of securities fraud, five counts of falsifying business records, and one count of insider trading. Enron was just the first chapter in what was to prove to be a series of corporate scandals of huge proportions.

WorldCom

In July 2005, Bernard J. Ebbers, former CEO of the telecommunications company, WorldCom, was sentenced to 25 years in prison for conspiracy to commit securities fraud, and false filing of 10Q and 10K income statements with the SEC. In the 31-page indictment, US Attorney David N. Kelley charged: "Rather than disclose WorldCom's true operating performance and financial condition, in or about April 2002, Ebbers and Sullivan instructed subordinates, in substance and in part, to falsely and fraudulently book certain entries in WorldCom's general ledger, which were designed to increase artificially WorldCom's reported revenue and to decrease artificially WorldCom's reported expenses, resulting in, among other things, artificially inflated figures for WorldCom's EPS, EBITDA, and revenue growth rate. These adjustments included (a) the improper capitalization of line cost expenses, and (b) increases to revenue, which in light of their departure from prior revenue recognition policies, and in light of their aggregate amount, made WorldCom's reported revenue materially misleading. Ebbers and Sullivan instructed others to make these adjustments solely in an effort to report results that would satisfy analysts' expectations, even though Ebbers and Sullivan knew that WorldCom's true results in fact failed to meet those expectations." (US Attorney David N. Kelley, UNITED STATES DISTRICT COURT NY, USA v. Bernard J. Ebbers, Defendant. INDICTMENT S3 02 Cr. 1144: 15)

WorldCom's CFO, Scott Sullivan received a 5-year sentence, significantly lighter for providing evidence and testifying against Bernard Ebbers. The jury found that Ebbers and Sullivan intentionally defrauded shareholders that owned the company, resulting in the biggest bankruptcy in American history, much larger than the Enron bankruptcy. Accounting fraud was at the center of the stage in the WorldCom bankruptcy, fraudulently reporting high revenues and low costs. Their favorite technique seemed to be moving operation expenses to capital expenditures so as not to be reflected as operating costs, but rather as capital investments.

Adelphia

Adelphia's founder, John Rigas, and his son Timothy, the cable company's former CFO, got 15 years and 20 years in prison sentences, respectively, for their role in fraud that led to the collapse of the US's largest cable companies. Prosecutors accused them of conspiring to hide $2.3 billion in Adelphia debt, stealing $100 million, and lying to investors about the company's financial condition.

Tyco International, Inc., a Bermuda company

In September 2002, the SEC indicted former Tyco International, Ltd., executives CEO Dennis Kozlowski, CFO Mark Schwartz, and General Counsel Mark Belnick on charges of civil fraud, theft, tax evasion, and not filing insider sales of the company's stock, as required by the SEC. (www.tycofraudinfocenter.com) They are accused of giving themselves interest-free or low interest loans for personal purchases of property, jewelry, and other items, which were neither approved by directors nor repaid to the company. Loan forgiveness of $37.5 million did not appear on Kozlowski's or Schwartz's income returns for 1999. Kozlowski and

Schwartz are also accused of issuing bonuses to themselves and others without the approval of Tyco's board of directors. It is alleged that these bonuses acted as de facto loan forgiveness for employees who had borrowed company money. They are also being indicted on charges of selling company stock without reporting their insider sales, fraud, and making fraudulent statements. All in all, Kozlowski and Schwartz were accused by the SEC of "looting" Tyco of $600 million. Both Kozlowski and Schwartz were found guilty in June 2005. On September 19, 2005, New York Justice Obus ordered Mr. Kozlowski to repay $97 million to Tyco International, Inc., and an additional $70 million in fines. Mr. Schwartz was ordered to pay $38 million to Tyco, and $35 million in fines. In addition, they have been sentenced to serve between 7 to 25 years in prison. Schwartz was released from prison in October 2013, while Kozlowski was released in January 2014.

A special committee of the publishing company, Hollinger International Inc., concluded in a report that Sir Conrad M. Black and F. David Radler ran a "corporate kleptocracy," diverting to themselves the company's entire earnings of $400 million over seven years. It also ordered certain directors, particularly Richard N. Perle, to return $5.4 million in pay for "putting his own interests above those of Hollinger's shareholders." It criticizes the payment of $226 million to Ravelston for management fees from 1996 to 2003—a company controlled by Sir Black that, in turn, essentially owned 68% of the voting shares of Hollinger. Mr. Perle is singled out for "flagrant abdication of duty" in signing bonuses and loans to Sir Black at the expense of shareholders. He is also said to have earned a bonus of $3.1 million from Hollinger Digital, his project, even though it lost $49 million. In the report's terms "It is hard to imagine a more flagrant abdication of duty than a director rubberstamping transactions that directly benefit a controlling shareholder without any thought, comprehension, or analysis. In fact, many of the consents that Perle signed as an executive committee member approved related-party transactions that unfairly benefited Black ... and cost Hollinger millions ... " (*New York Times*, September 1, 2004) Black served 3.5 years in prison, while Perle was not charged with wrongdoing.

Countrywide Financial

Angelo Mozilo, former chief executive of subprime lender Countrywide Financial Corp., paid $67.5 million in 2010 to settle civil fraud charges filed by the SEC. He didn't admit or deny wrongdoing. Countrywide was purchased by Bank of America Corp. in July 2008. Since then, BOA has been subjected to costly litigation on claims of fraudulent lending by Countrywide Financial. BOA's share, ticker symbol BAC, are worth $5.27 on December 28, 2011, while it was worth $33.61 at the close July 30, 2008, representing an 83% fall since the purchase of Countrywide. In a program at Countrywide known internally as "Friends of Angelo," mortgage loans were purportedly made on favorable terms to politicians and congressmen who could influence legislation and regulation in Countrywide's favor. BOA's price in November 2019 is $33.32.

Olympus, Japan

The Olympus accounting practice known as "tobashi," was used for "hiding bad loans" or "selling or divesting unwanted stocks." By selling loss-making assets or loans to dummy companies in a *tobashi deal*, losses can be shifted off Olympus financial statements. In 2008, Olympus bought Gyrus for $1.9 billion. Under the transaction, a financial adviser based in the Cayman Islands received a payout of $687 million—more than a third of the purchase price. Olympus also bought three small Japanese companies for a total of ￥73.49 billion ($940.1 million) from 2006 to 2008 that had little or no operational revenue. A year later, the company wrote down their value by nearly $700 million. Olympus admits to hiding losses. (*Wall Street Journal*, November 8, 2011)

The Sarbanes-Oxley Act of 2002

2002年《萨班斯-奥克斯利法案》(The Sarbanes-Oxley Act of 2002)：根据安然、世界通讯 (Worldcom) 等财务欺诈事件所暴露出的公司和证券监管问题，美国立法机构于2002年制定了该法案作为监管法规。

The recent scandals in corporate governance spawned new legislation—the U.S. Sarbanes-Oxley Act of 2002. Many companies are complaining about the higher than expected cost of compliance with "SOX" or "Sarbox", as the Act is commonly known. The Act addresses most major issues in corporate governance and disclosure, and has the following main titles:

Title I: Public Company Accounting Oversight Board which establishes an independent accounting oversight board with whom public accounting firms, including foreign ones that prepare audits, must register for inspection.

Title II: Auditor Independence prohibits a public accounting firm from providing non-audit services to its client, in particular:

(1) bookkeeping or other services related to the accounting records or financial statements of the audit client;

(2) financial information systems design and implementation;

(3) appraisal or valuation services, fairness opinions, or contribution-in-kind reports;

(4) actuarial services;

(5) internal audit outsourcing services;

(6) management functions or human resources;

(7) broker or dealer, investment adviser, or investment banking services;

(8) legal services and expert services unrelated to the audit; and

(9) any other service that the Board determines, by regulation, is impermissible.

(H. R. 3763-28 Sarbanes-Oxley Act of 2002, Sec. 201)

Title III: Corporate Responsibility requires that CEOs and CFOs certify in annual or quarterly reports that:

(1) the signing officer has reviewed the report;

(2) based on the officer's knowledge, the report does not contain any untrue statement of a material fact or omit to state a material fact ...

(3) based on such officer's knowledge, the financial statements, and other financial information included in the report, fairly represents in all material respects the financial condition and results of operations of the issuer as of, and for, the periods represented in the report.

(H. R. 3763-28 Sarbanes-Oxley Act of 2002, Sec. 302)

It also provides for forfeiture of bonuses and profits as a result of misreporting (Sec. 304), prohibits insider trades during pension fund blackout periods when the firm suspends the right of more than a majority of participants of pension plans from selling their shares in the company (Sec. 306), and provides for "disgorgement" or fair funds for investors whose rights are violated (Sec. 308).

Title IV: Enhanced Financial Disclosures requiring accurate compliance with GAAP principles (Sec. 401), disclosure of material off-balance sheet transactions, arrangements and obligations (Sec. 401), prohibits personal loans to executives (Sec. 402), requires greater disclosure of equity transactions involving management and principal stockholders (Sec. 403), establishes a code of ethics for senior financial officers (Sec. 406), and requires real time issuer disclosures of material changes in the financial condition or operations of the issuer (Sec. 409).

Title V: Analyst Conflicts of Interest requiring disclosure of:

(1) the extent to which the securities analyst has debt or equity investments in the issuer that is the subject of the appearance or research report;

(2) whether any compensation has been received by the registered broker or dealer . . from the issuer that is the subject of the appearance of research report . . .

(3) whether an issuer, the securities of which are recommended in the appearance or research report is, or during the 1-year period preceding the date of appearance or date of distribution of the report has been, a client of the registered broker or dealer, and if so, stating the types of services provided to the issuer.

(H. R. 3763-28 Sarbanes-Oxley Act of 2002, Sec. 15D)

Title VI: Commission Resources and Authority which appropriates monies for the Commission and its activities.

Title VII: Studies and Reports commissions the study of public accounting firms with the view of increasing competition by studying the factors that have led to industry consolidation (Sec. 701), the study of the role and function of the credit rating agencies in the evaluation of issuers of securities with a view to identifying conflicts of interest (Sec. 702), a report on the number of securities professions who have violated securities laws, which laws were violated, and what punishments, if any, were meted out (Sec. 703). Sec. 704 mandates a report on enforcement actions, while Sec. 705 requires a study ". . . on whether investment banks and financial advisers assisted public companies in manipulating their earnings and obfuscating their true financial condition."

Title VIII: Corporate and Criminal Fraud Accountability provides for criminal penalties for the destruction, alteration, or falsification of records in Federal investigations and bankruptcy (Par. 1519) and extends the statute of limitations for securities fraud from 2 to 5 years after the violation (Sec. 804).

Title IX: White-Collar Crime Penalty Enhancements raises from 5 to 20 years the possible punishments for mail and wire fraud (Sec. 903) and raises the monetary penalties from $5,000 to $100,000 in one case, and from $100,000 to $500,000 in another, and criminal penalties from one year to ten years for violations of the employee retirement income security act of 1974 (Sec. 904). Sec. 906 establishes corporate responsibility for financial reports, providing criminal penalties of up to $1,000,000 or 10 years in prison or both, for certifying a fraudulent report, and up to $5,000,000 or 20 years in prison or both for a corporate officer who "willfully certifies" a fraudulent statement that misrepresents the financial conditions and result of operations of the issuer (Par. 1350).

Title X: Corporate Tax Returns requires that the Federal income tax return of a corporation be signed by the chief executive officer.

Title XI: Corporate Fraud and Accountability proscribes the tampering with the records or impedes the carrying out of an investigation (Sec. 1102), increases criminal penalties of the SEC act of 1934 substantially, up to 10 or 20 years, as well as up to $5 million or $25 million, depending on the violation (Sec. 1106). Finally, it provides for criminal penalties up to 10 years and similar fines for retaliating against an employee who provides information on the company to any law enforcement officer (Sec. 1107). It is appropriately entitled "Retaliation Against Informants."

To sum up, the Sarbanes-Oxley Act of 2002 means business and severe penalties for knowingly committing securities fraud or false accounting. It also means significantly increased costs of compliance. One prominent accountant gave insight on remedies to fraud and SOX. "If you devote attention to safeguards for minimizing the immense risks of fraud that have happened all too frequently in the last five years especially, my sense of the key preventatives are:

1. The risks of financial ruin and long jail terms to perpetrators such as Ebbers. (If justice were quicker and harder, we wouldn't have needed SOX, though CEO certifications required by SOX are a positive reminder of the CEO's responsibilities.)

2. Independent, competent boards such as SOX supports.

3. A strong SEC-type body, perhaps international in scope, to regulate public companies.

4. More standardizing accounting rules for the various industries, enabling apples-to-apples comparisons.

5. More principles-based accounting; today there are in the US too many rules and not enough judgment, even on such issues as revenue recognition.

6. SOX rules on auditor independence, including a cooling off period

for hiring top level people from the audit firm, are a big step in the right direction. " (David Lieberman, CFO, University of Miami)

Other financial abuses

Retention bonuses are payments that a firm may pay to retain an employee. In principle, the firm should determine the unusually high or unique qualifications of the employee that makes it essential to retain an employee. Clearly, retention bonuses may have the opposite effect. For instance, if an employee is to be awarded a million dollars at the end of the year for staying on one year, he or she has an incentive to seek another job while remaining at his or her post for one year. In many cases, the firm is in financial distress, so the current management might award itself retention bonuses to manage its downfall or cash out its remaining assets. For the same reason, management may make itself personal loans, knowing that the company is headed for bankruptcy. This practice is now prohibited under SOX, but K-Mart managers cashed out a great deal before its bankruptcy through bonuses and personal loans. Retention bonuses are often abused—after all, the managers that took the firm into the ground should be considered for dismissal, let alone be awarded a bonus for poor performance. Days before Enron Corp. declared bankruptcy on December 2, 2001, it announced that it would not abide by severance payments to its employees. At the same time, the company gave executives retention bonuses totaling more than $55 million. The generous executive payouts, many of which were made on November 30, were approved by the new Enron management team—Jeff McMahon, Enron president, and Ray Bowen, the CFO. McMahon received a bonus of $1.5 million and Bowen got $750,000. Enron's practices seemed not to change; handsome rewards to executives days before reneging on its employee severance commitments. Enron's planned severance package—subsequently scrapped—cost $120 million and would have provided an average payment to employees of approximately $30,000. That plan was discarded. Instead, at least $105 million was distributed in executive bonuses. To add insult to injury, the Enron blackout of sales of Enron stock by employees, two thirds of their pension assets, was reported to have been accompanied by unreported insider sales by management. (*Washington Post*, *op. cit.*) Once again, this practice would be illegal under SOX, if discovered. Indeed, former CEO Jeffrey Skilling has been found guilty of one count of insider trading.

留职奖金(Retention bonuses):公司支付给员工以留住他的一笔报酬。

AMR

Shortly after two of its three unions had ratified $1.8 billion in annual wage and other concessions April 14, 2003. AMR (parent of American Airlines) filed its annual 10K report with the SEC revealing a retention bonus plan for the company's top seven executives of about $5 million each for another year of service and a bulletproof $41 million pension trust fund designed to protect executives' retirement monies from possible bankruptcy. AMR stood by its pension trust fund, but then AMR CEO Donald J. Carty and six other senior AMR executives gave up the retention bonuses on April 18. The remaining stewards union ratified the restructuring plan, despite the considerable anger provoked among union members. Neither plan was disclosed to shareholders, AMR's labor unions, or the SEC until the April 15, 2003 SEC filing. ("'Timely disclosure' at center of AA flap," *Dallas Business Journal*, April 28, 2003) In the end, the unions had no better alternative than to approve the restructuring plan. Carty has since been replaced as CEO of American Airlines.

Insider trading

内幕交易(Insider trading):知悉证券交易内幕信息的人员利用所知悉的内幕信息,自己进行证券交易或者泄露该信息或者建议他人进行证券交易的行为。

The term "insider trading" can mean the perfectly legal buying and selling of stock by a company's corporate insiders who comply by reporting their trading in advance. Insider trading is legal when these corporate insiders trade stock of their own company, but report in advance these trades to the U.S. Securities and Exchange Commission (SEC) and the firm's income statements contain all information relevant to the financial standing of the firm. The SEC discloses the insider's intention to sell on the EDGAR (Electronic Data Gathering and Retrieval) database. That way, the insider trading is disclosed and anyone can speculate about the corporate insider's opinion of the fortunes of his or her company. In the past, there have been loopholes that have allowed executives to skirt the disclosure rules, but SOX attempts to close them.

Insider trading is illegal when a person bases their trade of stocks in a publicly listed company on information that is not shared with the public. It is also illegal to give someone a tip, so they can trade on the inside information. In Europe, the possibility of insider trading in EADS, the Airbus consortium is being investigated by the French Finance Commission. Noël Forgeard, co-president of EADS, his three children and other French and German directors sold their shares in EADS in March 2006, three months before announcing further, lengthy delays in the delivery of the jumbo Airbus 380 jet which triggered a sharp fall in the value EADS shares. Mr. Forgeard claims it was not insider trading, that he had no idea that there would be further delays. Innocent until proven guilty, of course, but the Airbus workers were apparently aware that they were far behind schedule due to extreme "customizing" for each customer. The French press are having a heyday with the affair, saying that Forgeard was either a liar, incompetent, or both!

In the News: U.S. Congressional Insider Trading

Several academic studies show that the investment portfolios of congressmen and senators consistently outperform stock indices like the Dow and the S&P 500, as well as the portfolios of virtually all professional investors. Congressmen do better to an extent that is statistically significant, according to studies including a 2004 article about "abnormal" Senate returns by Alan J. Ziobrowski, Ping Cheng, James W. Boyd and Brigitte J. Ziobrowski in the *Journal of Financial and Quantitative Analysis*. Democrats' portfolios outperform the market by a whopping 9%. Republicans do well, though not quite as well. And the trading is widespread, although a higher percentage of senators than representatives trade—which is not surprising because senators outperform the market by an astonishing 12% on an annual basis. These results are not due to luck or the financial acumen of elected officials. They can be explained only by insider trading based on the nonpublic information that politicians obtain in the course of their official duties.

Source: "Congress's Phony Insider-Trading Reform", *Wall Street Journal*, December 13, 2011.

The punishment for illegal insider trading depends on the situation. The person can be fined, banned from sitting on the executive or board of directors of a public company and even jailed. The Securities Exchange Act of 1934 in the United States allows the SEC to give a person a reward—"a bounty"—to someone who gives the Commission information that results in a fine of insider trading. SOX 2002 makes it illegal to retaliate against whistle-blowers. Yet, it would be wise to think twice before blowing a whistle. The government may not be able to save your job. "Other reasons" might suffice, and you would have to pay lawyers to fight your company, not a pleasant thought.

> **In the News**: Expert Networks
>
> Raj Rajaratnam's, a billionaire and founder of Galleon, a hedge fund, was sentenced to 11 years in prison, the longest-ever term imposed in an insider-trading case. Expert networks are independent research networks that pay so-called experts for information on public companies. In fact, many of the experts were employed in the very same firm whose information they provided to Galleon on which to trade. In a revealing text message, Ray was told: Don't buy Polycom's stock "till I get guidance; want to make sure guidance OK," wrote Roomy Khan, a former Intel Corp. employee who had been suspected of providing inside information to sources. In another case, The U.S. accused Mr. Rajat Gupta, former director at Goldman Sachs Group, Inc. of passing along nonpublic information to Raj Rajaratnam, namely that Warren Buffet was buying shares in Goldman. Mr. Gupta and Mr. Rajaratnam, were good friends whose regular discussions of business included the illegal tips, according to authorities. The insider-trading investigation that has so far focused primarily on those who profited directly from stock tips, but is now examining a culture where prosecutors say secrets are swapped freely among powerful business figures. "There is a lot of insider trading—and some of that goes to high places," according to Charles Munger, vice chairman of Berkshire Hathaway Inc., whose investment in Goldman during the heat of the financial crisis in 2008 was one of Mr. Gupta's alleged leaks. While some expert networks may be legitimate, one of the biggest challenges they face is legal compliance with respect to information passed on from the expert to the hedge fund. In the absence of insider trading on private information, it is hard to see how some hedge funds that use experts are able to consistently rack up higher than market returns.
>
> Source: *The Wall Street Journal*, October 14, 2001.

Abusive tax schemes

滥用税收机制(Abusive tax schemes): 通过利用外国税收管辖权,达到避税的目的。有一些避税行为是合法的,另一些则不然。

Taxes may be evaded by using a foreign jurisdiction. Evasion can be as simple as depositing unreported cash or checks into a bank account in a tax haven. Others methods are more elaborate involving domestic and foreign trusts and partnerships. Some are perfectly legal. Others are not.

A U.S. resident receives checks from customers, the checks are sent for deposit in the resident's International Business Corporation (IBC) of an offshore bank. The foreign bank uses its correspondent bank account to process the checks. When the check clears, the taxpayer's IBC account is credited for the payments. The customer who receives the canceled check does not know that the payment was made offshore. However, the U. S. taxpayer has transferred the unreported income to an offshore tax haven. Interest income goes untaxed in the tax free jurisdiction. Some Florida dentists went afoul of the law when they were discovered using credit cards issued by the foreign bank in Nassau in order to transfer the monies back to the U. S. U. K. tax expatriates move to the Bahamas to live from the income transferred or earned there. Or they incorporate in the Bahamas or Bermuda, but avoid staying more than 180 days in the US over a three year period to avoid residency issues for the business. False billing scams abroad can also be used to evade taxation.

Undisclosed executive compensation

The SEC requires that income statements now expense beginning January 2006 the value of options granted to executives in order to "improve the value of the firm." The generosity of deferred compensation, bonuses, and options has sometimes only been revealed to shareholders as a result of accidental claims due to divorce proceedings. A former Chairman of General Electric is retained as a consultant at $86,000 a year after his retirement in 2001, including "lifetime access to company facilities and services comparable to those which are currently made available to him by the company." These benefits are "unconditional and irrevocable" according to a General Electric 2001 proxy statement. The former executive also has an $80,000 per month Manhattan apartment owned by the company, in addition to other perks of significant value, such as use of the company airplane. In this particular case, the executive probably deserves such a "golden parachute," but the shareholders should be informed of the package.

高管的秘密薪酬(Undisclosed executive compensation): 公司高管的薪酬、奖金以及期权有时并不会向股东披露。

Many managers "manage" to protect their pensions and health benefits, while defaulting on those of their employees. Some have the company pay their income taxes, unbeknown to the shareholders. Christopher Cox, the head of the SEC won unanimous support from SEC commissioners to overhaul proxy-statement disclosure of top executives in the following ways:

1. Require companies to provide a total compensation figure for executives.

2. Include a dollar value of stock options in the summary compensation table.

3. Disclose any executive perks that are more than $10,000 in value.

4. Provide an actual amount to specify what payments executives would receive should there be a change in control or change in responsibilities.

5. Create a new disclosure table that would cover the details of retirement plans, including what the executive would receive in potential annual payments and benefits.

6. Create a new director compensation table similar to the executive summary compensation table that would disclose payments received by directors in a given year.

(*Wall Street Journal*, January 10, 2006)

At least this is a step in the right direction, although Cox himself was totally unaware that Markopolous had persistently informed the SEC that Bernie Madoff was operating a Ponzi game. It is easier to pass regulations than to enforce them.

The shareholders should know what executive compensation is, and perhaps have an advisory say on it. Adam Smith hit the nail on the head, once again. As Professor Lucian A. Bebchuk, Director, Corporate Governance Program, Harvard University aptly put it: "The positive effect will be that on the margin—and it is an important margin—there will be a new so-called outrage constraint. The caveat is that even though there is an outrage constraint, shareholders have very limited power to do anything about it." (Stephen Labaton, "S. E. C. to Tighten Reporting Rules for Executive Pay," *New York Times*, January 18, 2006.) In the meantime, average chief executive pay of CEOs of Fortune 500 companies has risen from $2.82 million in 1990 to $11.8 million in 2004. Professor Bebchuk also found that in the S&P 500 companies, those with pension plans the median actuarial value given to chief executives is about $15 million (*op. cit.*).

Many of these abusive financial practices are subject to a "Wells letter". The SEC Wells notification letters are mandated under Exchange Rules 17.1 and 17.2, which provide that prior "to submitting its report [to the Business Conduct Committee], the staff shall notify the person(s) who is the subject of the report ... of the general nature of the allegations" in violations of exchange rules, such as conduct inconsistent with just and equitable principles of trade, failure to provide requested information and the like. This is to notify the person of the initiation of an investigation into possible exchange violations and to give that person the opportunity to respond to allegations within one year.

Derivative scandals and rogue traders

Barings Bank

Britain's oldest merchant bank had financed the Napoleonic wars, but was brought down by a single, rogue trader, Nick Leeson, then 28 years old, in February 1995. His losses were so great that Barings was unable to meet a SIMEX (Singapore International Monetary Exchange) margin call and was declared insolvent. In British Parliament, the Chancellor of the Exchequer announced somberly: "*With permission, Madam Speaker, I would like to make a statement about the insolvency of the merchant bank Barings. The Bank of England announced late last night, ahead of the opening of the Far East financial markets, that Barings was unable to continue trading...*" (February 27, 1995) At the time of the announcement, Leeson was on the run from the Singapore Branch of Barings where he was chief trader and settlements officer. Arrested in Frankfurt, Germany on March 3, 1995, he was returned to Singapore where he served 4 years of a 6.5 year sentence for fraud and forgery. Barings was sold to ING, a Dutch bank, for a symbolic £1 the same day of his arrest. ING assumed the liabilities of Barings.

Many have raised the twin questions: How did this happen and what are the lessons to be learned? There are two basic versions on how this happened, Nick Leeson's and Barings, but only one set of lessons that everyone seems to agree upon. Let's begin with the problems that led to the debacle with a view of drawing lessons.

Firstly, Nick Leeson was both chief trader and settlements officer, a conflict of interest that left his activity essentially unsupervised. "An internal memo dated in 1993 had warned the London headquarters about allowing Leeson to be both trader and settlement officer, 'We are in danger of setting up a system that will prove disastrous.'" ("Crime Case Closed", BBC)

Secondly, the absence of checks and balances allowed Leeson to set up an error account 88888 which started with £20,000 losses from one of the traders he recruited, but was transferred losses of £827 million, or $1.4 billion in the end. This was done by trading at a loss to other Barings accounts which profited, showering bonuses on Leeson and his associates.

衍生工具丑闻(Derivative scandals):衍生工具的交易员在缺乏有效监管的情形下,为了牟取个人利益而采取赌博式交易策略,从而给公司带来巨大的损失。

Thirdly, unauthorized trading for the account of Barings took place. Leeson and his traders were authorized to trade futures and options orders for clients or for other firms within the Barings organization, and were allowed to arbitrage price differences between Nikkei futures traded on the SIMEX and Japan's Osaka exchange. Neither of these activities would risk the assets of Barings, if conducted as authorized. Trading the futures and options for clients only risked the client's monies and margins, while arbitraging according to the law of one prices is riskless. Not realizing that Leeson was taking speculative positions, booking his losses in error account 88888, and his profits in other Barings accounts, the management in London did not fully realize the potential danger of his dual role—trader and settler.

Fourthly, doubling his positions when they moved against him. Leeson had the bad habit of doubling his losing position in the hopes of recovering his losses when the market moved in his favor, in this instance, a rise in the Nikkei Index. His long bet might have worked had not the January 17, 1995 Kobe earthquake rocked Japan and the Tokyo Exchange. In the words of authors Stephen J. Brown of the Stern School of Business, New York University and Onno W. Steenbeek of the Erasmus School of Finance, Rotterdam: "The empirical evidence suggests that Leeson followed a doubling positions strategy: He continuously doubled his position as prices were falling." Indeed, Leeson confirms that he followed this strategy. "I felt no elation at this success. I was determined to win back the losses. And as the spring wore on, I traded harder and harder, risking more and more. I was well down, but increasingly sure that my doubling up and doubling up would pay off... I redoubled my exposure. The risk was that the market could crumble down, but on this occasion it carried on upwards... As the market soared in July (1993) my position translated from a £6 million loss back into glorious profit. I was so happy that night I didn't think I'd ever go through that kind of tension again. I'd pulled back a large position simply by holding my nerve... but first thing on Monday morning I found that I had to use the 88888 account again... it became an addiction." (Leeson, 1996: 63-64). Doubling is disastrous when the market moves systematically against the trader. Yet, there is a temptation to win the money back by doing so. Ironically, 10 years later on the SIMEX, China Aviation Oil Corporation's (CAOC) Jiulin Chen, the 43-year-old CEO of Singapore-listed CAOC kept doubling his bet that oil prices would fall, which they never did while he was trading. This resulted in another SIMEX scandal. Both Leeson and Chen made margin deposits and margin calls until they could no longer do so. Both tend to fault SIMEX, but the exchange was just practicing prudent collateral requirements for a clearinghouse.

Fifthly, trading on margin affords a great deal of leverage, which can be your best friend if prices move in your direction, but your worst enemy when they move against you. Consider a security which you borrow from a broker with a margin account deposit of $5 and sell now at $100. You hope to buy it later at a lower price to return to the broker. If the market price rises 5% or more, your margin is wiped out and you may get a call for "margin maintenance". If you fail to maintain margin, the broker can close your position at a loss. The more leveraged you are, the smaller is the price movement against you that triggers a margin call. Leeson had plenty of these from SIMEX, and had to get the cash for margins from London. He argued that large transactions were needed to make small arbitrage profits and that both the SIMEX and Tokyo Exchanges required margin. Also, due to time differences he stated that there would be intra-day "advance margin calls" that Barings would have to meet due to time differences of location of the ultimate client. In other cases, he simply traded from account 88888. Leverage was also to play a big role in the downfall of China Aviation Oil Company and Long Term Capital Management.

Sixthly, Leeson was a good liar. In his ten year on article in *The Observer*, he notes: "Barings people had begun to ask some serious questions at last about the huge amounts of cash that had been disappearing in Singapore. Tony Railton, a senior bank official, had found a hole in the balance sheet—not the sort you plug by putting your finger in the dyke, more like one that threatens to wash the whole dam away. His colleague Tony Hawes, a London-based director, was on a tour of southeast Asia looking at funding requirements, and was due to be in Singapore on my birthday—25 February. But still they allowed me to fob them off with flimsy excuses for my cash-guzzling operation. I believe that they were all so desperate to believe in my success for personal reasons; their bonuses depended on it and there were only a few days before these were due to be signed off . . . By 23 February it all became too much. That day, which will be imprinted on my mind forever, my then-wife Lisa and I packed a couple of small suitcases and made our way to the airport." Since Leeson fled on February 23, leaving his letter of apology and tendering his resignation, it is clear he did not meet with Tony Hawkes when both realized the jig was up.

Seventhly, Leeson's trades were inherently risky. A short straddle on the Nikkei index is fine if there is low volatility in the Tokyo Exchange, but not when the volatility is high. A short straddle is a combination of a short call and a short put with the same exercise price. Thus as the seller of both a call and a put on the Nikkei Index, Leeson was betting there would be little movement, so he would gain the premiums. In the event, the city of Kobe had a major earthquake and he had to honor the put he had sold. Leveraged long positions in the Nikkei Index ate margin cash when the index fell. Matters became much worse when Leeson doubled his long positions in the Nikkei. Many brokerage houses have stop-loss rules requiring the trader to take the losses, preventing them from growing larger. Options trading is inherently risky since you lose 100% of your investment, the option premium, when it expires out of the money.

Eighthly, Leeson was, in his own words, "eager to please, eager to succeed." (*The Observer*, February 19, 2005) He seemed to have a big ego, anxious to be a star for Barings. So anxious to succeed, he falsified documents and trades to generate profits which would generate everyone, including himself, large bonuses. He told a pack of lies. It is also disingenuous to claim, as he does in *The Observer*: "The Bank of England, which a decade ago this weekend was sitting on a powder-keg with a burning fuse, was surely right not to have bailed Barings out. It was a comparatively small bank, poorly run, and an accident waiting to happen." Although it is certainly true, as he states: "Open-outcry trading pits are virtually a thing of the past and have been largely replaced with automated systems. Many of the anomalies that existed on the trading floor in my day, often bordering on the illegal, have been removed, and that can only be advantageous in promoting fair and accessible markets for everyone."

He is quick to note, however, that the China Aviation Oil Company scandal involving the same type of rogue trading and doubling of losing positions to recover losses happened again in 2005 on the SIMEX. Nick Leeson now lives in Galway, Ireland and is a motivational speaker.

China Aviation Oil Company

A Singapore-listed company, China Aviation Oil Company (CAOC) controlled by a Chinese state-owned enterprise, lost $550 million in 2004 from short sales of oil derivatives on SIMEX. (*New York Times*, December 2, 2004; *Wall Street Journal*, December 3, 2004; *Wall Street Journal*, December 6, 2004.) Jiulin Chen, the then 43-year-old CEO of China

Aviation Oil Company, Singapore, was taken into custody for investigation of Singapore's worst financial scandal in nearly a decade since Nick Leeson took down Barings in 1995 in unauthorized trading. Mr. Chen appears to have pursed the same dogged policy of doubling his short sales of oil futures in the hopes that oil prices would fall. For example, In April 2004, Chen decided to extend the maturity of the futures sales held by CAOC, as well as dramatically increase the size of their short position. Clearly, he and his risk management team felt that oil prices would fall. In the event, oil price rose continuously to record highs.

As oil prices kept rising, the margin requirement on CAOC's futures trading also surged, draining its cash flow. On October 10, 2004, CAOC's books showed losses of US $180 million, and it did not have the $80 million necessary to make the margin calls. On October 21, 2004, CAOHC, knowing that its Singapore affiliate was in financial distress, sold 15% of CAOC's shares to a few fund management companies without revealing its desperate financial condition, in violation of insider-trading regulations. The parent CAOHC immediately lent the $108 million in cash from the sale to CAOC in the hope of rescuing it.

Chen stated that he had no idea CAOC would be required to pay huge amounts in margin calls as a result of its trading. By engaging in speculative trading, Chen had violated strict prohibitions by Chinese regulators. His authorized trading purpose was to hedge fuel needs for Chinese aviation companies. In one example of a money-losing trade, CAOC entered into a derivative agreement on September 1, 2004 that involved 100,000 barrels of jet fuel. CAOC sold a call that the average monthly spot price for Singapore-traded jet fuel oil would not rise above $37 a barrel during October. Fuel prices rose to an average price of $61.25. CAO suffered a loss of $24.25 per barrel, or $2.4 million in total, having to honor the short call that was deep into the money.

CAOC filed for bankruptcy on November 30, 2004 citing losses of US $550 million from oil derivatives trading. Jiulin Chen and CAOC management lost money by doggedly gambling against rising oil prices, increasing the amounts of oil futures it sold. CAOC's short position increased losses from an initial US $5.8 million to a staggering US $550 million.

Time and again, Chen extended the maturity date of most of the short futures contracts CAOC held to 2005 and 2006, essentially doubling his position. CAOC's trading volume ballooned and oil prices kept rising. By engaging in speculative trading, Chen had violated strict prohibitions by

Chinese regulators and was accordingly jailed for fraud and the violation of security laws.

Some critics suspected that CAOC had no risk-control mechanism in place. But the mechanism did exist. The company's risk-control manuals were developed by the consulting firm Ernst & Young, and were similar to those of other international oil companies. In addition, CAOC had a seven-member risk-control committee, staffed by Singaporean employees. The company also had internal rules that any trader losing more than US $200,000 must report the losses to the committee. Losses above US $375,000 are to be reported also to the CEO personally. The rules also stipulate mandatory stop-loss sales of the position when they reach US $500,000. Chen claims: "The US $500,000 must refer to actual losses—all our losses were book-value losses at the time, which didn't count," he told *Caijing* on December 7, 2004. In China, airlines were expressing concern that the rescue operation will lead to surging fuel costs, since CAOHC was the country's sole importer of aviation fuel. Chen, the center of the scandal, did not lose confidence: "If I can get just another US $250 million, I am sure I will turn things around." he said in a mobile phone message to a *Caijing* reporter on December 9, after he was freed on bail. Chen also believed that the Chinese government had a responsibility to bail CAOC out, saying "CAOC represents a standard of Chinese enterprises overseas."

The Chinese State-owned Asset Supervision and Administration Commission (SASAC) was briefly supportive of a rescue plan. It asked for foreign currency quotas for hundreds of millions of US dollars from the State Administration of Foreign Exchange (SAFE), the exchange control body. The SASAC, however, changed its mind. It ruled instead that the state would not go against its own principles against rescuing an insolvent company. It recommended that senior management of the company be punished.

In the end, we have a Leeson-like story: Unauthorized trading, doubling of losing positions, and not informing the parent company until the subsidiary could not make its margin calls. In the case of Leeson, he doubled bets that the Nikkei Index would rise. In the case of Chen, he doubled bets that the oil price would fall. In both cases, they could no longer make margin calls and their firms went bankrupt.

UBS AG

A Swiss Bank, UBS, said a rogue trader, London employee Kweku Adoboli, incurred $2 billion in losses using the firm's own money. Apparently, the losses were from unauthorized derivatives trading. The bank said no client positions were affected, but top resignations and curtailing of proprietary trading at UBS resulted. ("UBS: Rogue Trader Hit Firm," *Wall Street Journal*, September 16, 2011)

Société Générale

Jérôme Kerviel, a trader at Société Générale, was sentenced to five years in jail, two of them suspended. He was also ordered to pay damages of €4.9 billion. The judge ruled that he had fraudulently manipulated his reported trades, concealing his losing trades from his colleagues with offsetting transactions. "Plus ça change, plus c'est la même chose" or "The more things change, the more they remain the same." (*Der Spiegel*, November 16, 2010) It is clear that the world's largest banks have increasingly greater difficulty monitoring their traders' activity. Electronic trading takes less than a second.

Long Term Capital Management

Long Term Capital Management (LTCM), a hedge fund, was founded in 1994 by John Meriwether. Nobel laureates Myron Scholes of Stanford University and Robert Merton of Harvard University were co-principals. LTCM's reputation afforded them greater leverage than other hedge funds: They reportedly were able to leverage $4.8 billion of investor and principal money into $100 billion of positions. In the end, this leverage was to prove their worst enemy.

长期资本管理公司 (Long Term Capital Management):一家对冲基金公司,于1994年成立。和其他的对冲基金相比,长期资本管理公司的声誉使其具备了很大的杠杆能力;据说公司可以用48亿美元对高达1 000亿美元的头寸进行杠杆操作。

In 1996 and 1997, LTCM had paid its investors high yields, nearly 40% annually. However, during 1998, the hedge firm engaged in a variety of leveraged bets on the convergence of corporate and sovereign bond yields, but they diverged. Apparently, they also expected sovereign credit spreads to decrease, but once again the spreads increased. LTCM bought Russian short-term sovereign GKOs and sold Japanese bonds. The hedge fund was wrong about the direction of Japanese yields and worse yet, Russia defaulted (Wilmott, 2000).

On August 21, 1998, LTCM is reported to have lost $550 million. It was felt that a LTCM bankruptcy was too risky on the grounds of its "systemic" impact on US financial markets. Alan Greenspan, then Governor of the Federal Reserve System, organized a recapitalization of $3.6 billion by 12 investment banks in return for a 90% stake in LTCM. In the event, LTCM recovered in the subsequent years, yielding a good return on investment to the banks.

This is a different story than the previous ones, although there are some similarities. The investors were hedge fund participants risking their own and investor's monies, there was far too much leverage in hindsight—apparently over 20 to 1, and the Russian default left many holding worthless securities. No one claims there was any fraud in LTCM, only high leverage and risky bets that went bad.

Backdating of options grants

期权授予回溯(Backdating of options grants): 管理者的期权授予日期总是被回溯到一个股票价格低点,从而使得管理者能够获得更大的收益。

In a blockbuster article March 18, 2006, "The Perfect Payday," the *Wall Street Journal* exposed the dating of options grants to executives at or near the lowest share price of the year, which is extremely unlikely. The options are then exercised at or near the high price when vested, or upon leaving the company. Consider the case of Affiliated Computer Services, Inc.'s former CEO: "It was the same through much of Mr. Rich's tenure: In a striking pattern, all six of his stock-option grants from 1995 to 2002 were dated just before a rise in the stock price, often at the bottom of a steep drop ... Just lucky? A *Wall Street Journal* analysis suggests the odds of this happening by chance are extraordinarily remote—around one in 300 billion ... The Securities and Exchange Commission is examining whether some option grants carry favorable grant dates for a different reason: They were backdated."

How can this be? Let's say Mr. Back Dater, CEO of XYZ Corp. is awarded one million call option grants on July 5, 2018 when the share price is $50 at 4:00pm of that or the previous day. They vest or can be exercised in one year. On July 5, 2019, Mr. Back Dater is eligible to buy at $50 and sell say at $60, the share price that day, earning $10 million—fair enough. However, in cahoots with the compensation committee or some board members, the options are backdated to May 5, 2018 when the stock was at its low point, $20 a share. Bingo, he has hit the jackpot: $40 million in the exercise of the options. Where does the extra $30 million come from? It comes from the shareholders, of course.

The *Wall Street Journal* reports other possible malfeasance: "On Oct.

13, 1999, William W. McGuire, CEO of giant insurer United Health Group Inc., got an enormous grant in three parts that ... came to $14.6 million in options. So far, he has exercised about 5% of them, for a profit of about $39 million. As of late February (2006) he had 13.87 million unexercised options left from the October 1999 tranche. His profit on those, if he exercised them today, would be about $717 million more. The 1999 grant was dated the very day UnitedHealth stock hit its low for the year. ... At Mercury Interactive Corp., a Mountain View, Calif., software maker, the chief executive and two others resigned late last year. Mercury said an internal probe found 49 cases where the reported date of options grants differed from the date when the options appeared to have been awarded. The company said it will have to restate financial results ... Another company, Comverse Technology Inc., said ... that its board had started a review of its past stock-option practices, including "the accuracy of the stated dates of options grants". Shares of Vitesse Semiconductor Corp ... now rest at about the level of a decade ago. But Louis R. Tomasetta, chief executive of the Camarillo, Calif., chip maker, reaped tens of millions of dollars from stock options. In eight of Mr. Tomasetta's nine option grants from 1994 to 2001, the grants were dated just before double-digit price surges in the next 20 trading days. The odds of such a pattern occurring by chance are about one in 26 billion." Following the *Wall Street Journal* story, there have been waves of resignations of top executives, some cashing out to boot, as well as an avalanche of new SEC investigations into possible backdating.

There are several obvious problems with the backdating of options: Firstly, it is illegal to forge or backdate options grants. Secondly, the shareholders are usually not informed. Thirdly, it mocks the supposed link of options grants to the incentives of executives to raise the profitability of the firm. Finally, it steals wealth from shareholders. While the practice also violates Sarbanes-Oxley's prompt disclosure rules, many corporate executives in the U.S. are apparently doing so with impunity, at least so far.

Money laundering

The list of financial *peccadillos* would be incomplete without the mention of money laundering. An interesting case has been under investigation for some years now, and is finally going to court in Germany.

> **In the News**: Five Indicted in German Money-Laundering Case
>
> German prosecutors indicted five men, including four German banking executives, on charges of laundering $150 million for a former Russian telecommunications minister in one of the highest-level criminal probes of a Russian official outside Russia. The indictments follow a six-year investigation into allegations that four current or former Commerzbank AG executives and a Danish lawyer, Jeffrey Galmond, assisted former Russian telecommunications minister Leonid Reiman in selling telecommunications assets he allegedly secretly controlled in offshore companies, while concealing who the true owner was. The prosecutors allege that Mr. Reimen had surreptitiously converted telecom businesses from state ownership to that of a number of foreign companies that he allegedly set up and controlled after the collapse of communism in the early 1990s.
>
> Source: David Crawford, "Five Indicted in German Money-Laundering Case," *The Wall Street Journal*, December 13, 2011.

Lessons learned

Many of the financial mishaps and schemes reviewed here resulted from under-estimating the risks of leverage. Borrowing to sell short can trigger margin calls as the asset rises in price. Stop losses rather than rolling over losing positions by doubling up are recommended by most internal risk management procedures. When there is too much leverage, a small move in the price of the asset in the wrong direction can initiate large losses and margin calls. That seems to be one lesson from Barings, LTCM, and CAOC.

Illegal insider trading, falsification of earnings to ensure gains in options and bonuses, moving losing positions off balance sheets, and other conscious corporate frauds that apparently took place at Enron and WorldCom would seem to merit greater punishments, in addition to the restoration of investor funds or worker pensions. Poor governance and the failure of checks and balances within the firm bring with them the risk of bankruptcy. Monitoring trading activities of rogue traders that set up offsetting positions and accounts that conceal their losses is a challenge to the investment banks.

Backdating of options grants is outright fraud, direct theft from the shareholders and should be prosecuted. Retention bonuses may retain talented officers, such as at Apple Computer following the tragic loss of Steve Jobs, but they often seem to be the last refuge of corporate scoundrels to finance a year of job-seeking in a troubled company. Debt forgiveness on personal loans to executives, now prohibited by SOX, is also a bad practice. Money laundering will always be an issue with illegal activities, as well as the transfer of funds to support terrorism.

Conclusion

Adam Smith was right in 1776. Managers will often put their own interest ahead of the interest of the shareholders. The so-called efforts to align the interest of the managers with those of the owners through stock options and grants, bonuses and other "incentive pay" linked to reported earnings has reaped a harvest of falsified earnings and backdated options grants. Poorly performing firms are rewarding their CEOs at record levels. Indeed, there seems to be little relationship between performance and executive reward. Shareholders are not always informed of executive compensation nor are they consulted, as they would surely balk. The Cox ruling attempts to remedy this, but it is unclear what shareholders can do about the issue. Accountants will say what they are told to say in many circumstances, though SOX will punish them severely if they are caught. SOX attempts to eliminate some of the conflicts of interest in auditing firms. There is an ethical crisis in management. At the same time, there will always be pyramid schemes that attract those seeking high short term gains. Leverage always compounds the risk, and margin calls can rise rapidly when a bad leveraged bet is doubled. It is difficult to foresee much change, despite the heavy penalties that are now being meted out. There are always other scandals about to happen.

> **In the News: Trolling for Outperforming Hedge Funds**
>
> In 2009, the SEC began developing a computer-powered system that now analyzes monthly returns from thousands of hedge funds. Officials won't say exactly how it works or how much it cost to build, but the agency has announced four civil-fraud lawsuits filed as a result of what it calls the 'aberrational performance initiative.' ... The hedge funds have one thing in common: Their performance seems too good to be true, with some trouncing the overall market and others churning out modest results without ever suffering a

> down month. Some funds on the list stumble but still always outperform rival hedge funds … In 2008, ThinkStrategy reported a 4.6% return on its Capital Fund—A hedge fund. It was the sixth year in a row that Chetan Kapur, a 36-year-old New Yorker, seemed to have a Midas touch. In contrast, the average hedge fund fell roughly 19% in 2008, with losses in 8 of the year's 12 months, according to data from Hedge Fund Research Inc. The SEC alleged in its civil-fraud suit against Mr. Kapur that the 4.6% return figure was faked. The hedge fund actually had a 90% loss in 2008, according to the SEC's lawsuit.
>
> Source: Jean Eaglesham and Steve Eder, "SEC Ups Its Game to Identify Rogue Firms," *The Wall Street Journal*, December 27, 2011.

Questions and problems

6.1 Pyramid investments

Pyramid investments of Fort Lauderdale, in business for two years, has promised to pay 3% per month on notes redeemable in one year. It has redeemed any notes presented for redemption so far.

a. Indicate the annual rate of return that is promised on these notes.

b. Why might there not have been any default on the notes to date?

c. Do you think that this investment is sustainable?

6.2 Insider trading

Some argue that insider trading "helps in price discovery" of a firm's true value since the inside traders have information material to the financial situation of the firm. Besides, even if they buy low and sell high, it is not to the same shareholder, so it does not matter. Do you agree or disagree with this argument? Explain why.

6.3 Doubling down

Rogue traders often seem to have a strategy of "doubling down" on their initial bet in the same, wrong direction, even though the price has moved in the opposite one. Explain why this strategy is highly unlikely to succeed in terms of movements in the future price of the asset.

6.4 Sarbanes-Oxley and Dodd-Frank

In your view, would these two Acts of Congress survive an economic cost-benefit analysis? Think like an economist, not a regulator.

6.5 Backdating of options grants

There are various problems involved with the backdating of options grants.

a. What are the legal ones?
b. What are the ethical ones?
c. Who gains and who loses financially in a backdating episode? Explain.

References and suggested reading

Behr, Peter and April Witt, "Concerns Grow Amid Conflicts officials Seek to Limit Probe, Fallout of Deals," *The Washington Post*, July 30, 2002.

Brown, Stephen J. and O. W. Steenbeek (2001), "Doubling: Nick Leeson's Trading Strategy," *Pacific-Basin Finance Journal*, 9(2): 83–99.

Forelle, Charles and James Bander, "The Perfect Payday: Some CEOs Reap Millions by Landing Stock Options When They are Most Valuable. Luck—or Something Else?" *The Wall Street Journal*, March 18, 2006.

Hoffman, William, "Timely Disclosure at Center of AA Flap," *Dallas Business Journal*, April 25, 2003.

Jarvis, Christopher (2000), "The Rise and Fall of Albania's Pyramid Schemes," *Finance and Development*, 37(1): 46–49.

Jorion, Philippe (1995), *Big Bets Gone Bad: Derivatives and Bankruptcy in Orange County*, San Diego: Academic Press.

Leeson, N. (1996), *Rogue Trader*, London: Little, Brown and Co.

Kindleberger, Charles (1989), *Manias, Panics and Crashes: A History of Financial Crises*," 2nd ed. New York: Basic Books.

Nimalendran, M., Ritter R. Jay, and Donghang Zhang (2004), "Are Trading Commissions a Factor in IPO Allocation?" Working Paper, University of Florida.

Niskanen, William (2005), *After Enron: Lessons for Public Policy*, Lanham, MD: Rowman and Littlefield Publishers.

O'Hara, Philip (2001), "Insider Trading in Financial Markets: Liquidity, Ethics, Efficiency," *International Journal of Social Economics*, 28(12): 1046–1062.

Prystay, Chris, "Five are Charged in Case Involving CAO Singapore," *The Wall Street Journal*, June 10, 2005.

Prystay, Chris, "Singapore Exchange to Bolster Listing Rules," *The Wall Street Journal*, May 31, 2005.

ERisk.com (2004), Barings Case Study, http://www.erisk.com/Learning/CaseStudies/ref_case_barings.asp

Quing, Hao (2004), "Laddering in Initial Public Offerings," Working

Paper, University of Florida.

Searsey, Dionne and Li Yuan, "Adelphia's John Rigas Gets 15 Years," *The Wall Street Journal*, June 21, 2005.

Western, David (2004), *Booms, Bubbles, and Busts in the U. S. Stock Market*, London & New York: Routledge.

Stigler, George (1971), "The Theory of Economic Regulation," *The Bell Journal of Economics and Management*, 2(1): 3-21.

Wilmott, Paul (2000), *Paul Wilmott on Quantitative Finance*, New York: John Wiley and Sons.

Witt, April and Peter Behr, "Losses, Conflicts Threaten Survival CFO Fastow Ousted in Probe of Profits," *The Washington Post*, July 31, 2002.

Tabasso, Gianfranco (2004), "A Modern Replica of Ponzi Finance: The Painful Lessons of the Parmalat Affair," *Treasury Management International*, 126:21-25.

Zuckoff, Mitchell (2005), *Ponzi's Scheme: The True Story of a Financial Legend*, New York: Random House.

CHAPTER 7 Financial Leverage, Moral Hazard and Counterparty Risk: The Financial Crisis of 2007-2009

金融杠杆、道德风险和对手风险:2007—2009年的金融危机

When housing prices and share prices fall, households suffer a loss in wealth. In particular, U.S. household net wealth fell $11 trillion in 2008, 77% of 2008 GDP. This loss in wealth curbed consumer spending. Households raised their savings rates to restore their wealth, pensions and savings. At the same time, falling asset prices bankrupted leveraged borrowers who were put in financial distress, default, or foreclosure. Leveraged banks, especially investment banks were also put on the brink of insolvency and negative equity. Bankruptcies raised the specter of counterparty risk, and credit, even interbank credit, came to a halt. The ultimate consequence of these developments led to the recession of 2008-2009 in the United States. It is useful to simplify the denouement of the financial crisis and its economic effects in a simple drawing, Figure 7.1.

Figure 7.1　The financial crisis of 2008–2009

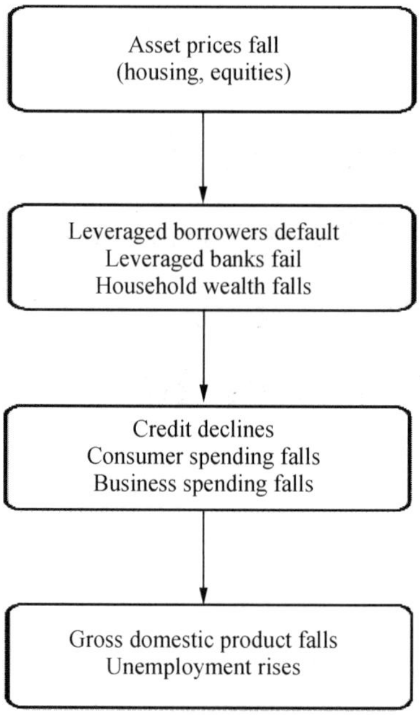

```
┌─────────────────────┐
│  Asset prices fall  │
│ (housing, equities) │
└──────────┬──────────┘
           ▼
┌──────────────────────────┐
│ Leveraged borrowers default │
│   Leveraged banks fail   │
│  Household wealth falls  │
└──────────┬───────────────┘
           ▼
┌──────────────────────────┐
│     Credit declines      │
│  Consumer spending falls │
│  Business spending falls │
└──────────┬───────────────┘
           ▼
┌──────────────────────────┐
│ Gross domestic product falls │
│    Unemployment rises    │
└──────────────────────────┘
```

Financial leverage

Financial leverage is the best friend of an investor when asset prices rise, but her worst enemy if asset prices fall. This is because the multiplied effect on equity depends on the degree of financial leverage. U.S. publicly-listed firms are required to file **balance sheets** quarterly, known as the 10Q, and at the end of their fiscal year, the 10K. The balance sheet of a firm measures the "probable" value of a firm's assets, A, and its liabilities or debt, D, defining stockholders equity, E, as the difference between its assets and its liabilities:

$$\text{Assets}(A) = \text{Liabilities}(D) + \text{Stockholders' Equity}(E)$$

Assets are defined as "*probable future economic benefits obtained or controlled by a particular entity as a result of past transactions or events*" (*Statement of Financial Accounting Standards* (SFAC 6, paragraph 25) of *the Federal Accounting Standards Board* (FASB) of the United States), while liabilities are "*probable future sacrifices of economic benefits arising from present obligations of a particular entity to transfer assets or provide services to other entities in the future as a result of past transactions or*

资产负债表（Balance sheet）：表示企业在一定日期的财务状况的主要会计报表。

资产 = 负债 + 所有者权益

events" (SFAC 6, paragraph 35).

Stockholder's equity is thus "*the residual interest in the net assets of an entity that remains after deducting its liabilities*" (SFAC 6, paragraph 49).

The *International Accounting Standards Board* (IASB) was established in 1973 to harmonize global accounting standards.

Market and impairment rules may require "markdowns" to the value of assets and liabilities, particularly in the accounting for investments in securities. Thus financial institutions are required to "mark to market" much of their assets to recognize probable losses. Marking to market has a multiplied effect on the equity held, and may result in negative equity or bankruptcy.

We have:
$$\text{Assets} \equiv \text{Liabilities} + \text{Equity} \equiv A \equiv D + E \quad (7.1)$$

Three definitions of financial leverage

1. For financial institutions in particular, the financial leverage ratio is often defined by the ratio of assets to equity:
$$\frac{\text{Assets}}{\text{Equity}} = \frac{A}{E} \quad (7.2) \qquad \frac{资产}{权益} = \frac{A}{E}$$

2. For firms, the debt to equity ratio is often used:
$$\frac{\text{Liabilities}}{\text{Equity}} = \frac{D}{E} \quad (7.3) \qquad \frac{负债}{权益} = \frac{D}{E}$$

Clearly, from the definition $A = D + E$ the relationship between these two measures of financial leverage is simply:
$$\frac{A}{E} = \frac{D}{E} + 1$$

Consequently, when liabilities are constant:
$$\frac{\Delta A}{A} = \frac{\Delta E}{A}$$

or
$$\frac{\Delta A}{A} = \left(\frac{E}{A}\right)\frac{\Delta E}{E}$$

Thus
$$\frac{\Delta E}{E} = \left(\frac{A}{E}\right)\frac{\Delta A}{A} \quad (7.4)$$

权益的变化百分比等于杠杆率与资产变化百分比的乘积。此公式表明，杠杆率放大了由资产变化而引起的权益变化。

Consequently, when debt is constant, the percentage change in the value of equity equals the degree of financial leverage times the percentage change in the value of assets. For instance, at purchase, a mortgage borrower that makes a 20% down payment has a financial leverage ratio of

$A/E = 5$, or $D/E = 4$. Since $\frac{\Delta E}{E} = \left(\frac{D}{E} + 1\right)\frac{\Delta A}{A}$, a change in the value of a home of 10% causes a 50% change in the borrower's home equity, as indicated in Figure 7.2. Financial leverage is a good friend when asset prices rise, but a poor one when they fall.

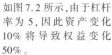
如图 7.2 所示,由于杠杆率为 5,因此资产变化 10% 将导致权益变化 50%。

Figure 7.2 The magnification effect of financial leverage on gains and losses

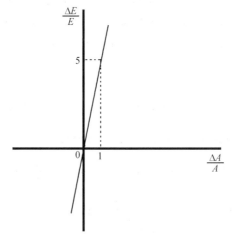

3. A third index of financial leverage is defined by debt to assets, or

负债/资产 = $\frac{D}{A} = \frac{D}{(D+E)}$

$$\frac{\text{Debt}}{\text{Assets}} = \frac{D}{A} = \frac{D}{D+E} \tag{7.5}$$

This is also given by the ratio of the first two measures of financial leverage since $\frac{D/E}{A/E} = \frac{D}{A} = \frac{D}{D+E}$. The third definition, $[D/(D+E)]$, has the merit of ranging from zero for the unlevered firm, to 1 for the bankrupt firm with zero equity.

A simple application of the leverage concept is to determine what percentage decline in the value of assets will make equity zero. In this case, with debt constant:

$$\Delta A = -E$$

or

$$\frac{\Delta A}{A} = -\frac{E}{A} = -\frac{1}{A/E}$$

That is, if the value of assets falls by the reciprocal of the financial average ratio, equity will be wiped out. For instance, an investment bank with a 30 to 1 degree of financial leverage would only be able to sustain a 1/30th fall in the value of its assets before becoming bankrupt, that is a 3.3% fall.

Securitization

Securitization stands for the bundling of contracts to future cash flows into a security that can be traded for the present value of its expected cash flow. Any asset that yields a future expected cash flow can, in principle, be bundled with other assets, either similar or unlike, that then are sold as a single security. The securitization of mortgage backed assets (MBAs) of different credit worthiness, including sub-prime or risky mortgages, was not a problem so long as housing prices kept rising. A typical mortgage backed asset would be composed of say 20% prime mortgages, 40% alternative A-paper (Alt A), of slightly less credit quality, then 40% subprime loans which have a higher risk of default.

The present value of the cash flow thus depends largely upon the likelihood of payment of principal and interest on the mortgages. With rising housing prices, the likelihood of default is small, thus the value of the MBA is great. The moment housing prices fell, this led to defaults by highly leveraged sub-prime borrowers, and thus a rapid fall in the value of MBAs. Indeed, MBAs became illiquid, in part due to the difficulty of evaluating their fundamental value, so the MBA market froze following the precipitous fall in their value. The FED ultimately purchased over a trillion dollars of MBAs in the open market to avert a collapse of the investment and commercial banks that held them. A **collateralized debt obligation (CDO)** is also a security backed by a bundle of other assets. A synthetic CDO is one that holds no underlying assets, so that a spot buyer is betting that the price will rise, while a spot seller is expecting the price to fall. If a synthetic CDO is bought for future delivery, it is a long position, while a sale for future delivery is a short position. It is said that Goldman Sachs (GS) shorted MBAs that it had structured and sold to investors, expecting to benefit from a fall in their price. In any case, GS settled with the Justice department for having possibly misled investors and betting against their position. In principle, there is nothing wrong with securitization. However, it plays a major role in passing on the risk to ultimate investors. For instance, the mortgage originator makes a loan to someone who does not otherwise qualify, but sells it immediately to Fannie Mae, Freddie Mac, or a Wall Street investment bank who bundles the mortgage with others to sell them to investors.

The mortgage lender has no credit risk, so there is said to be "moral hazard" in his or her mortgage origination. The original lender has "no skin in the game." That is, the original lender cannot lose if the borrower defaults. This insurance against loss does not provide the right incentives for the original lender to verify the credit worthiness of the borrower. The main incentive is to make the loan to collect the fees, then immediately sell it. The credit rating institutions typically scored the MBAs as AAA, the highest notation, which is fine while the market is rising. A triple A rating is necessary to be able to sell MBAs to some pension funds, such as CALPERS in California. There is thus said to be "moral hazard." Everyone gains while housing prices continue to rise, but they do fall!

Reduced mortgage leverage in China

在中国,部分城市首套住房的首付款比例(down payments) 已经提高到30%,第二套住房的首付款比例已经提高到50%。

In some cities of China, down payments have been increased to 30% for the first property and 50% for the second. This means that the financial leverage ratios are 3.33 and 2 respectively. Thus, at loan origination, it would take a 30% and 50% fall in the market value of the home before being "under the water" or in negative equity territory. This has the advantage of making strategic default less likely, but the disadvantage of raising the "cost of carry" of real estate.

Such stabilization measures, along with increased mortgage rates, should effectively reduce the rate of housing price rises. Economic growth in China has been fueled by construction, so the policy of slowing investment in housing must be done with extreme care. However, when the inflation rate rises relative to the nominal interest rate, the real cost of carry falls.

Financial leverage of some selected firms

Here are some measures of financial leverage reported in Table 7.1 for U.S. tech companies drawn from yahoo.finance, and some comparable Chinese companies listed as American Depositary Receipts in Table 7.2, as well as some comparable electric vehicle and computer companies in Table 7.3.

Table 7.1 Financial leverage of selected US technology and internet firms

	Apple (Nasdaq)	Amazon (Nasdaq)	Microsoft (Nasdaq)	Facebook (Nasdaq)	eBay (Nasdaq)
	11/21/2018	11/21/2018	11/21/2018	11/21/2018	11/21/2018
Market capitalization* (billions)	$839	$742	$792	$387	$27
Total debt (billions)	$114	$47	$83	$0.07	$9
Debt/Equity	13.6%	6.4%	10.5%	0.02%	34%
Debt/(Debt + Equity)	12.0%	6.0%	9.5%	0.02%	25%
Beta (3 Years, monthly)	1.21	1.94	1.09	0.62	1.41

* Market capitalization equals equity value.

Table 7.2 Financial leverage of selected Chinese technology and internet firms

	Alibaba (NYSE)	Baidu (Nasdaq)	Tencent (Nasdaq)	JD (Nasdaq)	Weibo (Nasdaq)
	11/21/2018	11/21/2018	11/21/2018	11/21/2018	11/21/2018
Market capitalization (billions)	$384	$64	$347	$29	$13
Total debt (billions)	$21	$7	$26	$3	$1
Debt/Equity	5.5%	12%	8%	11%	7%
Debt/(Debt + Equity)	5.2%	10%	7%	10%	6%
Beta	1.74	1.27	1.41	1.38	2.3

Table 7.3 Financial leverage of selected US and Chinese electric automobile and computer companies

	Tesla (Nasdaq)	NIO (NYSE)	Lenovo (OTC other)	IBM (Nasdaq)	Intel (Nasdaq)
	11/20/2018	11/21/2018	11/21/2018	11/20/2018	11/20/2018
Market capitalization (billions)	$58	$8	$9	$107	$215
Total debt (billions)	$14	$0.3	$4	$47	$28
Debt/equity	23%	3.3%	52%	44%	13%
Debt/(Debt + Equity)	19%	3.2%	34%	30%	11%
Beta	0.52	NA	1.12	1.84	0.8

In general, technology and internet firms have less leverage than manufacturing firms. Examples of highly leveraged automobile companies are General Motors with debt more than twice equity and Ford Motor Company with debt more than four times equity as of November 23, 2018.

Leveraged households

During the housing boom, mortgage loans were made at 20% down, 10% down, and in some cases zero down payment, implying financial leverage of 5, 10, and infinity respectively. Many of these mortgages were sold directly to Fannie Mae and Freddie Mac, who guaranteed them against default, bundled some and sold them as MBAs as well as holding some. Other mortgages were sold to Wall Street institutions who similarly bundled them, selling them to investors as MBAs or CDOs. In most cases, the mortgage lender passed on the credit risk as did the investment banks. However, both Fannie Mae and Freddie Mac kept many MBAs as security investments, thus holding the credit risk.

The role of the government: Fannie Mae and Freddie Mac

房利美(Fannie Mae): 联邦国民抵押贷款协会, 是美国最大的政府赞助企业, 主要业务是在美国房屋抵押贷款二级市场中收购贷款, 并通过向投资者发行机构债券或证券化的抵押债券, 以低成本集资, 赚取利差。

房地美(Freddie Mac): 联邦住房贷款抵押公司, 是美国第二大政府赞助企业, 商业规模仅次于房利美。

"Fannie Mae has expanded home ownership for millions of families in the 1990's by reducing down payment requirements," said Franklin D. Raines, Fannie Mae's (then) chairman and chief executive. "Yet there remain too many borrowers whose credit is just a notch below what our underwriting has required who have been relegated to paying significantly higher mortgage rates in the so-called sub-prime market." Fannie Mae, the nation's largest underwriter of home mortgages does not lend money directly to consumers, instead it purchase loans that banks make on what is called the secondary market. By expanding the type of loans that it will buy, Fannie Mae is hoping to spur banks to make more loans to people with less than-stellar credit ratings." (*New York Times*, September 20, 1999)

A prescient remark was made by Peter Wallison of the American Enterprise Institute at the time: "From the perspective of many people, including me, this is another thrift industry growing up around us ... If they fail the government will have to step up and bail them out the way it stepped up and bailed out the thrift industry."

Indeed, this is a prime example of moral hazard: Mortgage lending institutions such as Countrywide Financial made sub-prime loans on stated income with little likelihood of repayment if home prices did not rise, and sold the mortgages to Fannie Mae and Freddie Mac, thereby passing on the credit risk to the US taxpayer ultimately. Similarly, these loans could be sold to an eager Wall Street who bundled them as MBAs, passing on the default risk to investors who purchased them. The investment banks were also burned holding MBAs, especially Lehman Brothers and Citibank. As of 2011, the Federal rescue of Fannie Mae and Freddie Mac has cost the taxpayer over \$120 billion, nor has any meaningful reform of these now state owned institutions been implemented, including in the Dodd-Frank Act of 2010.

Rising and falling home equity

When housing prices are expected to rise forever as they did in the recent past, this is good news for the homeowner whose equity in the home rises (except for the increased property taxes). Even the NINJA borrower (no income, no job, and no assets) enjoys rising equity. Here is an example of a fixed interest rate mortgage of 6% that is serviced by the lender for one year. In light of rising prices, the amount of equity increases in Table 7.4, depending on the increase in the market value of the home, and the degree of financial leverage.

资产价格上升时,权益也随之增加。但权益的增加不仅由资产价格上升所决定,还取决于杠杆率的大小。

Table 7.4 Rising equity with rising home prices

Loan origination(8-15-2008, 6% fixed rate, 30 years)

Value of house	Down payment	Value of Mortgage	Equity
100	0	100	0
100	10	90	10
100	20	80	20
100	30	70	30

1 year later(9-15-2009, market rates remain at 6%)

Value of house	Down payment	Value of Mortgage	Equity
110	0	98.77	11.23
110	10	88.89	21.11
110	20	79.02	30.98
110	30	69.07	40.93

1 year later(9-15-2009, market rates remain at 6%)

Value of house	Down payment	Value of Mortgage	Equity
120	0	98.77	21.23
120	10	88.89	31.11
120	20	79.02	40.98
120	30	69.07	50.93

1 year later(9-15-2009, market rates remain at 6%)

Value of house	Down payment	Value of Mortgage	Equity
130	0	98.77	31.23
130	10	88.89	41.11
130	20	79.02	50.98
130	30	69.07	60.93

(Continued)

1 year later(9-15-2009, market rates remain at 6%)			
Value of house	Down payment	Value of Mortgage	Equity
140	0	98.77	41.23
140	10	88.89	51.11
140	20	79.02	60.98
140	30	69.07	70.93

However, when the market price of the home falls, the mortgage goes "under the water", exhibiting negative equity sooner, the greater the financial leverage and the greater the fall in the market price of the home. A striking example of the boom in housing prices took place in Miami, Florida as reported in Table 7.5. Home prices nearly tripled from January 2000 to December 2006, then plummeted in half by February 2011.

Table 7.5 The boom and the bust in Miami's home prices

Miami, Florida		
January 2000	100	% change
December 2006	281	181%
February 2011	138	−51%
Source: The S&P/Case-Shiller Home Price Index.		

This represents a compound annual rate of appreciation of 19% per year during the housing boom and a fall of 16% per year during the bust. For the United States 20 city index, prices doubled from January 2000 to July 2006 to a level of 206, then fell to 138 in February 2011. The boom increased household wealth through increasing equity values, then destroyed most of the wealth during the bust. Further, the bust gave rise to the problem of negative equity. Table 7.6 indicates the problem of falling equity when home prices decline.

Table 7.6 Falling equity with falling home prices

Loan origination(8-15-2008, 6% fixed rate, 30 years)			
Value of house	Down payment	Value of Mortgage	Equity
100	0	100	0
100	10	90	10
100	20	80	20
100	30	70	30

(Continued)

1 year later(9-15-2009, market rates remain at 6%)			
Value of house	Down payment	Value of Mortgage	Equity
90	0	98.77	−8.77
90	10	88.89	1.11
90	20	79.02	10.98
90	30	69.07	20.93
1 year later(9-15-2009, market rates remain at 6%)			
Value of house	Down payment	Value of Mortgage	Equity
80	0	98.77	−18.77
80	10	88.89	−8.89
80	20	79.02	0.98
80	30	69.07	10.93
1 year later(9-15-2009, market rates remain at 6%)			
Value of house	Down payment	Value of Mortgage	Equity
70	0	98.77	−28.77
70	10	88.89	−18.89
70	20	79.02	−9.02
70	30	69.07	0.93
1 year later(9-15-2009, market rates remain at 6%)			
Value of house	Down payment	Value of Mortgage	Equity
60	0	98.77	−38.77
60	10	88.89	−28.89
60	20	79.02	−19.02
60	30	69.07	−9.07

The positive and negative effects on mortgage holder equity can be vividly seen in the Home Price Index in Figure 7.3. From 1996 to 2007, a ten year period, housing prices rose at a near accelerating rate, topping out at 20% in 2005. In 2007, housing prices began falling.

The fall in housing prices of 2006–2007 were both dramatic and unanticipated. Once unsold inventories of existing and new houses reach ten or eleven months supply, and prices are cut, the drop was sharp and steep. As a fraction of GDP, residential construction fell from 6.2% in 2005 and 5.8% in 2006 to 4.2% in 2007. In terms of USD, that represents a decline in residential investment of 127 billion USD, as reported in Table 7.11. In over 6 years, from January 2000 to April 2006, the average housing price of the 20 major cities of the S&P/Case Shiller home price index in the United States more than doubled, rising at an annual rate of 17%. Due to the stock-flow nature of the housing cycle, the downturn was severe. The S&P/Case-Shiller index fell 32% in two years, from the peak of April 2006 to the trough of May 2008, a decline of 15% per annum. The slump remained in place for nearly another four years, from May 2008 at a home price index of 141 falling to an absolute low—an index of 137 in March 2012. In all, it took over 10 years for the home price index to reach its peak level of April 2006. In May 2019 the index is at 216, slightly above the boom period's peak.

Figure 7.3   The S&P/Case-Shiller U. S. National Home Price Index (January 2000 = 100)

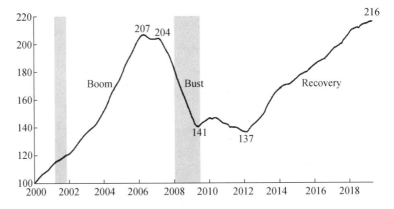

Shaded areas represent US recessions.

Note: The S&P/Case-Shiller home price index (SPCS20R) is a composite of the home price index for 20 major Metropolitan Statistical Areas in the United States. The index is published monthly by S&P. The Case and Shiller method adjusts for the quality of the homes sold.

Source: The Case-Shiller 20 City home price index accessed from the Federal Reserve Bank of St. Louis, FRED at fred.stlouisfed.org, August 2, 2019.

In the News: China's Real Estate Sector

China's real estate sector showed a slowdown of the rise in real estate prices during 2008, then a brief fall in early 2009, before rising again at high annual rates, as shown in Figure 7.4.

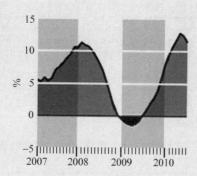

Figure 7.4 China: Sales price index of residential and commercial buildings in 70 large and medium size cities*

* percentage change from a year earlier.
Source: Chinese National Bureau of Statistics.

Floor space sold was at reduced rates during almost all of 2008, reflecting the fall in demand relative to a year earlier, consistent with the fall in prices in early 2009. Once again, the rise in sales of floor space resumed in 2009, but slowed somewhat in 2010, as shown in Figure 7.5.

Figure 7.5 China: Real estate floor space sold*

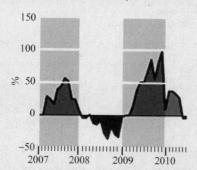

* percentage change in square meters from a year earlier.
Source: Chinese National Bureau of Statistics.

Table 7.7 reports China's policies to slow the rise in housing prices.

Table 7.7 China's policies to slow the rise in housing prices

APRIL 15, 2010	MAY 6, 2010	SEPT. 29, 2010	OCT.-NOV. 2010	OCT. 20, 2010	DEC. 25, 2010	JAN. 26, 2011	JAN. 28, 2011	FEB. 8, 2011
The State Council raises minimum down payments for second-home purchases to 50% from 40%.	Shenzhen restricts apartment purchases by foreigners and Hong Kong and Macau residents to one each until the end of the year.	New rules require a 30% down payment on putchases of primary residences. Banks are ordered to stop lending for third-home purchases.	Several local governments introduce limits on home purchases.	The central bank raises interest rates by a quarter percentage point.	The central bank raises interest rates by a quarter percentage point.	The State Council raises down-payment requirements for second-home purchases to 60% from 50%.	Shanghai and Chongqing start trials of an annual property tax.	The central bank raises interest rates by a quarter percentage point.

Note: Most recent figure is from December 2010; includes residential and commercial property.
Source: National Bureau of Statistics(property price); WSJ reporting(timeline).

Strategic default

策略违约(Strategic default):有支付能力的一方选择性停止对某项借款进行支付。

Falling housing prices often imply mortgage holders have negative equity, giving them an incentive to "walk away" from their mortgages. High leverage entailed in low down payments mean that small housing price declines may trigger a strategic default choice.

Default and foreclosure, by the same token, add to the momentum for housing prices to fall. A vicious cycle of falling housing prices, rising default rates and further falling prices as the foreclosed homes come onto the market is a key feature of the slowdown in real estate construction.

A potential buyer who has deposited $50,000 in earnest money to purchase a condominium under construction is under no obligation to buy the unit when it is finished. If the market price of the condominium has fallen $50,000 below its sales price, the potential buyer has the option to forfeit, leaving the $50,000 with the builder. Or she can recover some or all of the deposit by claiming that the contract conditions were not satisfied.

The importance of residential construction in investment has led to slowdowns in the major economies of the world from the problem of default in sub-prime mortgages, negative equity, and strategic forfeit of contracts. Figure 7.6 illustrates an optimal strategic default when equity is sufficiently negative to warrant the costs of default.

Figure 7.6 Optimal strategic default with negative equity

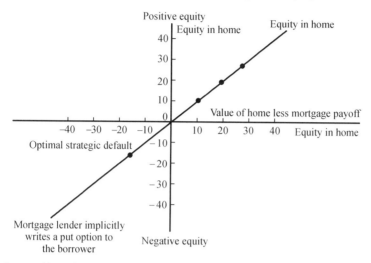

Source: Yong Chen, Michael Connolly, Wenjin Tang, and Tie Su (2009).

Applying the Concept: Foreclosure

Foreclosure is a process that allows a lender to recover some of the amount owed on a defaulted loan by selling or taking ownership (repossession) of the property securing the loan. The foreclosure process begins when a borrower/owner defaults on loan payments (usually mortgage payments) and the lender files a public default notice, called a Notice of Default or Lis Pendens. The foreclosure process can end one of four ways:

1. The borrower/owner reinstates the loan by paying off the default amount during a grace period determined by state law. This grace period is also known as pre-foreclosure.

2. The borrower/owner sells the property to a third party during the pre-foreclosure period. The sale allows the borrower/owner to pay off the loan and avoid having a foreclosure on his or her credit history.

3. A third party buys the property at a public auction at the end of the pre-foreclosure period.

4. The lender takes ownership of the property, usually with the intent to re-sell it on the open market. The lender can take ownership either through an agreement with the borrower/owner during pre-foreclosure or by

取消抵押品赎回权（Foreclosure）：允许债权人通过出售或获得所有权的方式，对违约贷款的损失进行一定程度的弥补的过程。

> buying back the property at the public auction. Properties repossessed by the lender are also known as bank-owned or REO properties (Real Estate Owned by the lender).
> Source: RealtyTrac, Inc., February 14, 2007.

In Colorado in 2009, the rate of foreclosure per 100 mortgages was 15.3%, 17.5% in Nevada, 11.3% in California, 11% in Michigan, and 8% in Florida.

The loan to value ratio

Home mortgages typically require a down payment. For instance, the benchmark down payment in the United States is 20%, while it is 30% in some cities of China on the first home. The **loan to value** (LTV) ratio in these two instances is 80% and 70% respectively. The LTV ratio represents the mortgage loan to the assessed value of the asset, the home in this instance, or $\frac{D}{A}$. Note that:

$$1 - LTV = \frac{A}{A} - \frac{D}{A} = \frac{E}{A}$$

Consequently, financial leverage equals:

$$\frac{A}{E} = \frac{1}{1 - LTV}$$

We can thus have a simple relationship between LTV, the percentage down payment, and financial leverage at loan origination in Table 7.8.

Table 7.8 Loan to value and financial leverage

Loan to value	Down payment	Financial leverage
0.99	0.01	100.0
0.95	0.05	20.0
0.90	0.10	10.0
0.85	0.15	6.7
0.80	0.20	5.0
0.75	0.25	4.0
0.70	0.30	3.3
0.65	0.35	2.9
0.60	0.40	2.5
0.55	0.45	2.2
0.50	0.50	2.0

Of course, a NINJA loan, no income, no job, no assets and a LTV = 1 would have infinite leverage!

Pre-construction "earnest money"

A good time to buy a real estate investment is during the pre-construction finance phase. A builder must pre-sell from 60% to 70% of his/her units to qualify for construction finance. In order to buy during this phase, a deposit of 10% of the sales prices is made. The "earnest money" is then deposited in a third-party escrow account until the development is completed and the closing can take place. In the meantime, the builder can obtain a "bridge" loan or mezzanine finance while the construction loan is pending.

保证金 (Earnest money):房产购买者付给开发商以确保未来购房的担保金。

This pre-construction finance period is thus critical to launch the development. If the builder fails to pre-sell sufficient units, the project is off and the deposits returned. What happens when a buyer purchases the unit early at a fairly good market price, the market price rises, then suddenly falls? This describes many condominium and apartment developments in US cities. The potential buyer, not having closed yet, is in a unique position of holding a call option to buy the unit at a sales or strike price determined in advance. If the market price is below the sales prices less the earnest monies, the buyer has the business option to forfeit.

Following the developer's filing of official condominium documents, the most the buyer can lose by failing to close is the initial deposit. This is a contractual forfeit. Say the buyer purchases the unit for delivery in one year for $500,000, depositing $50,000 in "earnest" or good faith money in the escrow account. In one year, if the unit appreciates 10%, the buyer will close, earning potential profits of $50,000. However, should the market price fall 10% or more, the buyer has the legal option to forfeit on the contract, forfeiting to the builder the initial $50,000 deposit. Some recovery of the initial deposit may also be possible.

Applying the Concept: Credit Default Swap

The buyer of a credit swap pays premia for credit protection against the default of a bond or firm, whereas the seller of the swap guarantees the credit worthiness of the product. The risk of default is transferred from the holder of the security to the seller of the swap. For example, the buyer of a credit swap will be entitled to the par value of the bond by the seller of the swap, should the bond default—fail to make its coupon payments.

信用违约互换 (Credit default swap):互换的购买者向互换的出售者支付一定费用,从而将违约风险转移给互换的出售方。

Figure 7.7 illustrates the cash flows between the protection buyer and seller when there is no default.

如图所示,互换的购买者持有债券,他因为持有债券而面临信用违约风险。因此,他向互换出售者购买互换,并支付一定的费用,当债券发行人违约时,债券持有人(即互换的购买者)并不会损失惨重,因为互换的出售者会把债券的面值支付给互换的购买者。

Figure 7.7 A credit default swap with no default

Credit default swap (No default)
Protection buyer
Quarterly payment of basis points per annum
Protection seller
Reference bond or notional amount

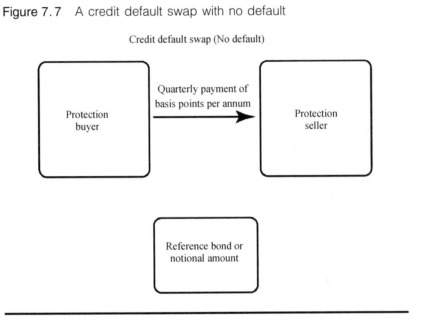

When a default occurs, the seller of the credit default insurance pays the protection buyer, as illustrated in Figure 7.8.

Figure 7.8 A credit default swap with default

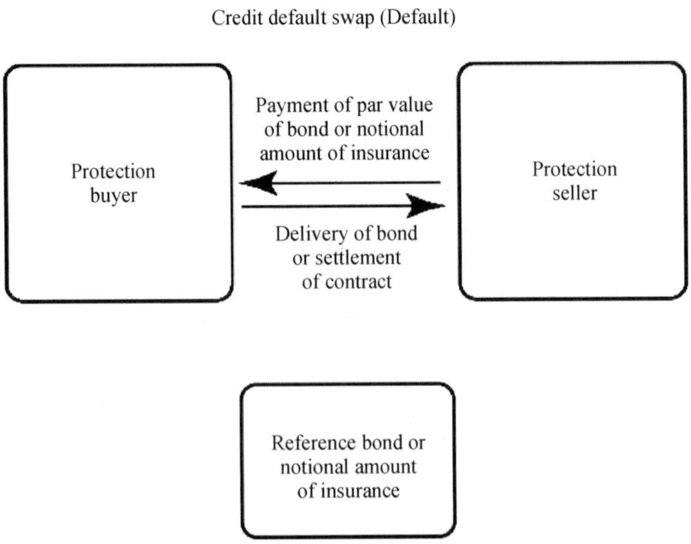

Credit default swap (Default)
Protection buyer
Payment of par value of bond or notional amount of insurance
Delivery of bond or settlement of contract
Protection seller
Reference bond or notional amount of insurance

The difference between a credit default swap and an insurance policy against default is that anyone can purchase the insurance, even those who have no direct interest in the loan. This type of investor is commonly referred to as a speculator, while the one holding the bond is referred to as a hedger. If the borrower defaults on the loan, not only does the lender receive payment by the insurance company, the speculator receives money as well. Speculation proved key to the massive losses by American International Group (AIG) when Lehman Brothers defaulted since AIG had sold credit default swaps against Lehman Brothers and other defaults. A significant portion of the AIG bailout monies of up to $173 billion were paid to investment banks that had purchased credit default swaps from AIG. Credit default swaps are not traded on an exchange and there is no required reporting of transactions to a government agency. This may be changed by the Dodd-Frank regulation bill, but that remains to be seen. A graphical representation of the major purchases of credit default insurance against the default of mortgage backed assets, including those of Lehman Brothers, is provided in Figure 7.9.

Figure 7.9 AIG's default swap insurance sold to five major Wall Street Banks

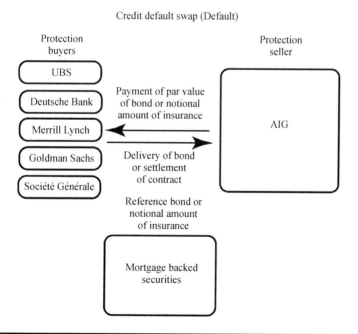

The payouts ranged from 3.3 billion dollars to UBS to 11 billion

dollars to the Société Générale, as illustrated in Figure 7.10. AIG, originally headquartered in Shanghai, received a TARP loan of $85 billion, most of which has been converted to preferred shares in AIG.

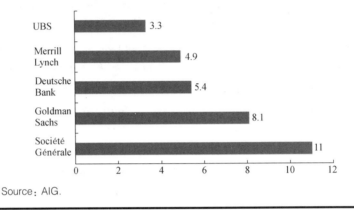

Figure 7.10 AIG's payments of default swap insurance sold to five major Wall Street Banks (USD billions)

Source: AIG.

Counter-party risk

交易对手风险(Counter-party risk):交易对手不履约的风险。

High leverage and securitization of assets compounds counter-party risk—the risk that default of a counter-party in a contract, loan or impairment of a security inflicting loss on the investor holding the counterpart, the lender, or the holder of the security. The securitization of mortgages and collateralization of debt obligations spreads leveraged counterparty risk throughout the financial system. At the height of the financial bubble, leveraged mortgage backed assets and collateralized debt obligations were held by Federal National Mortgage Association (FNMA), known as Fannie Mae, and the Federal Home Loan Mortgage Corporation (FHLMC), known as Freddie Mac, as well as investment banks and insurance companies. Fannie Mae and Freddie Mac were previously government sponsored enterprises but were put under the conservatorship of the Federal Housing Finance Agency (FHFA) September 2008 after their stocks fell to 50 cents and were delisted in June. Wall Street banks issued notes and shares rated investment grade to other investors and financial institutions worldwide. When the consumer defaults on the initial loan, the default spreads throughout the financial system, impairing the mortgage back assets and collateralized debt obligations on which they reside, as in Figure 7.9 elaborated by Wachovia Research in 1994.

Figure 7.11   Counterparty risk

如图所示,交易对手风险在金融系统中传递。

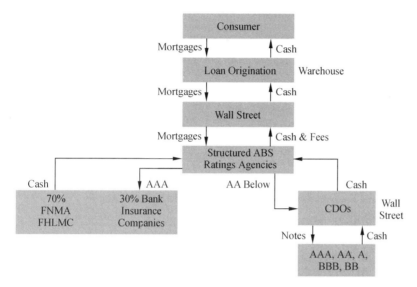

FNMA: Federal National Mortgage Association, commonly known as Fannie Mae.
FHLMC: Federal Home Loan Mortgage Corporation, known as Freddie Mac.
ABS: Asset Backed Securities.
CDOs: Collateralized Debt Obligations.
Ratings Agencies: S&P, Moody's, Fitch.
Source: Wachovia Research, 1994.

Defaults on such levered assets sends counterparty fear through the financial system, giving rise to the term "toxic" assets that ceased to be traded as financial markets froze, leaving investors holding illiquid assets of dubious value. Indeed, since trading in many markets came to a halt, it was difficult to value many assets. Thus, "marking to market" was not possible since there was no mechanism for price discovery. The US Treasury and the Federal Reserve Bank intervened by purchasing many of these assets and lending to the insolvent banks, thus providing a market for the assets and liquidity for the banks. Nowhere was the impact more important than on commercial and investment banks, as well as insurance companies holding these assets.

Leveraged financial institutions

Both commercial and investment banks were highly leveraged prior to the financial crisis. During the housing boom, this meant rising bank profits. Of course, during the bust in housing prices and the value of mortgage backed assets held by them as securities, many banks were technically bankrupt, i.e. had negative equity. While not insolvent, these banks could not continue for long as "zombie" banks. Consider *Levered Bank, Inc.* in Table 7.9 whose assets are 100 and liabilities are 95. Consequently, its book value or shareholders' equity is 5, implying financial leverage of 20.

Table 7.9 Bank leverage (Levered Bank, Inc.)

	Assets	Liabilities	
Reserves	10	95	Debt
Loans & securities	90	5	Shareholders' equity
	100	100	
Financial leverage			
Assets/Equity	20		
Debt/Equity	19		

Now suppose that the value of its loans and securities fall by 10%, and are "marked to market" at 91. Note: if the bank's assets are available-for-sale or traded securities, the balance sheet carrying value is the market value. If they are classified as held-to-maturity assets, they may be carried at cost. The hypothetical balance sheet in Table 7.10 would have negative shareholders' equity, that is, it would be bankrupt from an accounting point of view. Its book value would be negative.

Table 7.10 Bank leverage and accounting bankruptcy (Levered Bank, Inc.)

	Assets	Liabilities	
Reserves	10	95	Debt
Loans & securities	81	-4	Shareholders' equity
	91	91	

联邦存款保险公司(Federal Deposit Insurance Corporation, FDIC): 美国国会建立的独立的联邦政府机构,通过为存款提供保险、检查和监督金融机构以及接管金融机构,来维持美国金融体系的稳定性和公众信心。

If this were a single bank in isolation, the **Federal Deposit Insurance Corporation (FDIC)** could take over the operation of the bank, recapitalize it, and sell it when it has a healthier balance sheet. Or, it could liquidate the bank entirely.

However, when it is virtually all banks in financial distress, the monetary and fiscal authorities may decide that it is a "systemic crisis," a crisis of the financial system that has dire consequences for the economy as a whole. Then authorities may put in place an emergency Troubled Asset Relief Program (TARP) as in the United States to make loans to financial institutions and take ownership stakes in them, such as preferred or common shares. In the UK, Ireland, and Europe, some banks became state enterprises. The authorities may also attempt to merge weaker banks with stronger banks.

The harbinger of the crisis: Bear Stearns

Bear Stearns, a global investment bank headquartered in N.Y., engaged in securities trading and brokerage, until its collapse and distress sale at $10 a share to JP Morgan Chase in 2008, brokered by the FED. Bear Stearns held asset-backed securities which had lost significant value. In March 2008, the Federal Reserve Bank of New York provided an emergency loan to avert a sudden collapse of the company. However, on March 28, 2008, it was sold to JP Morgan Chase for ten dollars per share, financed by a loan from the FED, far below the 52-week high of $133.20 per share before the crisis. This was, however, an improvement on the two dollars per share originally agreed upon by Bear Stearns and JP Morgan Chase. The FED guaranteed against further losses by JP Morgan Chase in the risky loan to JP Morgan. At the same time, the FED launched its Primary Dealer Credit Facility to make loans to *primary dealers* —those that trade with the FED in its open market operations, including investment banks. The latter thus became eligible for emergency loans even though not being member commercial banks in the Federal Reserve System. Figure 7.12 reports losses in 2007 of global financial institutions.

贝尔斯登公司 (Bears Stearns): 成立于 1923 年, 曾是美国第五大投资银行, 在 2008 年的美国金融风暴中因亏损严重而被收购。

Among the top eleven losers in Figure 7.12, there are seven American financial institutions.

The bankruptcy of Lehman Brothers

Lehman Brothers, a N.Y. investment bank, borrowed significant amounts to fund its investments in the years leading to its bankruptcy in 2008. Much of its investing was in mortgage backed assets, making it vulnerable to a housing downturn. Its leverage ratio—assets to owner's equity, increased from approximately 24:1 in 2003 to 31:1 by 2007. The Fed and the Treasury attempted a sale of Lehman Brothers to Bank of America,

雷曼兄弟公司 (Lehman Brothers): 成立于 1850 年, 曾为美国第四大投资银行, 于 2008 年 9 月 15 日宣布申请破产保护。

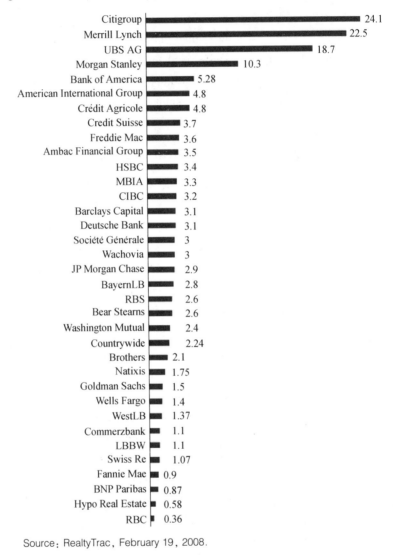

Figure 7.12 Losses to financial institutions in 2007 (USD billions)

Source: RealtyTrac, February 19, 2008.

but BOA's due diligence forecasted only negative equity and future operating losses. An offer by Barclays was rejected by the British monetary authorities, leading to the bankruptcy filing of September 15, 2008. The Lehman Brothers bankruptcy shook the financial world, raising the specter of counterparty risk and ushering in a flight to safety and cash.

While generating tremendous profits during the boom, Lehman Brothers leveraged position meant that just a 3.2% decline in the value of its assets would entirely eliminate its book value or equity. According to the bankruptcy court examiner's report: "On January 29, 2008, Lehman

Brothers Holdings Inc. (LBHI) reported record revenues of nearly \$60 billion and record earnings in excess of \$4 billion for its fiscal year ending November 30, 2007. During January 2008, Lehman's stock traded as high as \$65.73 per share and averaged in the high to mid-fifties implying a market capitalization of over \$30 billion. Less than eight months later, on September 12, 2008, Lehman's stock closed under \$4, a decline of nearly 95% from its value in January 2008. On September 15, 2008, LBHI sought Chapter 11 protection, in the largest bankruptcy proceeding ever filed. There are many reasons Lehman failed, and the responsibility is shared. Lehman was more the consequence than the cause of a deteriorating economic climate. Lehman's financial plight, and the consequences to Lehman's creditors and shareholders, was exacerbated by Lehman executives, whose conduct ranged from serious but non-culpable errors of business judgment to actionable balance sheet manipulation; by the investment bank business model, which rewarded excessive risk taking and leverage; and by government agencies, who by their own admission might better have anticipated or mitigated the outcome."

Accounting shenanigans at Lehman Brothers

"Lehman did not disclose, however, that it had been using an accounting device (known within Lehman as "Repo 105") to manage its balance sheet—by temporarily removing approximately \$50 billion of assets from the balance sheet at the end of the first and second quarters of 2008. In an ordinary repo, Lehman raised cash by selling assets with a simultaneous obligation to repurchase them the next day or several days later; such transactions were accounted for as financings, and the assets remained on Lehman's balance sheet. In a Repo 105 transaction, Lehman did exactly the same thing, but because the assets were 105% or more of the cash received, accounting rules permitted the transactions to be treated as sales rather than financings, so that the assets could be removed from the balance sheet. With Repo 105 transactions, Lehman's reported net leverage was 12.1 at the end of the second quarter of 2008; but if Lehman had used ordinary repos, net leverage would have to have been reported at 13.9. Contemporaneous Lehman e-mails describe the "function called repo 105 whereby you can repo a position for a week and it is regarded as a true sale to get rid of net balance sheet." Lehman used Repo 105 for no articulated business purpose except "to reduce balance sheet at the quarter-end." Rather than sell assets at a loss, "(a) Repo 105 increase would

雷曼兄弟公司的破产,一方面是因为其高杠杆率,另一方面是因为其利用"Repo 105"("回购105")隐瞒其杠杆率。

help avoid this without negatively impacting our leverage ratios."
Lehman's Global Financial Controller confirmed that "the only purpose or
motive for (Repo 105) transactions was reduction in the balance sheet"
and that "there was *no substance* to the transactions." (Report of Anton
R. Valukas, Examiner, *op. cit.*)

Lehman reported that it had been in talks with Bank of America and
Barclays for the company's possible sale. Bank of America declined, and
Barclays ended its bid to purchase all or part of Lehman when the UK monetary authorities rejected the deal. Lehman filed for Chapter 11 bankruptcy protection on September 15, 2008. The Dow Jones closed down over
500 points, −4.4%, on September 15, 2008, a drop subsequently exceeded by a −7.0% plunge on September 29, 2008.

The resultant credit squeeze due to counterparty risk— *Cash is king*!

Due to counterparty risk, bank lending virtually came to a halt, even
interbank lending. Commercial banks built up their excess reserves, as illustrated in Figure 7.13, following the bankruptcy of Lehman Brothers.

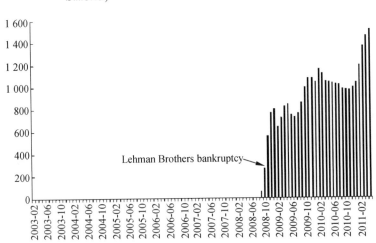

Figure 7.13 Excess reserves held by US depository institutions (USD billions)

Source: Federal Reserve Board, 2011.

As a result of the freezing of markets, the Federal Reserve Bank
stepped in to prevent failure of the major investment banks by providing a
Term Asset-backed Security Loan Facility (TALF) for the purchase of illiq-

uid assets, holding up to 1.5 trillion dollars of MBAs as well as 400 billion dollars of commercial paper. Governor Bernanke had broadly interpreted the emergency powers of the FED to purchase assets from non-member banks, including investment banks, as well as commercial paper from firms. At the time of the crisis, this provided the necessary liquidity and equity to prevent systemic bank failure.

Figure 7.14   Total borrowings from the Federal Reserve System (USD millions)

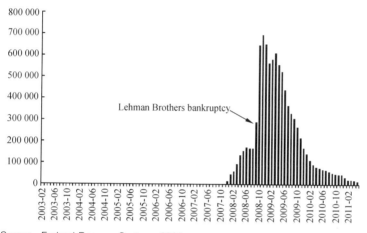

Source: Federal Reserve System, 2011.

The Bank of China

"Bank of China saw its Hong Kong stock price fall by as much as 8.1 percent Friday as investors sold shares in reaction to the bank's report it holds US $9.65 billion in subprime asset-backed securities and collateralized debt obligations, or CDOs. That's 3.8 percent of its total securities investments." ("Bank of China Reports Heavy Exposure to Subprime Crisis," The Associated Press, August 24, 2007.) Further, "Bank of China said Tuesday that third-quarter profit rose 22 percent, posting the slowest earnings growth among the country's largest lenders after a $322 million loss on U.S. subprime mortgage investments." (Luo Jun, "Bank of China Profit Hamstrung by Mortgage Losses," *Bloomberg News*, October 31, 2007.)

The macro-economic impact of the financial crisis

Residential construction, a spark-plug during the housing boom, sputtered during the bust, as recorded in Table 7.11.

Table 7.11 Residential investment as a share of GDP in the United States: 1999–2009

(USD billions)	1999	2000	2001	2002	2003	2004	2005	2006	2007	2008	2009
RI	426	449	472	509	578	681	775	762	629	472	352
GDP	9,354	9,952	10,286	10,642	11,142	11,868	12,638	13,399	14,062	14,369	14,119
RI as % of GDP	4.6%	4.5%	4.6%	4.8%	5.2%	5.7%	6.1%	5.7%	4.5%	3.3%	2.5%

Source: Bureau of Economic Analysis, Department of Commerce, September 1, 2010.

From 1999 to 2007, residential investment averaged 5.1% of GDP, reaching a peak of 6.1% in 2005. In 2008 and 2009, it averaged 2.9%, falling to a trough of 2.5% in 2009. The recession began in the third quarter of 2008 and ended in the third quarter of 2009, as indicated in Figure 7.15. A sharp contraction of 8.9% at an annual rate in GDP took place in the 4th quarter of 2008.

Figure 7.15 US GDP growth*

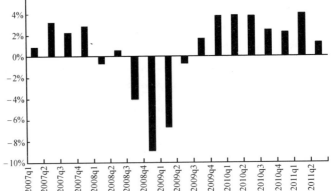

* percentage change at a seasonally adjusted annual rate.
Source: Bureau of Economic Analysis, Department of Commerce.

In the fourth quarter of 2008, the main negative forces were investment and consumption spending, as shown in Figure 7.16.

Figure 7.16 The contributions of consumption and investment expenditure to growth in real GDP*

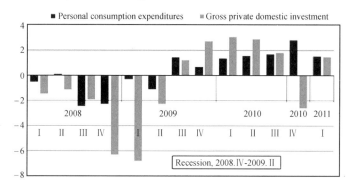

* Annual rate, seasonally adjusted.
Source: Bureau of Economic Analysis, Department of Commerce.

New "mark to model" rules for assets whose price discovery is difficult were put in place by the FASB (Federal Accounting Standards Board). This makes markdowns of "legacy" assets less severe, but will make price discovery more difficult and the banks less likely to sell the assets at a larger discount. The danger is that it could lead to "zombie" banks. Due to counterparty risk, liquidity risk, and increasing collateral requirements, interbank lending has frozen significantly. Efforts by the FED to increase liquidity to promote increased credit have not yet succeeded. The commercial banks hold the new liquidity created by the Fed—"cash is king", credit is risky.

In Europe, the recession was deep and recovery is slow, as seen in Figure 7.17.

当金融市场的流动性极低时,"mark to market"(逐日盯市)的定价方法便无法实现,因此,FASB(联邦会计准则委员会)允许金融机构运用"mark to model"(参照模型)方法来为难以估值的资产进行定价。通常来说,参照模型方法的估值会高于逐日盯市方法的估值。

Figure 7.17 Annualized quarterly change in GDP for the euro area

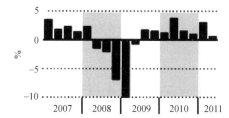

Source: *The Wall Street Journal*, November 7, 2011.

Europe's sovereign debt troubles have worsened since the recession.

In 2011, Greek debt was over 172% of GDP, Italian debt 120%, Irish 111%, Portuguese 114% and German 80% of GDP.

China's Purchaser's Manufacturing Index

The Purchaser's Manufacturing Index (PMI) is an index of manufacturing sector activity. Above 50 suggests an expansion and below 50 suggests a contraction. In China, the index is composed of 11 sector sub-indices, which are: output, new orders, new export orders, backlogs of orders, stocks of finished goods, purchases of inputs, input prices, imports, stocks of major inputs, employment, and supplier's delivery time. In the beginning of the second half of 2011, the HSBC PMI index for China was below 50, suggesting a slowdown of manufacturing activity for the first time in recent history, the 100 city average property price per square meter fell 0.25% in October 2011. (*The Wall Street Journal*, October 1, 2011)

The Troubled Asset Relief Program (TARP)

不良资产救助计划(Troubled Asset Relief Program): 为了应对2008年的次贷危机,美国政府通过收购金融机构的不良资产以稳定金融市场的计划。该计划于2008年10月3日由美国总统乔治·W. 布什签署生效。

The TARP was signed into law by U. S. President George W. Bush on October 3, 2008. It allows the United States Treasury to purchase or insure up to $700 Billion of "troubled assets", defined as "(A) residential or commercial mortgages and any securities, obligations, or other instruments that are based on or related to such mortgages, that in each case was originated or issued on or before March 14, 2008, the purchase of which the Secretary determines promotes financial market stability; and (B) any other financial instrument that the Secretary, after consultation with the Chairman of the Board of Governors of the Federal Reserve System, determines the purchase of which is necessary to promote financial market stability, but only upon transmittal of such determination, in writing, to the appropriate committees of Congress."

The TARP allows the Treasury to purchase illiquid, difficult-to-value assets from banks and other financial institutions. The targeted assets can be mortgage backed asset and collateralized debt obligations, which were sold in a booming market until 2007 when they were hit by widespread foreclosures on the underlying loans. TARP was intended to improve the liquidity of these assets by purchasing them using secondary market mechanisms, thus allowing participating institutions to stabilize their balance sheets and avoid further losses. Table 7.12 indicates the initial levels of support that financial and automotive firms received from the TARP.

Table 7.12 TARP loans to financial and automobile companies

Company	Preferred stock purchased (USD millions)
Citigroup	45,000
Bank of America	45,000
AIG (American International Group)	40,000
JP Morgan Chase	25,000
Wells Fargo	25,000
GMAC Financial Services (Ally)	17,300
General Motors	13,400
Goldman Sachs	10,000
Morgan Stanley	10,000
PNC Financial Services Group	7,579
U.S. Bancorp	6,600
Chrysler	4,000
Capital One Financial	3,555
Regions Financial Corporation	3,500
American Express	3,389
Bank of New York Mellon Corp	2,000 to 3,000
State Street Corporation	2,000 to 3,000
Discover Financial	1,230

Source: U.S. Treasury.

Indeed, under the Term Asset-Backed Securities Loan Facility Program, the FED has purchased commercial paper along with mortgage-backed assets to the tune of $400 billion and $1.2 trillion respectively. Under the TARP, many banks and financial institutions avoided bankruptcy and have mostly repaid their loans with interest. In the cases of AIG, the insurance company, and Citigroup, the Treasury became a majority shareholder. Loans to the automobile maker and the purchase of shares in General Motors, and Chryslev also made the US Treasury majority shareholders for a while.

The banks and AIG have fully repaid their loans with interest. General Motors and Chrysler have discharged their debts, but the automobile bailouts cost the US Treasury an estimated $10.2 billion (Kimberly Amadeo, "The Auto Industry Bailout", https://www.thebalance.com, November 6, 2019). Nobody knows what would have happened, of course, if GM and Chrysler had not been bailed out.

The Volcker Rule

沃克尔法则(Volcker Rule):由保罗·沃克尔提出,其内容是要求吸收存款的银行必须剥离其衍生产品业务。

保罗·沃克尔(Paul Volcker):美国经济学家,他曾在里根和卡特任职总统期间出任美联储主席,结束了美国20世纪70年代到80年代初的高通胀,受到广泛的赞誉。30年后,沃克尔以83岁高龄再度出山,担任经济复苏顾问委员会主席,帮助奥巴马推进经济复苏政策。

Paul Volcker served as governor of the Federal Reserve System from 1979 to 1987, putting a stop to the inflation of the late 1970s. As a person of great integrity, he also served as the Chairman of the Swiss Bank report on the holdings of assets of those that had died and lost them in World War II. Volcker challenges the conventional wisdom that financial innovations have contributed anything to economic growth, suggesting instead that they have created moral hazard and contributed to the financial crisis.

At the *Future of Finance Initiative* in January 2009, major questions about the future role of finance were raised. Volcker challenges the conventional wisdom in his answers.

> **In the News**: Does Financial Innovation Contribute to Economic Growth?
>
> You concluded with financial-services executives showing cultural sensitivity and responsible leadership. Well, I have been around the financial markets for 60 years, and how many responsible financial leaders have we heard speaking against the huge compensation practices?
>
> Every day I hear financial leaders saying that they are necessary and desirable, they are wonderful and they are God's work. Has there been one financial leader to stand out and say that maybe this is excessive and that maybe we should get together privately to think about some restraint?
>
> I hear about these wonderful innovations in the financial markets, and they sure as hell need a lot of innovation. I can tell you of two—credit-default swaps and collateralized debt obligations—which took us right to the brink of disaster. Were they wonderful innovations that we want to create more of?
>
> You want boards of directors to be informed about all of these innovative new products and to understand them, but I do not know what boards of directors you are talking about. I have been on boards of directors, and the chance that they are going to understand these products that you are dishing out, or that you are going to want to explain it to them, quite frankly, is nil.
>
> I mean: Wake up, gentlemen. I can only say that your response is inadequate. I wish that somebody would give me some shred of neutral evidence about the relationship between financial innovation recently and the growth of the economy, just one shred of information.

Do Innovations Do Much Good?

A few years ago I happened to be at a conference of business people, not financial people, and I was making a presentation. The conference was being addressed by a very vigorous young investment banker from London who was explaining to all these older executives how their companies would be dust if they did not realize the joys of financial innovation and financial engineering, and that they had better get with it.

I was listening to this, and I found myself sitting next to one of the inventors of financial engineering. I didn't know him, but I knew who he was and that he had won a Nobel Prize, and I nudged him and asked what all the financial engineering does for the economy and what it does for productivity.

Much to my surprise, he leaned over and whispered in my ear that it does nothing—and this was from a leader in the world of financial engineering. I asked him what it did do, and he said that it moves around the rents in the financial system—and besides, it's a lot of intellectual fun. Now, I have no doubts that it moves around the rents in the financial system, but not only this, as it seems to have vastly increased them.

How do I respond to a congressman who asks if the financial sector in the United States is so important that it generates 40% of all the profits in the country, 40%, after all of the bonuses and pay? Is it really a true reflection of the financial sector that it rose from $2\frac{1}{2}$% of value added according to GNP numbers to $6\frac{1}{2}$% in the last decade all of a sudden? Is that a reflection of all your financial innovation, or is it just a reflection of how much you pay? What about the effect of incentives on all our best young talent, particularly of a numerical kind, in the United States?

In Britain, I was just talking to a high-tech company about the immense attraction to go into finance when both Britain and the United States are suffering from a basic inability to produce things competitively, to keep up with the new economy. Is this a result of financial innovation that we should be really worried about?

Let us think about what structural changes are necessary to produce what is the heart of the problem, about too big to fail, moral hazard and the rest. As I say, I agree with many of your individual suggestions, but there were no suggestions in the area of moral hazard. It was suggested to improve regulation, and that may help, but having gone that far, it is better that you talk about some more serious structural changes.

I made a wiseacre remark that the most important financial innovation that I have seen the past 20 years is the automatic teller machine. That really helps people and prevents visits to the bank and is a real convenience.

> **What Is the Role of Commercial Banks?**
> Commercial banks are still at the heart of the system. In a crisis, everybody runs back to the commercial banks. They, after all, run the payment system. We cannot have this global economy without commercial banks operating an efficient payment system globally as well as nationally. They provide a depository outlet for individuals and businesses, and they are still big credit providers for small and medium-size businesses, but they backstop most of the big borrowers as well. The commercial-paper market is totally dependent on the commercial banking market. They are an essential financial institution that has historically been protected. It has been protected on one side and regulated on the other side.
>
> I think that fundamental is going to remain. People are going to think it is important, it is important, it needs regulation and in extremis it needs protection—deposit insurance, lender of last resort and so forth.
>
> I think that it is extraneous to that function that they do hedge funds, equity funds and that they trade in commodities and securities, and a lot of other stuff, which is secondary in terms of direct responsibilities for lenders, borrowers, depositors and all the rest.
>
> There is nothing wrong with any of those activities, but let you nonbank people do it and you can provide fluidity in markets and flexibility. If you fail, you're going to fail, and I am not going to help you, and your stockholders are going to be gone, and your creditors will be at risk, and that is the way that it should be.
>
> How can I be so blithe about making that statement? We need a new institutional arrangement which I believe has a lot of support. We need a resolution facility. What can that resolution facility do? If one of you fails and has systemic risk, then it steps in, takes you over and either liquidates or merges you, but it does not save you. That ought to be a kind of iron cross. How many other innovations can you tell me that have been as important to the individual as the automatic teller machine, which is in fact more of a mechanical innovation than a financial one?"
>
> Source: Paul Volcker's remarks, excerpted from Alan Murray, the *Journal Report*, the *Wall Street Journal*, December 14, 2009.

These thoughts gave rise to the Volcker Rule, where commercial banks making commercial loans are entitled to Federal Deposit Insurance and Federal Savings and Loan Insurance Corporation (FSLIC), but investment banks who risk their investors money in proprietary trading are not.

Thus, while investment banks were encouraged to take over and establish commercial banks to be entitled to TARP monies during the crisis, they are now urged to either do commercial and investment banking or investment banking with proprietary trading desks, but not both. In particular, Goldman Sachs has shed itself of its proprietary trading branch to remain qualified as a commercial bank.

The Dodd-Frank Act of 2010

To remedy the moral hazard problem, the Dodd-Frank Act of 2010 attempted to address the "**too big to fail**" problem. Partly, through the Volcker rule, the attempt is to restrain risk taking by commercial banks whose deposits are guaranteed by the FDIC. Investment banks who risk their investors' and their own money would, in principle, be allowed to fail. In practice, moral hazard is alive and well—large banks will probably never be allowed to fail, surely not *en masse*. The Lehman Bros. bankruptcy put the financial system at risk of systemic failure. As with the Sarbanes-Oxley Act of 2002, the fear is that regulatory costs will exceed the benefits of any regulation. Worse yet, a new Consumer Protection Agency will make consumer credit more costly and reduce credit to the consumer. The US regulatory environment for financial institutions is becoming less friendly, discouraging business in the US, encouraging it to take place elsewhere.

There were sufficient SEC regulations in place to stop the Madoff Ponzi game and sufficient warnings to the SEC to warrant a serious investigation of Madoff. However, as Stigler reminds us, regulators are typically "captured" by those they regulate. It is not clear how regulators will enforce the "5% skin in the game rule" for mortgage origination.

"大而不倒"("too big to fail"): 指当一些规模极大或在产业中具有关键性重要地位的企业濒临破产时，政府不能等闲视之，甚至要不惜投入政府资金相救，以避免那些企业倒闭后所掀起的巨大连锁反应造成社会整体更严重的伤害。

Conclusion

Milton Friedman once likened a business contraction to pulling down on a rubber band, with recovery snapping back. Most recoveries have been of the rubber band variety. This one is not.

Despite record liquidity, low Fed Fund and Treasury rates, businesses and banks have not yet regained enough confidence in the future to invest and lend at a greater stride. Consumer wealth in the form of stock market equities has recovered, as has wealth in home equity. Businesses, banks, and consumers have been de-leveraging, which makes recovery difficult since it curtails private spending. New business and financial reg-

米尔顿·弗里德曼(Milton Friedman): 美国经济学家,1976年因在消费分析、货币供应理论和历史以及稳定政策复杂性等范畴的贡献而获得诺贝尔经济学奖。

ulations as well as rapidly rising U.S. debt signals higher future taxes for businesses, banks, and households.

Government spending in the US has not followed a golden rule that deficits only be financed for public investment spending. On the contrary, the Economic Stimulus Act of January 2009 focused, as did most state and local spending, on government consumption spending: That is, on consumption smoothing during the recession. This did not lay a strong foundation of renewed infrastructure for long term economic recovery. Indeed, it would appear from Figure 7.18 that the economic stimulus program is a misnomer: it was instead a consumption smoothing scheme.

如图所示,经济刺激计划中,仅有约 5% 的资金投入基础设施建设。

Figure 7.18 The US economic spending plan of 2009, a consumption smoothing program

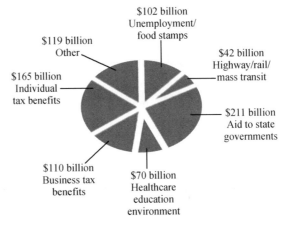

Source: Michael Kranish, Globe Staff, January 29, 2009.

罗伯特·巴罗(Robert Barro):哈佛大学经济学教授,美国著名古典宏观经济学家。他在 1990 年的研究中发现,在一个包含 98 个国家的样本中,政府支出的增长显著地减缓了真实经济增长。

Indeed, **Robert Barro**(1990) finds that increased government consumption spending significantly reduces real economic growth in a sample of 98 countries:

For the 98 countries for which g^c/y (government consumption as a fraction of GDP) was measured (Barro, 1990, table 1), a regression of the average annual growth rate of real per capita GDP from 1960 to 1985 on a set of explanatory variables yielded an estimated coefficient on g^c/y of -0.12 (standard error $= 0.03$). Thus there is an indication that an increase in resources devoted to non-productive (but possibly utility-enhancing) government services is associated with lower per capita growth. (Barro, *op. cit.*, S124.)

Policymakers have fooled themselves into believing in the Keynesian government spending multiplier. When households and businesses are taxed more in the present and the future to finance government consumption spending it is likely that the multiplier will be zero (**Ricardian Equivalence**), or negative if the deficit money is not well spent—i. e. on government consumption.

The US now seems hampered by slow growth and rapidly growing sovereign debt. The US benefits greatly, however, from the dollar being the world's reserve and settlement currency. However, no growth policy is in sight. Since government spending is rising—that is, *effective* taxes, now, in the future, or by inflation—are rising as a percent of income. The Congressional Budget Office projects total US governmental spending to grow at a 5.3% per annum rate in the next five years—2019 to 2023.

李嘉图等价 (Ricardian Equivalence): 在某些条件下, 政府无论用债券还是税收筹资, 其效果都是相同的或者等价的。

Questions and problems

7.1 Financial leverage

Consider the (approximated) consolidated balance sheet of Countrwide Financial Corporation as of June 30, 2008.

Countrywide Financial Corporation

30-Jun-2008 Balance sheet from 10Q report (unaudited) (USD billions)	
Assets	Liabilities and shareholders' equity
200	190 Liabilities
	10 Shareholders' equity
200 Total Assets	200 Liabilities plus shareholders' equity

Answer the following questions:

a. Compute three measures of financial leverage of Countrywide Financial.
   1.
   2.
   3.

b. What percent must the value of Countrywide Financial's assets be marked down (or fall) in order for it to have zero equity?

c. Discuss the following statement: "For a given level of debt, a 10% rise (or fall) in asset values implies a multiplied rise (or fall) in equity as a percent (of itself), depending upon the degree of financial leverage."

7.2 **The economic stimulus and Ricardian equivalence**

Consider an economic stimulus where every citizen receives a $1,000 lump-sum check from the Treasury, but government expenditure and current taxes remain constant. Thus, each payment must be financed by a $1,000 new issue of government bonds. Would you expect this economic stimulus package to have a large effect on spending? Why or why not?

References and suggested reading

Barro, Robert J. (1990), "Government Spending in a Simple Model of Endogeneous Growth," *The Journal of Political Economy*, 98(5), Part 2: S103–S125.

Chen, Yong, Michael Connolly, Wenjin Tang and Tie Su (2009), "The Value of Mortgage Prepayment and Default Options," *The Journal of Futures Markets*, 29(9): 840–861.

Holmes, Steven, "Fannie Mae Eases Credits to Aid Mortgage Lending," *New York Times*, September 20, 1999.

Mankiw, N. Gregory and Laurence M. Ball (2011), *Macroeconomics and the Financial System*, New York: Worth Publishers, 537–574.

CHAPTER 8 Cross Border Mergers and Acquisitions 跨国兼并与收购

Motives for M&A activity

There are many potential gains to mergers and acquisitions, including:

• Economies of scale—global output may be maintained by reducing inputs or output may be expanded at reduced average costs.

• Marketing economies—advertising costs are spread over the merged firm.

• Economies of scope—wider and complementary product range.

• Economies of global standardization of product and manufacturing processes.

• Exploitation of comparative advantage within the merged firm by greater vertical integration.

• Leapfrogging of import barriers by producing, distributing, and marketing locally.

• Anti-competitive acquisitions—reduce market competition and increase market share, at risk of violating anti-trust laws.

• Acquisition of technologies, patents, and know-how.

• Economies of R&D—sharing of fixed costs.

• Diversifying the risk of R&D—exploring competing technologies within the merged firm.

• Restructuring—eliminating inefficient and redundant management, reducing costs.

• Natural hedging—acquiring accounts payable in a currency in which there are accounts receivable.

跨国兼并与收购(cross border M&A):收购或兼并方和目标公司不在同一国家。

并购(M&A):兼并与收购。

规模经济(economies of scale):在总产出不变的情况下降低了投入,或者在平均成本降低的情况下增加了产出。

营销经济(marketing economies):广告费用得以在并购公司内进行分摊。

范围经济(economies of scope):更加广泛、更加互补的产品范围。

自然对冲(natural hedging):在拥有一种货币的应收账款时获得该货币的应付账款。

- Tax gains from the acquisition of tax shields from net operating losses.
- Vertical integration and avoidance of double marginalization—a downstream retailer charging a higher than profit maximizing price to earn a positive margin.

Cross border mergers and acquisitions have challenges too.

- Political risk, hostile trade unions, and excessive regulations are fraught with pitfalls.
- The firm's cultures may also differ significantly in terms of goals—maximizing shareholder value versus pleasing several "stakeholders", especially in the case of state enterprises and establishments.

The tax burden is invariably higher in developed countries, especially high payroll taxes to finance social programs—health, unemployment, retirement, and disability. As a result, the growth of temporary employment agencies in Europe, for example, is phenomenal. Temporary workers do not "benefit" from the same high payroll tax treatment.

Corruption—securing large contracts, for example, the exploitation of mineral rights, or the acquisition of a state enterprise that is being privatized, is often a matter of putting a bundle of cash on the President or Minister's desk, or depositing some percent of the contract in an offshore bank account in his or her name, or in a numbered account. In other cases, obtaining regulatory approval is costly and burdensome, and sometimes fails.

However, every foreign direct investor is guaranteed "National Treatment" by the WTO/GATT, meaning the same tax and regulatory treatment as domestic firms. In some cases, this is not particularly business friendly.

The ease of doing business abroad

The World Bank's ease of doing business index covers several areas of interest to potential cross border investors, as illustrated in Table 8.1.

Table 8.1 Ease of doing business index

Starting a Business	Protecting Minority Investors
Dealing with Construction Permits	Paying Taxes
Getting Electricity	Trading across Borders
Registering Property	Enforcing Contracts
Getting Credit	Resolving Insolvency

Source: https://data.worldbank.org/indicator/IC.BUS.EASE.XQ

Among countries, the United States is ranked 8/190, while China is 46/190 November 2018. Yet there are rewards from acquiring or starting a business abroad, as seen by Chinese M&A activity in Figure 8.1.

Figure 8.1 The value of Chinese global M&A transactions, 2010 – 2017 (USD billions)

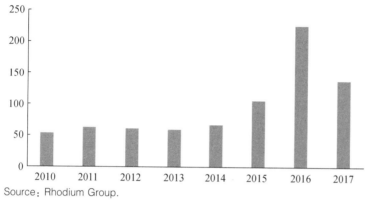

Source: Rhodium Group.

Chinese mergers and acquisitions in the United States represent a substantial portion of total overseas Chinese investment, as illustrated in Figure 8.2.

Figure 8.2 Chinese direct investment in the United States, 2009 – 2017 (USD billions)

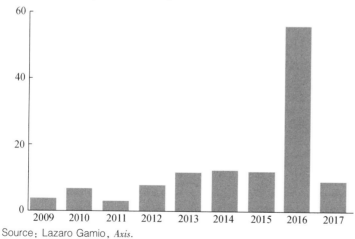

Source: Lazaro Gamio, *Axis*.

The nearly $55.7 billion direct Chinese investment in the U.S. in 2016 is an outlier: just four companies accounted for 61%, or $34 billion, of China's entire investment that year. The four companies were: Anbang Insurance, HNA Group, Oceanwide Holdings, and Wanda Group. However, the government seized control of Anbang and, in May 2018, imprisoned founder Wu Xiaohui, sentencing him to prison for 18 years. Further, under pressure from strict capital controls and high leverage ratios, Dalian's Wanda began to sell its properties in the U.S. and overseas, as did HNA. Oceanwide appears to be the exception, getting final approval for yet another U.S. deal—a $3.8 billion takeover of Genworth Financial, an insurance company. Chinese M&A has also slowed in 2018, as increased Chinese and U.S. regulations have narrowed the focus of Chinese investment in the U.S., as we shall review later in the chapter.

M&A structures

There are three main types of combinations of firms: a merger, an acquisition, and an asset purchase. Joint ventures are also a common measure for firms joining forces. Additionally, there are de-merger techniques such as "spinoffs" and "carve-outs". We consider each of these in turn.

A Merger

兼并(merger): 两家或更多的独立的企业合并组成一家企业,通常由一家占优势的企业吸收一家或更多的企业。

Two corporations "merge" or become one corporation pursuant to state corporation statutes.

- In the United States, the most prevalent is the General Corporation Law of the State of Delaware.
- The corporation that "survives" the merger, or remains in existence, is called the "surviving corporation."
- The surviving corporation succeeds to all of the assets and liabilities of the "disappearing corporations."
- The outstanding stock of both corporations is converted into cash, stock in the surviving corporation, or other property.

The structure of a merger can be illustrated in Figure 8.3.

Figure 8.3 A merger—or two firms merge and become one

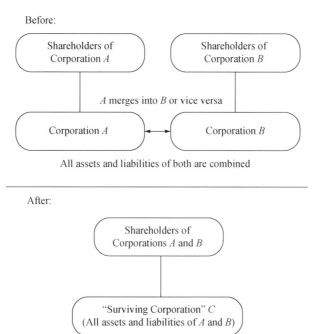

Source: Edward Miller Jr. *Mergers and Acquisitions: A Step-by-step Practical Guide*, John Wiley and Sons, 2008.

In the news: American Airlines and US Air Merger

American Airlines Group Inc. was born on Monday (Dec. 9, 2013) after AMR Corp.'s American Airlines stepped out of bankruptcy and merged with US Airways Group Inc. Shares of the combined company, now the world's largest airline by traffic, rose 2.7% to $24.60 in their first day of trading on the Nasdaq Stock Market ... Under the terms of the stock-swap merger, US Airways shareholders received 28% of the new company's shares, while AMR's creditors and equity interests are slated to receive the rest. The two-year restructuring and complex merger agreement will repay AMR's creditors with interest and give its big unions and common holders a big slab of equity in the new company—rare outcomes for a bankruptcy. Normally in airline restructurings, creditors receive cents on the dollar of their claims and common holders are wiped out. Holders of AMR common shares, which ceased trading Friday, received an initial distribution of roughly one AAL share for every 15 AMR shares held, which represents 3.5% of

> the new company. But if the stock price doesn't fall significantly in the next 120 days, AMR holders are in line to own nearly one-third of the combined company, or roughly $5 billion of equity. In 2014, American Airlines was the larger carrier with 88.4 million passengers that year, while US Air had 58.3 million. The merger retained US Air management but American Airlines' reservation system in the surviving American Air Group.
>
> Source: Susan Carey and Jack Nicas, American Airlines Steps out of Bankruptcy and Forms The World's Largest Airline by Traffic, *The Wall Street Journal*, Dec. 10, 2013.

A stock purchase

股权收购 (Stock purchase): 是指以目标公司股东的全部或部分股权为收购标的的收购。

An outright purchase of all the stock of the target company by cash is the best form of acquisition when the buyer does not want to have any remaining minority interest that could challenge governance. A stock purchase also avoids double taxation in the United States, as the target shareholders do not have to pay taxes on gains in their share value. If shares in the buyer are offered as consideration, the buyer then has minority shareholders.

Figure 8.4 A stock purchase

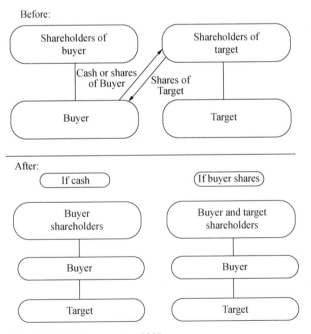

Source: Edward Miller Jr., *op. cit.*, 2008.

We will cover the ChemChina acquisition of Syngenta in 2017—an all stock purchase—at the end of this chapter.

An asset purchase

An asset purchase is a complicated form of acquisition because it cannot legally be used to acquire the "crown jewels" of a firm, leaving behind all its liabilities, even bankrupting the target. In an asset purchase:

资产收购(Asset purchase):一家公司以有偿对价取得另外一家公司的全部或者部分资产。

- All or selected assets are purchased.
- An asset purchase may be necessary because the target business is in a division and not a separate legal entity.
- Selected liabilities are assumed. An asset purchase of the "crown jewels" of a firm, leaving behind all its liabilities, is not legal.
- An asset purchase is tax favored in the U.S. to the buyer.
- It is possible to avoid a target stockholder vote if not substantially all assets are acquired.

Figure 8.5 An asset purchase—if only specific assets are desired

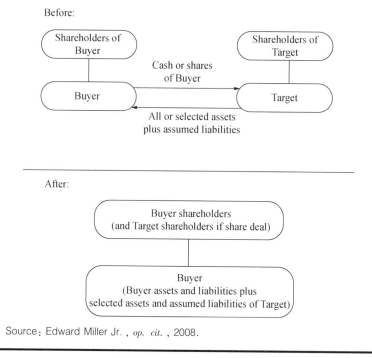

Source: Edward Miller Jr., *op. cit.*, 2008.

A good example of an asset purchase is the Lenovo acquisition of IBM's PC division for $1.2 billion in 2004: $600 million in cash and $600 million in Lenovo shares. IBM acquired 18.9% of Lenovo by this sale, signaling its support of the ThinkPad line would continue. (See "Lenovo: Building a Global Brand" by John Quelch and Carin-Isabel Knoop, Harvard Business School 9-507-014, Revised Oct. 19, 2006.)

A spinoff

分拆(Spinoff):母公司将其在子公司中所拥有的股份,按比例地分配给现有母公司的股东。

A corporation creates a spinoff by distributing 100% of its ownership interest in a business unit as a special stock dividend to existing shareholders. If properly structured, the dividend payment goes untaxed. In the United States, it is required that 20% of the spinoff business operations be at the core of the spinoff.

In general, spinoffs are divisions of companies or organizations that then become independent businesses with assets, employees, intellectual property, technology, or existing products that are taken from the parent company. Shareholders of the parent company receive equivalent shares in the new company in order to compensate for the loss of equity in the original stocks. Spinoffs tend to increase returns for shareholders because the newly independent companies can better focus on their core products or services. Both the parent and the spinoff tend to perform better as a result of the spinoff transaction—the sum of the separate parts is expected to be greater than the whole. Figure 8.6 illustrates the structure of a spinoff.

Figure 8.6 A spinoff into a subsidiary

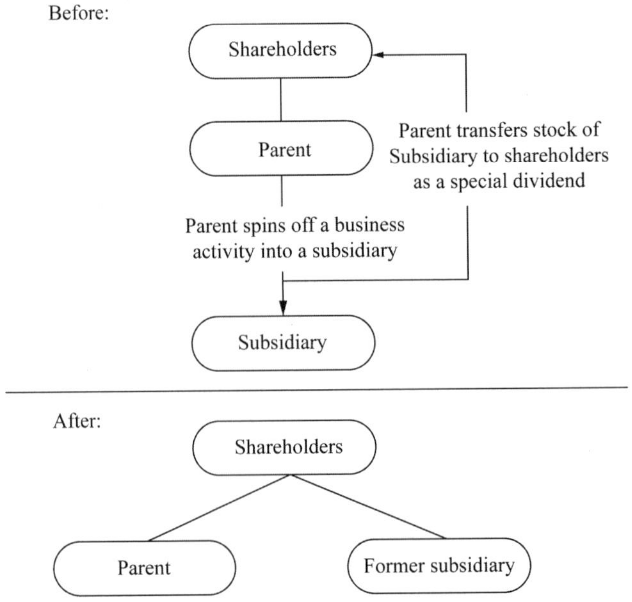

Source: Edward Miller Jr. op. cit. 2008

> **In the News**: **Spun-off Companies Tend to Perform Better Than the Broader Market and—Often—Than Their Former Parent**
>
> Among corporate executives, spinoffs of divisions have come in and out of favor over the years, but with one group they have been a steady crowd-pleaser: investors. Honeywell International Inc. plans to hive (*spin*) off major business units in an effort to sharpen the focus on their core operations. The moves served as a reminder that even though such activity has slowed, handing businesses to shareholders remains a popular tool as company executives, often besieged by activist investors, find it harder to justify a vast sweep of businesses and pivot toward leaner and more focused operations. Companies use spinoffs—the act of turning a unit into a separate, publicly traded company by issuing newly created stock to existing stockholders as a special dividend avoiding taxes—to simplify their operations and shed unrelated businesses while avoiding tax bills that sales of divisions often entail. For investors, the appeal of spinoffs lies in their long history of outperforming the broader market, particularly in the years immediately following separation from a corporate parent. Including dividends, the S&P U.S. Spin-off Index has outperformed the S&P 500 by nearly 190 percentage points over the past decade ... Companies leave the index after that time has passed ... In many cases, they have vastly outperformed the shares of their former parents.
>
> Source: Miriam Gottfried and Thomas Gryta, Spun-off Companies Tend to Perform Better Than the Broader Market and—Often—Than Their Former Parent, *The Wall Street Journal*, October 11, 2017.

An equity carve-out

An equity carve-out is a corporate reorganization, in which a company creates a new subsidiary, selling shares in it, yet retaining management control. Only a minority stake in shares is offered to the public, so the parent company retains the majority stake in the subsidiary. Typically, up to 20% of subsidiary shares is offered to the public. Equity carve-outs increase access to capital markets, giving the carved-out subsidiary strong growth opportunities, while avoiding the negative signaling associated with a further issue of the parent's equity.

股权切离（Carve-out）：母公司出售一家子公司的少数权益。

Figure 8.7 An equity carve-out

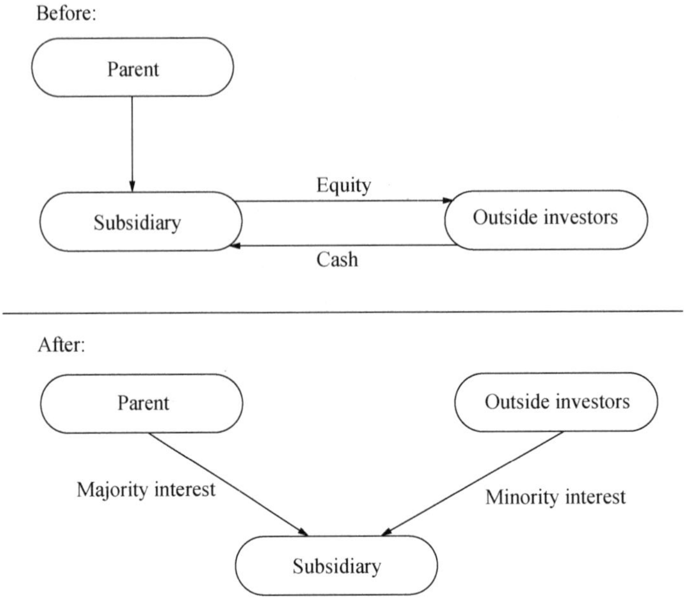

Before:

Parent → Subsidiary

Subsidiary ⇄ Outside investors (Equity / Cash)

After:

Parent — Majority interest → Subsidiary ← Minority interest — Outside investors

Source: Edward Miller Jr., *op. cit.*, 2008.

McKinsey has noted:

"Many CEOs consider equity carve-outs too good to miss: a financial instrument that increases company stock price without sacrificing control of a valuable business unit. However, an analysis we conducted of 200 major carve-outs across the world over the past ten years[①] shows that this perception is not entirely accurate. We found that the vast majority of carve-outs ultimately lead to changes in corporate control, and very few produce significant share price increases for the parent. Most actually do not create shareholder value unless the parent company follows a plan to subsequently fully separate the carved-out subsidiary. The initial carve-out minority interest is usually less than 20% in the U.S. This is not to say that carve-outs, executed wisely, are not useful tools in an executive's restructuring toolbox." An advantage of an equity carve-out is that it allows a prior evaluation of the subsidiary's market value and creates price valuation if the parent company wants to fully divest the subsidiary.

---

① https://www.mckinsey.com/business-functions/strategy-and-corporate-finance/our-insights/do-carve-outs-make-sense

Joint Ventures

A joint venture is a good way to combine efforts in a common project without merging the other activities of the parent companies.

合资企业（Joint ventures）：共同出资、共同经营、共负盈亏、共担风险的企业。

Figure 8.8　A joint venture (JV)

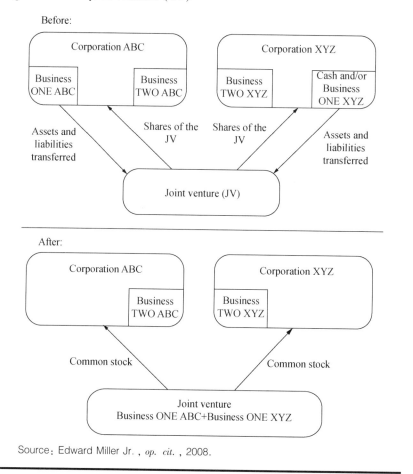

Source: Edward Miller Jr., *op. cit.*, 2008.

In China, a joint venture is particularly helpful when a state-owned enterprise (SOE) combines its ownership with a foreign firm's to collaborate in a partnership. Usually, the Chinese company retains majority ownership of the joint venture, thus facilitating technology transfer while maintaining governance.

国有企业（State-owntd enterprise, SOE）：国家的中央政府或地方政府投资或参与控制的企业。

A leveraged buyout with cash

Debt can be used to acquire an asset or firm by the buyer borrowing

杠杆收购(Leveraged buyout, LBO):利用收购目标的资产作为债务抵押,收购另一家公司的策略。

against the asset to be acquired. This is known as a leveraged buyout (LBO). The simplest LBO is a mortgage where the borrower puts up some equity and acquires debt secured by title to the house as collateral. As in this case, financial leverage can be the buyer's route to a multiplied gain, but also carries the risk of magnified financial distress if the acquisition does not prove profitable.

Figure 8.9 A leveraged buyout with cash

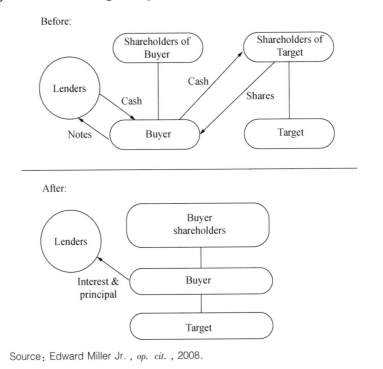

Source: Edward Miller Jr., *op. cit.*, 2008.

Due diligence

尽职调查(Due diligence):对企业的历史数据和文档、管理人员的背景、市场风险、管理风险、技术风险和资金风险做全面的审核。

The term "due diligence" is broadly used to mean the investigation that an investor or a buyer undertakes of a prospective investee or target. The due diligence process is extremely important because it affects the buyer's decision whether to invest in or acquire the target, on what terms, and for what price. Due diligence may also be done on the buyer by the target in a transaction in which the target's shareholders are to receive stock of the buyer as part of the buyer's purchase in acquiring the target. In effect, the target's shareholders are buying the buyer's stock in the acquisition and need to perform due diligence.

Business due diligence is the process whereby the business development and financial personnel of the buyer, and their investment banker if one is hired, examine the target to see if the acquisition makes sense from a financial and strategic perspective. Due diligence also should ascertain any soured business relations, technological obsolescence and unreported legal and business claims.

The buyer initiates the process by giving the target a due diligence checklist. Some investment banks and consultants offer due diligence and transition services as a separate business line.

In legal due diligence, the buyer's in-house counsel—or outside law firm—examines the legal affairs of the target to uncover any undisclosed legal obligations or threats. Intellectual property (IP) is any intangible asset that consists of knowledge and ideas, or real-world representation of them. IP due diligence refers to research and procedures designed to identify and protect intellectual property held by the target firm such as patents, copyrights, trademarks, and trade secrets. If IP is not properly protected by the target, that fact diminishes the value of the target to a prospective buyer or may even make the target unsellable.

知识产权 (Intellectual property, IP): 权利人对其智力劳动所创作的成果和经营活动中的商标、商誉所依法享有的专有权利。

As a practical matter, there is typically a period between the acquisition agreement and the definitive settlement. There are some common lock-up arrangements to make it difficult for the target to breach the agreement, though the target has a fiduciary duty to its shareholders to entertain better offers:

1. No-shop agreements. A no-shop agreement says that the target will not seek other bids, may not negotiate with, or furnish confidential information to other prospective bidders.

排他性谈判协议 (No-shop agreements): 在协议期间目标公司不可寻找其他投资方的协议。

These provisions are included because there necessarily is a delay between signing and closing due to the need to hold a shareholder meeting. In that interim period, an upset bid can emerge. In the definitive agreement, the target is also required to use its best efforts to secure shareholder approval, and the board is required to recommend the deal to the target's shareholders.

No-shop agreements, however, typically have fiduciary clauses that allow the target to negotiate with and furnish information to a prospective bidder if the target board receives legal advice that the board's fiduciary duty requires it to do so.

终止协议费用(Break-up fee):已经达成了并购协议的情况下,如果目标公司单方面终止了并购协议,那么买家将会得到一定金额的补偿。

2. Break-up fee. The no-shop agreement is typically combined with a provision that the target can terminate the acquisition agreement if it gets a superior proposal, but only if it pays the original suitor a break-up fee and/or a topping fee. This means that the target, in order to terminate the agreement, must pay the original suitor expenses (sometimes unaccountable and sometimes actual out-of-pocket expenses, possibly with a cap plus a fixed fee and/or a fee equal to a percentage of the amount that the new bid exceeds the original deal). In some cases, a reverse break-up fee requires the suitor to pay the break-up fee. A key question here is when the fee has to be paid. These fees are usually very substantial, even so high that the target may not have the cash to pay it.

顶尖业务(Crown jewels option):一家企业最有价值的业务单位。

3. Crown jewels option. The original lock-up devices included a crown jewels option that gave the buyer the option to buy a critical piece of the target's business, or the "crown jewels," if the deal didn't close for any reason other than the buyer's breach (e.g., in the event the target's shareholders did not vote for the deal, particularly if they did not approve the deal after another bidder announced that it would pay more).

股东表决(Voting agreements):全体或一部分股东就特定的股东大会决议事项进行表决。

4. Voting agreements. The bidder gets agreements from key shareholders that they will vote for the bidder's deal and will not tender their shares into a tender offer made by a rival bidder. They may be required to vote for the original deal regardless, or they may be required to vote for it only if the merger agreement is not terminated. Given that the original deal needs majority shareholders' approval and that bidders have threshold requirements as to how much stock they have to acquire, these agreements make it harder (and maybe impossible) for an upset bid to emerge.

A lock-up device often effectively precludes another bidder from scooping up the deal, even if the bidder offers a significantly better price for the target. These preclusive lock-ups were invalidated by the courts on a number of occasions as a breach of fiduciary duty on the part of the board of directors of the target, which rendered the merger agreement unenforceable.

In addition to lock-up devices in negotiated deals, potential targets have implemented defensive measures that are meant to make difficult (or perhaps impossible) the completion of a hostile bid. These devices include the poison pill, staggered terms for directors, and other devices. The other procedural aspect that must be kept in mind in public company deals is that mergers are subject to shareholder approval that can only take place well after signing. If the board agrees to a particular deal with a bidder that includes the most stringent of lock-up provisions, or anti-takeover devices, the shareholders still may not vote for that deal. So even if some of these clauses and devices can discourage another deal, they cannot ensure that the negotiated deal will be completed.

One possibility then is that the target does not have to terminate the signed merger agreement and pay a break-up fee—it can simply wait for the shareholders to veto the deal. What happens to the original bidder under those circumstances: Does it get a break-up fee? The answer is usually "yes", but that may be a financial stress for the target if the break-up fee is payable in cash, since a new bidder may not have emerged that can pay the break-up fee for the target.

Due diligence valuation

1. Discounted cash flow (DCF) analysis is based on estimated free cash flows (FCFs) achievable in the future before financing activities. These cash flows are discounted using the weighted average cost of capital (WACC) in order to reflect their present value. This yields the firm's **enterprise value (EV)**—its discounted free cash flow. Then, deducting net liabilities—existing debt minus cash on hand—from enterprise value, gives an estimated standalone equity value of the target. The present value of **net synergies** (synergies less costs of integration) are then added to estimate the value of the acquisition, including synergies. Of course, it is also possible to include the synergies and the costs of integration in an estimate of free cash flow of the merged firm—buyer plus target—in a single spreadsheet exercise of valuation.

Steps in discounted cash flow analysis

DCF analysis looks at cash flows which are, in principle, available to the providers of both debt and equity capital. The free cash flows of the target firm are established by utilizing the business plan drawn up by the target's management, then discounting these by the weighted average cost of capital (WACC). The WACC reflects the return expected by its creditors and shareholders. The cost of equity capital is derived based upon the capital asset pricing model (CAPM). The present value is then obtained by discounting the free cash flows and the terminal value using the WACC. The DCF itself yields the enterprise value.

If the Target is expected to continue its business activity beyond the business plan period, a **terminal value** is calculated as a discounted per-

现金流折现法(Discounted cash flow, DCF): 把企业未来特定期间内的预期现金流量还原为当前现值,因考量企业未来的盈利能力而普遍被当作估值的首选方法。

加权平均资本成本(Weighted average cost of capital, WACC): 企业以各种资本在企业全部资本中所占的比重为权数,对各种长期资金的资本成本加权平均计算出来的资本总成本。

企业价值(Enterprise value): 企业本身的价值,等于其未来所有自由现金流的现值。

净协同效应(Net synergies): 并购后净现金流量减去并购开销。

终值(Terminal value): 因无法估算无限的现金流而采用的简化计算方法,把未来现金流假定为按照固定速度永远增长,再折算至可估算现金流的最后一年的价值。

petuity based upon assumptions made about sustained free cash flow. To calculate the terminal value, future cash flows subsequent to the business plan period are usually estimated as a perpetuity—either a level one or one that grows at a constant rate (less than the WACC, otherwise the terminal value is infinite!). The enterprise value is made up of the present value of free cash flows during the business plan period and the present value of the terminal value.

To estimate the terminal value, the first n years of free cash flow can be forecast, then the free cash flow is assumed to be a constant flow or grow at a constant rate forever to infinity. Consequently the net present value of the firm—its **enterprise value**—is estimated as:

$$PV = FCF_0 + \frac{FCF_1}{1 + WACC} + \frac{FCF_2}{(1 + WACC)^2} + \cdots + \frac{FCF_{n-1}}{(1 + WACC)^{n-1}} + \frac{\frac{FCF_{n-1}(1 + g)}{(WACC - g)}}{(1 + WACC)^{n-1}} \quad (8.1)$$

Where g is the constant growth rate of FCF in the n'th year and forever.

The **equity value** is then obtained by deducting existing debt and liabilities from the enterprise value and adding cash and cash equivalents. Dividing the equity value by the number of shares outstanding yields the estimated value per share.

2. Analysis of comparables

可比公司分析(Analysis of comparables):利用同类公司的各种估值倍数对目标公司的价值进行推断。

Comparable companies identified should include other firms whose core business is similar to the target's, ruling out firms which have substantial other lines of business.

For the group of comparable companies selected, the enterprise value is calculated on the basis of their current market capitalization and the latest available actual net debt/cash position (including debt-like and cash-like items), where enterprise value equals equity value plus net debt.

EBITDA:计算利息、税项、折旧及摊销前的利润。

For each of the selected comparable companies, the EV/EBITDA multiple (transaction multiple) is calculated, where EBITDA is earnings before interest, taxes, depreciation, and amortization. The median from the resulting trading multiples is applied to the target's EBITDA estimate based on the business plan, producing an enterprise value of the target. That is, the estimated enterprise value of the firm is obtained by:

Estimated EBITDA of target × (EV/EBITDA) multiple from comparable companies = estimated EV of target.

To derive the equity value, enterprise value adjustments—net debt (debt less cash)—is deducted from the enterprise value. Dividing by the number of shares outstanding of the target, yields an estimate of the share value.

3. Analysis of precedent transactions

Relevant recent M&A transactions for similar companies are taken into account.

For the selected precedent transactions, the implied enterprise value (EV) and the implied historical EV/EBITDA multiple (transaction multiple) are calculated.

The median of the calculated transaction multiple is multiplied by the target's comparable historical EBITDA, producing an enterprise value for the target. To derive the equity value, enterprise value adjustments of net debt are deducted from the enterprise value. Dividing the equity value by the number of shares outstanding of the Target, yields an estimate of the share value.

交易先例分析(Analysis of precedent transactions): 参考涉及类似并购交易的已完成案例来评估一家企业的价值。

4. Analysis of takeover premium

In some circumstances, potential acquirers are willing to pay significant control premia.

This is especially true in contested takeover situations, where potential acquirers outbid each other resulting in higher premiums paid. The winning bidder suffers the "winner's curse," valuing the target firm more than its next highest value. In a worst case, the buyer may end up suffering "buyer's remorse," taking an impairment charge after the acquisition. In general, if the bidder already owns a controlling share in the target, the willingness to pay an additional control premium on the share price is typically lower.

溢价收购分析(Analysis of takeover premium): 收购方公司为取得目标公司的股权而向目标公司股东支付高于市场价格的价值。

Applying the concept: A Squeeze Out Acquisition—Minority Shareholders Are Frozen Out

In a squeeze out acquisition, "the Parent Buyer would acquire a majority of the shares of the Target for cash usually in a tender offer. The Parent forms a shell subsidiary (Merger Sub) that merges into the Target. Since the Parent owns a majority of the stock of the Target, it can approve the merger and "squeeze out" the minority shareholders of the Target. Following the merger agreement, the shares of the Target that are owned by its minority shareholders would be converted into the right to receive cash. The shares of the Merger Sub owned by the Parent would be extinguished since

排挤式合并(A squeeze out acquisitions): 一家公司在获得对另一家公司的控制权后,在其所作出的与该公司合并的决议中以现金交付的方式将该公司的少数股东排挤出公司。

> that entity is disappearing. As a result, the Parent would own all of the shares of the Target since the shares of the Target it acquired in the first instance would be the only shares of the Target outstanding."
>
> Sources: Ed Miller Jr. (2008), *Mergers and Acquisitions*, Wiley and Sons.

When the present value of synergies less costs of integration are determined, it is important not to offer the entire gains from net synergy to the target in the premium. Current shareholders of the buyer would not, in this case, benefit from the acquisition, seeing their shares diminish in value. While the shares of both the target and the buyer should immediately rise if investors regard the acquisition as a good one, overpaying often leads to an immediate decline in the price of the buyer's shares.

5. Equity research analysis

证券分析 (Equity research analysis): 通过金融模型和预测等手段分析公司的财务报告, 给出公司股票的目标价格及投资建议。

This analysis is based on a review of target prices published by equity research analysts covering the target firm. A target price can generally be taken as the value an equity research analyst expects a company's share price to reach within the next 12 months. The target price can be forecast either as a standalone value, or include a control premium for the takeover of the target firm.

In acquisitions of small high technology companies with no earnings and even no revenue, the price paid is simply determined by negotiation. "Comparables" are similar technology companies.

Cash and share consideration

A merger is the absorption of one firm by another. Firm A might acquire firm B by offering two shares in A for each share of B. B would then cease to exist, though its shareholders would own shares in A. Typically, a majority of the voting shares in the firm must approve the merger, and in some cases, a supermajority—2/3 vote. In general, a merger is only worthwhile if there is some synergy in combining the firms.

$$V_{AB} > V_A + V_B \tag{8.2}$$

That is to say, the value of the merged firm should be greater than the standalone value of the individual firms taken alone. When firm A and firm B consolidate into a new firm C—the surviving corporation—in general it should be true that:

$$V_C > V_A + V_B \tag{8.3}$$

In practical terms, a consolidation is equivalent to a merger. Synergy itself, S, is measured by:

$$S = V_{AB} - V_A - V_B \qquad (8.4)$$

That is, the value of the merged firm less the sum of the standalone values must be positive for a worthwhile merger.

Acquisition by cash

现金收购(Acquisition by cash):收购方支付一定数量的现金,以取得目标公司的所有权。

Table 8.2 Standalone values of Firms A and B

	Firm A	Firm B
Value	$100	$50
Shares outstanding	20	10
Share value	$5	$5

Let's say that after the acquisition, the combined firms are worth $170. Synergy is thus $20. Firm A could acquire firm B by paying $60 in cash, a premium of $10 over its market value in order to secure the majority vote necessary of B's shareholders. Each share would be tendered at $6 while it was previously worth $5. For firm A to benefit from this, the combined value of the firms must increase to more than $160 (the sum of their standalone values, $150, plus the synergy kept, $10). After the acquisition, the combined firms are worth $170. The value of firm A after the acquisition will therefore be $170 minus the $60 paid to B's stockholders. Firm A is thus worth $110 after the acquisition, as illustrated in Table 8.3.

Table 8.3 An outright cash acquisition of B by A

	Firm A
Value	$110
Shares outstanding	20
Share value	$5.5

The acquisition has a positive net present value, increasing shareholder's value. The price of the share rises to $5.50. Shareholders of both firms benefit and should approve the merger. The firms share equally in the synergy. Notice that if the NPV of firm B were $60, but it had present value of debt of $10, firm A could equivalently offer cash of

$50 and assumption of debt of $10.

换股收购 (Acquisition by stock) : 收购方通过发行新股票的方式替换目标公司原来的股票。

Acquisition by stock

It would seem that the same purchase price of $60 could be paid by the issue of 12 shares of A in exchange for the 10 shares of B. At the current market value of $5 for A's shares, this would appear to be equivalent to $60. However, this is not correct, because due to the rise in the value of A after the merger, 12 shares would be worth more than $60. To see this, consider the exchange ratio 12:10. Firm A would then look like this in Table 8.4.

Table 8.4 An acquisition of B by A through an incorrect share offer

	Firm A
Value	$170
Shares outstanding	32
Share value	$5.31

Former stockholders in B, would now own $5.31×12 = $63.75 worth of A's stock, receiving more than the purchase price of $60 in cash. How many shares should A therefore offer to B's shareholders? The correct amount would equal the ratio: $\alpha \times 170 = 60$, giving them shares worth $60. That is, $\alpha = 60/170 = 0.353$ of the combined company. Setting this ownership share equal to the fraction of new shares in the merged company, we can solve for n_w the number of new shares issued in addition to the existing number of shares outstanding, 20.

$$\alpha = \frac{n_w}{n + n_w} \tag{8.5}$$

Solving for n_w:

$$n_w = \frac{\alpha n}{(1 - \alpha)} = 10.90909 \tag{8.6}$$

Firm A's situation is now shown in Table 8.5.

Table 8.5 An acquisition of B by A through a correct share offer

	Firm A
Value	$170
Shares outstanding	30.91
Share value	$5.50

The 10.91 shares offered to shareholders of B are worth exactly $60 at the new share price of $5.50!

Acquisition by stock and cash

Suppose firm A acquires firm B by an offer of both cash and stock, for instance, $30 in cash and the rest in stock. How many shares of stock will firm A have to offer? Firm A will therefore be worth $140 after the cash payment of $30. In this case α = 30/140 = 0.2143, or inputting the basic data directly into equation (8.6).

$$n_w = \frac{\left(\frac{30}{140}\right) \times 20}{\left(1 - \frac{30}{140}\right)} = 5.45455 \qquad (8.7)$$

By offering exactly 5.45455 shares and $30 in cash, firm A would be offering the same premium as with pure cash or pure stock. Notice that the 5.45455 new shares are worth exactly $30 at the new share price of firm A, $5.5. Firm A's new situation would be as follows in Table 8.6.

混合收购 (Acquisition by stock and cash): 收购方以现金、股票等复合方式实现对目标公司的控制。

Table 8.6 An acquisition of B by A through a combination of cash and share offer

	Firm A
Value	$140
Shares outstanding	25.45
Share value	$5.5

The ChemChina acquisition of Syngenta

Timeline of the acquisition

- On August 15, 2015, the US's Monsanto, offered CHF 470 per share, roughly $460 per share at the time to acquire Syngenta. While it had been rejected twice previously, Monsanto argued it would make both firms more efficient by developing seeds and pesticides in tandem and integrating sales and distribution strategies for the two product categories.

- July 2015, Syngenta argued that the deal faced tough regulatory hurdles, especially anti-trust issues that Monsanto has not addressed and that the offer undervalues the company. "We said no in 2011, we said no

中国化工集团公司 (ChemChina): 简称中国化工,为中央企业,中国最大的化工公司。

先正达 (Syngenta): 瑞士的一家化工公司,全球最大农药生产商之一,于2017年被中国化工收购。

in 2012, we said no in 2015. What part of no don't they understand?" Chief Executive Michael Mack told a press conference at the group's Basel, Switzerland headquarters.

- In August 2015, Syngenta's Board of Directors again rejected an improved offer of $46 billion by Monsanto—a revised cash (45%) and stock (55%) takeover offer of CHF 470 a share, plus a $3 billion break-up fee—on the grounds that Monsanto had not addressed the regulatory obstacles, and that the offer undervalued Syngenta, despite a premium of 27% of Syngenta's standalone value before the Monsanto bid. Monsanto then dropped its offer.
- Aug. 26, 2015—"Syngenta's shares, which had been buoyed by Monsanto's bid, fell 18% to 309.90 francs in Swiss trading. Further, Syngenta American depository receipt shares (ADS) trading on the New York Stock Exchange fell over 15%. The market value of Syngenta as a standalone company was evidently 51% lower than the Monsanto offer! Shares in Monsanto rose over 7% to $95.76 on the news." (*The Wall Street Journal*, August 26, 2015) Some Syngenta shareholders were angered by the Board of Director's rejection of the offer by Monsanto, and with the subsequent offer withdrawal.
- On October 17, 2015, a group of disgruntled investors created the Alliance of Critical Syngenta Shareholders, sending a letter that day to Chairman Michel Demaré: "The Alliance urges the board to thoroughly evaluate all options for value creation without prejudice and to ensure that promises are kept, financial targets are met and shareholders are informed in a timely and open manner." (*Reuters*, August 25, 2015)
- In December 2015, in response, Chairman Michel Demaré implicitly acknowledged that Syngenta might need to be sold to provide shareholder value that Syngenta was unlikely to create as a standalone company—its previous standalone share price was CHF 370. Chairman Michel Demaré stated: "I would not say there were any mistakes in the way we negotiated with Monsanto. As I said, frankly, the responsibility for the deal not going through was more on their side. Monsanto tends to play the runaway bride, coming close and then escaping at the last moment. ... We had very specific questions that were left unanswered: On the synergies, tax benefits, regulatory risks. There was nothing else we could do." However, "in these circumstances, where our shareholders have a kind of benchmark share price, what they think this company is worth, it is very difficult to say that we can deliver this in the next twelve months," thereby

acknowledging the company needed to be sold. (*Finanz und Wirtschaft*, December 22, 2015)

- In February 2016, ChemChina (The China National Chemical Corporation) offered to purchase Syngenta for $43 billion (CHF 480 per share), representing nearly three times the purchase price of the largest previous Chinese acquisition, the $15.2 billion acquisition of Canada's energy company Nexen by CNOOC.

- The offer was "unanimously recommended to shareholders" by the Syngenta Board of Directors.

- In April 2017, U.S. and European regulatory authorities approved the acquisition, allowing the largest foreign takeover in Chinese history to proceed. ChemChina agreed to divest pesticide production of paraquat, abamectin, and chlorothalonl.

- Beijing, May 5, 2017, ChemChina announced the acquisition of Syngenta offer interim voting results. As of May 4, the end of the main contract, according to preliminary statistics, 80.7% of Syngenta shareholders accepted the offer.

- As of May 26, 2017, ChemChina's plan to purchase Syngenta for $44 billion neared completion, with ChemChina amassing "huge bridge loans" to pay Syngenta stockholders.

- May 31, 2017, Beijing China Chemical Group announced the end result of the Syngenta offer, with approximately 94.7% of the shares accepting the offer.

- Beijing June 7, 2017, ChemChina announced the completion of the second delivery of Syngenta offer. Shareholders who received the offer after May 4, 2017 received a consideration of $465 per share on June 7, 2017, and ADS holders received a consideration of $93 per ADS.

- China Chemical now has 94.7% stake in Syngenta and will "squeeze out" the remaining minority shareholders.

- Syngenta stock was withdrawn from the SIX Swiss Exchange on January 8, 2018, and its ADS were withdraw from the NYSE on January 18, 2018.

Swiss Exchange: 瑞士证券交易所。

- Some observers noted: "The acquisition of Syngenta by ChemChina has major implications for food security in China. The country is eager to bring home new technologies for genetically modified crops, fertilizers and pesticides, and the deal fits that overall demand to boost its capabilities in those areas." (*The Financial Times*, May 31, 2017)

ChemChina

In May 2004, the State Council of the People's Republic of China approved a merger of companies formerly under the Ministry of Chemical Industry as the China National Chemical Corporation (ChemChina). Ren Jianxin, who had founded Bluestar, a solvents company in 1984, became its CEO in 2004 and the chairman of the board of directors in 2014. Its main business is in materials science, life sciences, high-end manufacturing and chemicals. China Chemical is headquartered in Beijing and has production, research and development bases and marketing systems in 150 countries and regions. It is the largest chemical enterprise in China, ranking 234th of the world's top Fortune 500 companies.

ChemChina is 100% state owned, its parent being the State-owned Assets Supervision and Administration Commission (SASAC) of the State Council. As such, it does not have publicly listed shares on an exchange that could be used in payment for an acquisition. Consequently, an all cash offer to Syngenta shareholders is the consideration in the acquisition. An important exception to majority controlled state enterprises using cash only was Lenovo's 2004 acquisition of IBM's PC division for $1.2 billion, including $600 million of common stock. In that case, IBM, the corporation itself, in taking a stake in Lenovo, was signaling continued support of the ThinkPad and other PC products following the sale to Lenovo. IBM shareholders themselves might not have taken Lenovo shares as consideration. The IBM logo was authorized for use for five years on the state of the art laptop, the ThinkPad. IBM held 18.9% of Lenovo shares in December 2004, then 13.2% in 2005 following private equity investments in Lenovo. (John Quelch and Carin-Isabel Knoop, *op cit.*)

> SASAC:国务院国有资产监督管理委员会,简称国资委。

Product lines

ChemChina's website boasts of the following main product lines:
- "New and specialty chemical production: silicone, fluorine rubber, methionine, metallurgical solar grade polysilicon and other ... PVC production ranks first in the country, including PVC paste resin production in Asia, the world's third largest ...
- Petroleum processing and refining products: China Chemical has nine refineries, crude oil processing capacity of 25 million tons ...
- Agricultural chemicals: China Chemical is currently the world's largest non-patented pesticide producers, products cover herbicides, pesti-

cides, fungicides and plant growth regulators…

• Rubber products with special high elasticity, excellent wear resistance, shock absorption, insulation, and sealing performance … China Chemical has tires and rubber products, latex products and other production enterprises, the production of various tires, polysulfide rubber, special rubber products, new technology, such as carbon black high-tech, high value-added products. All steel radial tires, semi-steel radial tires, aviation tires, giant engineering tires (with a total capacity of more than 12 million tires).

• Chemical equipment manufacturing industry … providing production technology and equipment manufacturing industry, is the basis for the development of chemical industry. Rubber and plastics machinery manufacturing … ranks third in the world."

Other cross border acquisitions. ChemChina acquired a 60% stake in Israel-based ADAMA Agricultural Solutions—a manufacturer of generic pesticides—in a 2.4 billion US dollar acquisition. The chemical materials and specialty chemicals group acquired the French Adisseo Group, a global animal nutrition feed firm that specialized in producing methionine, vitamins, and biological enzymes. Another French acquisition was the organic silicon and sulphide business of Rhodia, becoming the third largest producer in the world of organic silicon. The petrochemical processing division also operates refineries, including small ones known as teapot plants, giving it an oil processing capacity of 500,000 barrels per day. In March 2015, it acquired the Italian Pirelli, the world's fifth-largest tire manufacturer for 7.1 billion euros.

About Syngenta

Syngenta, headquartered in Basel, Switzerland, is a global agribusiness operating in the crop protection, seeds, and lawn and garden markets in over 90 countries. Through state-of-the-art science and worldwide operations, the Company's mission is increasing crop productivity and improving global food security. It posted sales of $13.4 billion in the fiscal year 2015, an EBITDA of $2.8 billion, and net income of $1.4 billion. It was listed on the SIX Swiss Exchange since 2000 following the merger of the Zeneca and Novartis agricultural businesses.

Syngenta's operations are divided into three businesses (Crop Protection, Seeds, and Lawn and Garden) and four sales regions: Europe, Africa, Middle East, North America, Latin America and the Asian Pacific. Syngenta operates five main global R&D centers in China, India, Switzerland, the UK, and the USA.

- The Crop Protection business offers herbicides (Acuron, Axial), fungicides (Amistar, Elatus), insecticides (Actara, Durivo) and seedcare (Cruiser, Vibrance), designed to improve crop yield and performance, increase plant vigor and reduce yield losses during periods of drought or heat. Crop protection represented 74% of sales in 2015.

- The Seeds business encompasses a variety of seed products and brands including corn and soybean (Golden Harvest, Enogen), diverse field crops (NK oilseeds, Hilleshog), and vegetables (S&G, Rogers), among others. The products help to provide higher yields as well as to increase performance. Seeds represented 21% of sales in 2015.

- The Lawn and Garden business offers plant health solutions for turf professionals, growers, and pest managers. The products help to increase productivity and protect the environment. Lawn and garden revenues were 5% of sales in 2015.

In the Syngenta Chairman's words: "China needs food security and technology to feed its population, because they don't have the resources to produce all the food needed in China. They need to invest globally and need to identify strategic partners in terms of food security. So there are quite some potential synergies." It also provides distributional and geographic synergies, adding cash flows and financial capacity in USD and other currencies.

ChemChina benefitted greatly from the rejected Monsanto offer of CHF 470 per Syngenta share plus a breakup fee of $3 billion.

Syngenta, a global agribusiness, argued the deal faces tough regulatory hurdles that Monsanto has not addressed and that the offer undervalues the company. The Syngenta board of directors rejected the sweetened offer, promising instead high organic growth as a standalone seed, crop protection, and company headquartered in Switzerland. Syngenta shareholders were not convinced: they had urged the board of directors to negotiate and indeed favored its sale. Upon the rejection, the share price immediately fell 18% to CHF 309.90.

Evidently, the market also estimated that the standalone value of Syngenta was 51% lower than the revised CHF 470 per share offer of Aug. 18, 2016. Syngenta, which makes large research and development (R&D) investments in crop technology to increase the productivity of crops such as corn, soybeans, sugar cane, and cereals, was apparently worth much less as a standalone company.

N + 1 SWISS CAPITAL's fairness opinion on behalf of Syngenta

The Syngenta's Board of Directors retained N + 1 SWISS CAPITAL to prepare a fairness opinion on the financial adequacy of the ChemChina offer from the point of view of the public shareholders of Syngenta. ChemChina's offer to acquire Syngenta had two big advantages: Firstly, less regulatory opposition than Monsanto's would have faced, particularly from the U. S. Treasury, and secondly, it was all cash, no shares were involved in the consideration.

To estimate the standalone value of Syngenta using discounted cash flow, N + 1 SWISS CAPITAL first forecasts future free cash flow.

Table 8.7 outlines the procedure to compute free cash flow.

公平意见书 (Fairness opinion):涉及并购项目主要细节的意见书,由合格的分析员或顾问向决策人出具。

Table 8.7　Calculation of free cash flow

Total Revenue
less Total Costs
equals Operating Income
less Taxes
equals Operating Income after Taxes
plus Depreciation and Amortization
less change in New Working Capital
less Capital Expenditures
equals Free Cash Flow

N + 1 SWISS CAPITAL used the following valuation assumptions in Table 8.8.

Table 8.8　Syngenta valuation assumptions

- Valuation date: 26 January 2016
- Enterprise value adjustments: USD 3,348 million
- WACC: 8.0%–8.5%
- Perpetual growth rate: 2.0%–2.5%
- Diluted shares outstanding: 92.6 million
- Avg. sales growth (FY 2016 to 2030): 4.6% (CAGR)
- Avg. EBITDA margin (FY 2016 to 2030): 24.5%
- Avg. tax rate (FY 2016 to 2030): 21.8%
- Avg. capex (FY 2016 to 2030): 4.6% of sales
- Avg. D&A (FY 2016 to 2030): 81.9% of capex
- Avg. net working capital (FY 2016 to 2030): 25.5% of sales

Source: N + 1 SWISS CAPITAL.

Recall that the cost of capital is a weighted average of the after-tax cost of borrowing (D) and the cost of issuing equity (E).

$$\text{WACC} = r_D(1 - t_C)\left(\frac{D}{D+E}\right) + r_E\left(\frac{E}{D+E}\right) \tag{8.8}$$

where WACC indicates the weighted average cost of capital, r_D indicates the cost of debt, r_E indicates the cost of equity, and t_C indicates the marginal corporate tax rate.

边际公司所得税税率(Marginal corporate tax rate):根据公司收入多少分段的公司所得税税率。

The cost of equity can be estimated using the capital asset pricing model (CAPM):

$$r_E = r_f + \beta(r_M - r_f) \tag{8.9}$$

风险溢价(Risk premium):投资人要求较高的收益以抵消更大的风险。

市场回报率(Market rate of return):市场上所有股票组成的证券组合的报酬率。

国债利率(Treasury rate):国库券的利率。

where the return on equity equals the risk free rate on Treasuries, plus the equity's β—measuring market risk—times the market risk premium, ($r_M - r_f$), where $\beta = \dfrac{\text{Cov}(r_E, r_M)}{\text{Var}(r_M)}$, r_M and r_f indicate the market rate of return and the Treasury rate respectively. N + 1 SWISS CAPITAL thus estimates the WACC of Syngenta to be 8.3% in USD, as indicated in Figure 8.10.

Figure 8.10 Syngenta's weighted average cost of capital

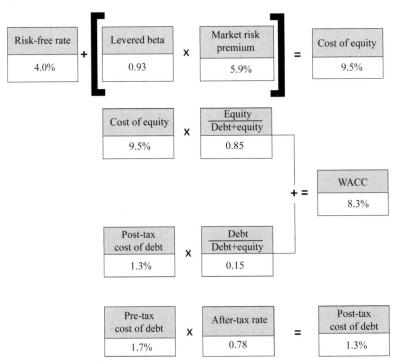

Source: N + 1 SWISS CAPITAL.

N + 1 SWISS CAPITAL estimated the discounted cash flow (DCF) plus terminal value on January 26, 2016 using this WACC—8.3%—as the discount rate, an average sales growth rate of 4.6%, an EBITDA margin of 24.5%, a tax rate of 21.8%, CAPEX to sales of 4.65, depreciation and amortization of 81.9% of CAPEX, and net working capital of 25.5% of sales. These operational assumptions are maintained until 2030, at which point a terminal value is estimated by discounting as a perpetuity sustained free cash flow at the weighted average cost of capital. The terminal value in 2030 is then discounted to the present, again at the WACC of 8.3%. The DCF and terminal values yielded an enterprise value of $42.49 billion as of January 26, 2016, from which debt net of cash of $3.348 billion was deducted, leaving an equity value of $39.347 billion. Dividing the equity value by 92.6 million shares outstanding, yielded a standalone share value of $422.82, or CHF 430.05, as indicated in Table 8.9.

Table 8.9 Calculation of value per Syngenta share

USD millions (unless otherwise stated)	
Present value of free cash flows	20,949
Present value of terminal value	21,545
Enterprise value	**42,494**
Net debt	(3,348)
Equity value	**39,147**
Shares outstanding (millions)	92.6
Value per share (USD)	**422.82**
USD/CHF exchange rate	1.0171
Value per share (CHF)	**430.05**
Net debt (USD millions)	
Financial debt	3,887
Pensions and retirement benefits	605
Cash and cash equivalents	(1,144)
	3,348

Note: Enterprise value = equity value + debt − cash = equity value + net debt, or, equity value = enterprise value − net debt.
Source: N + 1 SWISS CAPITAL.

The 60-day VWAP (Volume-weighted average price) was CHF 370.70 on 26 January 2016, which we can use as a "stand alone value." In addition to DCF, market-value-based valuation methods were also used as

成交量加权平均价(VWAP):将多笔交易的价格按各自的成交量加权而算出的平均价。

benchmarks to evaluate the fairness of the ChemChina offer. These included:

- Equity research analyst's target prices
- Analysis of comparable companies
- Analysis of precedent transactions
- Analysis of takeover premia

The final report by N + 1 SWISS CAPITAL summarized the ChemChina offer relative to the valuation benchmarks indicated in Table 8.10.

Table 8.10 Valuation analysis of Syngenta

Premium of mid-point analysis of the Chemchina offer (CHF 489* per share)

	CHF per share (midpoint valuation)	% premium of CHF 489 offer
• Discounted cash flow (DCF)	430	13%
• Equity research	328	49%
• Comparable companies	294	67%
• Precedent transactions	326	50%
• Takeover premium over standalone value	371	32%

* Equivalent to $481 as of valuation date, January 26, 2016.
Note: The Swiss franc (CHF) estimates are the mid-point of the range: high plus low value divided by 2.
The standalone value is CHF 370.70 per share, prior to the Monsanto offer.
Source: N +1 SWISS CAPITAL and author's calculations.

The report remarked in conclusion: "The ChemChina Offer of CHF488.95 per share represents a premium of 31.9% compared to the 60-day VWAP of 370.7 as at 26 January 2016. Considering the prolonged speculation on merger discussions, we believe that the current VWAP already contains some element of (unquantifiable) takeover premium. Applying the premium calculation to a potentially 'unaffected' VWAP (CHF 329.83) results in a premium of 48.2%."

On May 5, 2017, "China National Chemical Corporation (ChemChina) ... announced the provisional interim results for ChemChina's offer to acquire Syngenta. At the end of the Main Offer Period on May 4, based on preliminary numbers, around 80.7 percent of shares have been tendered. Subject to confirmation in the definitive notice of interim results scheduled for May 10, the Minimum Acceptance Rate condition of 67 percent of issued Syngenta shares has been met. As of June 7, 2017, ChemChina has completed the second settlement for shares tendered for the acquisition of Syngenta, the companies said Wednesday. It was reported last week that the deal has received support from 94.7 percent of the Swiss pesticides and seeds company's stockholders during two settlement periods."

In the News: **ChemChina Raises $20 Billion for Syngenta Deal via Perpetual Bonds and Preferred Shares**

ChemChina has raised $20 billion in perpetual bonds and preferred shares to finance its acquisition of Swiss seeds maker Syngenta, according to a regulatory filing by the state-owned Chinese company. ChemChina has restructured the financing of its Syngenta deal to take on more equity and reduce its short-term debt burden, but will still have nearly $20 billion in loans to refinance within 18 months …

Bank of China (BoC) has invested $10 billion via a perpetual bond, making the Chinese lender the single largest financier in the $44 billion deal, according to the May 18 filing which also shows state-owned asset manager China Reform Holdings Corp Ltd has provided $7 billion via a perpetual bond. China's Industrial Bank Co. Ltd has invested $1 billion through the same means, while Morgan Stanley has provided $2 billion via convertible preferred shares. Perpetual bonds are financing instruments that can act as both equity and debt. They are typically treated as equity under accounting standards but rating agencies may still treat them as debt depending on the circumstances. Because perpetual bonds have no maturity date, the new financing should help improve ChemChina's overall debt position … The deal gives China a portfolio of top-tier chemicals and patent-protected seeds to improve agricultural output, but has also left ChemChina facing a hefty debt burden which it has been seeking to reduce by bringing in more equity investors and replacing short-term loans with longer-term debt.

Source: Carol Zhong and Julie Zhu, "ChemChina Raises $20 Billion for Syngenta Deal via Perpetual Bonds and Preferred Shares," *Reuters*, May 25, 2017.

FYI: **New US Regulations on Foreign Mergers and Acquisitions**

- The **Foreign Investment Risk Review Modernization Act** (FIRRMA)—signed by President Trump August 13, 2018 expands the authority

外国投资风险审查现代化法案(FIRRMA)扩大了美国外国投资委员会(CFIUS)的权限。

出口管制改革法案(ECRA)对美国军民两用商品的出口进行管制。

of the Committee on Foreign Investment in the United States (CFIUS) to analyze, monitor, and budget for an extensive range of transactions that go beyond corporate acquisitions.

- The **Export Control Reform Act**(ECRA), August 13, 2018, provides sweeping statutory authority for regulation of commodities and technology, including in-country transfers and changes in an item's use in foreign countries.

New regulations in the U.S.

The new laws potentially apply to these types of transactions (*Forbes*, August 13, 2018):

- Acquisitions of U.S. companies holding "critical technology" by non-U.S. acquirers.
- Minority investments by non-U.S. investors in U.S. companies holding "critical technology".
- Investment in U.S. venture capital funds by foreign investors.
- Investment in U.S. private equity funds by foreign investors.
- Sales, licenses, or export of technology to non-U.S. companies.
- Acquisition or lease of certain types of U.S. real estate by foreign entities.

As a result of these new regulations in 2018, some proposed mergers by Chinese companies in the U.S. were rejected.

Table 8.11 lists proposed mergers that failed in the first half of 2018.

Table 8.11 Selected Chinese acquisitions terminated in the first half of 2018 due to U.S. regulations

Chinese Company	US Target	Value ($ millions)
Chongqing Casin	Chicago Stock Exchange (CHX)	N/A
Ant Financial	Moneygram	1.200
Sino IC, Unic Capital	Xcerra	580
HNA	Skybridge Capital	200
BlueFocus	Cogint	100
China National Heavy Duty Truck	UQM Technologies	28
Dabeinong	Waldo Farm	16.5
Shenzhen Selen	Akron Polymer	9.9

Source: Rhodium Group.

New regulations in China

The National Development and Reform Commission (NDRC), and the Ministry of Commerce (MOFCOM) are now reviewing Chinese M&A agreements. The two bodies are asking companies looking to buy assets overseas to justify terms, including target valuations, deal premiums, and financing arrangements, particularly with target companies not seen by the Chinese government as "strategic." The tightening of regulatory oversight for outbound purchases comes as Beijing is cracking down on some large domestic conglomerates for their debt-fueled acquisitions abroad of assets ranging from hotels to movie studios. The regulatory measures will deter some companies from making overseas acquisitions.

NDRC: 中华人民共和国国家发展和改革委员会, 简称发改委。

MOFCOM: 中华人民共和国商务部。

Table 8.12 outlines a time sequence of regulations issued by Chinese authorities.

Table 8.12 Regulatory guidance on outbound investment issued by Chinese authorities

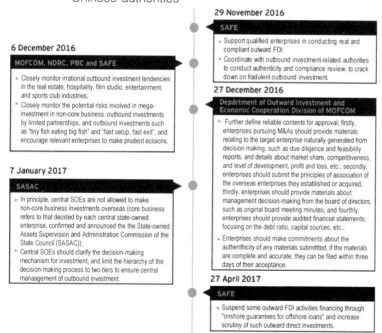

(MOFCOM)—Ministry of Commerce
(NDRC)—National Development and Reform Commission
(PBC)—People's Bank of China
(SAFE)—State Administration of Foreign Exchange
(SASAC)—State-owned Assets Supervision and Administration Commission of the State Council

Source: Xinhua News Agency, China Go Abroad (6th issue), *Strategic collaboration—How inclusive management helps Chinese enterprises win overseas*, August 2017.

As a result of the new Chinese policy towards overseas M&A activity:

- The government seized control of Anbang and, in May 2016, imprisoned founder Wu Xiaohui, sentencing him to prison for 18 years for corruption.
- Pressured by capital controls and high leverage, Dalian's Wanda began to sell its properties in the U.S. and overseas.
- HNA has also begun to sell its overseas properties not designated as strategic in order to reduce its leverage in U.S. dollars.

Some interesting new positive developments in China

> **In the news**: Foreign Ownership in Some Joint Ventures Raised Above 50%
>
> China is again gradually reforming its ownership structure, now that the joint venture model has proven its value in technology transmission. In 2022, BMW, the German automobile manufacturer, will own 70% of its joint venture in Shanghai, while Tesla is beginning production at its 100% Tesla-owned factory in Shanghai. On April 2018, Chinese regulators moved to lift the ceiling on foreign ownership of money management firms licensed to offer mutual funds to retail investors on the Chinese mainland to 51% from 49%. On May 14, 2018, J.P. Morgan Chase announced it will seek a majority stake in its joint venture since 2014 with Shanghai Pudong Development Bank, which currently owns 51% of the joint venture.
>
> Source: Douglas Appell, Pensions and Investments Money Management, May 14, 2018, www.pionline.com.

Conclusion

Cross border mergers and acquisitions raise a number of interesting and subtle additional issues due to cultural, legal, regulatory, and other differences—among these are currency conversion and convertibility. Here, we outline some approaches that buyers have taken to structure the offer and integrate the target.

ChemChina has retained the management and strategic mission of Syngenta while not retaining minority shareholders. It has signaled a desire to reap the synergies from integrating Syngenta, its research and know-how, into ChemChina's global operations rather than replacing its management or changing its business culture. The financing of the takeover of Syngenta was a leveraged buyout, with the loans to ChemChina coming from the Bank of China lending $10 billion, China Reform Holdings $7 billion, and Industrial Bank $1 billion. Morgan Stanley also bought $2 billion of convertible preferred shares. A 100% state-owned enterprise, ChemChina made a full cash offer. The strategic deal will play an important role in improving the future food supply of China and enable ChemChina to increase its global presence.

An important and exciting aspect of globalization is cross border mergers and acquisitions. These allow for the transmission of technology as well as more efficient production, management, and distribution worldwide. The policy pendulum has recently swung against globalization, both in trade and foreign direct investment. It will swing back again to reap the gains from international trade and the free movement of capital.

As free trade equalizes arbitrage prices of goods and services, capital mobility and arbitrage equalizes risk-adjusted rates of return globally. As free trade distributes goods and services from abundant low price regions to scarce high price regions, free capital mobility distributes capital from low return to high return areas. The world is gradually moving to globalization, a cause for optimism for global growth.

References and suggested readings

Weinland, Don, "ChemChina Edges Closer to Sealing Syngenta Deal," *The Financial Times*, May 31, 2017.

Erel, Isil, Rose C. Liao, and Michael S. Weisbach (2012), "Determinants of Cross-Border Mergers and Acquisitions," *Journal of Finance*, 67(3): 1045-1082.

Clark, Harry L. and Richard D. Harroch, "Mergers, Acquisitions and Investments Involving U. S. Companies With Chinese & Other Foreign Parties," *Forbes*, August 13, 2018.

Dittli, Mark and Andreas Meier, "Going Alone is Hardly an Option Anymore," *Finanz und Wirtschaft*, December 22, 2015, https://www.fuw.ch/Syngenta Chairman

Stone, Mike and P. J. Huffstutter, "Monsanto Sweetens Offer for Syngenta, Values Firm at $47 billion," *Reuters*, August 25, 2015.

Miller, Edward Jr. (2008), *Mergers and Acquisitions: A Step-by-step Practical Guide*, John Wiley and Sons.

N+1 Swiss Capital, "Fairness Opinion-Syngenta AG: Fairness Opinion of the ChemChina National Chemichal Corporation to Acquire Syngenta AG," March 4, 2016, http://www.n1swisscap.com

Quelch, John and Carin-Isabel Knoop (2006), "Lenovo: Building a Global Brand," Harvard Business School Case 9-507-014: 1-10.

Reuters, http://www.reuters.com

Rhodium Group, "China Investment Monitor: Capturing Chinese Foreign Investment Data in Real Time," http://www.rhg.com

"Syngenta Shares Fall on Rejection of Monsanto Offer," *The Wall Street Journal*, August 26, 2015.

Questions and problems

8.1 Mergers and acquisitions

Consider the net present value of firms A and B.

	Firm A	Firm B
Value	$20	$10
Shares outstanding	10	10

Answer the following questions:

a. What is the current value of the shares of each firm?

b. If firm A acquires firm B, and the value of the combined firm A is $40, what is the value of synergy?

c. Suppose that firm A offers cash of $15 to the shareholders of firm B, what is the premium A is offering?

d. Do you think firm B will accept firm A's offer if a majority vote of shareholders is required?

e. If they do, what will be the new value of firm A?

f. If firm A were instead to offer shares in the new, combined firm A, how many shares in the new firm would they have to offer to make a share offer equivalent to cash of $15?

g. Now suppose that firm A offers $10 in cash and the rest in shares in the new firm A. How many shares would it have to offer in order to make the equivalent of the cash offer of $15?

8.2 Mergers and acquisitions

Consider the data below indicating the standalone net present values of firms A and B.

	Firm A	Firm B
Value	$40	$10
Shares outstanding	20	10

Firm A's due diligence indicates that it will have costs of integration the first year of $2, but a perpetual increase in profits of $1 per year beginning the first year. Its cost of capital is 10%.

Answer the following questions:

a. What is the current value of the shares of each firm?
b. What is the value of synergies, net of integration costs?
c. Suppose that firm A offers cash of $14 (including a standalone value of $10 and $4 in synergy) to the shareholders of firm B, what is the premium A is offering?
d. Do you think they will accept the offer (a majority vote is required)?
e. If they do, what will be the new value of firm A?
f. If firm A were instead to offer only shares in the new, combined firm A, how many shares in the new firm would they have to offer to make a share offer equivalent to cash of $14?

8.3 An international business plan

Consider whether or not to acquire a subsidiary that has the following cash flow in euros. There is no terminal value. You are given the basic data below, and the WACC in euros is 10%.

Year	0	1	2	3	4	5
Free-cash flows(€)	(50)	10	10.5	11.0	11.6	12.2
Present value(€)	(50.0)					
NPV(€)						
Spot exchange rate(£/€)	0.71					
NPV(£)						

Appendix

The Time Value of Money

利息(Interest)是时间偏好的结果。消费者总是偏好即期消费,而不是未来消费。因此,他们在储蓄时要求获得利息收入。

Interest is the result of time preference: consumption now is preferred to consumption in the future. To renounce consumption, households require interest in order to save. In a closed economy, savings finances investment and therefore economic growth. The same is true for open economies: excess national savings translates into a current account surplus which finances other countries savings deficiency, a current account deficit.

There are several truisms regarding interest:

1. Higher expected inflation causes nominal interest rates to rise by the same amount to compensate savers for the expected loss in principal: the decline in purchasing power of the savings put aside. This is known as the Fisher equation.

2. The risk of default causes nominal interest rates to rise according, paying a risk premium to the saver willing to take the risk of default.

3. The nominal interest rate must be above the expected rate of inflation plus the default risk premium, so that the real rate of interest on savings is positive.

This yields the risk-augmented Fisher equation where:

$$1 + r = (1 + R)(1 + \pi)(1 + \rho) \qquad (A.1)$$

where

r = the nominal rate of interest

R = the real rate of interest

π = the expected rate of inflation

ρ = the default risk premium

When there is no risk of default, say for the moment on US Treasuries, $\rho = 0$. Thus we have for default free assets:

$$1 + r = (1 + R)(1 + \pi) \qquad (A.2)$$

The expected real rate of interest is:

$$R = \frac{r - \pi}{1 + \pi} \qquad (A.3)$$

which is always positive in a free capital market. However, if the actual inflation exceeds the expected inflation sufficiently, the realized real rate R^* may be negative:

当真实的通货膨胀率大大超过预期通货膨胀率时,真实的利率可能为负。

$$R^* = \frac{r - \pi^*}{1 + \pi^*} \qquad (A.4)$$

Indeed, the worst rate of realized return is -100%. When π^* is very large, R^* approaches minus one. That is, the entire investment is lost:

$$\lim_{\pi^* \to \infty} = \frac{r - \pi^*}{1 + \pi^*} = -1 = -100\% \qquad (A.5)$$

When a default occurs, the real rate of return can also be negative. In the case of full default on interest and principal, the real rate of return is once again -100%. The interest rate is a truly important price. It is the price of present consumption in terms of future consumption.

Notation:

t = time in years

m = frequency of interest payment per year (number of conversion periods per year)

r = nominal rate of interest rate per annum

i = interest rate of the conversion period

P = present value

A = accumulated value

r_e = effective rate of interest per annum

For example, if the original principal is P dollars and the interest is compounded per period at the rate of i, then at the end of the first period, the new principal, or accumulated amount, will be the sum of principal plus interest on principal.

$$A_1 = P + iP = P(1 + i)$$

The interest earned at the end of the second period is computed on A_1, so at the end of the second period, the accumulated amount will be:

$$A_2 = A_1 + iA_1 = (1 + i)A_1 = (1 + i)(1 + i)P = (1 + i)^2 P$$

Similarly at the end of the $n'th$ period, the accumulated amount will be:

$$A_n = P(1 + i)^n \qquad (A.6)$$

To convert the annual nominal rate of interest, r, to a periodic interest rate, we divide r by m, so that $i = \frac{r}{m}$ where m is the number of payment or conversion periods per year. Consequently, $n = mt$. We substitute these in (A.6) to derive the equation that indicates the accumulated value of a present sum P yielding annual interest of r paid m times per annum:

$$A = P\left(1 + \frac{r}{m}\right)^{mt} \qquad (A.7)$$

复利(Compound interest):复合利息,它是指每一期的利息还可以在以后的时期内产生利息,也即它的利息要并入本金中重复计息。

If interest earned is added to the principal and thereafter earns interest itself at the same rate, it is called **compound interest**. For example, in Table A.1 a sum of \$1,000 principal paid now will accumulate into the following amounts after three years, $t = 3$, with payments of 5% interest m times a year:

Table A.1 Accumulated interest after three years depending on the frequency of interest payments per year

t	m	r	P	$A(3\text{ years})$
3	1	0.05	\$1,000	\$1,157.63
	2			\$1,159.69
	4			\$1,160.75
	12			\$1,161.47

Notice that monthly interest payments, $m = 12$, yield a slightly higher accumulated sum than quarterly, $m = 4$, semi-annual, $m = 2$, or annual, $m = 1$, payments. In general, the more frequent the interest payment the greater the accumulated value.

Present value

现值(Present value):对未来现金流量以恰当的折现率进行折现后的价值。

Thus, the present value of the initial investment to be set aside at an annual rate of interest r with m conversion periods per year is indicated by (A.8). In Table A.2, the present value of one thousand dollars to be received in three years is calculated as a function of the number of conversion periods per year.

$$P = A\left(1 + \frac{r}{m}\right)^{-mt} \qquad (A.8)$$

Table A.2 calculates the present value of a sum to be paid depending on the number of conversion periods.

Table A.2 The present value of 1,000 dollars paid in year 3 using a discount rate of 5%, depending on the number of conversion periods paying r on P

t	m	r	$A(3\ \text{years})$	P
3	1	0.05	$1,000	$863.84
	2			$862.30
	4			$861.51
	12			$860.98

The interpretation of this result is that you only need to make an initial investment of $860.98 to accumulate one thousand dollars in three years if the 5% interest on $860.99 is paid monthly, $m = 12$. However, if the 5% interest is paid only quarterly, $m = 4$, you must set aside today a slightly higher amount, $861.51 dollars to accumulate one thousand dollars in three years.

The effective rate of interest per annum is simply:

$$r_e = \left(1 + \frac{r}{m}\right)^m - 1 \quad \text{since} \quad t = 1 \quad (A.9)$$

You are promised a 2% monthly rate of return, say by Bernie Madoff. The effective rate of interest per annum, if you indeed receive 2% a month, is:

$$r_e = \left(1 + \frac{0.02 \times 12}{12}\right)^{12} - 1 = 26.8\%$$

Similarly, when you are paid 2% quarterly, this represents an effective rate of 8.24% per annum:

$$r_e = \left(1 + \frac{0.02 \times 4}{4}\right)^4 - 1 = 8.24\%$$

The simple rates of interest are $2 \times 12 = 24\%$ and $2 \times 4 = 8\%$ respectively.

When this rate of interest is promised, *caveat emptor*!

Table A.3 indicates the effective rate of interest, depending on the number of conversion payments.

Table A.3 The effective rate of interest depending on the number of conversion payments

r	m	r_e
5%	1	5%
	2	5.06%
	4	5.095%
	12	5.116%

Continuously compounded interest

连续复利(Continuously compounded interest): 在期数趋于无穷大的极限情况下得到的利率,此时不同期之间的间隔很短,可以看作无穷小量。

Let $x = \dfrac{m}{r}$. Then in (A.7) we have

$$A = P\left(1 + \frac{1}{x}\right)^{xrt} = P\left[\left(1 + \frac{1}{x}\right)^{x}\right]^{rt} \quad (A.10)$$

In the limit as x approaches infinity:

$$\lim_{x \to \infty} A = P\left[\lim_{x \to \infty}\left(1 + \frac{1}{x}\right)^{x}\right]^{rt}$$

but

$$\lim_{x \to \infty}\left(1 + \frac{1}{x}\right)^{x} = e$$

Therefore

$$\lim_{m \to \infty} P\left[\left(1 + \frac{r}{m}\right)^{\frac{m}{r}}\right]^{rt} = Pe^{rt} \quad (A.11)$$

This yields the accumulated value continuously compounded:

$$A = Pe^{rt} \quad (A.12)$$

There is little difference between daily compounding and continuous compounding, as seen in Table A.4. Table A.4 indicates the accumulated value of discrete and continuous compound interest payments on an initial investment of $1,000, depending on the number of conversion payments.

Table A.4 Accumulated values of an initial payment of $1,000 with continuous versus discrete conversion payments of interest r percent per year paid on P

m	r	P	A 1 year	A 2 years	A 3 years	A 4 years	A 5 years
1	0.05	$1,000	$1,050.00	$1,102.50	$1,157.63	$1,215.51	$1,276.28
2			$1,050.63	$1,103.81	$1,159.69	$1,218.40	$1,280.08
4			$1,050.95	$1,104.49	$1,160.75	$1,219.89	$1,282.04
12			$1,051.16	$1,104.94	$1,161.47	$1,220.90	$1,283.36
360			$1,051.27	$1,105.16	$1,161.82	$1,221.39	$1,284.00
Continuous			$1,051.27	$1,105.17	$1,161.83	$1,221.40	$1,284.03

The corresponding present value is indicated by equation (A.13) and shown in Table A.5.

$$P = Ae^{-rt} \qquad (A.13)$$

Table A.5 Present values of $1,000 paid in each year

m	r	P	P year 1	P year 2	P year 3	P year 4	P year 5	P every year*
1	0.05	$1,000	$952.38	$907.03	$863.84	$822.70	$783.53	$4,329.48
2			$951.81	$905.95	$862.30	$820.75	$781.20	$4,322.01
4			$951.52	$905.40	$861.51	$819.75	$780.01	$4,318.19
12			$951.33	$905.03	$860.98	$819.07	$779.21	$4,315.61
360			$951.23	$904.84	$860.72	$818.74	$778.81	$4,314.35
Continuous			$951.23	$904.84	$860.71	$818.73	$778.80	$4,314.31

*If the cash flow of $1,000 is received every year.

Once again, the present values are the amounts that must be set aside now at interest rate r with m conversion periods per year to yield $1,000 in the year indicated.

In general, if a project or firms is expected to generate "free cash flow" of $1,000 a year for five years, we then add the corresponding present values. For simplicity, consider only annually compounded interest at 5%. A firm generating free cash flow of $1,000 a year for five years would have an equity value today of $4,329.48, as shown in Table A.6.

Table A.6 Present values of free cash flow of $1,000 per year every year for 5 years

m	r	Free cash flow every year	P year 1	P year 2	P year 3	P year 4	P year 5	Sum of Ps Net Present value (equity value)
1	0.05	$1,000	$952.38	$907.03	$863.84	$822.70	$783.53	$4,329.48

The general formula for the net present value of an investment yielding free cash flow or a coupon payment of Π_i in period i for n periods is given by:

$$P = \Pi_0 + \frac{\Pi_1}{(1+r)} + \frac{\Pi_2}{(1+r)^2} + \frac{\Pi_3}{(1+r)^3} + \cdots + \frac{\Pi_n}{(1+r)^n} \tag{A.14}$$

This is perhaps the most important formula in finance for the valuation of assets, securities and firms.

A related formula is the **return on investment (ROI)** which is that rate of discount, δ, which makes the present value equal to zero, or:

$$0 = \Pi_0 + \frac{\Pi_1}{(1+\delta)} + \frac{\Pi_2}{(1+\delta)^2} + \frac{\Pi_3}{(1+\delta)^3} + \cdots + \frac{\Pi_n}{(1+\delta)^n} \tag{A.15}$$

which is a polynomial equation often yielding multiple solutions.

An example might be as illustrated in Table A.7.

Table A.7 The internal rate of return

	$(6,666.67)	$1,000.00	$1,000.00	$1,000.00	$1,000.00	$7,666.67
IRR	15%					

Ranking investments or securities is better done by their net present value, particularly when the discount rate includes an appropriate risk and inflation premium. A special but important case is that of perpetuities that pay a sum in perpetuity.

Perpetuities

Let K be the dividend or sum paid in perpetuity. A no-growth perpetuity of K dollars has a present value:

$$P = \frac{K}{r} \quad (A.16)$$

A perpetuity of K dollars growing at the rate g has a present value:

$$P = \frac{K}{r - g} \quad (A.17)$$

These two formulas can be derived in different ways.

• **Continuous discounting**: $1 growing at the continuous rate g in perpetuity discounted at the rate r yields a present value of:

$$\int_0^\infty e^{-(r-g)t} dt = \frac{1}{r - g} \quad (A.18)$$

found by taking the integral and evaluating in the limit as t approaches infinity and at $t = 0$ provided that $r > g$. If r were less than g, the perpetuity value would be unbounded, i.e. infinite.

• **Discrete discounting**: A perpetuity of $1 growing at the rate g per period forever discounted at the rate r per period yields a present value of:

$$\frac{1}{r - g} \quad (A.19)$$

Let Z the present value of a one dollar perpetuity growing at g per period:

$$Z = \frac{1}{1 + r} + \frac{1 + g}{(1 + r)^2} + \frac{(1 + g)^2}{(1 + r)^3} + \cdots + \frac{(1 + g)^{n-1}}{(1 + r)^n}$$

Multiply both sides by $\frac{1 + g}{1 + r}$ and subtract the result, yielding:

$$Z - \left(\frac{1 + g}{1 + r}\right)Z = \frac{1}{1 + r} - \frac{(1 + g)^n}{(1 + r)^{n+1}}$$

or

$$Z \left[\frac{1 + r}{1 + r} - \left(\frac{1 + g}{1 + r}\right)\right] = \frac{1}{1 + r} - \frac{(1 + g)^n}{(1 + r)^{n+1}}$$

or

$$Z \left(\frac{r - g}{1 + r}\right) = \frac{1}{1 + r} - \frac{(1 + g)^n}{(1 + r)^{n+1}}$$

or

$$Z = \frac{1}{r - g} - \left(\frac{1}{r - g}\right)\frac{(1 + g)^n}{(1 + r)^n} = \frac{1}{r - g} - \left(\frac{1}{r - g}\right)\left(\frac{(1 + g)}{(1 + r)}\right)^n$$

When $0 < g < r$, in the limit as n approaches infinity, the right hand term approaches zero, so:

$$Z = \frac{1}{r - g} \quad (A.20)$$

Remarks:

• A level perpetuity: When a one dollar perpetuity does not grow, its discounted value is simply:

$$\frac{1}{r} \quad (A.21)$$

Applications:

1. Terminal values

When $g > r$, the perpetuity has infinite value, i.e. is unbounded from above. Consequently, as g approaches r, the terminal value of a business approaches infinity. Terminal values of a business are useful in discounting free cash flow. The first three years of free cash flow can be forecast, then the third year free cash flow can be assumed to be constant thereafter to infinity. Consequently the net present value of the firm is estimated as:

$$P = \Pi_0 + \frac{\Pi_1}{(1+r)} + \frac{\Pi_2}{(1+r)^2} + \frac{\Pi_3}{(1+r)^3} + \frac{T_3}{(1+r)^3} \quad (A.22)$$

where

$$T_3 = \frac{\Pi_3}{r} \quad (A.23)$$

If the last year's free cash flow grows forever at the rate g, the terminal value is indicated by:

$$T_3 = \frac{\Pi_3}{r - g} \quad (A.24)$$

As a practical matter, the assumption of a high growth rate in free cash flow relative to a low weighted average cost of capital implies a high terminal value even when discounted at 3 or 5 years, over-estimating the value of the business. That is, the lion's share of the present value of the business is its terminal value, which may not be credible. In Table A.8, an example of equity valuation might be:

终值(Terminal value): 如果第三年到未来的现金流可以被认为恒定,那么终值公式可以用式(A.23)表示;如果从第三年起未来的现金流以增长率 g 增长,那么终值公式可以用式(A.24)表示。

当永续年金的增长率大于贴现率时,永续年金的价值为无穷大。

Table A.8 The net present value of free cash flow plus terminal value

	year 1	year 2	year 3	year 4	year 5	Sum of NPVs
Free cash flow	$1,000	$1,000	$1,000	$1,000	$7,666.67	(equity value)
NPV at 15%	$869.57	$756.14	$657.52	$571.75	$3,811.69	$6,666.67

In year 5, the free cash flow is $1,000 plus $1,000 divided by 0.15—the value of the firm as a perpetuity beginning in year 6—or $6,666.67.

2. A coupon bond

A bond with a fixed coupon of C payable annually for n years, at which time a face value of F_n is also paid, is worth today:

$$P = \frac{C_1}{(1+r)} + \frac{C_2}{(1+r)^2} + \frac{C_3}{(1+r)^3} + \cdots + \frac{F_n + C_n}{(1+r)^n} \quad (A.25)$$

where r is the per annum market rate of interest. The coupon payments can be split from the face payment, so that the discounted coupon flow when it is paid annually is worth:

$$P = \frac{C_1}{(1+r)} + \frac{C_2}{(1+r)^2} + \frac{C_3}{(1+r)^3} + \cdots + \frac{C_n}{(1+r)^n} \quad (A.26)$$

while the face payment is treated as a **zero coupon bond** with maturity n. Consequently, its value is:

$$P = \frac{F_n}{(1+r)^n} \quad (A.27)$$

零息债券 (Zero coupon bond): 以贴现方式发行,不附息票,而于到期日按面值一次性支付本利的债券。

If the same bond pays the coupon semiannually, twice a year, it is worth:

$$P = \frac{C_1}{\left(1+\frac{r}{2}\right)^{2\times 0.5}} + \frac{C_2}{\left(1+\frac{r}{2}\right)^{2\times 1}} + \frac{C_3}{\left(1+\frac{r}{2}\right)^{2\times 1.5}}$$
$$+ \frac{C_3}{\left(1+\frac{r}{2}\right)^{2\times 2}} + \cdots + \frac{(F_n + C_n)}{\left(1+\frac{r}{2}\right)^{2n}} \quad (A.28)$$

For example, Table A.9 values a 2 year coupon bond with interest paid every six months.

Table A.9 The net present value of a semi-annually paid 5% coupon bond with face value of $1,000

r	m	t	A	P	Coupon	Face	Coupon + Face
0.05	2	0.5	$50	$48.78	$48.78		
		1	$50	$47.59	$47.59		
		1.5	$50	$46.43	$46.43		
		2	$1,050	$951.25	$45.30	$905.95	
				$1,094.05	$188.10	$905.95	$1,094.05

3. China versus the United States in real GDP: an arithmetic calculation

If income per capita in the US grows at the rate γ_{us} and income per capita in China grows at the rate γ_c, we have: $y^{us} = y_0^{us} e^{\gamma_{us} t}$ and $y^c = y_0^c e^{\gamma_c t}$.

China's income per capita overtakes that of the US when:

$$y_0^c e^{\gamma_c t} = y_0^{us} e^{\gamma_{us} t}$$

or

$$\frac{y_0^{us}}{y_0^c} = e^{(\gamma_c - \gamma_{us})t}$$

That is:

$$\ln\left[\frac{y_0^{us}}{y_0^c}\right] = (\gamma_c - \gamma_{us})t$$

or

$$\hat{t} = \frac{\ln\left[\frac{y_0^{us}}{y_0^c}\right]}{(\gamma_c - \gamma_{us})} \qquad (A.29)$$

If China grows 7% faster than the U.S., China's income per capita in purchasing power parity terms (Source: www.cia.org/worldfactbook, June 2011) overtakes that of the US in 26.5 years.

$$\hat{t} = \frac{\ln\left[\frac{47,400}{7,400}\right]}{0.07} = \frac{\ln[6.4]}{0.07} = \frac{1.86}{0.07} = 26.5$$

In terms of absolute levels of income in purchasing power of billions of US dollars, China's real GDP overtakes that of the United States in 5.7 years.

$$\hat{t} = \frac{\ln\left[\frac{14,720}{9,872}\right]}{0.07} = \frac{\ln[1.491]}{0.07} = \frac{0.3995}{0.07} = 5.7$$

李嘉图等价 (Ricardian equivalence): 在某些条件下,政府无论通过债券还是税收筹资,其效果都是相同的或者等价的。

4. Ricardian equivalence

In his "Essay on the Funding System" (1820) David Ricardo studied whether it makes a difference to finance a war with the £20 million in current taxes or to issue government bonds with infinite maturity and annual interest payment of £1 million in all following years financed by future taxes. At the assumed interest rate of 5%, Ricardo concluded that ...

"In point of economy there is no real difference in either of the modes, for 20 millions in one payment, 1 million per annum for ever ... are precisely of the same value."

That is:

$$P = \frac{K}{r} = \frac{1}{0.05} = 20$$

When households and businesses are taxed more in the present and the future to finance current government consumption spending, it is likely that the spending multiplier will be zero (Ricardian Equivalence), or even negative if the deficit money is not well spent.

5. Sovereign debt

The primary fiscal deficit is written:

$$G_t + V_t - T_t$$

Where G_t is governmental spending on goods and services, V_t is governmental transfer payments (from Jane to Paul), T_t is governmental revenues from taxes, The total fiscal deficit includes interest payments at r on the Treasury's debt D_t.

Consequently, the total deficit may be written:

$$G_t + rD_{t-1} + V_t - T_t \quad (A.30)$$

It is often useful to express the total deficit as a percentage of GDP, Y_t.

$$\frac{G_t + rD_{t-1} + V_t - T_t}{Y_t} \quad (A.31)$$

Several countries have had total deficits that are a high fraction of GDP, such as Ireland, 32%, and Greece, 14%, in the recent past.

Consequently, debt this year is indicated by last year's debt, plus the interest payments on the debt, plus this year's primary deficit.

$$D_t \equiv (1+r)D_{t-1} + G_t + V_t - T_t \quad (A.32)$$

As a fraction of GDP, the debt to GDP ratio is indicated by:

$$\frac{D_t}{Y_t} \equiv (1+r)\frac{D_{t-1}}{Y_t} + \frac{G_t + V_t - T_t}{Y_t} \quad (A.33)$$

As a rule of thumb, when debt to income rises above 100%, a risk premium emerges. Greece's debt to income ratio is currently 1.5 for instance.

The financing of a deficit is necessary, so that:

$$G_t + rD_{t-1} + V_t - T_t \equiv \Delta H_t + \Delta D_t \quad (A.34)$$

Where ΔH_t is newly printed high-powered, base money (i.e. Federal Reserve Bank purchases of US Treasury bonds), also known as "the printing press", and ΔD_t is the sale of new Treasury bonds to the public, domestic and foreign (approximately 52% of Treasuries are sold to US investors and banks, and 48% to foreign investors and banks, including Central Banks).

The increase in total Treasury debt, ΔB_t, is the sum of Treasuries sold to the FED and those sold to domestic and foreign individuals, firms, and banks, that is:

$$\Delta B_t = \Delta H_t + \Delta D_t \quad (A.35)$$

The **no Ponzi game (NPG) condition** is written, with constant interest rate r, in the continuous case for convenience:

$$\lim_{t \to \infty}[D(t)e^{-rt}] = 0. \quad (A.36)$$

That is, debt cannot increase faster asymptotically than the interest

总财政赤字(Total fiscal deficit):在主要财政赤字的基础上,还包括国债的利息支出。

财政赤字的融资(Financing of deficit)主要有两种方式:一是发行高能的基础货币,也即政府开动"印钞机器";二是通过新发债券融资。

无庞氏骗局条件(No Ponzi game condition):政府债务的增长速度不能大于利率的增长速度,否则就会产生违约风险,也即产生所谓的"庞氏骗局"。

rate. This gives an inter-temporal budget constraint for the government. In the case of most European governments and the US government in 2011, the inter-temporal budgets constraint does not seem to be satisfied. Should that continue, we can expect many sovereign defaults, including that of the US Treasury, either by explicit default by missing a payment or implicit default by unanticipated inflation.

6. Interest and default risk

Default or credit risk is measured by the percentage discount of the market value of an asset relative to the present value of its payments at a risk-free interest rate (say a AAA US Treasury rate, held till August 4, 2011). In the Figure A.1, the present value of sovereign bonds as a fraction of GDP is indicated along the horizontal axis, discounted by the risk-free rate. If there is no default risk, the market value of the bonds plotted on the vertical axis would be the same, as plotted along the 45-degree line from the origin. When there is default risk, the market value falls below the risk-free value indicated along the 45-degree line. As indebtedness increases relative to income, holding other things such as income constant, it becomes more difficult to service the debt, so a discount emerges. It is entirely conceivable that additional debt might reduce the expected present value of repayment—more debt would have in fact less market value. In that case, the market value curve slopes downward. In the previous example of a risky coupon bond with a present value of 100% of GDP at the risk-free rate, the present value of expected repayment is only 75% in one year. The default-risk premium is 25/75 = 35.33%.

违约风险(Default risk) 由信用风险溢价度量。信用风险溢价是由无风险利率折现的资产现值与资产实际价值的差值。

Figure A.1 Measuring default risk

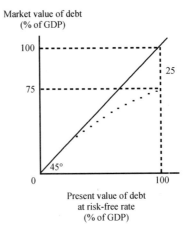

7. The rule of 70

How long does it take for a variable to double, such as GDP per capita, if the growth rate is g percent? If y is growing at the rate γ percent, we have:

$$y = y_0 e^{\gamma t}$$

To double, the variable must be $2y$ or:

$$y_0 e^{\gamma t} = 2y_0$$

or

$$e^{\gamma t} = 2$$

Taking natural logarithms, and solving:

$$\gamma t = \ln(2) = 0.693147 \approx 0.7$$

or

$$t \approx \frac{0.7}{\gamma} \tag{A.37}$$

In words, anything that grows at 7% will double every ten years. If y grows at 3.5%, it will double every twenty years, while if it grows at 14%, it will double in 5 years. Compound growth takes place more rapidly than simple growth. Just divide 70 by the rate of growth to get the number of years it takes for something to double.

> 70 法则 (The rule of 70): 用 70 除以增长百分比即可得到价值翻倍所需的时间。例如，如果某一资产价值以 7% 的年增长率增长，则需要 70/7 = 10 年的时间使资产价值翻倍。

8. A Ponzi Game

When interest promised on an investment is "too good to be true" it is usually *not* true. Suppose that you are offered two percent a month compounded on an investment that is to be redeemed in one year, but not before. The compounded annual rate of return on this investment is:

$$r_e = (1 + r_{12})^{12} - 1 = (1.02)^{12} - 1 = 26.8\%$$

Unless this investment scheme can manage to gain new investors, there are few, if any, investments that can *ex ante* yield 26.8%, so there is a high possibility of default—that this is a Ponzi Game. *Ex post*, there are many realized returns exceeding 27%, the problem is identifying them beforehand.

9. Interest rate parity

When two assets are default risk free, the interest rate differential on the two assets reflects the expected percentage currency rate change between them. Interest rate parity says:

$$\frac{F_{\$/£}}{S_{\$/£}} = \frac{(1 + r_{us})}{(1 + r_{uk})} \tag{A.38}$$

Subtracting unity from each side of (A.38) and simplifying, we have:

$$\frac{F_{\$/£}}{S_{\$/£}} - 1 \equiv E(s)$$

$$= \frac{(1+r_{us})}{(1+r_{uk})} - 1 = \frac{(1+r_{us})}{(1+r_{uk})} - \frac{(1+r_{uk})}{(1+r_{uk})} = \left(\frac{r_{us} - r_{uk}}{1 + r_{uk}}\right) \quad (A.39)$$

Note that the expected percentage increase in the dollar price of the pound, indicated by $E(s)$, is indicated by:

$$E(s) = \frac{r_{us} - r_{uk}}{1 + r_{uk}} \cong r_{us} - r_{uk} \quad (A.40)$$

Thus, the expected dollar depreciation—or pound appreciation—is equal the percentage difference in interest rates. If the interest rate on US Treasuries is two percent greater than on UK Treasuries, the dollar price of the pound is expected to rise by approximately 2%. That is, the dollar is expected to depreciation 2% or the pound to appreciate 2%. In the Fisher equation, this reflects typically a higher expected rate of inflation in the US compared to the UK.

10. Synergy

AT&T offered Deutsche Telecom $39 billion for its USA T-Mobile network. AT&T's due diligence estimated (approximately) costs of integration of $1 billion a year for two years, then synergies of $3 billion forever thereafter. Consequently, if AT&T's cost of borrowing is say 5%, the acquisition would add value to AT&T, about $11 billion, as shown in Table A.10.

Table A.10 The net present value of estimated synergies and integration costs

	year	year	forever	Total synergy
Borrowing cost	1	2	In perpetuity	
5%	$(1.00)	$(1.00)	$3.00	
			$60	
NPV	$(0.95)	$(0.91)	$51.83	$49.97

However, the ROI is only 8%, so that higher borrowing costs would not make the acquisition worthwhile, as shown in Table A.11.

Table A.11 The internal rate of return on AT&T's offer to Deutsche Telecom

	$(39.00)	$(1.00)	$(1.00)	$60.00
IRR	17%			

The due diligence agreement with T-Mobile was that AT&T would pay between $3 billion and $6 billion in broadband spectrum should the deal fall through for any reason. Due to regulatory opposition by the US Justice Department, the FCC, and a suit by Sprint, AT&T has withdrawn its offer. It paid a penalty fee of 4 billion USD.

Conclusion

The payment of interest on securities reflects the fact that money today is usually worth more than money tomorrow. (Negative interest rates on sovereign bonds reflect expansionary monetary policies by the European Central Bank and the Bank of Japan. The 10-year German Bund yields -0.29% per annum, so that a buyer pays 102.83 euros on December 6, 2019 to receive no coupon, only 100 euros in 10 years. Remarkably, this reflects a high storage cost and risk to hold large sums of cash.) Nevertheless, in normal times, putting aside money today will bring money plus interest tomorrow. This appendix reviews the mechanics of compound interest and uses it for discounting future cash flows; receipts and payments. The analysis applies to business planning, terminal values, Ricardian Equivalence, coupon bonds, credit risk, and the inter-temporal budget constraint. The power of saving in building wealth is amplified by compound interest. Saving in secure assets that pay compound interest is often a more sure way of building wealth than counting on asset appreciation. Indeed, growth models focus upon saving and investment along with technological change as the source of growth in income and the capital stock. In this context, saving is income that is not consumed.

章后习题答案

Solutions to Problems

1.1 Yes, due to different jurisdictions having different regulations, tax rates, accounting procedures, forms of business organization, and bankruptcy laws.

1.2 The purpose of the SEC is to provide transparency to investors through timely disclosure of income statements, the balance sheet, and information material to the financial condition of the firm. The idea is to level the playing field to combat illegal insider trading and abuses. Documents can be falsified, but now under Sarbanes-Oxley of 2002 require the signature of the Chief Executive Officer (CEO) and Chief Financial Officer (CFO) attesting to their veracity to the best of their knowledge.

2.1 a. The functions of money are (1) a unit of account to measure value (2) a medium of exchange to facilitate transactions and (3) a store of value as a temporary abode of purchasing power.

b. The cost of mining, refining, and minting metallic monies is a natural brake to the overproduction of metallic money. The mint profits—value as money less cost of production—are significantly less than with paper money. Robert Mundell put it succinctly, "You cannot print gold, and you cannot melt paper." If inflation takes place, the commodity value of the coin is greater than its face value as money, so it gets melted. Thus, growth in the hard money supply stops.

2.2 a. Cross rates determine the fixed parity of two monies fixed to gold. That is:

$$\frac{\$/G}{£/G} = \$/£ = 2$$

b. Yes, because an arbitrage profit can be made.

c. Ignoring transaction costs, a "round trip" beginning and ending in pounds would involve the following steps:

1. Sell one pound for $2.01 on the foreign exchange market.

2. Buy an ounce of gold from the Bank of the United States for $2,

profiting by 1 cent.

3. Sell an ounce of gold to the Bank of England for one pound.
4. Keep one cent profit in USD.
5. Convert to 1/2.01 cent profit in pounds, to finish the round trip.

d. The money supply of England goes up by one pound, while the money supply in the United States falls by two dollars. In other words, the Bank of England buys one ounce of gold from the public, while the Bank of the United States sells one ounce of gold to the public.

e. Yes, the Bank of the United States could buy $2 worth of bonds from the public, while the Bank of England could sell one pound of bonds to the public. The monetary effects of the gold flows would be neutralized.

3.1 a. The net present value of and rate of return on the flow of payments and receipts in pounds is given by using the = NPV(values; rate) less initial cost and = IRR(values, guess) formulas in Excel:

Net present value and rate of return

Interest rate	10%
Initial investment	−£100
Year 1 income	£50
Year 2 income	£50
Year 3 income	£50
Net present value (NPV)	£24
Internal rate of return (IRR)	23.4%

Alternatively, the NPV and ROI can be calculated manually from the formulas:

$$\text{NPV} = -100 + \frac{50}{1.1} + \frac{50}{(1.1)^2} + \frac{50}{(1.1)^3}$$

and

$$100 = \frac{50}{1+\delta} + \frac{50}{(1+\delta)^2} + \frac{50}{(1+\delta)^3}$$

b. If you were to sell this investment worth £24 at 1.76 dollars per pound, it would be worth £24.34 × 1.76 = $42.84.

3.2 a. Setting the quantity supplied equal to the quantity demanded in the foreign exchange market and solving for S yields an equilibrium exchange rate of 20 pesos per dollar. That is:

$$90 - 2S = -10 + 3S \quad \text{yields} \quad 5S = 100 \quad \text{or} \quad S = \frac{100}{5} = 20$$

b. If the Central Bank maintained a fixed exchange rate of 15 pesos per dollar, there would be an excess demand for dollars equal to $25. That is:

$$Q_D - Q_S = 90 - 2(15) + 10 - 3(15) = 100 - 75 = 25$$

c. If the Central Bank had only $15 million left in foreign reserves, it could devalue to 20 to reach equilibrium without selling reserves, or partially devalue and sell some reserves. It could borrow additional reserves and sell them on the exchange market. To maintain its reserves for a rainy day, it could float the currency, letting supply and demand equilibrate at 20. The imposition of exchange controls would only create a parallel market, an implicitly floating exchange rate.

d. If the Central Bank instead wanted to add $10 million to its holdings of foreign reserves, it could depreciate the exchange rate to 22 pesos per dollar. Adding 10 to the demand curve, and solve for S by setting supply equal to demand. That is:

$$100 - 2S = -10 + 3S \quad \text{yields} \quad 5S = 110 \quad \text{or} \quad S = \frac{110}{5} = 22.$$

3.3 a. With a floating exchange rate, the equilibium rate is determined by the supply equals demand equilibrium. By inspect of Figure 3.2 the equilibrium exchange rate would be 1.2 pesos per dollar.

b. To maintain a one-to-one exchange rate the central bank must supply an additional $10 million to the foreign exchange market, just enough to satisfy total demand at that price. Essentially, the Central Bank adds horizontally $10 million to the supply curve, shifting total supply to the right by that amount.

c. The sale of dollars by the central bank to the foreign exchange market reduces the money supply held by commercial banks and the public. As the money market in Argentina becomes less liquid, interest rates in pesos rises and the rate of inflation falls. This reduces the demand for dollars and simultaneously increases its supply in the foreign exchange market. The graphic illustrates the flows of funds from foreign exchange market purchases and sales of foreign exchange.

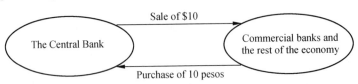

3.4 a. The bid-ask spreads are indicated in the table below. Recall the rule that 1/bid in one quotation equals the ask in the other. Similarly, 1/ask in one quotation equals the bid in the other.

	European Quotations (£/$)		American Quotations ($/£)	
	Bid	Ask	Bid	Ask
Spot	0.56577086	0.56596299	1.7669	1.7675
Spread	0.00019212		0.0006	
Mid-point	0.56586692		1.7672	

b. The spreads are simply the difference between the ask and the bid.

c. The mid-point equals the sum of the bid and the ask divided by two.

d. In both cases, the bid-ask spread as a percent of the mid-point is 0.033952, or about 3%.

3.5 a. Recalling the rule that 1/bid in one quotation equals the ask in the other and 1/ask in one quotations equals the bid in the other, we have:

	European Quotations (£/$)		American Quotations ($/£)	
	Bid	Ask	Bid	Ask
Spot	0.5658	0.5660	1.7668	1.7675
Spread	0.0002		0.0007	
Mid-point	0.5659		1.7671	
Spread/Mid-point(%)	0.0004		0.0004	

b. The bid-ask spread is 0.0002 in pounds and 0.0007 in dollars.

c. The mid-points are 0.5659 pounds per dollar and 1.7671 dollars per pound respectively

d. The bid-ask spread is 0.04 percent in terms of each quotation.

3.6 Since the points quotation is lower than the offer, add 0.0214 to the one month spot outright bid and 0.0220 to the outright offer. Similarly, add the points of the two and three month divided by 10,000 to obtain the two and three month forward outright quotations.

	European Quotations (£/$)	
	Bid	Ask
Spot	1.7669	1.7675
Points	Bid	Ask
1 month	214	220
2 months	283	298
3 months	388	416
	American ($/£)	
	Bid	Ask
1 month	1.7883	1.7889
2 months	1.7952	1.7967
3 months	1.8057	1.8085

3.7 a. By inspection, the forward premium on the pound is 2%, while US Treasuries are 1% higher than UK Treasuries at point Z. Consequently, the gain on forward cover in selling the pound will more than offset the loss on investing in UK Treasuries.

b. Ignoring transactions costs, the steps taken in this riskless arbitrage opportunity are:

    1. Sell US Treasuries (r_{us} rises)

2. Buy pounds spot (sell dollars spot) (S rises)
3. Buy UK Treasuries (r_{uk} falls)
4. Sell pounds forward (buy dollars forward) (F falls)

The net gain for the individual arbitrageur would be 1%, a 2% gain on forward cover and a 1% loss on the interest rate differential. As a result of many arbitrageurs taking advantage of this profit opportunity $\left(\frac{F-S}{S}\right)$, the premium on the pound falls, and $(r_{us} - r_{uk})$, the interest rate difference in favor of US Treasuries, rises.

3.8 a. The absolute version of purchasing power parity predicts that the exchange rate will reflect the different costs of purchasing the same bundle of goods (the inverse of the absolute purchasing power of each currency in terms of goods). Consequently, the PPP rates are indicated in the table:

	Cost of Basket	Purchasing Power Parity Rates
U.S.	$60	1.666667 dollars per pound
England	£36	0.6 pounds per dollar
Mexico	N$540	9 pesos per dollar

b. No, because the market exchange rates do not accurately predict the true purchasing powers of different currencies. Those countries with relatively cheap labor-intensive goods such as haircuts, a non-traded good, will find that the equilibrium rate does not fully reflect the purchasing power of the currency. There is little arbitrage in non-traded goods such as haircuts.

c. Therefore it is not a surprise to find that the PPP prediction for the pound is fairly accurate, but the equilibrium rate of 11 pesos per dollar "overvalues" the dollar in terms of the purchasing power parity rate of 9 pesos per dollar.

d. Taking the current equilibrium rates as given, the purchasing power parity predictions are:

Initial equilibrium rates	Relative PPP	PPP forecast
0.566	1.5	0.849 pounds per dollar
11	1.5	16.5 pesos per dollar

Essentially, take the initial equilibrium rates as the base rates for the forecast, then multiply by 3/2, the expected inflation differential relative to the United States. While the absolute PPP forecast may be significantly off, the relative PPP is still the best forecast of the movement in future exchange rates. It is embodied in the nominal interest rate on risk free Treasuries, which do not exist in Mexico due to previous default. For this reason, the relative PPP forecast may be the most accurate.

e. Mexico and England are both net oil exporters, while the US is a net oil importer. A rise in the price of oil would appreciate the pound and the peso relative to the PPP forecast. It would cause a real appreciation of the pound and the peso. However, a rise in the price of wheat would be likely to cause a real appreciation of the dollar.

4.1 a. "I never hedge, since it reduces my bottom line!"

This CFO has reckoned the costs of hedging foreign exchange risk against the benefits, and concluded that the costs exceed the benefits. This is likely to be a firm that does not face significant losses due to being exposed to foreign exchange risks in operations and contracts. This firms has a low probability of bankruptcy costs. As a result, it does not perceive any benefits in lowered borrowing costs due to risks of financial distress from foreign exchange losses. The cost of the hedges clearly outweighs the benefits in lowered risk of financial distress. Put simply, the foreign exchange exposure of this firm may be minimal.

b. "I always hedge, since I cannot take the risk of exchange rate losses bankrupting my firm."

This firm is likely to have significant foreign exchange exposure, so that its value at risk from unanticipated changes in the exchange rate is high. Higher earnings in foreign exchange must be volatile and/or the exchange rate volatile. The high risk of financial distress from going unhedged would significantly increase its borrowing costs. Investing in the hedges provides the benefit of significantly lowering the chances of financial distress and bankruptcy costs. In this situation, the CFO chooses to hedge. It may even increase the net present value of the firm due to lowered borrowing costs. Put simply, the foreign exchange exposure of this firm is large.

4.2 a. Its yield to maturity, r, is solved for by:

$$\$80 = \frac{\$100}{1+r} \quad \text{or} \quad r = \frac{\$100}{\$80} - 1 = 0.25 = 25\%$$

b. Its risk premium, ρ, is approximately $25\% - 5\%$, or 20%. More precisely, it is solved by:

$$(1.05)(1+\rho) = 1.25 \quad \text{or} \quad \rho = \frac{1.25}{1.05} - 1 = 19.05\%$$

4.3 a. Your options expire today out of the money. You would never buy at £80 when the spot price is £50. Consequently, your total annual compensation is £12,000.

b. Zero percent since they are out of the money.

If today's share price is instead £100.

a. Your options are now in the money—profitable if exercised. Since you buy at £80 and sell at £100 you make £20 in profits on each share. Buying

1,000 shares at £80 and selling them at £100 earns you £20,000 today. Your total compensation is thus £32,000.

b. Consequently, the percent of your total compensation in the form of stock options is $\frac{£20,000}{£32,000} - 1 = 62.5\%$.

4.4 a. She made 2 cents per option upon exercise, but paid 1 cent for each one. Her profit per option was 1 penny. She thus made only $1 in net profits.

b.

1. The put was in the money—the buyer bought at $1.20 and sold at $1.25, making 5 cents per option.

2. Tomas lost 4.5 cents per option or $40.50 in total. His gain from the sale of the option of half a cent was outweighed by losses of 5 cents per option.

3. Yes, the writer or seller of the option is contractually obligated to honor the option if it is presented for exercise. Otherwise, he is in default. If it expires out of the money, the writer keeps the premium.

4.5 i. Martha might sell £100 thousand for delivery in 90 days. She would lock in the bid price of the pound now, $1.78, for settlement in 90 days. This would be a forward market hedge.

ii. She might purchase a put option to sell pounds sterling at a strike price of $1.78 and a cost per option of $.0028 per pound, or $280 for a notional amount of £100,000. This would be an options hedge.

iii. She might borrow £100/1.02 = £98.04 thousand today for 3 months, sell the pounds spot, having no further pound exposure. With the proceeds from accounts receivable, she would pay the principal, £98.04, and interest, £1.96, in pounds, exactly equaling her expected receipts in pounds. This would be a money market hedge.

iv. She invoices British Baking Imports in US dollars to shift the exchange rate exposure to the importer. She thus invoices $178 thousand dollars deliverable in 90 days.

v. British Baking can similarly buy dollars forward, purchase an option to buy dollars at a strike price, or make today a money market loan in USD that matures in 90 days with principal and interest of $178 thousand.

4.6 a. The translation of these assets into US dollars on the consolidated balance sheet of the US parent firm would have a favorable effect on this portion of the balance sheet:

Assets	Original value	New Value
€ 200	$200	$240

b. Some alternative balance sheet hedges would be:

1. Acquire short term debt, an equal liability, of 200 euros.
2. Sell the 200 euros spot (i.e. buy dollars spot), thus removing the exposure from the balance sheet.
3. Acquire accounts payable of 200 euros.

4.7 a. As a French company, I am exposed to operating exposure next year. If the dollar falls below 0.8 euros, I will lose, while if it rises above 0.8 euros, I will gain. My exposure equals $\$10 \times 110 = \$1,100$.

b. Operating exposure can be hedged in a number of ways: some involve financing others involve operations. Firstly, I can borrow in dollars so that my revenues from the sale of widgets in dollars are offset by payments of interest and principal on a matching basis. If my comparative advantage is borrowing in euros, I could do so then swap the euro loan for a dollar loan. These would be a financial hedge. In terms of operations, I could move production from France to the United States, thereby acquiring a "natural hedge" involving payroll, rent and other expenses in US dollars. These are just two techniques for hedging my operating exposure. A risk-sharing currency contingency clause or invoicing in euros would also be techniques for managing exchange rate exposure. All these techniques of hedging involve some costs.

4.8 a. If the exchange rate unexpectedly changes to $0.25 per peso, "operating losses" due to not hedging would equal 25 cents per peso, or $2,500.

b. Since this is ongoing operating exposure, Tiny Tots could seek a loan in pesos and use the earnings from accounts receivables in pesos to service the loan. Any loss on the peso would be offset by an equal gain on its peso loan. To obtain the loan on favorable terms, Tiny Tots could borrow in USD, its currency of comparative advantage, then swap the USD loan for an Argentine peso loan. Indirect financing could also be done by back-to-back parallel loans whereby Tiny Tots makes a dollar loan to an Argentine subsidiary in the U.S., and Argentine headquarters makes a similar loan to Tiny Tots in pesos. Relocating production to Argentina would also give Tiny Tots a "natural hedge"— matching expenditures in pesos.

c. If Tiny Tots relocates production to Argentina and expects second quarter costs of production and distribution to be 5,000 pesos, the net exposure would only be 5,000 pesos. Only that amount would need to be hedge to be "perfectly" hedged.

d. Theoretically, profitability could go either way. The costs of the hedges might be offset by lowered borrowing costs. In this case the NPV of Tiny Tots would rise. The more likely case is that the cost of the hedges would reduce the

NPV of the firm.

4.9 a. Headquarters gains because euro denominated assets are 400, while liabilities are 300. There is a net 100 long position in euros on the balance sheet.

b. The gains of $0.10 \times 100 = \$10$ would be added to the cumulative translation adjustment line in the balance sheet.

c. Some alternative ways of acquiring a perfect balance sheet hedge would be to pay off 100 euros of in accounts payable or debt in advance, sell the 100 euros in cash for dollars, or increase short term debt in euros by 100.

5.1 a. The weighted average cost of capital in euros would be, using a European marginal income tax rate of 45%:

$$WACC = 0.3[10(1 - 0.45)] + 0.7(15) = 12.15\% \text{ in euros}$$

If IBM is able to apply the higher tax as credits against other income, it would imply an effective marginal income tax rate of 35%. In this case, the WACC in euros would be:

$$WACC = 0.3[10(1 - 0.35)] + 0.7(15) = 12.45\% \text{ in euros}$$

b. In terms of USD, the weighted average cost of capital would be:

$$1.1245 \left(\frac{1.03}{1.02}\right) - 1 = 0.13552 = 13.552\% \text{ in USD}$$

using the US marginal income tax rate.

5.2 a. The profit maximizing level of sales is 100 since the marginal cost of the bundled product equals its marginal revenue at that level of output.

b. The firm will charge the final customer $7.00 per unit, found by the demand for that quantity of output (its average revenue).

c. To guarantee that the production unit provides exactly the optimum amount to the marketing division, the latter will pay the production unit a transfer price of $3.00. The production unit in turn maximizes its profits by setting marginal production cost equal to the fixed transfer price.

5.3 The WACC in pounds sterling is indicated below as 13.9%:

	U.S. & U.K. data (percent per annum)
U.S. inflation rate	3
U.K. inflation rate	2
U.S. Treasury	5
U.K. Treasury	4
$WACC_\$$	15
$WACC_£$	13.9

which is solved for either by using PPP or IRP, that is:

$$\text{WACC}_{\mathcal{L}} = (1.15)\left(\frac{1.02}{1.03}\right) - 1 = 0.139 = 13.9\%$$

or, using Treasury rates,

$$\text{WACC}_{\mathcal{L}} = (1.15)\left(\frac{1.03}{1.04}\right) - 1 = 0.139 = 13.9\%$$

b. The NPV in USD differs only by rounding done by both methods:

Method A

Discount foreign currency flows to the present at the foreign currency discount rate, then convert the NPV in forex to home currency at the spot rate.

	Year		
	0	1	2
Free cash flows (£)	−100	60	70
Present value of cash flow (£)	−100	52.68	53.96
NPV (£)	6.64		
Spot exchange rate ($/£)	1.77		
NPV ($)	11.74		

Method B

Convert foreign currency cash flows to home currency, discount to the present at the home currency discount rate.

	Year		
	0	1	2
Free cash flows (£)	−100	60	70
Exchange rate forecast	1.77	1.787	1.8042
Free cash flows ($)	−177	107.22	126.29
Present value of cash flow ($)	−177	93.24	95.50
NPV ($)	11.73		

5.4 Your shipment of 100 computers worth $2,000 each amounts to $200,000 in export revenues. Here are some of the international means of payment and who bears the counterparty risk:

a. Cash in advance guarantees the exporter of payment, but does not guarantee the importer of shipment. The importer bears the counterparty risk.

b. An open account into which the importer pays upon delivery of the shipment puts the counterparty risk on the exporter. The exporter could ship coincidentally with the payment, the bank invoicing the importer, receiving the funds at the same time the exporter delivers the bill of lading to the bank.

c. A documentary letter of credit is a guaranteed means of payment for goods which, when confirmed, substitutes the bank's credit for that of the importer. The bank bears the counterparty risk. In return, it collects fees for issuing the letter of credit.

5.5 a. If you need Bahamian dollars today, you can sell (discount) the letter of credit today since it is confirmed and irrevocable. The L/C is a negotiable instrument.

b. The L/C is virtually riskless, so you might use the Bahamian Treasury rate of 6% per annum, representing nearly a half a percent per month (0.486755 percent per month). The discounted value of the L/C would therefore be worth 11,628,800 Bahamian dollars at a compound monthly rate of 0.49 percent and 11,618,932 at a simple monthly rate of 0.5 percent.

	1	2	3	4	5	6	7	8	9	10	11	12
PV at 0.487%	1,000,000	1,000,000	1,000,000	1,000,000	1,000,000	1,000,000	1,000,000	1,000,000	1,000,000	1,000,000	1,000,000	1,000,000
	995,156	990,336	985,538	980,764	976,014	971,286	966,581	961,899	957,239	952,603	947,988	943,396
Sum of PV	11,628,800											

	1	2	3	4	5	6	7	8	9	10	11	12
PV at 0.5%	1,000,000	1,000,000	1,000,000	1,000,000	1,000,000	1,000,000	1,000,000	1,000,000	1,000,000	1,000,000	1,000,000	1,000,000
	995,025	990,075	985,149	980,248	975,371	970,518	965,690	960,885	956,105	951,348	946,615	941,905
Sum of PV	11,618,932											

5.6 a. If fees are about 1%, Citybank would stand to earn annually about $10,000, hardly worth the money laundering.

b. Yes the cash deposit is over $10,000 so would have to be reported to the U.S. Treasury.

c. The transfer would also constitute money laundering and thus be in violation of anti-money laundering laws and conventions. The fees are certainly not worth the reputational risk.

5.7 a. The coefficient of risk aversion is 4, since $A/2 = 2$, $A = 4$.

b. The optimal fraction of the complete portfolio held in the form of risky assets is given by: $z = \dfrac{E(r_P) - r_f}{A\sigma_P^2} = \dfrac{0.15 - 0.05}{4(0.1)} = \dfrac{0.1}{0.4} = 25\%$. Consequently, 75% is held in the risk-free asset.

c. The expected rate of return on the complete portfolio is given by:
$$E(r_C) = 0.05 + 0.25(0.15 - 0.05) = 0.075 = 7.5\%$$

d. The variance of the complete portfolio is:
$$\sigma_C^2 = z^2\sigma_P^2 = (0.25)^2 \times 0.1 = 0.00625$$

e. The level of utility of this investor is indicated by:
$$U = E(r_C) - 2\sigma_C^2 = 0.075 - 2(0.0065) = 0.0625$$

5.8 a. The expected rate of return on the complete portfolio is a weighted average of returns on the risky and the risk free assets:
$$E(r_C) = 0.5(0.20) + 0.5(0.05) = 0.125 = 12.5\%$$

b. The variance of the complete portfolio is:
$$(0.5)^2 0.4 = 0.1 = 10\%$$

c. The standard deviation or volatility of the complete portfolio is the square root of its variance, or:
$$\sqrt{0.10} = 0.3162 \text{ or about } 32\%$$

5.9 At a transfer price of q_t, the downstream retailer would maximize profits by charging p_r, selling q_r units. Profits would thus be the dashed rectangle above marginal revenue, rather than the solid rectangle. Profits to the upstream manufacturer would be the small dashed rectangle below marginal revenue.

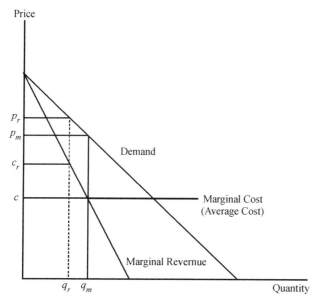

5.10

a.

i. *XYZ, Inc. N.Y.* makes $0 profits.

ii. *XYZ, Europe, S.A.* makes $0 profits.

iii. *XYZ FSC, Nassau* makes $3 profits.

b. If the profits are repatriated, the tax paid is $1.

c. If the profits are not repatriated, the taxes are $0 because there are no income taxes in Nassau.

6.1 A Ponzi scheme is an investment that relies upon new debt paying interest, dividends, and redemptions from old debt. Usually there is no underlying asset, proving ultimately unsustainable.

a. It is unlikely that there is an underlying asset that bears 43% per annum, *ex ante*. Such high rates of return indicate high credit risk and likelihood of default.

b. Because the sellers of the investment are initially able to pay the first investors with money from new investors.

c. No, because past performance is not a good indicator of future performance, and additionally, they are unlikely to rise at this rate.

6.2 Insider trading involves trading on inside information on the potential future financial performance of a firm. As such, some investors benefit from unshared information at the expense of others. The SEC views insider trading as a form of theft. Firms are required to disclose all information material to their financial health and performance. Insider trading is thus both illegal and unethical. Its price discovery role is too late for the uninformed investor.

6.3 The doubling down strategy is tempting since the investor can recover initial losses if the price of the asset moves in the right direction. However, there is a great risk of increased leverage, particularly since the asset has already moved out of the money. The likelihood that doubling up will work is increasingly remote.

6.4 On the one hand, the benefit of SOX and Dodd-Frank is to delineate what is appropriate and what is inappropriate financial behavior. SOX also increased penalties to meaningful ones, and prohibited some previously common practices, such as lending to CEOs. On the other hand, compliance with SOX and Dodd-Frank is costly, prohibitively so for small firms. Regulators are usually not vigilant and enjoy being "captured." On balance, these Acts probably have costs that outweigh their benefits.

6.5 a. Forgery and perjury are illegal. Stating a false issue date for grants of shares or options for illicit gains is against the law.

b. Fraudulently taking money from a firm is unethical. The managers' are supposed to be loyal to the owners, the shareholders.

c. The undetected back dater gains financially at the expense of the shareholders. If the fraud is detected, the back dater loses financially, but the shareholders do not gain.

7.1 a.

1. $\dfrac{\text{Assets}}{\text{Equity}} = \dfrac{A}{E} = \dfrac{200}{10} = 20$

2. $\dfrac{\text{Liabilities}}{\text{Equity}} = \dfrac{D}{E} = \dfrac{190}{10} = 19$

3. $\dfrac{\text{Debt}}{\text{Debt} + \text{Equity}} = \dfrac{D}{A} = \dfrac{190}{200} = 0.95$

b. For a given level of debt, $\Delta A = -E$ implies

$$\dfrac{\Delta A}{A} = -\dfrac{E}{A} = -\dfrac{1}{A/E} = -\dfrac{1}{20} = -5\%$$

c. When debt is constant, we have:

$$\dfrac{\Delta E}{E} = \left(\dfrac{A}{E}\right)\dfrac{\Delta A}{A}$$

That is, the percentage change in equity equals the degree of financial leverage, a multiple of the percentage change in the value of assets.

7.2 Ricardian equivalence states that the present value of new taxes to be levied in the future will exactly equal $1,000 per citizen. Therefore, if full

Ricardian equivalence held, consumers and investors know that the present value of their wealth is unchanged. Consequently, they will not change their expenditures. On the other hand, older generations know they will escape some of the new taxes, so if they do not have a strong bequest motive, they will increase their spending. In general, a lump sum check from the Treasury financed by a new bond issue will have a limited effect on spending because permanent income is unchanged.

8.1 a. By inspection, the value of Firm A is $20 and of Firm B is $10.

b. If the value of the consolidated firm is $40, synergy is $10 since the separate firms only have a combined value of $30.

c. If Firm A offers cash of $15 a share to the owners of Firm B, they are offering a premium of 50%, that is, a premium of $5 per share.

d. It is likely that 2/3 of the shareholders will accept the premium, unless management of Firm B activate an extremely effective poison pill defense or the shareholders want to hold out for another bidder or an improvement in the initial bid.

e. Firm A would be worth $25 if it offers $15 in cash for Firm B: That is, $40 − $15.

f. Using the formula $\alpha = 15/40$, and solving

$$n_w = \frac{\alpha n}{(1-\alpha)} = \frac{\frac{15}{40}(10)}{\left(1 - \frac{15}{40}\right)} = 6 \text{ shares.}$$

g. If Firm A offered $10 in cash and the rest in shares, it would have to offer:

$$n_w = \frac{\alpha n}{(1-\alpha)} = \frac{\frac{5}{30}(10)}{\left(1 - \frac{5}{30}\right)} = 2 \text{ shares.}$$

This is because after the $10 cash offer, Firm A would be worth $30 and the new shares would have to be 5/30th or 1/6th of the new firm's value.

8.2

a. Firm A's shares are worth $2.00 and Firm B's shares are worth $1.00.

b. The value of synergies, net of integration costs, is $10 − $2 = $8.

c. A 40% premium.

d. Probably, unless the shareholders want to hold out for a better offer.

e. With the cash offer, the new value of Firm A will be $58 − $14 = $44. There are still only 20 shareholders, so the share price is now $2.20.

f. $n_w = [(14/58) \times 20]/[(1 - 14/58)] = 6.36364$ shares. Then Firm A's share is worth: $58/26.36364 = 2.20. This is the same value as with the cash offer.

8.3 At a 10% cost of borrowing in euros, this investment would have a negative net present value. It should not be undertaken.

	Year					
	0	1	2	3	4	5
Free cash flows (€)	(50.0)	10.0	10.5	11.0	11.6	12.2
Present value (€)	(50.0)	9.1	8.7	8.3	7.9	7.5
NPV (€)	(8.5)					
Spot exchange rate (£/€)	0.71					
NPV (£)	−6.00					

教辅申请说明

北京大学出版社本着"教材优先、学术为本"的出版宗旨，竭诚为广大高等院校师生服务。为更有针对性地提供服务，请您按照以下步骤在微信后台提交教辅申请，我们会在 1~2 个工作日内将配套教辅资料，发送到您的邮箱。

◎手机扫描下方二维码，或直接微信搜索公众号"北京大学经管书苑"，进行关注；

◎点击菜单栏"在线申请"—"教辅申请"，出现如右下界面：

◎将表格上的信息填写准确、完整后，点击提交；

◎信息核对无误后，教辅资源会及时发送给您；
如果填写有问题，工作人员会同您联系。

温馨提示：如果您不使用微信，您可以通过下方的联系方式（任选其一），将您的姓名、院校、邮箱及教材使用信息反馈给我们，工作人员会同您进一步联系。

我们的联系方式：

北京大学出版社经济与管理图书事业部
北京市海淀区成府路 205 号，100871
联 系 人： 周莹
电   话： 010-62767312 /62757146
电子邮件： em@pup.cn
Q Q： 5520 63295（推荐使用）
微信：北京大学经管书苑（pupembook）
网址： www.pup.cn